Collaborative Technologies and Applications for Interactive Information Design:
Emerging Trends in User Experiences

Scott Rummler
Researcher, USA

Kwong Bor Ng
Queens College, CUNY, USA

INFORMATION SCIENCE REFERENCE

Hershey · New York

Director of Editorial Content:	Kristin Klinger
Senior Managing Editor:	Jamie Snavely
Assistant Managing Editor:	Michael Brehm
Publishing Assistant:	Sean Woznicki
Typesetter:	Sean Woznicki
Cover Design:	Lisa Tosheff
Printed at:	Yurchak Printing Inc.

Published in the United States of America by
Information Science Reference (an imprint of IGI Global)
701 E. Chocolate Avenue
Hershey PA 17033
Tel: 717-533-8845
Fax: 717-533-8661
E-mail: cust@igi-global.com
Web site: http://www.igi-global.com/reference

Library of Congress Cataloging-in-Publication Data

Collaborative technologies and applications for interactive information design
: emerging trends in user experiences / Scott Rummler and Kwong Bor Ng,
editors.
    p. cm.
  Includes bibliographical references and index.
  Summary: "This book covers emerging topics in collaboration, Web 2.0, and
social computing"--Provided by publisher.
  ISBN 978-1-60566-727-0 (hbk.) -- ISBN 978-1-60566-728-7 (ebook) 1.
Information technology. 2. Computer software--Development. 3. Cooperation.
I. Rummler, Scott, 1962- II. Ng, Kwong Bor.
  T58.5.C655 2010
  302.30285--dc22
                            2009007014

British Cataloguing in Publication Data
A Cataloguing in Publication record for this book is available from the British Library.

Table of Contents

Section 1
Patterns of User Experience for Collaboration

Detailed Table of Contents

Section 1
Patterns of User Experience for Collaboration

Chapter 1

    Gwen L. Kolfschoten, Delft University of Technology, The Netherlands
    Robert O. Briggs, University of Nebraska at Omaha, USA
    Gert-Jan de Vreede, University of Nebraska at Omaha, USA; Delft University of Technology,
        The Netherlands

This chapter describes how to build a tool for pattern based collaboration process design following the Collaboration Engineering approach and geared toward process managers designing collaboration processes for organizations. To support the design task, describes best practices or design patterns can be used as building blocks. It describes the requirements for a tool for pattern based collaboration process design, specifically for design efforts following the Collaboration Engineering approach.

Chapter 2

    Stephan Lukosch, Delft University of Technology, The Netherlands

Dr. Lukosch describes how to design tools for collaborative knowledge management. For designing and developing successful tools, it is crucial to involve end-users in the development process and to create shared understanding of the requirements as well as the solutions among the end-users and developers. Describes typical problems encountered when developing tools for computer-mediated interaction and presents a pattern-based approach for supporting developers and integrating end-users in the development process.

Chapter 3

Andy Polaine, The University of New South Wales, Australia
Rick Bennett, The University of New South Wales, Australia

This chapter describes a project for designing critical healthcare information in local communities in Africa. Design benefits from many levels of collaboration, especially when dealing with complex policy issues facing today's world. This project shows the results that can be produced through careful facilitation among online collaborators. 100 graphic designers joined forces with a similar number of pharmacists from over 40 countries worldwide to produce graphic proposals for public awareness campaigns about six health issues seriously affecting the people of a village community in Kenya.

Chapter 4

Monica Liljeström, Umeå University, Sweden

This chapter presents a model for online education that suggests that online education may have advantages over traditional classroom settings. The program gives students the opportunity to share, interpret and discuss criteria in order to gain a deeper understanding of their tacit dimensions. It also shows what peer assessment in the form of peer review contributes to enhancing the students' learning in online courses, and presents a design for a peer assessment element. It concludes by reporting some early findings from the project.

Chapter 5

Marjorie Darrah, West Virginia University, USA
Angela Dowling, Suncrest Middle School, USA

Offers insight into the types of collaborative experiences needed to spur innovation. Companies have realized that collaboration is a key competency for the global economy. This chapter discusses the steps the US is taking to ensure that its citizens remain innovative, how the business community is using collaboration to be competitive, and the issues encountered in education as schools attempt to teach innovation.

Chapter 6

Yasmin Ibrahim, University of Brighton, UK

The advent of the Internet hailed the ability of users to transform their identity and expression and articulation of the 'self' through their digital interactions. The Internet in its early days enabled the user to re-define identity through the text-based environment of the internet without declaring their offline persona or identity. In comparison new social software like Facebook have brought about a narcissistic turn where private details are placed on a global arena for public spectacle creating new ways of connecting and gazing into the lives of the others. It raises new social issues for societies including the rise of identity fraud, infringement of privacy, the seeking of private pleasures through public spectacle as well as the validation of one's identity through peer recognition and consumption.

Section 2
Interactive Tools for Collaboration

Chapter 7

Dr. Kussmaul examines how collaboration and knowledge management (KM) can be supported using Wikis and related tools. Describes what Wikis are and how they can be used to support collaboration and KM. Describes various approaches and factors. Systems should be off-the-shelf, avoid "either-or" conflicts, and provide structures to facilitate common tasks. Identifies best practices grouped into categories. The chapter also discusses future directions and implications in these rapidly changing areas.

Chapter 8

This chapter shows how the information glut compounded by many collaborative systems can be managed by using the topics the systems generate. This chapter discusses limitations of current information organization approaches and how to incorporate ontology into information organizations, thus enhancing collaboration possibilities. This chapter compares the two ontology languages, RDF and Topic Maps, addresses the selection guidelines between the two ontology languages, and presents user performance using a Topic Maps-based ontology.

Chapter 9

Dr. Sun presents a new take on the critical search functionality. Collaborative search generally uses previous search information to assist in future searches. However, users with the same expressed query topic may need different information. This chapter proposes to enrich the context of query representation to incorporate non-topical properties of user information needs, which appears to improve the results of collaborative search.

Dr. Ng describes a system for determining quality Wiki content using stepwise discriminative analysis and machine learning. Wikis make collaborative knowledge building easy. Since any registered member can change the content of a Wiki page, quality control becomes an issue. This paper reports a pilot study of factors that can enhance the quality of contents built by open collaborative knowledge building. Using stepwise discriminant analysis and logistic regression, several variables were identified that could contribute positively to the identification of high-quality Wiki pages. The result was analyzed using Receiver Operating Characteristic (ROC) curves from signal detection theory. The predictor worked well, with a high detection rate and a low false-alarm rate. This finding can help programmers and architects of open collaborative knowledge building systems to design and implement mechanisms that will facilitate high quality content creation.

Section 3
The Design of Information Spaces for Next-Generation Collaboration

Describes how to unleash the "dark side" of collaboration: listening, and how to collaborate in a true discussion that provides valuable content. Listening is key because simply adding data to a "knowledge base" does not make it better, just as adding "eyeballs" to a web site does not make it more significant. He argues from the lead user's perspective. His objective: to propose enhancements to a hypothetical system, increasing the amount of "Listening" (that is content consumption rather than production) in online collaboration. This approach can help to foster the true, valuable discourse that collaborative discussion has been promising to deliver.

This chapter provides an open usability engineering method for use in distributed projects. Free and open source software (F/OSS) developers tend to ignore the necessity of usability in the resulting product. This chapter examines different types of collaboration methods used by usability experts and developers, focusing particularly on open source projects, and associated communication issues. It describes the collaboration trends and patterns of HCI experts, developers and users with an emphasis on concerns related to inefficient exploitation of current tools and technologies and provides an open usability engineering method which could be used in distributed open-source projects.

Chapter 13
Lesley Farmer, California State University, USA

Dr. Farmer shows how collaborative videoconferencing can be used as a tool to build professional networks and best practices. Using video conferencing, teacher librarians have a unique opportunity to build a strong collaborative, professional network that benefits best practices and raises awareness of twenty-first century librarianship. Critical elements and practices used to build communities of practice and support teacher professional development are identified. Key aspects of video conferencing are detailed, and a case study on the use of video conferencing explains how to facilitate a nation-wide community of practice among teacher librarians.

Chapter 14
Scott Rummler, laserthread.com

Presents a system for using collaboration in risk-based environments such as finance, healthcare, and insurance. Collaboration can be an effective tool for managing risk and improving decision-making. This chapter presents a model in which organizations collaborate by trading risk-based product utilizing Web Services to facilitate transactions. Knowledge management of risk information can be facilitated by the development of an Ontology used to describe Web Semantics. A user interface for knowledge management that incorporates collaborative mapping, filtering, and community discussion is presented based on an ontology and Web Semantics. By improving security, transparency, and effectiveness, this model might have mitigated the impact of risk-based problems on the current financial crisis.

Section 4
Selected Readings

Chapter 15
Anita Mirijamdotter, Växjö University, Sweden
Mary M. Somerville, University of Colorado, Denver, USA

Within the context of a three year applied research project conducted from 2003-2006 in a North American university library, staff were encouraged to reconsider organizational assumptions and design processes. The project involved an organizational leader and an external consultant who introduced and collaboratively applied Soft Systems Methodology (SSM) practice. Project results suggest the efficacy of using 'soft' systems thinking to guide interaction (re)design of technology-enabled environments, systems, and tools. In addition, participants attained insights into their new roles and responsibilities within a dynamically changing higher education environment. Project participants also applied SSM to redesign 'in house' information systems. The process of employing systems thinking practices to activate and advance organizational (re)learning, and initiating and elaborating user-centered interaction (re)design practices, culminated in a collaborative design (co-design) approach that readied participants for nimble responsiveness to continuous changes in the dynamic external environment.

Chapter 16

Angel Luis Meroño-Cerdán, Universidad de Murcia, Spain
Pedro Soto-Acosta, Universidad de Murcia, Spain
Carolina López-Nicolás, Universidad de Murcia, Spain

This study seeks to assess the impact of collaborative technologies on innovation at the firm level. Collaborative technologies' influence on innovation is considered here as a multistage process that starts at adoption and extends to use. Thus, the effect of collaborative technologies on innovation is examined not only directly, the simple presence of collaborative technologies, but also based on actual collaborative technologies' use. Given the fact that firms can use this technology for different purposes, collaborative technologies' use is measured according to three orientations: e-information, e-communication, and e-workflow. To achieve these objectives, a research model is developed for assessing, on the one hand, the impact of the adoption and use of collaborative technologies on innovation and, on the other hand, the relationship between adoption and use of collaborative technologies. The research model is tested using a dataset of 310 Spanish SMEs.

Chapter 17

Luca Iandoli, University of Naples Federico II, Italy
Mark Klein, Massachusetts Institute of Technology, USA
Giuseppe Zollo, University of Naples Federico II, Italy

The successful emergence of on-line communities, such as open source software and Wikipedia, seems due to an effective combination of intelligent collective behavior and internet capabilities However, current internet technologies, such as forum, wikis and blogs appear to be less supportive for knowledge organization and consensus formation. In particular very few attempts have been done to support large, diverse, and geographically dispersed groups to systematically explore and come to decisions concerning complex and controversial systemic challenges. In order to overcome the limitations of current collaborative technologies, in this article, we present a new large-scale collaborative platform based on argumentation mapping. To date argumentation mapping has been effectively used for small-scale, co-located groups. The main research questions this work faces are: can argumentation scale? Will large-scale argumentation outperform current collaborative technologies in collective problem solving and deliberation? We present some preliminary results obtained from a first field test of an argumentation platform with a moderate-sized (few hundred) users community.

Chapter 18

Anna Michailidou, University of Macedonia, Greece

Anastasios Economides, University of Macedonia, Greece

Computer supported collaborative learning environments (CSCLEs) is one of the innovative technologies that support online education. Successful design and implementation of such environments demand thorough analysis of many parameters. This chapter studies the impact of diversity in learner-learner interactions in collaborative virtual teams through a social and cultural perspective. Social differences include gender, race, class, or age. Cultural differences refer to matters like how an individual's cognition, values, beliefs, and study behaviors are influenced by culture. Instructors must take into consideration the factors that influence individuals' diversity, and invent new ways to implement successful collaboration. This is crucial, especially regarding teams scattered on different countries or even continents. Social and cultural differences influence an individual's performance in a learning environment. Such differences must be adequately studied by both the educational organization and the instructors in such a way that the learning procedure will become a positive experience for all the members involved.

Foreword

We are social animals and as such we develop considerable skills and tools that help us to communicate, compete and cooperate. Governments and cultural institutions arise out of the need to share resources efficiently, and libraries are one important kind of cultural institution that have long exemplified cooperative sharing. Collaboration is a special kind of cooperation that assumes strong intrinsic intention to achieve a common goal and in many cases is used as a metaphor for cooperation and sharing. Collaboration has become the go to strategy for attacking complex problems. This trend is illustrated in all arenas of endeavor from industry (partnerships and cooperative agreements) to science (collaboratories and translational research) to education (social learning and distributed cognition). Collaboration and implicit cooperation are supported by the emerging cyberinfrastructure that makes possible the WWW and today's social networking services.

Wherever one looks, the messages of our culture promote collaboration as the way to improved use of resources and outcomes. Open access information, open standards, and open source software all emanate from the desire to share intellectual and physical resources and invite collaboration and cooperation. Clearly, collaboration is a significant driver of human progress and considerable efforts are given to create tools and services to support it (e.g., the CSCW research and development community).

In addition to the explicit collaboration that people undertake, cyber-infrastructure allows people and machines to leverage the implicit activities of people as they work and play online. Although not true collaboration, such systems have become known as recommender systems that depend on collaborative filtering algorithms. We are thus witnessing increasing examples of cooperation and collaboration among collectives of people and machines.

As with all important ideas, collaboration can become dogma if it becomes the default rather than a choice. It is just important that we ask, "When is collaboration not effective and what are its limitations?" as it is to ask, "Why it is effective and how can we best apply it." Certainly collaboration comes with costs associated with communication overhead and additional monitoring support. Moreover, collaboration requires personality traits and organizational cultures that help or hinder effectiveness. Any serious treatment of collaboration must at least state underlying assumptions and better yet question them. To do so seriously yields a strong basis upon which theoretical and empirical evidence of the effects of collaboration stand. The collection of papers in this book presents cases of collaboration and cooperation from a range of these perspectives.

Dr. Gary Marchionini
Chapel Hill, North Carolina

Gary Marchionini is Cary C. Boshamer Professor in the School of Information and Library Science at the University of North Carolina where he teaches courses in human-information interaction, interface design and testing, and digital libraries. He heads the Interaction Design Laboratory at SILS. His Ph.D. is from Wayne State University in mathematics education with an emphasis on educational computing. He was previously professor in the College of Library and Information Services at the University of Maryland and a member of the Human-Computer Interaction Laboratory. Dr Marchionini is President-Elect (2008-09) of the American Society for Information Science and Technology . He is editor for the Morgan-Claypool Synthsis Series of lectures/monographs on Information Concepts, Retrieval, and Services. He was Editor-in-Chief for the ACM Transaction on Information Systems from 2002-2008. Professor Marchionini has had grants or contracts from the National Science Foundation, Council on Library Resources, the National Library of Medicine, the Library of Congress, Bureau of Labor Statistics, Kellogg Foundation, and NASA, The National Cancer Institute, Microsoft, among others. He has published over 180 articles, chapters and reports in a variety of books and journals. He is author of a book titled Information Seeking in Electronic Environments published by Cambridge University Press. He serves or has served on the editorial boards of the Journal of the American Society for Information Science, Information Processing and Management, Journal of Biomedical Discovery and Collaboration, Library and Information Science Research (1997-2007), Information Retrieval, Journal of Network and Computer Applications (1996-2007), Journal of Digital Information, Educational Technology, ACM Journal on Computers and Cultural Heritage (JOCCH), New Review of Multimedia and Hypermedia, and the International Journal on Digital Libraries. Dr Marchionini is President-Elect (2008-09) of the American Society for Information Science and Technology . He is editor for the Morgan-Claypool Synthsis Series of lectures/monographs on Information Concepts, Retrieval, and Services. He was Editor-in-Chief for the ACM Transaction on Information Systems from 2002-2008. Professor Marchionini has had grants or contracts from the National Science Foundation, Council on Library Resources, the National Library of Medicine, the Library of Congress, Bureau of Labor Statistics, Kellogg Foundation, and NASA, The National Cancer Institute, Microsoft, among others. He has published over 180 articles, chapters and reports in a variety of books and journals. He is author of a book titled Information Seeking in Electronic Environments published by Cambridge University Press.

Preface

Collaborative approaches facilitate user participation via interaction in order to solicit, collect, and integrate input from users to improve the quality of the output. Traditionally it was done by proper implementation of incentives and rewards to invoke actions from stake holders through some structured communicative channel. With the appearance of all kinds of social software, the landscape is changing, and so emerges the new paradigm of collaboration.

Now, collaboration is often thought of a relatively new yet rapidly maturing kind of technology. Wikis, blogs, and other tools have been mainstreamed over the last few years. Many organizations have found that collaboration suffers from common problems: people do not use it because it creates additional work or does not meet an existing need; a proliferation of ad-hoc tools and widgets creates an unproductive working environment; collaboration becomes an end in itself rather than serving a useful purpose.

As a result, organizations are rethinking their approaches to these tools, and in considering the business case for their use, are seeing a need for 'deep collaboration' – that which enables an organization's core business processes to be carried out more productively in a collaborative fashion than otherwise.

This book is geared toward those who have encountered either the theoretical or practical aspects of collaboration and have wanted a grounding, framework, unified theory, or set of best practices. In some cases they will be business practitioners who are evolving new business models; in other cases, policy experts attempting to grapple with emerging crises, or researchers who are interested in contributing to the emerging body of knowledge in an area which seems set to transform many of the areas with which it intersects.

From one vantage point, the Web was created in order to do collaboration and is just now getting up to the task. It now seems fitting that, with the rising need for more meaningful interactions, collaboration might once again be seen as the main thing, and the Web its byproduct.

In this framework, collaboration is emerging as the new 'bricks and mortar' of purposeful activity. Many organizations have 'gone digital' – replacing bricks and mortar with a digitized presence - only to find that a key element, that of collaboration and its valuable creative, decision-making, information-sharing, and inclusive power, was missing. As evidence of this, one need only look to the confusion and time involved in sending out trillions of emails as a substitute for collaboration that works.

This book is organized into three general themes: patterns of user experience, interactive tools, and information spaces.

Section 1: Patterns of User Experience for Collaboration

The key to reaping the benefits of deep collaboration lies in modeling the distinctive processes that constitute an organization's differentiating factors, the reason it exists in the first place. These patterns of collaborative user experience form the building blocks, the new bricks and mortar, for organized activity.

In *A Technology for Pattern-Based Process Design and its Application to Collaboration Engineering*, Gwen Kolfschoten notes that many business processes are inherently collaborative in nature. This chapter shows how managers can design collaboration processes for an organization, and how best practices or design patterns can be used as building blocks. It describes how to build a tool for pattern based collaboration process design following the collaboration engineering approach. This CASE tool supports both users and designers in a continuous learning cycle.

Pattern-Based Tool Design for Shared Knowledge Construction, by Stephan Lukosch, shows how to design tools for collaborative knowledge management. These tools pose unique challenges, as they must accommodate interdependent patterns of use by multiple users. The major problems involved are assessed, and a pattern-based process with example tools are introduced.

Creative Waves: Exploring Emerging Online Cultures, Social Networking and Creative Collaboration Through e-Learning to Offer Visual Campaigns for Local Kenyan Health Needs, by Andy Polaine, describes a project for designing critical healthcare information in local communities in Africa. It shows how the user experience of collaboration can address some of the most complex communication issues facing today's world. In an online project, graphic designers joined forces with Pharmacists from over 40 countries to produce graphic proposals for public awareness campaigns for health issues affecting the people of a village community in Kenya. The task was extremely difficult because it encompassed educational, technical, and governmental/administrative dimensions. Nevertheless, the project met with success. This type of multidimensional, collaborative user experience may prove crucial in developing technical and policy approaches (such as preparing the way for research and development) in areas that have previously met with little success.

Enhancing University Students' Interaction and Learning Through Formative Peer-assessment Online, by Monica Liljeström, presents a model for online education that raises interesting questions for curriculum theory. Students were given the opportunity to collaborate in the educational process by giving feedback on each other's work. Early results indicate that this type of interaction can be an important adjunct to formal instruction. In an era where online education and lifelong learning are so important, and in which the role of technology in education has had mixed reviews, this approach shows that online education may have advantages over traditional classroom settings.

Preparing the Next Generation of Innovators through Collaboration, by Marjorie Darrah, offers insight into the types of collaborative experiences needed to spur the innovation. This chapter discusses the steps the United States is taking to ensure that its citizenry remains innovative: how the business community is using collaboration to be competitive, the issues encountered in schools to meet challenges of the 21st Century, and evidence that education is changing in response to the need to produce the next generation of innovators. These collaborative experiences in innovation will help to achieve 'technology transfer' – moving new ideas from academia into business implementation, in key areas like energy and healthcare.

Social Networking Sites (SNS) and the 'Narcissistic Turn': The Politics of Self-Exposure, by Yasmin Ibrahim, discusses a recent change in online communities: from using them to conceal one's identity to using them to expose one's identity. A new economy based on these transactions is emerging, which uses the sharing of personal information as a kind of currency. This economy revolves around the risks and rights associated with exposing personal information in anticipation of some future gain. These transactions involve social and cultural assumptions and expectations that are not always well understood by parties of different cultural backgrounds. This raises the issue of how identity and authority are constructed, which is a major theme of Continental philosophy. Identities, roles, rights, and actions will need to be formalized so that they can be incorporated into a SNS. This presents the interesting challenge of moving from Continental philosophy to its more Analytic counterpart. The impact of cultural differences on technology design is made clear when one considers the very different approach to mobile use in Europe vs. the United States. SNS user experience patterns that are sensitive toward identity and political concerns might be used to improve challenging collaborative exchanges, such as those between the U.S. and Islamic communities, or to facilitate ecommerce initiatives between the huge, culturally diverse, emerging economies of India and China.

Many popular SNS, such as Facebook, Craigslist, and MySpace, have been notable for succeeding in spite of a lack of user experience design, which may help explain why their effectiveness has been hard to duplicate. In the next section are examples of collaborative tools that can be replicated across environments.

Section 2: Interactive Tools for Collaboration

New interactive tools are needed for designing collaboratively generated information. The tools shown here synergize collaborative activity by adding contextual value to information. The information is then used systematically to perform key functions (search, knowledge management, information organization). Once collaborative information is used systematically, quality metrics and best practices can be applied, thus providing the crucial link between collaborative possibilities that 'seem like a good idea', and those which show measurable results.

Wikis for Collaboration & Knowledge Management: Current Practices & Future Directions, by Cliff Kussmaul, describes clearly how Wikis can support collaboration and Knowledge Management. It also reviews effective tools and techniques, describes how they can be used for prototyping, and discusses future directions in these rapidly changing areas. It identifies best practices grouped into categories.

Maximizing Collaboration Using Topic Maps-based Ontology, by Myongho Yi, shows how the information glut compounded by many collaborative systems can be managed by using the topics the systems generate. This chapter discusses limitations of current information organization approaches in the digital age and shows how to incorporate ontology into information organizations in ways that facilitate collaboration. This chapter compares the two ontology languages, RDF and Topic Maps, provides guidelines for deciding which to select, and concludes by presenting user performance results of a Topic Maps-based ontology.

Collaborative Retrieval Systems: Reusable Information Quests, by Ying Sun, presents a new take on the critical search functionality. Current collaborative search uses previously collected search sessions as a recommendation. However, users with same expressed query topic may need different information. This chapter proposes a model for next generation search which enriches the context of query representation by incorporating non-topical properties of user information needs. This approach appears to improve the results of collaborative search.

Automatically Evaluating the Quality of Contents Created in Collaborative Knowledge Building: A Pilot Study Using Wiki, by Kwong Bor Ng, addresses one of the key challenges of using Wikis: content quality. While a system that allows anyone to contribute has its advantages, an obvious drawback is that of quality control. This paper describes a pilot study that identifies factors that can enhance the quality of contents built by open collaborative knowledge building. Using stepwise discriminative analysis and logistic regression, several variables were identified that could contribute positively to the high quality of Wiki pages. A machine learning method was applied to create a quality predictor based on these variables to test if a machine could automatically estimate the quality of a Wiki page. The result was analyzed using Receiver Operating Characteristic (ROC) curves from signal detection theory. The predictor worked remarkably well, with high correct prediction rates and low false-alarm rates. As more online publications move toward embracing user-generated content, but want to maintain quality, compliance of various types, and the integrity of editorial control, this approach fills a critical need.

Section 3: The Design of Information Spaces for Next-Generation Collaboration

These new user experiences and tools require new user interface designs. In many cases, the business or organizational framework of collaboration will determine the design of the information that is presented to the user. Whereas the original Wikis functioned similarly regardless of where they were deployed, in the case of deep collaboration, form follows function.

Speak First, Then What?, by Jay Heuer, describes a large, often-overlooked aspect of collaboration. According to Jakob Nielsen, "90% of users are lurkers who never contribute, 9% of users contribute a little, and 1% of users account for almost all the action." In addition, it is sometimes the case that people post their own ideas without listening to others, defeating the purpose of having an online discussion. This chapter describes how to unleash the "dark side" of collaboration: listening, and how to collaborate in a true discussion that provides unique content.

Collaboration in Open Source Domain: A Perspective on Usability by Görkem Çetin, provides an open usability engineering method for use in distributed projects. Software designers in this area tend to build around features rather than user-centered design principles. As a result, it is easy to see the drawback to free software: it is hard to use compared to its commercial counterpart. The chapter examines collaboration methods, trends, and patterns of usability experts, users, and developers, with emphasis on concerns about inefficient exploitation of current tools and technologies.

Teacher Librarians 2.0: Lights, Camera, Action! Via Video Conferencing, by Lesley Farmer, shows how collaborative videoconferencing can be used as a tool to build professional networks. Professional associations are known for their importance in professional development and in being a clearinghouse for specialized expertise. Both of these aspects hinge on a level of personal interaction that is beyond that of a text-based collaborative system. Collaboration and videoconferencing are often studied independently; here they are presented in a system that has benefits for Teacher Librarians and potentially other groups. Best practices in facilitating Communities of Practice (COPs) and supporting teacher librarian professional development are identified. The components of video conferencing are detailed, and a case study explains how to facilitate a nation-wide community of practice among teacher librarians.

Collaboration in Risk Markets, by Scott Rummler, presents a system for using collaboration in risk-based environments such as finance, healthcare, and insurance. A structured environment for sharing critical risk information can improve decision-making. The chapter describes a business framework and an interface in which organizations might collaborate by trading risk-based products and information using an ontology, Web Services, and Peer-to-Peer technology. The chapter suggests that this type of environment might have been used to mitigate the impact of risk-based problems such as the current financial emergency. In conclusion, it is posited that a new type of product could emerge which incorporates the social-computing value of risk.

CONCLUSION

As readers will see and learn from this book, in the new collaboration paradigm, just letting stakeholders participate through some predefined channels to shape the final product is not enough to facilitate a productive process. "Collective" is not "collaborative". Constructive collaboration needs active coordination, common goal synchronization, proper social technologies utilization, and supportive cooperation.

This book is a good first step in understanding how to overcome the limits of current collaborative activities. The best practices in user experience, interactive tools, and information design shown here illustrate how a richer, more creative, and evolving research framework can be used to design and implement practical collaborative technologies and applications.

Acknowledgment

Many thanks to IGI-Global for filling this key publishing and scholarly niche, and for seeing the value in this project. Special thanks to Julia Mosemann at IGI for her unrelenting assistance at each step along the way.

Thanks to Lou Rosenfeld at Rosenfeld Media for telling me about Dr. Gary Marcionini and to Gary for the Foreword.

Scott Rummler
Researcher, USA

Kwong Bor Ng
Queens College, CUNY, USA

Section 1
Patterns of User Experience for Collaboration

Chapter 1

A Technology for Pattern-Based Process Design and its Application to Collaboration Engineering

Gwendolyn L. Kolfschoten
Delft University of Technology, The Netherlands

Robert O. Briggs
University of Nebraska at Omaha, USA

Gert-Jan de Vreede
University of Nebraska at Omaha, USA
Delft University of Technology, The Netherlands

ABSTRACT

As many business processes are collaborative in nature, process leaders or process managers play a pivotal role designing collaboration processes for organization. To support the design task of creating a new collaborative business process, best practices or design patterns can be used as building blocks. For such purposes, a library of design patterns and guidelines would be useful, not only to capture the best practices for different activities in the process in a database, but to also offer the users of this database support in selecting and combining such patterns, and in creating the process design. This chapter describes the requirements for a tool for pattern based collaboration process design, specifically for design efforts following the Collaboration Engineering approach.

1. INTRODUCTION

With collaboration and team work becoming the organizational norm to innovate and create value (Frost & Sullivan, 2007), new business processes predominantly involve collaborative work practices. A *work practice* is a set of actions carried out repeatedly to accomplish a particular organizational task (Briggs, Kolfschoten, Vreede, & Dean, 2006). A task is said to be *collaborative* if its successful completion depends on joint effort among multiple individuals. Process design and deployment has

DOI: 10.4018/978-1-60566-727-0.ch001

become the basis for most approaches to support change, improvement, and innovation in organizations. *Collaboration engineering* is an emerging approach to designing collaborative work practices for high value recurring tasks and deploying them to practitioners to execute for themselves without ongoing support from professional facilitators. Collaboration engineering researchers have distilled a number of collaboration principles, techniques and best practices, and codified them into a design pattern language (Briggs et al., 2006; Briggs, Vreede, & Nunamaker, 2003). This design pattern language provides Collaboration Engineers with reusable elements for designing collaborative work practices, and for specifying the technological capabilities a group will need to support its efforts. While such repositories of best practices support the design of collaborative work practices, this paper proposes a design for a technology to further support the design of collaborative work practices using a pattern language.

While new technologies can be a driver for changes of work practices, they often do not prescribe a new way of working, but rather offer the tools to support the new way. Workflow management (Aalst, Hofstede, & Kiepuszewski, 2003) approaches and business process engineering (Grover & Kettinger, 1995) methods offer an overview of tasks and processes, but do not provide the detailed 'how to' instructions to initiate and prescribe change. To change a collaborative work practice, groups need to be trained or require facilitation support (Briggs, 2006). The transition of new collaborative work practices is a complex task because a new work practice needs to be accepted and adopted by its users. A key requirement is the users' willingness to change. Briggs describes a Value Frequency Model to explain the behavioral intention (willingness) to change a work practice (Briggs, 2006). In this model, the willingness to change is caused by an individual judgment of the value of change and the expected frequency in which this added value

is experienced. Therefore, in order to transfer a new collaborative work practice, it needs to be designed in a way that offers its users a recurring added value.

The design of a new collaboration process poses several, sometimes conflicting, requirements: It needs to improve productivity of the organization, it needs to offer recurring value to the users, resources for the process are limited by definition, and the skills of process leaders might also present a limitation (Kolfschoten, Vreede, Briggs, & Sol, 2007). While many design approaches to collaboration support exist (Schwarz, 1994; Sheffield, 2004; Zigurs & Buckland, 1998), they merely offer a high level process structure, not the details on choices in tool configuration, combined with specific instructions. Research shows that such small configuration can have large impact on outcomes in group processes (Santanen & Vreede, 2004; Shepherd, Briggs, Reinig, Yen, & Nunamaker, 1996). To design new collaboration processes such that these requirements are met with some certainty, the designer can use best practices or design patterns – solutions that work and that can be combined to offer the prescription of an instrumental, predictable and transferable collaborative work practice (Coplien & Harrison, 2005; Schümmer & Lukosch, 2007). Design patterns are re-usable solutions to address frequently occurring problems. In Alexander's words: "A pattern describes a problem which occurs over and over again and then describes the core of the solution to that problem, in such a way that you can use this solution a million times over, without ever doing it the same way twice (Alexander, Ishikawa, Silverstein et al., 1977, p. x)."

A pattern language offers a designer or community of designers a library of best practices for a specific domain and product that can be used and combined to create solutions to problems in the organization. Furthermore it can support this community in providing a shared language, a coherent basis for their design and a way to document and transfer knowledge in this domain

(Alexander, 1979). Alexander's design patterns are used to design towns and buildings, but the design pattern concept was adopted in various other domains, including software engineering (Gamma, Helm, Johnson, & Vlissides, 1995; Lukosch & Schümmer, 2006; Rising, 2001), workflow management (Aalst et al., 2003), e-learning (Niegemann & Domagk, 2005), Project management (Khazanchi & Zigurs, 2007), and Collaboration Engineering (Kolfschoten, Briggs, Vreede, Jacobs, & Appelman, 2006; Vreede, Briggs, & Kolfschoten, 2006).

While a pattern language offers support in documenting and sharing best practices in process design and process support, it does not directly offer support on how to use these best practices. Design patterns are currently shared in books (Coplien & Harrison, 2005; Schümmer & Lukosch, 2007), or libraries on the internet (Hillside, 2008a; Yahoo, 2008). Therefore, to increase the usefulness of a pattern language and to evolve it to being more than a mere database of best practices, this chapter explores tool support for pattern-based design efforts. Such tools exist for software design patterns (Budinsky, Finnie, Vlissides, & Yu, 1996), and some social software could offer a starting point for such tools, such as wiki software (Hillside, 2008b). In the field of software engineering where design patterns have been adopted successfully as a way to share best practices, the use of Computer Aided Software Engineering (CASE) tools has been an important development. The IEEE standard for the adoption of CASE tools describes three gains from the use of CASE tools: increased design productivity, improvements in the quality of the software produced and improved consistency and uniformity of the design approach (IEEE Std 1348, 1995). Process design and deployment could gain from the development of a similar class of tools which we will label a Computer Aided Process Engineering tools, CAPE tools. Like a CASE tool, a CAPE tool is expected to increase process design productivity, process quality and consistency and uniformity of the process design and deployment approach.

Process analysis and design are often aimed at process change or improvement. Approaches to process improvement (Total Quality Management, Six Sigma, Deming Cycle, Capability Maturity, etc.) are not linear but cyclic, to support that lessons learned, measured performance and experience feed back to improve the best practices they were built upon. Therefore, a natural extension of a CAPE tool would be to integrate it with tools for management and evaluation of process change projects. Such integration is valuable not only to offer full support for process engineering, but especially to ensure that patterns do not become static documents but evolve to living documents that continuously improve and evolve based on experience and lessons learned.

In this chapter we explore the use of design patterns in collaboration process design; to create reusable sequences of activities that can be deployed in organizations to change collaborative work practices. For this purpose we will derive requirements for a Computer Aided Process Engineering tool that is offered as a design interface to a pattern language. The tool will offer support for the documentation of design patterns, their selection and combination into a sequence of activities, their implementation in a process design and their deployment in the organization. Further the tool will support learning from use and deployment of patterns to support continuous improvement of design patterns. We will derive our requirements based on the example of Collaboration Engineering, an approach to the design and deployment of repeatable collaboration processes. The challenges in Collaboration Engineering will pose several additional requirements to the resulting collaboration process design, and thus to the CAPE tool.

The remainder of this chapter is structured as follows. The next section describes a generic background on process design and deployment. Based on this foundation, the third section describes relevant aspects of the Collaboration

Table 1. Cyclic change cycles

Deming	Six Sigma	Capability Maturity	Process Reengineering Life Cycle
Plan	Define	Initial	Envision
Do	Measure	Reusable	Initiate
Check	Analyze	Defined	Diagnose
Act	Improve	Managed	Redesign
	Control	Optimized	Reconstruct
			Monitor

Engineering approach, while the fourth section defines the support required for the design and deployment of collaboration processes according to the Collaboration Engineering approach. The chapter ends with conclusions and recommendations for future research.

2. BACKGROUND: PROCESS DESIGN

Process design has been studied in a variety of closely related domains, in particular Business Process Change (Grover & Kettinger, 1995), Business Process Reengineering (O'Neill & Sohal, 1999), and workflow management (Aalst et al., 2003). Designs of processes and workflows in essence describe a sequence of tasks or steps for which actors, roles or agents are defined and for which technology support, objects, or applications are used. In workflow management there is a large role for "flow of execution control" decisions or choices that determine when the next step in the sequence is activated (Aalst et al., 2003). The same concepts are also used in modeling languages with a process perspective such as Data Flow models, IDEF0 (Mayer, 1990), and SADT models (Marca & McGowan, 1987).

To support process design, process modeling languages are supported with software tools that enable the user to drag and drop blocks representing activities and arrows representing process flow into a diagram and to specify a variety of

attributes of the activities, the process flow and the roles, routines, objects, decisions, etc. involved. Patterns in such system are used mostly to provide templates for the documentation of these elements and the different types of combinations that are used to sequence the process such as the AND-join pattern for synchronization in work flow (Aalst et al., 2003; Castano, Antonellis, & Melchiori, 1999) or the decision node in process flow models.

Process design as any other design effort has similar phases as a process for decision making, and problem solving (Ackoff, 1978; Checkland, 1981; Couger, 1995; Mitroff, Betz, Pondly, & Sagasty, 1974; Simon, 1973; Sol, 1982). It consists of an analysis of the current situation, possibly involving a decision about the need for a new approach or change. Next, through decomposition an initial sequence of steps is created. Alternative solutions to change and support the process are then identified and evaluated to eventually choose a sequence of steps and supporting tools that are validated (pilot, test case) to be ultimately implemented. As discussed modern approaches for process change such as the Business Process Reengineering Lifecycle (Guha, Kettinger, & Teng, 1993), the Deming cycle (Deming, 2000), the Capability Maturity Model (Paulk, Weber, Curtis, & Chrissis, 1995) and Six Sigma (Snee, 2004) are more incremental and cyclic (see table 1), working to establish and document the current process based on performance measurement and lessons learned to continuously improve and

Figure 1. Community based pattern development & sharing

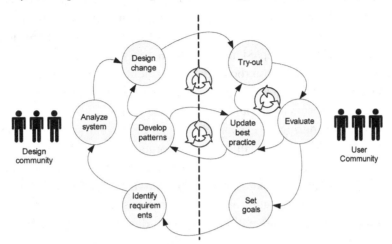

adapt the process.

We start our cycle with envisioning a goal, setting requirements, analyzing the current system, designing change, trying this change in the field and evaluating its effects to set new goals. Using a cyclic design approach connects the user and designer community, and creates a cycle of mutual learning. In this cycle the designer community analyses the system and based on design patterns derived from their expertise and experience, they propose changes. These changes are implemented and evaluated by the user community who identify best practices in their ways of working, reinforcing the design patterns. The design patterns based on best practices create a short-cut in this learning cycle in which both the user community and the designer community learns from the evaluation of changes to improve design and system performance (see Figure 1).

3. BACKGROUND: COLLABORATION ENGINEERING

Collaboration Engineering is an approach to designing collaborative work practices for high-value recurring tasks, and deploying those designs for practitioners to execute for themselves without

ongoing support from professional facilitators (Briggs et al., 2006; Briggs et al., 2003; Vreede & Briggs, 2005). In this approach an expert in collaboration support or facilitation designs a repeatable collaborative work practice based on design patterns, and transfers this work practice to practitioners in the organization who will use it to support their groups in the collaborative work practice.

For Collaboration Engineering it is critical that the design of the collaborative work practice is robust, that it creates predictable outcomes, that it is reusable in different instance of the task, that it is efficacious to the collaborative goal, that it is acceptable for the participating stakeholders, and that it is transferable to practitioners. For this purpose, thinkLets are developed. ThinkLets are named, scripted, reusable, and transferable collaborative activities that give rise to specific known patterns of collaboration among people working together toward a goal with predictable results (Briggs et al., 2006). For instance a LeafHopper thinkLet (Kolfschoten, Briggs et al., 2006) is used to let participants brainstorm ideas in multiple categories. This gives rise to the collaboration pattern "generate" where the group moves from having fewer to having more concepts in the pool of concepts shared by the group (Briggs et al.,

2006), and results is a set of categorized ideas that might contain redundant and double ideas.

A collaboration process design mostly consists of a sequence of thinkLets, which is scripted in a manual for practitioners (Kolfschoten, Kosterbok, & Hoekstra, 2008; Vreede & Briggs, 2005). Furthermore, practitioners get a process model and a set of cue cards to support them during the execution of the process design (Kolfschoten & Hulst, 2006). The information required for the designer of a collaboration process, i.e. the Collaboration Engineer, is different from the information required by the practitioner. While the Collaboration Engineer needs information to support the selection and combination of thinkLets, the practitioner only needs the information required to understand and execute the thinkLets in different instance of the collaborative work practice.

Since the robustness of the collaboration process design is of critical importance, there is large emphasis on the validation of the design before it is transferred to practitioners in the organization. For this purpose, quality dimensions of a collaboration process design are distinguished, as described above (efficacious, predictable, transferable, reusable, acceptable). These dimensions also offer a framework for the analysis of the task (efficaciousness), stakeholders (acceptance), available resources (reusability), and practitioners (transferability) (Kolfschoten & Rouwette, 2006b; Kolfschoten, Vreede et al., 2007; Kolfschoten, Vreede, Chakrapani, & Koneri, 2006). Once the requirements and constraints to the collaboration process are known, a first sequence of activities is determined. Then for each activity a thinkLet is be selected resulting in a sequence of thinkLets. Additionally other activities such as breaks, presentations and introductions are placed in the sequence. For each activity, additional information should be specified. For instance in the example of the LeafHopper thinkLet, the collaboration engineer should specify the type of contributions, (e.g. solutions, risks, problems), the categories in which the group should brainstorm contributions,

the topic of the brainstorm in general and the time for the thinkLet. Thus, if the LeafHopper were used to have a group brainstorm requirements for a new tool, categories could be hardware requirements, software requirements and network requirements, while the time for the activity could be one hour.

Once all activities are specified, the collaboration process design can be validated based on a number of criteria. Some characteristics of thinkLets can be used to determine generic characteristics of the entire process design such as its duration, complexity, and the amount of discussion. These factors influence the acceptance of the work practice. This validation activity can be automated, such that an alert is issued when the collaboration process design does not meet some or all of the criteria, e.g. too many complex thinkLets are used, or too little discussion is included in the design. Other validation criteria can be offered as a checklist for consideration. After validation, a process manual for the practitioner should be created containing a process model, the script for each activity, a summary of the analysis, and cue cards to support execution (Kolfschoten & Hulst, 2006). Furthermore, the execution of the collaboration process can be supported with tools such as Group Support Systems, for which the information of the activity scripts needs to be instantiated as well.

Over the past five years, the Collaboration Engineering research community has developed a number of 'paper-based' tools to support the Collaboration Engineering efforts. First, the design approach as described above, was developed and evaluated based on feedback from facilitators and students using the design approach (Kolfschoten, Hengst, & Vreede, 2007; Kolfschoten & Vreede, 2007). The thinkLet pattern concept has been introduced by Briggs and de Vreede (Briggs et al., 2003; Briggs, Vreede, Nunamaker, & David, 2001; Vreede & Briggs, 2001), and was further developed into its current form (Kolfschoten, Appelman, Briggs, & Vreede, 2004; Kolfschoten,

Briggs, Appelman, & Vreede, 2004; Kolfschoten, Briggs et al., 2006; Kolfschoten & Houten, 2007; Kolfschoten & Hulst, 2006; Kolfschoten & Santanen, 2007; Vreede et al., 2006).

Second, to support the analysis of work practices, we asked facilitators about the information required to design a collaboration process (Kolfschoten, Hengst et al., 2007). Third, to support the selection and combination of thinkLets we performed a pattern analysis to derive frequently occurring thinkLet combinations, i.e. we identified patterns in thinkLet sequences (Kolfschoten, Appelman et al., 2004) and we performed in-depth interviews with facilitators to elicit the criteria they use to choose among thinkLets (Kolfschoten, Appelman et al., 2004; Kolfschoten & Rouwette, 2006a, 2006b). The insights on choice criteria also helped us to develop a validation framework. Finally, a facilitation process model was developed to visualize thinkLets-based collaboration process designs (Vreede & Briggs, 2005), and a first prototype of a design support tool was developed (Kolfschoten & Veen, 2005).

4. COMPUTER AIDED PROCESS DESIGN

To support design efforts in information systems, the Software Engineering discipline has introduced the use of CASE tools. A CASE tool is defined as *"a software tool that aids in software engineering activities including, but not limited to requirements analysis and tracing, software design, code production, testing, document generation, quality assurance configuration management and project management (IEEE Std 1348, 1995)."*

To support pattern-based process design, we can use this definition to define a CAPE tool as *"a software tool that aids in process design activities including but not limited to situation analysis, process decomposition, process design, process visualization, selection, storage and addition of process design patterns, process validation,* *process specification, process documentation, process implementation and project management."* A CAPE tool supports the user in following the process design approach and simplifies the choices that need to be made during the design effort. It does not render a process design or implementation based on a set of requirements.

When a pattern language is used, design patterns are used as building blocks. This will change the process design effort slightly from the steps described above. While the original approach assumes that alternative solutions have to be created, evaluated, compared, and selected, using design patterns, this changes into an approach in which a design pattern is selected based on known properties of this design pattern that fit the requirements for the process. As these known properties support the choice of design patterns, they also prescribe the information required to make this choice (Kolfschoten & Veen, 2005). It can thus offer a checklist for analysis of the current situation. Furthermore, design patterns are descriptions of solutions but like object oriented class descriptions, they need to be instantiated in the specific context of the process design. Finally, design patterns contain information about their applicability and thus they contain information that can be used to validate the process resulting from the design effort. When the pattern library does not offer a pattern that solves the specific requirements of the process task, a new pattern or a variation on an existing pattern should be added.

Thus process design with the support of design patterns offers process engineers valuable information to create and instantiate a process design. A tool to support such efforts should offer functionality to:

- Store design patterns to avail them to the community.
- Add new design patterns and to add variations to design patterns.
- Enable a community of users to discuss the

design patterns.

- Support the analysis of the situation sharing tools and methods for this.
- Share knowledge to support the decomposition of the process.
- Share knowledge to support the selection and combination of design patterns.
- Support visualization of the process flow to support transfer of the process.
- Support precise specification of the design patterns to improve shared understanding.
- Implement the design patterns in a process manual and in technology support to reduce cognitive load of their use.
- Support project management for change processes.

5. THE CACE TOOL

When we want to change work practices to make them collaborative work practices, we can benefit from a library of design patterns to support collaborative work practices, such as the thinkLet library. However, the design of a collaborative work practice with thinkLets required insight in design choices related to the selection of thinkLets and their instantiation to support specific organizational tasks. To avail this knowledge we can capture it in a design support environment based on the Computer Assisted Process Engineering tool proposed above. To support the design of collaboration processes according to the Collaboration Engineering approach we need to adapt the requirements for a CAPE tool to support thinkLet documentation, use, design, specification, and implementation. Further we need to incorporate different tools and methods to support the analysis, of the task, the decomposition of the process, the visualization of the process flow, the creation of output documents and the project management of a Collaboration Engineering project to change individual work practices to become collaborative work practices, increasing their efficiency and

effectiveness, though the benefit of integrating multiple perspectives and visions in an efficient way. In summary, we propose that a CACE tool, a specific type of CAPE tool, a tool to support collaboration process design following the Collaboration Engineering approach, should offer functionality to share design patterns, support the steps of the design approach, and support the project to change the work practice to become collaborative (see Table 2).

Based on these requirements, we created a conceptual model of the CACE tool (Figure 2). The model is an object model, but describes the functionalities on a high level than required for functional requirement specification. In the subsections below, we elaborate on the key components of the CACE tool in more detail.

5.1 Tools for Sharing Design Patterns

The Pattern Database

To share design patterns in a way that supports communication and mutual understanding a 'master' thinkLet should be developed to offer a template for documentation of the thinkLets. Besides knowledge about the techniques attributes can then be stored that can be used to support the selection and validation process. See (Kolfschoten, Briggs et al., 2006; Kolfschoten & Houten, 2007; Vreede et al., 2006) for a class diagram of the detailed content of the thinkLet concept. ThinkLets mostly contain textual information, but also a picture, some numeric information and video's of thinkLets. Not all users should be able to add or alter thinkLets, so a separate role should be developed for this purpose.

To keep the pattern language coherent, relations between thinkLets, such as combinations and alternatives, should be documented. This represents a complex aspect of the thinkLet pattern database: when a thinkLet is added not only the new thinkLet must be adjusted, but also the

Table 2. Requirements for a CACE tool

Support for the sharing of design patterns; to support the community in sharing their thinkLets and experiences with them.	Share thinkLets, including relevant information for both the collaboration engineer and the practitioner.
	Add new thinkLets and to add variations to thinkLets.
	Enable a community of collaboration engineers, facilitators, and practitioners to discuss thinkLets.
Support the key steps of the design approach; to share best practices, tools and methods to improve the quality of the thinkLet based designs.	Support the analysis of the collaborative task to be supported.
	Support the decomposition of the collaboration process.
	Support the selection and combination of thinkLets.
	Support the specification of thinkLets.
	Support the visualization of the collaboration process flow.
	Support the validation of the collaboration process design.
Support the deployment of the work practice; the transfer of the collaboration process design to practitioners in the organization, and to support their adoption and ownership of the project around the collaborative work practice.	Support the creation of different types of output documents such as an agenda, a process manual, cue cards, and collaboration technology configuration settings, based on the thinkLets used in the collaboration process design.
	Support for project management.
	Support for practitioners to share experiences

other thinkLets must be updated, as (potential) combinations with the new thinkLet must be evaluated. If the person who added the thinkLet does not know how it will combine with other thinkLets, experts in collaboration process design should be asked to contribute these aspects. For this purpose it would be useful to include a wizard that supports the user though the process of sharing a new thinkLet.

It would also be useful to store the thinkLet library in multiple languages. If the system offers multiple languages than language selection should be one of the first steps in the design process, to make each specification fit the selected language. For the community using the CACE tool it would be best if the comments on thinkLets and the thinkLet names are in one language so that a shared meaning of thinkLet labels remains.

Collaboration engineers and facilitators that use the pattern language and the CACE tool should be able to comment on attributes of the thinkLet and to offer suggestions for alternations of standard attributes of the thinkLets. They can customize the thinkLets in their design, but should

not be allowed to alter the structure of the master thinkLet. Besides discussing thinkLets, the system should also enable storage of complete process designs, which can be shared with other designers/facilitators and with practitioners. These users should be able to comment both on the entire process design and on the individual thinkLets within the design. The users maintaining the master thinkLets should regularly check these comments and when necessary alter the master thinkLet. In this way the community of collaboration process designers can share and maintain an intergraded library of design patterns.

5.2 Tools to Support the Design Approach

Analysis Support

The support for analysis should consist of a checklist that helps the Collaboration Engineer to gather all information required to design the collaboration process. However, with many users and stakeholders in the process, it is useful to first analyze (part of) the required information though a survey. In such case it would be useful if the information required was listed as pre-defined

interview questions. While not all stakeholders have similar information about the process or decision power when choices are to be made,

Figure 2. Class Model of the CACE tool

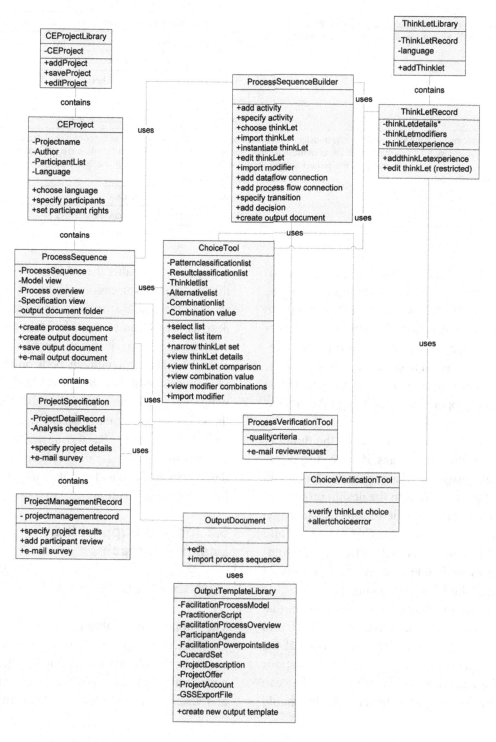

the collaboration engineer can assign questions to respondents, and automatically mail them the survey. Based on this information interviews and sessions to design and validate the process can be more efficiently organized and executed. Some of the information that is to be analyzed is used as a basis for the design effort or for the validation. In this way the feedback from the user community can be used to improve the design patterns.

Process Sequence Builder

Based on the information in the analysis support part of the CACE tool, a first set of constraints to the process design should be available: for example, the time frame for the collaboration process execution is fixed, and some elements like a lunch break, a introduction presentation etc. are automatically scheduled. The next step in the design effort is to create the sequence of activities. For this purpose, the collaboration engineer adds and labels the activities in the collaboration process such as "brainstorm ideas", "select key ideas", etc. After such a sequence of activities is created the collaboration engineer can start choosing and importing thinkLets using a choice tool. Some more experienced collaboration engineers "think in terms of thinkLets" meaning that they want to directly select thinkLets into the process. Furthermore, the selection of a specific thinkLet will sometimes change the sequence of activities, therefore activities should be visualized as a kind of placeholders, that can be replaced by one or more thinkLets. By default, the thinkLet should take on the activity name of the sequence. A collaboration engineer can import thinkLets into the process sequence, and can be supported in different ways to select a thinkLets, for example:

1. From an alphabetical list and from a list in which the thinkLet pictures are visualized.
2. Based on classifications of the patterns of collaboration or the results of the thinkLet.

3. Based on a set of thinkLets that can use the outcome of the previous thinkLet as input (combination patterns).
4. From a set of alternatives, this can be automatically derived from the above classifications, allowing the user to choose among alternatives with a similar result, or with a similar pattern of collaboration.

ThinkLets can be classified among several aspects (patterns of collaboration or results), so the collaboration engineer should be able to select an aspect on the list and thus narrow the set of available thinkLets. During the selection process, detailed information on the thinkLets should be available to the collaboration engineer. For example through a single click on the thinkLet, its attributes relevant for selection should be visible. We think of these selection methods as topics in a topic map, where the classification term is the topic, and the relations between thinkLets are the associations, and the patterns in the library are the occurrences (Techquila, 2007).

A specific combination of thinkLets will have specific added value or risks. Such information should be provided by the CACE tool as well when a combination is tested. Information about combinations is of course only valid when the output of one thinkLet is used as input for the next thinkLet. Further, a collaboration engineer needs a functionality that enables him to compare thinkLets on their applicability. Finally, thinkLets can be modified to create small changes in the patterns of collaboration they create or in the result they create. Such modifications will also support the collaboration engineer in selecting a thinkLet. Therefore, the sequence builder and the choice tool should allow the collaboration engineer to select modifiers.

Besides a fit to the task and the existing thinkLet sequence, the choice of a thinkLet should also be aligned with the available resources, the group, and the practitioner. Key aspects in this respect include (obviously, for some thinkLets other aspects may affect acceptance by the group participating in the collaboration process, but such specific considerations should be deliberated by the collaboration engineer based on the thinkLet description):

- The timeframe.
- The group size.
- The scope of the task.
- The complexity for the practitioner.
- The complexity for the group.
- The available technological resources, especially the availability of parallel input, anonymity and data processing abilities as offered in Group Support Systems.

To further verify the choice of a thinkLet, the CACE tool will compare information in the project description with information in the thinkLet. Furthermore, each of these factors affects the time required for the thinkLet. While the collaboration engineer should be free to specify the time frame for the thinkLet differently, the system should calculate a suggested time frame for each thinkLet based on the earlier field experiences with the particular thinkLet and these factors. When the thinkLet time estimated based on these factors does not fit the timeframe proposed by the collaboration engineer, an alert should be given. Similar intelligent design support will alert the facilitator when the thinkLet does not fit the group size or the complexity it can handle, when it does not fit the breadth of the scope, when it does not work without certain resources available or when it is too complex for the practitioners involved.

Based on the above, not only the thinkLet sequence which determines the process flow can be created, but also the data flow should also be specified and the decisions and transitions in the process should be specified. Further, based on the time frame of the meeting and the time estimation of the individual activities in the collaboration process design, the starting time and duration can be specified. Yet, starting times and durations may be altered, and there should be an option to automatically update the other times in the process sequence.

For some thinkLets several aspects need to be further specified. First of all, as mentioned earlier, most thinkLets have variations named modifiers. Modifiers can be selected, and they also alter the results, patterns of collaboration and in some cases the time and resources required for the step. Once the modifiers are selected, some other aspects of the thinkLets may need to be instantiated:

- Roles involved in the process can be labeled.
- Constraints to the data input or modifications can be specified such as topics, category names, and voting criteria.
- Capabilities should be instantiated with resources available.

Besides instantiation, the collaboration engineer will want to alter some descriptions or information in the thinkLet to further customize the design. It should therefore also be possible to edit the thinkLets in the project record without changing the same thinkLet entries in the thinkLet library.

Validation

A number of thinkLets attributes can be used to perform an overall assessment of the collaboration process design, for example in terms of its complexity, the amount of discussion, the amount of input required from the participants, and the need for consensus or agreement. These aspects give a first indication of the acceptance of the process. The choice verification system described above will check for most of the 'resource fit' and alert the collaboration engineer when the process does not fit the resources available. The system can render a list of skills required to run the process to evaluate the fit to the practitioner. Furthermore, for each thinkLet a list of challenges is specified which indicates what might go wrong or what might be difficult. This set can be used to assess the acceptance and transferability of the process, and may additionally give an indication of the predictability of the process.

For each quality dimension of the collaboration process design (as described above: efficacious, predictable, transferable, reusable, acceptable) the criteria are specified and can be used as a framework for evaluation. A collaboration engineer can go through this a list to validate his own design, but the list can also be used to ask users or other collaboration experts to validate the process design. In this case the evaluation framework is used in a similar way as the analysis checklist, where questions are selected for respondents and the design with the script are send out for review. Jointly these tools can help a community of collaboration engineers to develop collaborative work practices and to give each other feedback on their designs.

5.3 Tools to Support Deployment of the Collaborative Work Practice

Project Library

Each CE project will be stored in a separate file. For this CE project record, the participants (practitioner, project manager, collaboration engineer, facilitator, and session participants) and their rights can be specified. Different users will have different rights. For example, while practitioners must be able to review thinkLets and add their experience with the project, participants should only have access to an evaluation survey and the participant agenda. The project author should select a language to work in.

Output Documents

The thinkLet sequence should be visible for the collaboration engineer during the design effort as a Facilitation Process Model (Kolfschoten &

Hulst, 2006; Kolfschoten, Vreede et al., 2006; Vreede & Briggs, 2005). In such models, thinkLets are connected with arrows to represent process flow and data flow. It should be possible for the collaboration engineer to rearrange the thinkLets to smoothen the layout of the process model. The CACE tool will enable the user to drag and drop the thinkLets and other activities in a field where these can be connected into a sequence. The system should also offer an "edit" button for each thinkLet that opens a menu for selection of an alternative thinkLet or for specification of the thinkLet. Furthermore, with a single click, the user should be able to starting editing or fine-tuning the script of the thinkLet for the manual.

Besides the model and the design description there are several other output documents are used. These include the script for the practitioner, the slides for the introduction of the collaboration process, an agenda or invitation for the participants, a project offer or account, and an export document that can be imported into a Group Support System to instantiate the capabilities required for the process. A key output template that should be created is the manual for practitioners. This manual has four elements: the facilitation process model, the script, the cue cards, and a summary of the analysis as background material (Kolfschoten & Hulst, 2006). For each of these elements text selected from the thinkLet master in the database should be instantiated and displayed in a specific format so it can be printed in a useful way. Since the script might need to be altered for a specific collaboration process or context, each aspect of the script should be editable. Users should be able to create new output document templates and to store a collaboration process design in different document types such as word, pdf, and html.

Project Management

Apart from 'standard project management' support (which can be offered by many standard applications), it would be useful to monitor the performance of the practitioners and to collect feedback from participants in the process. For example, each practitioner can enter his experiences for each time he executed the process, and participants of the process can offer feedback through a questionnaire. These sources can be combined to gain insight in the success of the deployment of the collaboration process, and they can offer a basis for meetings in which practitioners share experiences, tips and tricks. Together these tools support the deployment of the work practice in the organization, and the transfer of responsibilities and ownership of the change project from the collaboration engineer to the community of practitioners.

6. FURTHER RESEARCH DIRECTIONS

The concepts advanced in this paper have been applied in an international initiative to create the ActionCenters platform, which will be the first full-featured CACE environment. This platform will support the complete Collaboration Engineering development cycle, from establishing the goals and deliverables of a group to pattern-based designs for their collaborative work practices, to configuring purpose-build collaborative software applications specifically tailored to move groups through particular high-value recurring tasks. Various developers of Group Support Systems have been approached to see if they are interested in participating in the project in an open source community.

Initial funding for the ActionCenters project has been obtained from a government agency. The Institute of Collaboration Science at the University of Omaha at Nebraska, Delft University of Technology, and other government agencies, and partners from private industry committed resources to bring the project to fruition.

Future research efforts will focus on further elaborating on the CACE tool's functional re-

quirements through experiences with prototypes such as described in (Kolfschoten & Veen, 2005), and designing an overall architecture for the tool. However, the conceptual integration of pattern based cyclic process design to enhance mutual learning in user and development communities is a model that also requires further evaluation and refinement. Finally the ThinkLet concept, in which design patterns for designers and best practices for users are combined in one concept, can be generalized to support the use of design patterns in a process design in general. While the conceptualization of design patterns is now very generic to support both communities, the actual patterns are often written for one of both audiences. To serve both communities, it is important to create a more detailed pattern documentation template in which joint and separate information requirements are integrated.

7. CONCLUSION

This chapter presents an overview of a CACE tool, a tool to support pattern-based design of collaboration processes following the Collaboration Engineering approach. The design of the tool is grounded in the requirements of a general computer-assisted process design tool. Initial prototypes of selected elements of the tool have been developed and tested (see e.g. Kolfschoten and Veen 2005), while others are currently in progress. The chapter shows a design based on a view in which the use of design patterns is combined with process design according to the new, more cyclic paradigms for continuous improvement of processes and therewith performance. To support pattern based design in this fashion, a CAPE tool should not only support design steps and choices but should support an overall project support in which experiences and performance are captured to support pattern development and improvement. In this way a CAPE tool supports both users and designers in a continuous learning cycle.

REFERENCES

Ackoff, R. L. (1978). *The Art of Problem Solving*: New York: John Wiley & Sons.

Alexander, C. (1979). *The Timeless Way of Building*. New York: Oxford University Press.

Alexander, C., Ishikawa, S., Silverstein, M., Jacobson, M., Fiksdahl-King, I., & Angel, S. (1977). *A Pattern Language, Towns, Buildings, Construction*. New York: Oxford University Press.

Briggs, R. O. (2006). *The Value Frequency Model: Towards a Theoretical Understanding of Organizational Change*. Paper presented at the International Conference on Group Decision and Negotiation, Karlsruhe, Germany.

Briggs, R. O., de Vreede, G. J., & Nunamaker, J. F. Jr. (2003). Collaboration Engineering with ThinkLets to Pursue Sustained Success with Group Support Systems. *Journal of Management Information Systems, 19*(4), 31–63.

Briggs, R. O., de Vreede, G. J., Nunamaker, J. F., Jr., & David, T. H. (2001). *ThinkLets: Achieving Predictable, Repeatable Patterns of Group Interaction with Group Support Systems*. Paper presented at the Hawaii International Conference on System Sciences, Waikoloa, HI.

Briggs, R. O., Kolfschoten, G. L., de Vreede, G. J., & Dean, D. L. (2006). *Defining Key Concepts for Collaboration Engineering*. Paper presented at the Americas Conference on Information Systems, Acapulco, Mexico.

Budinsky, F.J., Finnie, M.A., Vlissides, J.M., & Yu, P.S. (1996). Automatic Code Generation from Design Patterns. *Object technology, 35*(2), 151-172.

Castano, S., de Antonellis, V., & Melchiori, M. (1999). A methodology and tool environment for process analysis and reengineering. *Data & Knowledge Engineering, 31*(3), 253–278. doi:10.1016/S0169-023X(99)00028-2

Checkland, P. B. (1981). *Systems Thinking, Systems Practice*. Chichester, UK: John Wiley & Sons.

Coplien, J. O., & Harrison, N. B. (2005). *Organizational Patterns of Agile Software Development*. Upper Saddle River, NJ: Pearson Prentice Hall.

Couger, J. D. (1995). *Creative Problem Solving and Opportunity Finding*: Danvers, MA: Boyd and Fraser.

de Vreede, G. J., & Briggs, R. O. (2001). *ThinkLets: Five Examples Of Creating Patterns Of Group Interaction*. Paper presented at the International Conference on Group Decision and Negotiation, La Rochelle, France.

de Vreede, G. J., & Briggs, R. O. (2005). *Collaboration Engineering: Designing Repeatable Processes for High-Value Collaborative Tasks*. Paper presented at the Hawaii International Conference on System Science, Los Alamitos.

de Vreede, G. J., Briggs, R. O., & Kolfschoten, G. L. (2006). ThinkLets: A Pattern Language for Facilitated and Practitioner-Guided Collaboration Processes. *International Journal of Computer Applications in Technology, 25*(2/3), 140–154. doi:10.1504/IJCAT.2006.009064

Deming, W. E. (2000). *Out of the Crisis: For Industry, Government, Education*. Cambridge, MA: MIT Press.

Frost, & Sullivan. (2007). *Meetings around the World: The Impact of Collaboration on Business Performance*.

Gamma, E., Helm, R., Johnson, R., & Vlissides, J. (1995). *Elements of Reusable Object-Oriented Software*. Reading, MA: Addison-Wesley Publishing Company.

Grover, V., & Kettinger, W. J. (1995). *Business Process Change; Reengineering Concepts, Methods and Technologies*. Hershey, PA: Idea Group Publishing.

Guha, S., Kettinger, W. J., & Teng, T. C. (1993). Business Process Reengineering: Building a Comprehensive Methodology. *Information Systems Management, 10*(3), 13–22. doi:10.1080/10580539308906939

Hillside. (2008a). *hillside pattern languages.* Unpublished manuscript.

Hillside. (2008b). Wiki for pattern sharing. Retrieved August 26, 2008, from http://hillside.net/Wiki/

IEEE Std 1348. (1995). IEEE Recommended Practice for the Adoption of Computer-Aided Software Engineering (CASE) Tools.

Khazanchi, D., & Zigurs, I. (2007). *An Assessment Framework for Discovering and Using Patterns in Virtual Project Management.* Paper presented at the Hawaii International Conference on System Science, Waikoloa, HI.

Kolfschoten, G. L., Appelman, J. H., Briggs, R. O., & de Vreede, G. J. (2004). *Recurring Patterns of Facilitation Interventions in GSS Sessions.* Paper presented at the Hawaii International Conference on System Sciences, Waikoloa, HI.

Kolfschoten, G. L., Briggs, R. O., Appelman, J. H., & de Vreede, G. J. (2004). *ThinkLets as Building Blocks for Collaboration Processes: A Further Conceptualization.* Paper presented at the CRIWG conference, San Carlos, Costa Rica.

Kolfschoten, G. L., Briggs, R. O., de Vreede, G. J., Jacobs, P. H. M., & Appelman, J. H. (2006). Conceptual Foundation of the ThinkLet Concept for Collaboration Engineering. *International Journal of Human Computer Science, 64*(7), 611–621. doi:10.1016/j.ijhcs.2006.02.002

Kolfschoten, G. L., & de Vreede, G. J. (2007). *The Collaboration Engineering Approach for Designing Collaboration Processes.* Paper presented at the CRIWG Conference, Bariloche, Argentina.

Kolfschoten, G. L., de Vreede, G. J., Briggs, R. O., & Sol, H. G. (2007). *Collaboration Engineerability.* Paper presented at the Group Decision and Negotiation conference, Mt Tremblant, Canada.

Kolfschoten, G. L., de Vreede, G. J., Chakrapani, A., & Koneri, P. (2006). *A Design Approach for Collaboration Engineering.* Paper presented at the First HICSS Symposium on Case and Field Studies of Collaboration, Kauai, HI.

Kolfschoten, G. L., den Hengst, M., & de Vreede, G. J. (2007). Issues in the Design of Facilitated Collaboration Processes. *Group Decision and Negotiation, 16*(4), 347–361. doi:10.1007/s10726-006-9054-6

Kolfschoten, G. L., Kosterbok, J., & Hoekstra, A. (2008). *A Transferable ThinkLet based Process Design for Integrity Risk Assessment in Government Organizations.* Paper presented at the International Conference on Group Decision and Negotiation, Coimbra, Portugal.

Kolfschoten, G. L., & Rouwette, E. (2006a). *Choice Criteria for Facilitaition Techniques.* Paper presented at the First HICSS Symposium on Case and Field Studies of Collaboration, Kauai, HI.

Kolfschoten, G. L., & Rouwette, E. (2006b). *Choice Criteria for Facilitation Techniques: A Preliminary Classification.* Paper presented at the International Conference on Group Decision and Negotiation, Karlsruhe, Germany.

Kolfschoten, G. L., & Santanen, E. L. (2007). *Reconceptualizing Generate ThinkLets: the Role of the Modifier.* Paper presented at the Hawaii International Conference on System Science, Waikoloa, HI.

Kolfschoten, G. L., & van der Hulst, S. (2006). *Collaboration Process Design Transition to Practitioners: Requirements from a Cognitive Load Perspective.* Paper presented at the International Conference on Group Decision and Negotiation, Karlsruhe, Germany.

Kolfschoten, G. L., & van Houten, S. P. A. (2007). *Predictable Patterns in Group Settings through the use of Rule Based Facilitation Interventions.* Paper presented at the International Conference on Group Decision and Negotiation conference, Mt. Tremblant, Canada.

Kolfschoten, G. L., & Veen, W. (2005). *Tool Support for GSS Session Design.* Paper presented at the Hawaii International Conference on System Sciences, Waikoloa, HI.

Lukosch, S., & Schümmer, T. (2006). Groupware Development Support with Technology Patterns. *International Journal of Human Computer Systems, 64*(7), 599–610. doi:10.1016/j.ijhcs.2006.02.006

Marca, D. A., & McGowan, C. L. (1987). *SADT: Structured Analysis and Design Technique.* New York: McGraw Hill, Inc.

Mayer, R. (1990). *IDEF0 Functional Modeling.* College Station, TX: Knowledge Based Systems, Inc.

Mitroff, I. I., Betz, F., Pondly, L. R., & Sagasty, F. (1974). On Managing Science In The Systems Age: Two Schemas For The Study Of Science As A Whole Systems Phenomenon. *TIMS Interfaces, 4*(3), 46–58. doi:10.1287/inte.4.3.46

Niegemann, H. M., & Domagk, S. (2005). *ELEN Project Evaluation Report.* Retrieved from http://www2tisip.no/E-LEN

O'Neill, P., & Sohal, A. S. (1999). Business Process Reengineering, A Review of Recent Literature. *Technovation, 19*(9), 571–581. doi:10.1016/S0166-4972(99)00059-0

Paulk, M. C., Weber, C. V., Curtis, B., & Chrissis, M. B. (1995). *The Capability Maturity Model: Guidelines for Improving the Software Process.* New York: Addison-Wesley.

Rising, L. (2001). *Design Patterns in Communication Software.* Cambridge, UK: Cambridge University Press.

Santanen, E. L., & de Vreede, G. J. (2004). *Creative Approaches to Measuring Creativity: Comparing the Effectiveness of Four Divergence ThinkLets.* Paper presented at the Hawaiian International Conference on System Sciences, Waikoloa, HI.

Schümmer, T., & Lukosch, S. (2007). *Patterns for Computer-Mediated Interaction.* West Sussex, UK: John Wiley & Sons Ltd.

Schwarz, R. M. (1994). *The Skilled Facilitator.* San Francisco: Jossey-Bass Publishers.

Sheffield, J. (2004). The Design of GSS-Enabled Interventions: A Habermasian Perspective. *Group Decision and Negotiation, 13*(5), 415–435. doi:10.1023/B:GRUP.0000045750.48336.f7

Shepherd, M. M., Briggs, R. O., Reinig, B. A., Yen, J., & Nunamaker, J. F. Jr. (1996). Social Comparison to Improve Electronic Brainstorming: Beyond Anonymity. *Journal of Management Information Systems, 12*(3), 155–170.

Simon, H. A. (1973). The Structure of Ill Structured Problems. *Artificial Intelligence, 4*(3-4), 181–201. doi:10.1016/0004-3702(73)90011-8

Snee, R. D. (2004). Six-Sigma: the evolution of 100 years of business improvement methodology. *International Journal of Six Sigma and Competitive Advantage, 1*(1), 4–20. doi:10.1504/IJSSCA.2004.005274

Sol, H. G. (1982). *Simulation in information systems development.* Groningen, the Netherlands: Rijksuniversiteit Groningen.

Techquila. (2007). Retrieved from http://www.techquila.com/topicmaps.html

van der Aalst, W. M. P., ter Hofstede, A. H. M., & Kiepuszewski, B. (2003). Workflow Patterns. *Distributed and Parallel Databases*, *14*(1), 5–51. doi:10.1023/A:1022883727209

Yahoo. (2008). *Design Pattern Library*. Retrieved from http://developer.yahoo.com/ypatterns/atoz.php

Zigurs, I., & Buckland, B. (1998). A Theory of Task/Technology Fit and Group Support Systems Effectiveness. *Management Information Systems Quarterly*, *22*(3), 313–334. doi:10.2307/249668

Chapter 2
Pattern–Based Tool Design for Shared Knowledge Construction

Stephan Lukosch
Delft University of Technology, The Netherlands

ABSTRACT

Shared knowledge construction aims at supporting the creation and gathering of new knowledge. It relies on tools for computer-mediated interaction. The design and development of these tools is difficult, as not only the interaction of one user with the tool but also the interaction among the users themselves has to be taken into account. For designing and developing successful tools, it is crucial to involve end-users in the development process and to create shared understanding of the requirements as well as the solutions among the end-users and developers. In this chapter, the author analyzes the problems when developing tools for computer-mediated interaction in general and present a novel pattern-based approach for supporting developers as well as integrating end-users in the development process. The author shows the applicability of this approach by introducing tools for shared knowledge construction and describing their pattern-based design. The author concludes by giving an outlook on future research directions.

INTRODUCTION

The rapid evolution and development of computing systems and networking technologies resulted in the use of the Internet as a global communication infrastructure. Every day new computers or local area networks are connected via gateways and Internet service providers to the Internet and contributes to its exponential growth. The popular-ity of the Internet is largely due to the influence of the World Wide Web (WWW). The WWW is the fastest growing segment of the Internet and is now accepted as the standard information support system in many important sectors of life activities such as finance, education, travel, business, science, health care, art etc. Nowadays, the WWW is the platform for all kinds of information sharing and cooperation as well as communication forms. Furthermore, the WWW is currently performing a shift from the single-user-centered usage to support

DOI: 10.4018/978-1-60566-727-0.ch002

multi-user needs covering many social aspects and collaboration forms.

Our current knowledge and information society considers knowledge as intellectual capital. Knowledge is an important resource for companies, organizations, and individuals. Knowledge is often defined as information of which a person, organization, or a group is aware. Implicit knowledge cannot be formalized and is based on personal experiences, skills, or a combination of both. Compared to this, explicit knowledge is more comprehensible as it is often formalized, e.g. in mathematical expressions. For constructing knowledge, individuals reflect on their experiences and organize these experiences. Thus, knowledge is a cognitive learning process which uses and converts external forces to structure the environment. Shared knowledge construction goes a step further as it requires a group to interact and create a shared understanding of knowledge. Shared knowledge construction is a process in social sciences as well as pedagogy. It enhances traditional knowledge construction by using tools for computer-mediated interaction. Due to the popularity of the Web, these tools are often web-based.

The development of tools for computer-mediated interaction is difficult as not only the interaction of one user with the tool but also the interaction among a number of users has to be taken into account when designing these tools. For designing and developing successful tools, it is crucial to involve end-users in the development process (Schümmer, Lukosch, & Slagter, 2006). Involving end-users in the development process requires that end-users and developers can communicate using a common language. This language has to allow end-users and developers to identify and specify requirements as well as solution. Often this language does not exist. Furthermore, the necessary background knowledge for developing tools for computer-mediated interaction is often not part of the professional training for software engineers. These issues make it difficult to develop

successful tools for computer-mediated interaction in general and particularly for shared knowledge construction. We propose to overcome these issues by providing developers and end-users with a pattern language for communicating with each other and a development process which involves the end-users.

In this chapter, we first analyze the problems when developing tools for computer-mediated interaction in general. Then, we present a novel pattern-based approach for supporting developers as well integrating end-users in the development process. We report on our experiences when using the pattern language to design and specify tools for shared knowledge construction. We conclude the chapter by giving an outlook on future research directions.

BACKGROUND

The development of tools for computer-mediated interaction is a challenging task. Apart from the actual task of the application, e.g. editing texts or spreadsheets, developers have to consider various aspects ranging from low-level technical issues up to high-level application usage. Among others, network connections between the collaborating users have to be established to enable communication, parallel input from the collaborating users has to be handled, specific group functions have to be included to provide group awareness, and the data has to be shared and kept consistent to allow users to work on common task at all (Ellis, Gibbs, & Rein, 1991). These issues are often not part of the professional training of software engineers. Instead, software engineers learn the basic principles that empower them to create any kind of software.

Development frameworks, like e.g. *NSTP* (Patterson, Day, & Kucan, 1996), *GroupKit* (Roseman & Greenberg, 1996), *COAST* (Schuckmann, Kirchner, Schümmer, & Haake, 1996), *Habanero* (Chabert, Grossman, Jackson, Pietrovicz, &

Seguin, 1998), or *DreamObjects* (Lukosch, 2003), are prominent means to support developers. They offer solutions for the development of tools for computer-mediated interaction as pre-fabricated building blocks. These frameworks help during the development process by providing components that hide most of the *dirty and difficult* work such as network connection management, process scheduling, data sharing, or data consistency. They also impose a specific way of shaping the group process by, e.g., providing means for starting a collaborative session. If the framework perfectly matches the requirements of the project, it will simplify the development. Unfortunately, this is often not the case.

During the development of several tools for computer-mediated interaction in national or international projects, we experienced and identified several properties that complicate the use of frameworks (Lukosch & Schümmer, 2006a):

- *Programming language*: Framework developers often chose the programming language that is currently en-vogue or that has been used in other projects before. Reuse is thus limited by the chosen programming language.
- *Distribution architecture*: As with the programming languages, framework developers often limit the applicability of the framework by offering only one distribution architecture that fits the first intended applications best. This may mean that the framework for instance only supports a client/server-architecture or that it uses peer-to-peer mechanisms.
- *Framework dominance*: Framework developers often assume that the application can be created on top of exactly one framework. They design the framework as center around which the application should be built. The framework in this case dominates the application structure and complicates application development when the

application could benefit from more than one framework (Fayad & Schmidt, 1997).

- *Black-box components*: Frameworks often only provide black-box components. These components are designed for a specific context like a specific structure of the underlying data model or specific mechanisms for processing user input and normally cannot be adapted.
- *Lack of documentation*: Most groupware frameworks have emerged from research projects. Thus, the main focus has been on the functional aspects of the framework rather than the documentation of the framework for novices. However, a didactically sound description of the framework's dynamic aspects is crucial for training developers in using the framework.
- *Communication problems*: Groupware frameworks often address the problem space from a technical perspective rather than approaching the problem space from a human-computer interaction view. The interaction design thus often becomes technology driven. Developers continue to use their technical language while clients and end-users express their requirements with terms used in the specific interaction setting. The problem of communication between end-users and developers stays an open issue in these cases.

From these observations, we conclude that the framework approach is not sufficient for supporting the development of tools for computer-mediated interaction. As other authors pointed out for general software development (e.g. (Johnson, 1997), (Brugali & Sycara, 2000), or (Biggerstaff & Richter, 1987)), we argue that the development of tools for computer-mediated interaction should focus on design reuse rather than code reuse. The developers should be trained in a way so that they can understand and reproduce the framework developer's design decisions.

Taking a closer look on the communication problem between end-users and developers, it becomes obvious that one of the most difficult problems in the interaction between software developers and prospective users is the understanding of requirements. A lack of end-user participation when designing software often leads to invalid requirements, low end-user acceptance, and inadequate systems. The problem is that the developer has to foresee situations in which the user will make use of the system and think about potential variations in these situations. While this is already a complex task, it becomes much more difficult when the developer has to consider groupware applications. Apart from just addressing the interaction of one user with a computer system, the developer has to take the interaction between all groupware users into account. The interaction is mediated by the groupware system which implies that the groupware system has to fit the requirements and preferences of all users. This shows that the design of computer mediated interaction is much more complex than the design of human computer interaction. We argue that this complexity can only be managed by fostering interaction between end-users and developers during the whole life cycle of the development and use of groupware.

In summary, it is crucial for a successful tool for computer-mediated interaction to capture and reuse design insights and to involve end-users in the development process (Schümmer et al., 2006). Therefore, developers and end-users should be able to communicate with each other for a better understanding of the requirements. In our opinion, these goals can be reached by using patterns in a development process involving end-users.

A PATTERN-BASED DESIGN APPROACH

In this section, we will introduce the concept of socio-technical patterns, a pattern language for computer-mediated interaction, and a development process that makes use of the patterns as well as the pattern language to support successful tool development for computer-mediated interaction.

Socio-Technical Patterns

The idea of patterns originates from Christopher Alexander's work (Alexander, 1979; Alexander et al., 1977) in urban architecture. According to Alexander, 'patterns describe a problem which occurs over and over again and the core of the solution to that problem'. Each pattern includes a problem description, which highlights a set of conflicting forces and a proven solution, which helps to resolve the forces.

After using the first patterns with end-users and software developers, it became clear that patterns for computer-mediated interaction need a special form to be understood by end-users as well as software developers. The main reason for this is that the patterns address a *socio-technical* problem: they have to describe the *technology* that supports the *group process* and therefore include a technical and a social aspect. Patterns for computer-mediated interaction are thus *socio-technical patterns*. The socio-technical perspective on groupware design has to be aware of three key aspects (Bikson & Eveland, 1996):

- It is difficult to predict the reciprocal effect of changes to either the social or the technical system.
- The process used to create the socio-technical system will affect the acceptance of the system.
- Both social and technical systems change over time.

Patterns are a good means for empowering the user and the groupware developer so that they can react to the changing requirements during the group process. Besides the standard elements of a design pattern, i.e., a context description, a problem statement, a solution statement, and a collection of examples where the solution is in place, we identified several aspects that should be included in a pattern that addresses socio-technical problems.

Our pattern structure is shaped to meet both end-user's and developer's needs for detail and illustration. The *pattern name* is followed by the *intent*, and the *context* of the pattern. All these sections help the reader to decide, whether or not the following pattern may fit into his current situation.

Then follows the core of the pattern composed of the *problem* and the *solution* statement separated by a *scenario* and a *symptoms* section. The *scenario* is a concrete description of a situation where the pattern could be used, which makes the tension of the *problem* statement tangible. The *symptoms* section helps to identify the need for the pattern by describing aspects of the situation more abstract again.

After the *solution* section, the solution is explained in more detail and indications for further improvement after applying the pattern are provided. The *participants* section explains the main components or actors that interact in the pattern and explains how they relate to each other. The *rationale* section explains, why the forces are resolved by the pattern. The *check* section lists a number of questions, one has to answer before applying the pattern in a development context. Unfortunately, the application of a pattern can in some cases raise new unbalanced forces. These counter forces are described in the section labeled *danger spots*.

The solution presented in a pattern represents a proven solution to a recurring problem, so the *known uses* section provides well-known examples where this pattern is applied. Finally, the *related patterns* section states what patterns are closely related to this one, and with which other patterns this one should be used.

A Pattern Language for Computer-Mediated Interaction

An interconnected set of patterns is called a pattern language. Patterns of a pattern language are intended to be used together in a specific problem domain for which the pattern language guides the design decisions in the specific problem domain.

Links between patterns are an important criterion for organizing a pattern language. Forces of a pattern or 'requirements interact (and are therefore linked), if what you do about one of them in a design necessarily makes it more difficult or easier to do anything about the other' (Alexander, 1964). Thus, 'each pattern sits at the center of a network of connections which connect it to certain other patterns that help to complete it. [...] And it is the network of these connections between patterns which creates the language.' (Alexander, 1979) In case of patterns in the same problem domain, this results in a densely connected graph of patterns with links of different relevance.

The application of a pattern language brings up additional relations between patterns, called *sequences*. A sequence describes the order in which patterns can be or were applied in the context of a specific use case. Since the pattern approach demands that developers focus on one pattern at a time and thus improve the system incrementally in piecemeal growth (Alexander, Silverstein, Angel, Ishikawa, & Abrams, 1980; Schümmer & Lukosch, 2006; Schümmer et al., 2006) we can create a linear sequence by ordering the patterns according to the point in time when they were used. A sequence is then a sentence spoken in the pattern language that changes all forces addressed by the patterns used as words in the sentence.

In the pattern language for computer-mediated interaction, we consider patterns on two levels, each with a different target group (Lukosch & Schümmer, 2006a):

Figure 1. Layers in the pattern language for computer-mediated interaction

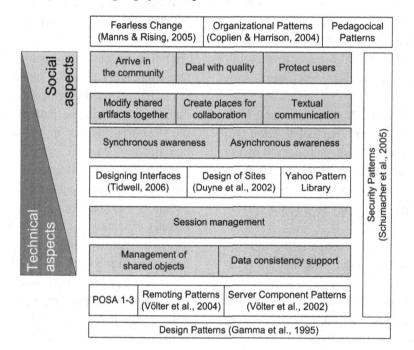

- High-level patterns describe issues and solutions typically targeted at end-users.
- Low-level patterns describe issues and solutions typically targeted at software developers on a more technical level.

Both low-level and high-level patterns can be positioned on a seamless abstraction scale. The more a pattern discusses technical issues; the lower is its level. Low-level patterns deal with class structures, control flow, or network communication. High-level patterns focus on human interaction and address computer systems just as tools to support the human interaction. In the extreme, high-level patterns would describe how the end-user can compose off-the-shelf components and embed them in his work process. This would then mean that the software developer would no longer need to assist the end-user in implementing the pattern.

In the pattern language for computer-mediated interaction (Schümmer & Lukosch, 2007a), we identified 11 clusters that group our patterns ac-

cording to the patterns' most important forces. Figure 1 shows the different clusters of our language as shaded boxes. The top level clusters, i.e. from *Arrive in the community* to *Protect users*, address issues at a community level and contain high-level patterns. The clusters in the middle layer, i.e. from *Modify shared artifacts together* to *Asynchronous awar*eness, address issues on a group level and contain a mixture of high-level and low-level patterns. Finally, the clusters on the lower levels address technical issues and contain low-level patterns. The white boxes represent complementary pattern languages.

Oregon Software Development Process

The main reason for us to require patterns on different levels of abstraction is based in the intended use of the patterns in the Oregon Software Development Process (OSDP) (Schümmer et al., 2006). This process fosters end-user involvement by means of socio-technical patterns. End-users interact with developers in different iteration types. OSDP proposes three different types of iterations:

1. In *conceptual iterations* users envision the scenarios of system usage.
2. In *development iterations* users and developers collaborate to build the required groupware infrastructure.
3. In *tailoring iterations* users appropriate the groupware system to changed needs.

In conceptual iterations, the end-users outline future scenarios of use. This is informed by the use of high-level patterns that describe how group interaction can be supported with tools for computer-mediated interaction.

The scenarios are implemented during development iterations. Here, the software developers are the main actors. They translate the scenarios to working solutions using low-level patterns as a development guideline. End-users closely interact with the developers by proposing the application of patterns from the pattern language and identifying conflicting forces in the current prototype.

As soon as the tool for computer-mediated interaction can be used by the end-users, the tailoring iterations start. End-users reflect on the offered tool support. Whenever the support can be improved, they either tailor the tool by using high-level patterns or escalating the problem to the developers who then start a new development iteration.

As OSDP is an iterative approach, each iteration may actually be performed multiple times: in fact, developers and end-users may even choose to go back to a previous iteration type. In all iteration types, the patterns primarily communicate design knowledge to the developers and the users. The participants of the OSDP learn how conflicting forces should be resolved instead of just using pre-fabricated building-blocks. This empowers them to create customized solutions that better suit their requirements.

EXPERIENCES

Patterns are independent from programming languages. They help educating developers by providing well-known design insights and thereby foster design reuse. Links between the patterns point to other relevant issues and thereby support a piecemeal growth of the application under development. Finally, they improve the communication between clients, end-users, and developers, when used in a iterative development process like OSDP.

In this section, we show how patterns for computer-mediated interaction help to design tools for shared knowledge construction. For this purpose, we introduce a web-based collaborative environment and some its extensions that foster shared knowledge construction. When describing the design of these tools we highlight and provide thumbnails of the patterns[1] that were used to implement the tools.

CURE in a Nutshell

In this section, we introduce the web-based collaborative system *CURE* (J. M. Haake, Schümmer, Haake, Bourimi, & Landgraf, 2004). *CURE* is used for collaborative work and learning. Typical collaborative learning scenarios are collaborative exercises, tutor-guided groups with collaborative exercises, collaborative exam preparation (Lukosch & Schümmer, 2006b), virtual seminars, and virtual labs (Schümmer, Lukosch, & Haake, 2005). When considering collaborative work typical use cases include group formation, group communication, document sharing, collaborative writing, collaborative task management etc. All these scenarios have in common that users interact to create shared knowledge.

Users can structure their interaction in groups that inhabit virtual Rooms. Room metaphors (Greenberg & Roseman, 2003; Pfister, Schuckmann, Beck-Wilson, & Wessner, 1998) have been widely used to structure collaboration. Figure 2

Figure 2. CURE abstractions

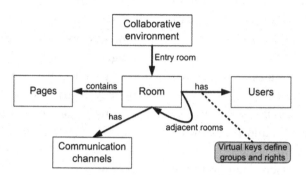

shows the abstractions that are offered by *CURE*. Users enter the cooperative working/learning environment via an entry room that is called *Hall*. Rooms can contain pages, communication channels, e.g. chat, threaded mail, and users. Users, who are in the same room at the same time, can communicate by means of a synchronous communication channel, i.e. by using the chat that is automatically established between all users in the ROOM. They can also access all pages that are contained in the ROOM. Changes of these pages are visible to all members in the ROOM.

ROOM

Problem: Users use different tools for communication, file transfer, application sharing, and other tasks that are needed in group interaction. In most cases, these tools are used together. However, setting up the tools is difficult and time-consuming.

Solution: Model a virtual place for collaboration as a room that can hold documents and participants. Ensure that users who are in the same room can communicate by means of a communication channel that is automatically established between all the users in the room. Make sure that all users can access all documents that are in the room and make these documents persistent. Changes to the documents should be visible to everyone in the room.

The concept of a virtual key is used to express access permissions of the key holder on ROOMs. Each key distinguishes three different classes of rights (J. M. Haake, Haake, Schümmer, Bourimi, & Landgraf, 2004): key-rights defining what the user can do with the key, room-rights defining whether or not a user can enter a ROOM or change the ROOM structure, and interaction-rights specifying what the user can do in the ROOM. ROOMs with public keys are accessible by all registered users of the system.

Users can enter a ROOM to access the communication channels of the room and participate in collaborative activities. Users can also create and edit pages in the ROOM. Pages may either be directly edited using a simple wiki-like syntax (Leuf & Cunningham, 2001), or they may contain binary documents or artifacts, e.g. JPEG images, Microsoft Word documents etc. In particular, the syntax supports links to other pages, other ROOMs, external URLs or mail addresses. The server stores all artifacts to support collaborative access. When users leave the ROOM, the content stays there to allow users to come back later and continue their work on the ROOM's pages.

Figure 3 shows a typical ROOM in *CURE*. The numbers in the figure refer to details explained in the following paragraphs. A ROOM (1) contains documents (cf. CENTRALIZED OBJECTS) that can be edited by those users, who have sufficient edit

Figure 3. A ROOM in CURE

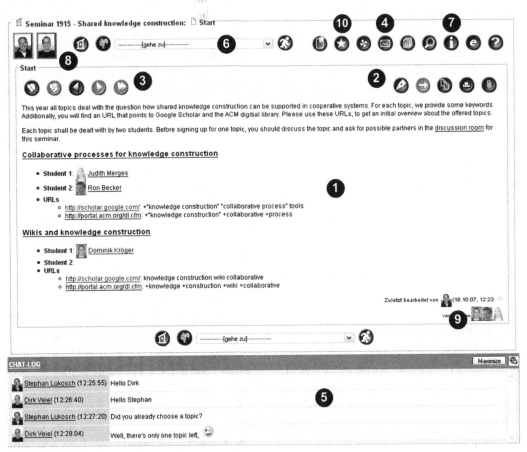

rights (2).

CENTRALIZED OBJECTS

Problem: To enable collaboration, users must be able to share data.

Solution: Manage the data necessary for collaboration on a server that is known to all users. Allow the users to access the data on the server.

CURE stores all versions of a page as IMMUTABLE VERSIONS.

IMMUTABLE VERSIONS

Problem: Performing complex modifications on a shared object usually takes time and requires cognitive effort on the part of the user. If users act on the same shared objects, the probability of conflicting changes increases. However, to discard one of the conflicting changes is inappropriate, since its originator has already expended much effort in performing the change.

Solution: Store all shared objects in a version tree. Make sure that the versions stored in the version tree are immutable, such that they cannot afterwards be changed. Store modifications of a shared object as new versions. Ask users to merge parallel versions in the version tree unless they explicitly branch the version tree.

Users can browse different versions (3) to understand their colleagues' changes (cf. TIMELINE).

TIMELINE

Problem: Not all users participate in collaborative sessions continuously. This makes it hard to understand who is working with whom on what topic. Without such an understanding, however, users lack the orientation and coordination required for group interaction.

Solution: Display the activities that took place in a workspace as a timeline.

Communication is supported by two room-based communication channels, i.e. a FORUM (4) and an EMBEDDED CHAT (5). Users can use the room-based e-mail to send a mail to the room. Users of the ROOM that have sufficient communication rights will receive this message like being a member of a mailing list.

FORUM

Problem: Users want to communicate about a specific topic. Without knowing people interested in the same topic, this is difficult.

Solution: Create a forum as a central place for communication in which all group members can discuss asynchronously by reading and writing messages. Keep forum messages persistent.

EMBEDDED CHAT

Problem: Users need to communicate. They are used to sending electronic mail. But since e-mail is asynchronous by nature, it is often too slow to resolve issues that arise in synchronous collaboration.

Solution: Integrate a tool for quick synchronous interaction into your cooperative application. Let users send short text messages, distribute these messages to all other group members immediately, and display these messages at each group member's site.

By providing a plenary ROOM, sharing and communication in a whole class or organization can be supported. By creating new ROOMS for subgroups and connecting those to the classes' or organization's ROOM, work and collaboration can be flexibly structured. Starting from the plenary ROOM users can navigate to the connected subrooms (6).

For user coordination, *CURE* supports various types of awareness information. Users can see in the ROOM's properties who else has access to this ROOM (7). Users can see in a USER LIST (8) who else is currently in the same ROOM.

USER LIST

Problem: Users do not know with whom they are interacting or could interact. Consequently, they do not have a feeling of participating in a group.

Solution: Provide awareness in context. Show who is currently accessing an artifact or participating in a COLLABORATIVE SESSION. Ensure that the information is always valid.

If the EMBEDDED CHAT (5) is enabled in the ROOM, users can directly start chatting to each other. Users can trace who has previously edited the current page (9) (cf. ACTIVE NEIGHBORS).

ACTIVE NEIGHBORS

Problem: The USER LIST pattern only shows users with the same focus. If users work on related artifacts, they are not aware of each other, which implies that no collaboration will be established.

Solution: Make users aware of other users who are currently performing semantically related activities on the same or related artifacts.

PERIODIC REPORTS automatically posted to all users of a ROOM include all changes made since the last report was sent.

PERIODIC REPORTS

Problem: Changes in indirect collaboration are only visible by inspecting a changed artifact. Users want to react to actions on artifacts, but they cannot predict when these actions will take place.

Solution: Inform users periodically about the changes that took place between the time of the current report and the previous one.

Additionally, users can lookup recent changes individually for each ROOM (10) (cf. CHANGE INDICATOR).

CHANGE INDICATOR

Problem: While users work on independent local copies of artifacts, their checkout frequency for the artifacts may be low. As a result, they may work on old copies, which leads to potentially conflicting parallel changes. The conflict is worse if two parallel modifications have contradictory intentions.

Solution: Indicate whenever an artifact has been changed by an actor other than the local user. Show this information whenever the artifact or a reference to the artifact is shown on the screen. The information should contain details about the type of change and provide access to the new version of the artifact.

In summary, *CURE* enables shared knowledge construction as users can meet in a ROOM to start collaboration. The different communication channels and awareness mechanisms ensure that users are aware of changes and the collaboration process. Finally, the wiki in *CURE* allows users to capture knowledge and to organize it in a form that best fits to the requirements of the group.

Game-Based Learning

In the default version of CURE, as described above, students mainly use *CURE* to form learning groups upon teacher's request. In these groups, they discuss course content, solve assignments, or collaboratively write a seminar thesis. This cooperation and discussion works well as long as there is a group task given by the teachers. If the given tasks are accomplished, the collaboration in most cases stagnates or even finally stops. A learning community could increase collaboration among the students and foster shared knowledge construction. However, communities cannot be designed. Instead, learning communities evolve through the collective building of shared knowledge and the shifting participation of their members (Lave & Wenger, 1991) and only the software that supports the community is designed (Preece, 2000). There are some key factors for a successful online community. Participation and practice are the key factors for developing a learning community (Haythornthwaite, Kazmer, Robins, & Shoemaker, 2000; Wenger, 1998) and community members must have possibilities for shared knowledge construction (Palloff & Pratt, 1999).

To establish a learning community in *CURE*, students have to be motivated to a higher degree of collaborative interaction and shared knowledge construction. Game-based learning approaches (Prensky, 2001) can be used to increase the motivation for more frequent collaborative interaction and may result in the construction of shared knowledge (Lukosch, 2007). Therefore, we extended *CURE* with game-based learning tools which can be added to the interaction possibilities of a ROOM in *CURE* by simply creating a new page. In the following, we present with *Fountain of Wisdom* one of these game-based learning tools and highlight which patterns for computer-mediated interaction especially influenced its design.

Fountain of Wisdom is based on a 3D virtual maze in which two teams compete with each other by answering questions. Additional teams can play in parallel in the same maze. Users can meet on a so-called 3D marketplace, use the EMBEDDED CHAT to socialize with co-learners, propose a game on a specific topic, and to send INVITATIONS to other users for participating in a COLLABORATIVE SESSION. The COLLABORATIVE SESSION, i.e. the game, can be limited in time or limited to a number of questions. Independent from the specified limit, the team that correctly answered most questions wins the game.

COLLABORATIVE SESSION

Problem: Users need a shared context for synchronous collaboration. Computer-mediated environments are neither concrete nor visible, however. This makes it difficult to define a shared context and thereby plan synchronous collaboration.

Solution: Model the context for synchronous collaboration as a shared session object. Visualize the session state and support users in starting, joining, leaving, and terminating the session. When users join a session, automatically start the necessary collaboration tools.

INVITATION

Problem: One user wants to interact with another. The other user may be unavailable or busy in another context so that an immediate collaboration would disturb them.

Solution: Send and track invitations to the intended participants. Include meta-information on the intended COLLABORATIVE SESSION. Automatically add all users who accept the invitation to the COLLABORATIVE SESSION.

After the teams formed, the 3D game maze is initiated. Users that later on visit the marketplace can join the game and decide in which of the two possible teams they want to participate. The underlying system then performs a STATE TRANSFER.

STATE TRANSFER

Problem: Users are collaborating in a COLLABORATIVE SESSION but not all of them participate from the beginning. Due to this, some do not know the intermediate results of the COLLABORATIVE SESSION which makes it difficult for them to collaborate.

Solution: Transmit the current state of shared objects to latecomers when they join a COLLABORATIVE SESSION. Since all current participants have the most recent state of the session's shared objects, the system can ask any of the existing clients to perform the state transfer. Ensure the consistency of the state.

The maze provides fountains from which team members have to obtain a question. Complementary to the fountains, there are several sinks in the maze where possible answers to the questions can be found. Each sink contains answers to a number of questions. When users step onto a sink, their view changes and displays the answers to all questions associated with the sink. From this list of possible answers the user has to choose the correct ones knowing only the number of correct answers. Each correct answer counts for individual and team points.

Figure 4 shows the normal maze view of *Fountain of Wisdom*. From the view of the local user, you can see another user, i.e. the snowman

Figure 4. Fountain of Wisdom maze view

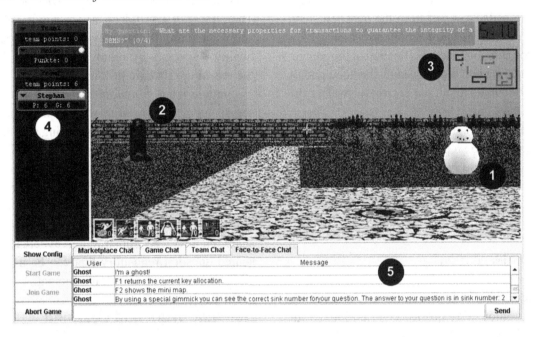

(1) on the right side, and one bad ghost (2) on the left side. The upper right corner of the 3D view shows a small ACTIVE MAP (3) of the maze with the positions of the other users in the maze and the time that is left in this match. Left to the 3D view, you can see the USER LIST (4), which highlights the teams competing with each other. The bottom of the screenshot shows the EMBEDDED CHAT (5).

ACTIVE MAP

Problem: To orient themselves and interact in space, users have to create a mental model that represents the space and the artifacts and users it contains. This is a difficult task.

Solution: Create a reduced visual representation of the spatial domain model by means of a map. Show other users' locations on the map. Ensure that the map is dynamic for artifacts and users, but static with respect to landmarks.

At the bottom of the 3D view you can see different chats, i.e. one for the marketplace, one for all participants of the current game, one for the team, and one for the user next to oneself. The chats can be used to gain information about where to find the correct sink for a question and to discuss possible answers with team members.

Apart from bad ghosts there are also good ghosts in the maze. Good ghosts help the players by e.g. giving tips on the correct answer to a question or giving away gimmicks that allow the user to perform special actions, e.g. to move faster or beam from one place to another in the maze. If a player comes to close to a bad ghost, this may steal the current question and the player has to get a new one.

Prior to a game, students can define questions and answers for a specific topic as *CURE* pages. *CURE* supports so-called Wiki-templates (A. Haake, Lukosch, & Schümmer, 2005), which allow end-users to define form-based pages. These Wiki-templates can be used to structure shared knowledge and simplify its construction. For all question and answer pages the same Wiki-template is used to enable re-use in different learning gadgets. Apart from the question, such a page consists of a number of correct answers, a question category, the specification of the course, and a helping text that is used by the good ghosts to provide hints about the correct answer of the question.

The question and answer pages are elements of a shared question repository in *CURE* and define the topics that are available for a game. To ensure the quality of the questions, *CURE*, implements a combination of the patterns QUALITY INSPECTION and VOTE.

QUALITY INSPECTION

Problem: Members participate in a community to enjoy high-quality contributions from fellow members. However, not every contribution has the same quality. Low-quality contributions can annoy community members and distract their attention from high-quality gems.

Solution: Select users as moderators and let them release only relevant contributions into the community's interaction space. Give moderators the right to remove any contribution and to expel users from the community.

VOTE

Problem: It is hard to work out the distribution of opinions in the community. However, good understanding of other users' attitudes can be important when making decisions.

Solution: Provide an easy means of setting up and running a poll. Show a virtual ballot in a prominent place in the community. After the vote is over, present the result.

Due to the implementation of the patterns QUALITY INSPECTION and VOTE, students can rate the quality of a question and the corresponding answers using a question overview page *CURE* provides. The ratings of all students are accumulated and shown as stars. Additionally, students can act as quality inspectors by removing questions from the repository that are of low quality.

Summarizing, *Fountain of Wisdom* increases social interaction, as students can meet on the marketplace to form teams and during a game the different chats allow cross-group interaction. It allows students to self-organize their learning and their interaction, as each user can create rooms in *CURE* and define the interaction possibilities of a room. Finally, *Fountain of Wisdom* supports shared knowledge construction by creating a shared question repository that can be used by all students of the *CURE* environment.

Nomadic Work and Learning

Nowadays, more and more users make use of web-based collaborative systems. Users participate in communities or search for and provide information in web-based systems. They access shared resources which they need for their professional life or for learning. One of the major prerequisites of such web-based systems is that users have to be connected to the network. But life has become much more mobile over the last years. While traveling, e.g. to the office or the university, users often are disconnected from the network. This makes it difficult to interact with other users or to access shared resources. An application supporting a seamless transition between connected and disconnected phases would allow users to work at any time and place while maintaining the advantages of a web-based collaborative system once they are online again. For that purpose, we extended *CURE* with a communication interface and an independent application, called *offlineCURE* (Lukosch, 2008), that allows users to interact with the system while being disconnected. In the following, we describe *offlineCURE* while again highlighting the patterns form computer-mediated interaction that influenced its design.

Figure 5. offlineCURE user interface

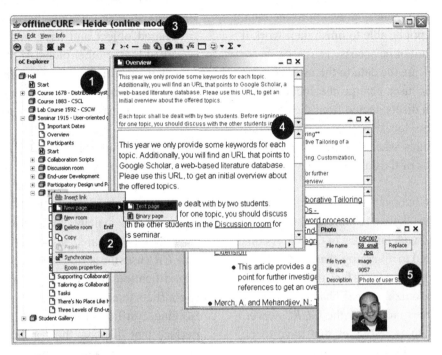

Figure 5 shows the user interface of *offline-CURE*. The left area of the user interface shows a tree-based overview of the content that is locally available (1). Compared to the web interface, this simplifies the navigation, since users always have an overview of the local content available. Context-sensitive menus allow users to perform actions in relation to the selected object, e.g. create a new sub-room in a room or delete a page (2). Additionally, the *offlineCURE* user interface offers static menus, keyboard shortcuts, and a toolbar which provides support for incorporating wiki-tags into the page text (3).

Figure 5 also shows three windows in which the user currently edits *CURE* pages (4) or views a binary page (5). Both edit windows are split horizontally. The upper part is used for editing Wiki pages while the lower shows a real-time preview of the rendered page. The size of the edit and preview areas is variable, i.e. users can decide to display only the edit area while working on a long document, or use the preview area on its own for browsing *CURE* content offline.

The real-time preview shows the page content like it would be rendered in the user's browser when working with the *CURE* server. This also includes usable links to other documents, external URLs etc. Support for creating complex structures is given by indicating whether internal links on a page are valid, i.e. whether the linked content is locally available and allowing users to conveniently create content via context sensitive menus attached to links. Compared to the web interface, the *offlineCURE* user interface thereby significantly improves the usability and workflow when editing *CURE* content.

For working nomadically, *offlineCURE* allows users to select the content for the disconnected phases. This selected content is replicated to the client application by using the NOMADIC OBJECTS pattern.

NOMADIC OBJECTS

Problem: Users may not have a permanent connection to the system where relevant data is kept. Without a permanent connection, or with just a poor connection to the data, users will not be able to finish their work if the data cannot be accessed.

Solution: Replicate the data to the user's device and let the user change the local replica even when disconnected from the network. Update the local replicas and distribute local changes whenever two systems that hold copies of the data connect.

An OPTIMISTIC CONCURRENCY CONTROL approach ensures that the shared resources can still be modified via the web interface of *CURE*. As this approach can lead to diverging shared resources, *offlineCURE* provides means for CONFLICT DETECTION and synchronizing local shared resources with the resources stored on the *CURE* server. *offlineCURE* detects resources that have to be synchronized by using modified bits and comparing the local version number with the most recent one at the *CURE* server.

OPTIMISTIC CONCURRENCY CONTROL

Problem: You want to ensure consistency but you want to ensure that changes to the replicated objects are propagated in minimum time.

Solution: Perform changes to local replicas immediately. If another client has earlier performed a conflicting change, roll back or transform your change.

CONFLICT DETECTION

Problem: If two or more users change the same data at the same time, changes interfere. This can lead to inconsistent data or contradict the users' intentions. If the users are unaware of this conflict, they will no longer have a common base for collaboration.

Solution: Let each client remember all local changes that have not yet been applied by all other clients. Whenever a change

is received from another client, check it against those changes that affect the same shared object and have not yet been applied by the other client. If performing the changes will produce a conflict, then undo or transform one of the changes such that all clients have a consistent state.

Apart from diverging shared resources, the NOMADIC OBJECTS can also lead to conflicting modifications of the same shared resource. Approaches that automatically resolve conflicts can only ensure the syntactical but not the semantic correctness of a shared resource. Therefore, *offlineCURE* uses the IMMUTABLE VERSIONS that keeps all modifications and lets users manually resolve the conflicts to ensure semantic correctness. For resolving conflicts, *offlineCURE* offers a user interface that displays the conflicts and allows the users to create a merged version.

In summary, *offlineCURE* enhances the possibilities for constructing shared knowledge as it enables users to work nomadically. While being nomads, users can access shared knowledge and also construct new knowledge which upon network connection can be integrated in the shared knowledge repository.

FUTURE RESEARCH DIRECTIONS

CURE and its extensions *Fountain of Wisdom* and *offlineCURE* are tools for computer-mediated interaction. While *CURE* offers basic support for shared knowledge construction, its extensions focus on fostering shared knowledge construction by offering means to establish a community and to work nomadically.

The design of these tools has been carried out using patterns for computer-mediated interaction. For this design, high-level as well low-level patterns have been used. During the design and development, we experienced that the patterns served as an educative means both for novice as well as more experienced developers. The known uses section of the patterns helped to select required technology from larger frameworks for groupware applications. For involving end-users, the patterns provided the developers with a common language and metaphors that eased the communication within the development team and between the team and the end-users. The check section of each pattern helped the designers and developers to focus their design on the important issues. The related patterns section pointed the developers to related problems and solutions which they could have ignored otherwise. Finally, the patterns helped to focus development activities on small problems and thus encourage iterative development and piecemeal growth of all tools.

In future research, we want to empirically evaluate the use of patterns when designing tools for computer-mediated interaction. For that purpose, we are developing questionnaires that will allow us to measure the usefulness of a pattern as well as the learning effect of a pattern. We will use these questionnaires in future development projects for tools for computer-mediated interaction.

The above examples already indicate that some patterns are used more often when developing tools for computer-mediated interaction, e.g. USER LIST or EMBEDDED CHAT. Other tools or extensions to *CURE*, e.g. support for visual tailoring (Lukosch & Bourimi, 2008), merging diverging pages (Lukosch & Leisen, 2008), or structuring wiki pages (A. Haake et al., 2005), support this finding. This raises the research question whether there is a canonical set of patterns for computer-mediated interaction that are necessary for building a successful tool. To pursue this question, we will analyze existing tools for computer-mediated interaction and describe their design using patterns. We will also carry on using patterns for computer-mediated interaction in future development projects. We expect that this analysis and usage will reveal a canonical set of patterns which then can be used in teaching as well as professional development to improve the quality of tools for computer-mediated interaction.

CONCLUSION

Shared knowledge construction aims at supporting the creation and gathering of new knowledge. It relies on tools for computer-mediated interaction. The design of tools for computer-mediated interaction is a challenging task. To develop a successful tool, end-users have to be involved in the development process, developers have to be educated, and a shared understanding of the requirements and solutions between the developers and the end-users has to be established.

In this chapter, we analyzed the problems when developing tools for computer-mediated interaction in general. To overcome the identified problems, we presented a pattern-based approach for supporting developers as well integrating end-users in the development process. This development process is based on a pattern language for computer-mediated interaction that can like other patterns (Erickson, 2000) serve as a *Lingua Franca* for designing tools for computer-mediated interaction. We showed how this pattern language influenced the design and specification of tools for shared knowledge construction by introducing *CURE*, *Fountain of Wisdom*, and *offlineCURE*.

The patterns for computer-mediated interaction have been used in several other projects. In these projects it became clear that some patterns are used more often than others. Future research will reveal if there is a canonical set of patterns that can improve teaching as well as professional development of tools for computer-mediated interaction. If this canonical set can be identified the end-user oriented development of tools for computer-mediated interaction and the tools themselves can be improved.

REFERENCES

Alexander, C. (1964). *Notes on the Synthesis of Form* (7th Ed.). Cambridge, MA: Harvard University Press.

Alexander, C. (1979). *The timeless way of building*. New York: Oxford University Press.

Alexander, C., Ishikawa, S., Silverstein, M., Jacobson, M., Fiksdahl-King, I., & Angel, S. (1977). *A pattern language*. New York: Oxford University Press.

Alexander, C., Silverstein, M., Angel, S., Ishikawa, S., & Abrams, D. (1980). *The Oregon Experiment*. New York: Oxford University Press.

Biggerstaff, T., & Richter, C. (1987). Reusability Framework, Assessment, and Directions. *IEEE Software*, *4*(2): 41–49. doi:10.1109/MS.1987.230095

Bikson, T. K., & Eveland, J. D. (1996). Groupware implementation: reinvention in the sociotechnical frame. In *CSCW '96: Proceedings of the 1996 ACM conference on Computer supported cooperative work* (pp. 428-437). New York: ACM Press.

Brugali, D., & Sycara, K. (2000). Frameworks and pattern languages: an intriguing relationship. *ACM Computing Surveys*, *32*(1es), 2. doi:10.1145/351936.351938

Chabert, A., Grossman, E., Jackson, L., Pietrovicz, S., & Seguin, C. (1998). Java Object-Sharing in Habanero. *Communications of the ACM*, *41*(6), 69–76. doi:10.1145/276609.276622

Coplien, J. O., & Harrison, N. B. (2004). *Organizational Patterns of Agile Software Development*. Upper Saddle River, NJ: Prentice Hall.

Duyne, D. K. V., Landay, J., & Hong, J. I. (2002). *The Design of Sites: Patterns, Principles, and Processes for Crafting a Customer-Centered Web Experience*. Reading MA: Addison-Wesley.

Ellis, C. A., Gibbs, S. J., & Rein, G. L. (1991). Groupware some issues and experiences. *Communications of the ACM*, *34*(1), 39–58. doi:10.1145/99977.99987

Erickson, T. (2000). Lingua Francas for design: sacred places and pattern languages. In *Proceedings of the conference on Designing interactive systems* (pp. 357-368). New York: ACM Press.

Fayad, M. E., & Schmidt, D. C. (1997). Object-oriented Application Frameworks. *Communications of the ACM*, *40*(10), 32–38. doi:10.1145/262793.262798

Gamma, E., Helm, R., Johnson, R., & Vlissides, J. (1995). *Design Patterns: Elements of Reusable Object-Oriented Software*. Reading, MA: Addison-Wesley.

Greenberg, S., & Roseman, M. (2003). Using a Room Metaphor to Ease Transitions in Groupware. In M. Ackermann, V. Pipek & V. Wulf (Eds.), *Sharing Expertise: Beyond Knowledge Management* (pp. 203-256). Cambridge, MA: MIT Press.

Haake, A., Lukosch, S., & Schümmer, T. (2005). Wiki-Templates: Adding Structure Support to Wikis On Demand. In *WikiSym 2005 - Conference Proceedings of the 2005 International Symposium on Wikis* (pp. 41-51). New York: ACM Press.

Haake, J. M., Haake, A., Schümmer, T., Bourimi, M., & Landgraf, B. (2004). End-User Controlled Group Formation and Access Rights Management in a Shared Workspace System. In *CSCW '04: Proceedings of the 2004 ACM conference on Computer supported cooperative work* (pp. 554-563). New York: ACM Press.

Haake, J. M., Schümmer, T., Haake, A., Bourimi, M., & Landgraf, B. (2004). Supporting flexible collaborative distance learning in the CURE platform. In *Proceedings of the Hawaii International Conference On System Sciences (HICSS-37)*. New York: IEEE Press.

Haythornthwaite, C., Kazmer, M. M., Robins, J., & Shoemaker, S. (2000). Community Development Among Distance Learners: Temporal and Technological Dimensions. *Journal of Computer-Mediated Communication*, *6*(1).

Johnson, R. E. (1997). Frameworks = (Components + Patterns). *Communications of the ACM, 40*(10), 39–42. doi:10.1145/262793.262799

Lave, J., & Wenger, E. (1991). *Situated Learning Legitimate Peripheral Participation.* Cambridge, UK: Cambridge University Press.

Leuf, B., & Cunningham, W. (2001). *The WIKI way.* Boston: Addison-Wesley.

Lukosch, S. (2003). *Transparent and Flexible Data Sharing for Synchronous Groupware.* Köln, Germany: JOSEF EUL VERLAG GmbH Lohmar.

Lukosch, S. (2007). Facilitating shared knowledge construction in collaborative learning. *Informatica, Special Issue on 'e-Society', 31*(2), 167-174.

Lukosch, S. (2008). Seamless Transition between Connected and Disconnected Collaborative Interaction. *Journal of Universal Computer Science, 14*(1), 59–87.

Lukosch, S., & Bourimi, M. (2008). Towards an Enhanced Adaptability and Usability of Web-based Collaborative Systems. *International Journal of Cooperative Information Systems, Special Issue on 'Groupware: Implementation, Design, and Use'.*

Lukosch, S., & Leisen, A. (2008). Dealing with Conflicting Modifications in a Wiki. In *WEB-IST 2008 - Proceedings of the 4th International Conference on Web Information Systems and Technologies* (Vol. 2, pp. 5-15). Madeira, Portugal: INSTICC - Institute for Systems and Technologies of Information, Control, and Communication, Universidade da Madeira.

Lukosch, S., & Schümmer, T. (2006a). Groupware Development Support with Technology Patterns. *International Journal of Human Computer Studies, Special Issue on 'Theoretical and Empirical Advances in Groupware Research', 64*(7), 599-610.

Lukosch, S., & Schümmer, T. (2006b). Making exam preparation an enjoyable experience. *International Journal of Interactive Technology and Smart Education, Special Issue on 'Computer Game-based Learning', 3*(4), 259-274.

Manns, M. L., & Rising, L. (2005). *Fearless Change: Patterns for Introducing New Ideas.* Reading, MA: Addison-Wesley.

Palloff, R. M., & Pratt, K. (1999). *Building Learning Communities in Cyberspace - Effective Strategies for the Online Classroom.* San Francisco: Jossey Bass Wiley.

Patterson, J. F., Day, M., & Kucan, J. (1996). Notification Servers for Synchronous Groupware. In *Proceedings of the ACM 1996 Conference on Computer Supported Cooperative Work* (pp. 122-129), Boston.

Pfister, H.-R., Schuckmann, C., Beck-Wilson, J., & Wessner, M. (1998). The Metaphor of Virtual Rooms in the Cooperative Learning Environment CLear. In N. Streitz, S. Konomi & H. Burkhardt (Eds.), *Cooperative Buildings - Integrating Information, Organization and Architecture. Proceedings of CoBuild'98* (pp. 107-113). Heidelberg, Germany: Springer.

Preece, J. (2000). *Online Communities.* Chichester, UK: John Wiley & Sons, Inc.

Prensky, M. (2001). *Digital Game-Based Learning.* New York: McGraw-Hill Education.

Roseman, M., & Greenberg, S. (1996). Building Real-Time Groupware with GroupKit, A Groupware Toolkit. *ACM Transactions on Computer-Human Interaction, 3*(1), 66–106. doi:10.1145/226159.226162

Schuckmann, C., Kirchner, L., Schümmer, J., & Haake, J. M. (1996). Designing object-oriented synchronous groupware with COAST. In *Proceedings of the ACM 1996 Conference on Computer Supported Cooperative Work* (pp. 30-38), Boston.

Schümmer, T., & Lukosch, S. (2006). Structure-preserving transformations in pattern-driven groupware development. *International Journal of Computer Applications in Technology, Special Issue on 'Patterns for Collaborative Systems', 25*(2/3), 155-166.

Schümmer, T., & Lukosch, S. (2007). *Patterns for Computer-Mediated Interaction.* Chichester, UK: John Wiley & Sons, Inc.

Schümmer, T., Lukosch, S., & Haake, J. M. (2005). Teaching Distributed Software Development with the Project Method. In T. Koschmann, D. D. Suthers & T.-W. Chan (Eds.), *Computer Supported Collaborative Learning 2005: The Next 10 Years!* (pp. 577-586). Mahwah: Lawrence Erlbaum Associates.

Schümmer, T., Lukosch, S., & Slagter, R. (2006). Using Patterns to empower End-users - The Oregon Software Development Process for Groupware. *International Journal of Cooperative Information Systems, Special Issue on '11th International Workshop on Groupware (CRIWG'05)', 15*(2), 259-288.

Tidwell, J. (2006). *Designing Interfaces.* Sebastopol, CA: O'Reilly.

Völter, M., Kircher, M., & Zdun, U. (2004). *Remoting Patterns - Foundations of Enterprise, Internet, and Realtime Distributed Object Middleware.* Chichester, UK: John Wiley & Sons, Inc.

Völter, M., Schmid, A., & Wolff, E. (2002). *Server Component Patterns: Component Infrastructures Illustrated with EJB.* Chichester, UK: John Wiley & Sons, Inc.

Wenger, E. (1998). *Communities of Practice: Learning, Meaning, and Identity.* Cambridge, UK: Cambridge University Press.

ENDNOTE

[1] Pattern names are set in SMALL CAPS and can be found in (Schümmer & Lukosch, 2007).

Chapter 3

Creative Waves

Exploring Emerging Online Cultures, Social Networking and Creative Collaboration through e-Learning to Offer Visual Campaigns for Local Kenyan Health Needs

Andy Polaine
The University of New South Wales, Australia

Rick Bennett
The University of New South Wales, Australia

ABSTRACT

The past few years have seen the promise of online collaboration vastly augmented by developments in online technologies and emerging creative practices. Through our work with the Omnium Research Group, the authors argue that design should never be a solitary activity and benefits from many levels of collaboration - never more so than when dealing with complex issues facing today's world. The highly connected global society in which many of us now live frequently uses web-technologies to enhance nearly every facet of day-to-day life. The authors strongly believe that design education should not isolate itself from such communal and collaborative potential. This chapter explores what happens when online creative collaboration is applied to a real-world design project tackling critical health issues affecting local communities in Africa. It offers an account of the most recent, fully-online Creative Waves project - Visualising Issues in Pharmacy (VIP) that saw over 100 graphic designers join forces with a similar number of pharmacists from over 40 countries worldwide to produce graphic proposals for public awareness campaigns about six health issues seriously affecting the people of a village community in Kenya. The three-month VIP project is explained in relation to its aims, objectives and graphic outcomes, as well as the online environment in which it took place. Creative Waves is a concept created in 2005 by the Omnium Research Group, based at The University of New South Wales in Australia, to form online communities of design students from many institutions around the globe. Consisting an array of

DOI: 10.4018/978-1-60566-727-0.ch003

enthusiastic students, teaching staff, professional practitioners and luminaries invited as special guests, these online creative communities have proved that amazing results can be produced through careful facilitation between distanced individuals who will most likely never meet. The Creative Waves concept has to date been offered twice in collaboration with Icograda and the Icograda Education Network.

INTRODUCTION: EMERGING ONLINE CULTURES AND SOCIAL CHANGE

Before we examine the role of online communities and global creative collaboration within the most recent *Creative Waves '07* project, offered by the *Omnium Research Group* (Australia) in collaboration with Icograda and its education network (IEN), it is important to take account of vast social and cultural changes emerging online over the last few years. As we will see, the philosophy of online creativity and collaboration from which Omnium was borne a decade ago has since become part of the fabric of many online cultures. Such change poses great impact in academic settings because students today are some of the most 'savvy' users of ever-evolving digital and web-based technologies. For the current generation these technologies, that have been the subject of so much academic research and speculation, are now so everyday that we need to take account of new ways of working, socialising and collaborating that have subsequently emerged. As we have argued elsewhere (Bennett, Chan, & Polaine, 2004), we are beyond asking "should we use these technologies within education?" and now have much to learn from a generation that have already been using them for most of their lifetime.

Quite apart from their use in educational settings, the impact of the kinds of collaborative processes we will outline below are affecting the world of professional practice and wider society in extraordinary ways. The Internet has clearly changed the nature of communications and communities in the last decade and this has led to new ways of living and working (Castells, 2000;

Johnson, 2001; Rheingold, 2003; Leadbeater, 2008; Weinberger, 2007).

Blogs and blogging are possibly the most well known explosion in this area. Blogging has grown so fast that statistics are continually out of date (and thus hard to measure), but at in late 2007 the blog tracking service, Technorati, was tracking over 72 Million blogs and the 'blogosphere' was over 100 times bigger than it was just three years before (Sifry, 2007). YouTube, another famous online success story, was already serving 100 million videos per day and received over 65,000 video uploads daily back in 2006 (YouTube, 2006). These successes are not just digital – the Jubilee Debt campaign started with one person in a shed in London and gathered enough momentum and 24 million signatures which helped force Western governments to cancel US$36 billion of debt owed by Third World countries and developing nations (Leadbeater & Miller, 2004, p. 54).

There are three emerging and overlapping areas to examine in the context of the *Creative Waves* projects:

- Social networks and communities
- Collaboration, open-source and the rise of the pro-ams
- Organisational change

Social Networks and Communities

In recent years the rise of portable or time-shifted media (such as podcasts, the iTunes Music Store and the video equivalents), blogs and social networks have created enormous shifts in traditional relationships to everything from media, to education, to consumer and political behaviour.

Collectively, web applications such as YouTube, Flickr, GoogleMaps, Digg, Facebook, MySpace, Last.FM and WIkipedia are known (and hyped) as Web 2.0 applications (O'Reilly, 2005); a term that describes some of the technical approaches to their creation, but generally describes the idea that users and their audience create the content and form communities around this content, sometimes known as the 'read/write' or 'living' web.

The very first Omnium project in 1999 (Bennett, 2000) was developed through an awareness that the landscape of design *practice* was changing and that design *education* was failing to keep in step with these changes. It is essential to explore these emerging trends in order to better understand the role of online creative collaboration within educational settings because our younger students are the age group that are at the forefront of this change (Lenhart, Madden, & Hitlin, 2005; McMillan & Morrison, 2006; Green & Hannon, 2007; Holden, 2007). How this demographic of young people experience the world will have an enormous effect on the way we all teach, learn and work. In fact, the *way* in which our students learn is possibly becoming far more important than *what* they learn.

The strength of social networks and online communities is that they provide both a way through the enormous amount of information on the web as well as creating social bonds and capital. The collaborative filtering evident in contexts like Amazon.com and iTunes ("people who bought X also bought Y") or recommendations from social networks like Last.FM are very different from the paradigm of searching, which is currently the process generally taught in information literacy courses in universities and colleges. When you *search* you know what you are looking for, you just need to find it. When you click through recommendations via *collaborative filtering* you don't know what you are looking for but find things of value to your tastes by following the connections that other people have made, often without realising it. *You find what you never knew you were looking for*. This is a very powerful process indeed, as anyone who has spent a fortune on Amazon.com in one sitting can confirm.

This process can either happen by accident (e.g., we don't pay that much attention to what we buy, but Amazon's tracking database does) or more deliberately by tagging content and adding our own connections to the group pool. People can also add to your tags and content and here we see the rich abilities of re-mix culture come into play, something that is central to the *Creative Waves* projects.

In terms of education, the value here is that we make connections between areas that appeared to be unrelated at first glance, and this encourages inter-disciplinarity. It also solves the oft-asked student question, "How do I know what to do when I don't know what I can do?" All the while strengthening the bonds between people with shared interests and creating communities of practice.

A final aspect to this is that people who are used to working in socially networked communities often harbour a set of values that are worth encouraging. Yahoo!'s Tom Coates (Coates, 2006) sums up the three main requirements for any social software application thus:

- An individual should get value from their contribution
- These contributions should provide value to their peers as well
- The organisation that hosts the service should derive aggregate value and be able to expose this back to the users (Coates, 2006)

This is an excellent blueprint for any endeavour, yet the ability of most existing educational structures to change in this direction is questionable. Indeed, providing advice and value to peers would often result in accusations of plagiarism, yet these are powerful *social values* in which the value of your own interests also creates value for those around you and the environment you are working in, much like open-source projects.

Collaboration, Open-Source and the Rise of the Pro-Ams

As Charles Leadbeater and Paul Miller argue in *The Pro-Am Revolution* (Leadbeater & Miller, 2004), a combination of technical and social changes have led to the rise of 'professional amateurs' or Pro-Ams. These groups generate a great deal of social, as well as financial capital and, according to Leadbeater and Miller, are "the new R&D labs of the digital economy" (2004, p. 67).

From astronomy to activism to software design and saving lives, the Pro-Ams are a powerful force and one in which collaboration, often via the Internet, is key:

Traditional innovation policies subsidise R&D and accelerate the transmission of ideas down the pipeline and into the market. Pro-Ams are helping to turn this closed model on its head... ideas are flowing back up the pipeline from avid users to the technology producers. (Leadbeater & Miller, 2004, p. 64)

Open-source software projects, in which many hundreds and thousands of people voluntarily contribute to the greater good, are the clearest example of this. Software projects are so complex it is virtually impossible for a single entity (even a company as large as Microsoft) to manage the process. By creating an open environment in which anyone can contribute changes thousands of workers and testers are brought into play and they can apply multiple minds to the complexity of the problem.

All these people contribute their time for free, on the understanding that the more they contribute the more they receive in the end (because the software is improved) and there is also a social kudos to this. Again, this is a valuable ideal for educational situations in which groups are col-

laborating, but it is also a powerful *social charter* that ripples upwards into the professional world as much as the corporate landscape is starting to change from above. Put simply, many hands make light work.

Organisational Change

Working Progress, also by Demos (it is interesting in itself that this research has not come from an academic institution, but an independent one who's motto is 'building everyday democracy' – they work outside of, but often advise the UK government), examines the nature of organisational change and the 'disconnect' between young people and employers (Gillingson & O'Leary, 2006). The authors reveal that organisations are finding it difficult to recruit graduates with the right skills even though they acknowledge that graduates are more highly qualified than ever: Graduates used to working in the peer-to-peer environment of the university find it hard to shift to organisational hierarchies and difficult to relate to their bosses (*Ibid.* p. 14).

At the same time, these organisations themselves are changing and the hope is that these two changing patterns, from what has traditionally been seen perhaps as the 'top' and the 'bottom', have a chance of meeting in the middle. They argue that hierarchical companies are slowly shifting and being replaced by the networked, organisational structures that we have already seen online.

Gillingson and O'Leary (2006, p.38) surveyed Human Resources directors from FTSE200 companies and the top four employee qualities the directors rated most highly were:

- Communications/communicating ideas
- Problem-solving
- Team-working
- Creativity and Innovation

These are several of the qualities we have researched and engendered in our past Omnium projects to date. For example, anyone can learn how to use Photoshop or Illustrator - they are tools just like a pencil - however design, creativity and collaboration *is* about process more than skilful practice (though it requires that too). The Creative Waves VIP project, detailed further in part two of this paper, was a collaboration between pharmacy students, lecturers and professionals as well as the same within design disciplines. It became clear during the duration of the project that many of problems relating to six health issues faced by the village of Winam in Kenya were not through a lack of medical knowledge or research, but a lack of communication of that knowledge effectively. Once again, we see that it is not the *specific knowledge of information* that it is important, for that is easy to come by these days, but *how to create new knowledge, make new connections and how to communicate* that are the fundamental qualities required of the 21st Century graduate and the rest of us:

If innovation flourishes within and across teams, then we need to be able to work within them. If the formalities of hierarchy are being overlaid with social networks inside organisations, then we need to negotiate our way through them. (Gillingson & O'Leary, 2006, p. 40)

The Omnium Project and Online Collaborative Creativity (OCC)

Initially founded as an individual research project in 1998, The Omnium Project has grown considerably through its ongoing online initiatives and creative activities to become a well-established research group based at the College of Fine Arts (COFA), the University of New South Wales in Sydney.

Omnium's continuing research focuses on exploring the notion of online collaborative creativity (OCC) and how the Internet can be best used to help geographically distanced individuals interact and work together creatively from any location worldwide. For nearly a decade, Omnium has offered a range of fully-online creative communities, facilitated a series of global and fully-online collaborative creative projects, as well as designed and written some ground breaking e-learning courses and programs. In addition, by designing and producing the unique Omnium® Software, specifically for online creative collaboration, and offering it as either a serviced package or an open-source option to other institutions around the world, Omnium has to date linked over 10,000 creative students, educators, professional practitioners, theorists and writers from over 50 countries worldwide.

Omnium has always maintained two underlying aims through all its online creative and e-learning projects and courses: to design, produce, test and evaluate:

- a revised online creative process through exploration into the generation of creative ideas and concepts, collaboratively, digitally, and across distance by individuals in collaboration via the Internet.
- a unique technical platform that enables the application of such a revised online creative process within a technical interface that uses 'virtual' space for its classrooms and studios.

In summary, Omnium bases its research investigations upon two significant and rapidly changing paradigms:

Education: Observing and contributing to the changing face of education through the availability and affect of web technologies and how these are challenging many well established principles upon which many education institutions have traditionally been founded.

Creativity: From predominantly individual production through to increasingly collaborative and collective approaches that have emerged increasingly over the last decade within many creative industries, studios and agencies.

Omnium's Five-Stage Process for Online Collaborative Creativity (OCC)

Although originally constructed by recollecting our own collective educational experiences throughout art and design colleges, and later our experiences in professional settings as designers and educators, we have continued to adapt and modify a five-stage online collaborative & creative (OCC) process by aligning our own perceptions to achieve an effective, analytical and intelligent working, teaching and learning methodology (Figure 1):

- **Socialising:** The first stage of Omnium's online collaborative creativity process aims to encourage initial individual involvement by all participants to not only introduce their own work, but introduce themselves through early discussions and autobiographies. Through construction orientation tasks requested by project facilitators participants are also subtly introduced to the technicalities of the user-interface without tedious formalities of a technical 'how-to-use' guide.

- **Gathering:** The second stage of the process aims to encourage initial individual contribution from all participants, while simultaneously producing process work that provides the project with a rich and varied mixture of cultural and personal backgrounds. It is a chance for each participant to feel they have contributed to the project and grow in confidence as a rich resource of visual research material, ongoing discussions and suggested links to other online resources grows. This stage is also the beginning of an array of feedback to the students in their working teams from the

range of free-roaming mentors and invited special guests.

- **Identifying:** Following the more individual 'gathering' stage of the process, a project will subtlety evolve into a more collaborative community at this stage where emphasis is placed on each creative team recognising, via discussions and dialogue, points of contact, commonality, difference and overlapping interests arising from process works being produced as a result of the initial activities. It is also a stage within the process to begin identifying what a creative team may aim achieve as a result of the project and delegating roles for each member to take responsibility for.

- **Distilling & Abstracting:** During the *distilling and abstracting* stage each working team continues to discuss their intended creative direction and establish their collaborative working process. This stage breaks down ideas from the works produced from the preceding *gathering* and *identifying* stages and places an increasing demand on the participants' abilities to critically assess their combined creative outcomes through discussion and feedback. Working collaboratively as small teams, this stage is most interesting in regard to the collective decisions made to keep and/or discard ideas previously offered and challenges the notion of individual possession of ideas and promotes issues of collective ownership.

- **Resolving:** The final *resolving* stage ultimately leads to the production of collaborative final submissions. The execution of final works provides opportunities for participants to then reflect upon the entirety of their creative process: from the individual beginnings of a project to the collaborative and collectively examined outcomes. In a project such as Creative Waves 07, there is arguably a further stage of *implementation* where the outcomes are manufactured or produced and implemented to the communities that a project is aiming to assist.

The Omnium five-stage OCC process, described above, is not intended to be totally linear in progression, and would often be applied in different depths depending upon time available for a project. It would be recommended that participants using this process always reflect both individually and collaboratively on each stage and use a reiterative process en route. Each stage is designed to include both individual and collaborative components; contributions which steadily progress each student from a valued individual contributor with elements of collaborative discussion (stage 1), through to a fully interactive collaborative contributor who is still required to make individual contributions in terms of messaging, debate reflection and critique (stage 5).

On reflection, Omnium five-stage online collaborative creativity process shares many ideologies with previously identified characteristics of more traditionally defined creativity and creative interaction. Graham Wallas (1926) describes a four-phase process for creative thinking: *preparation, incubation, illumination, and verification.* This too was derived from his own introspection and observations, rather than systematic empirical observations, although has since become widely accepted by theorists of creativity. Catherine Patrick (1937) proceeded to confirm Wallas' process through a more systematic and psychological research study. Analysing her findings, she confirmed Wallas' four-phases although added revision to accompany the final *verification* stage.

The way in which Omnium's own five-stage OCC process is applied through a learning context also closely mirrors established models for learning within online environments. Perhaps the most notable of these is the Five Stage Model offered by Prof. Gilly Salmon (2000) in which a suggested progression for online learning is illustrated and described from both a facilitators and learners

Figure 1. The Omnium Five-Stage Online Collaborative & Creative (OCC) Process

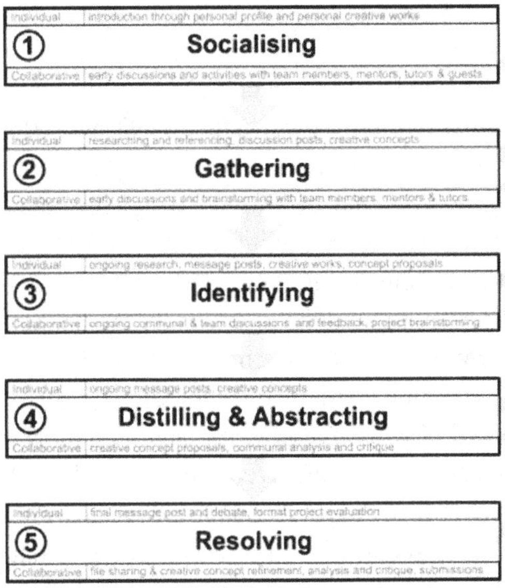

perspective. Salmon's Five Stage Model, describing processes of *access and motivation, online socialisation, information exchange, knowledge construction, and development,* also views the online learning process from both an e-moderating and technically supported perspective.

Throughout the entirety of the Omnium's OCC process, a project and its participants are supported by a series of specifically written lectures or readings, online activities to support those lectures and constant feedback from fellow students, project coordinators, roaming mentors and the invited special guests. It is the incredible amount of interactivity between participants in both social and working discussions that make Omnium's online studios consistently reported as highly social communities and free of the scourge of isolation reported by many e-learning or distance education offerings.

CREATIVE WAVES: AN OMNIUM INITIATIVE IN COLLABORATION WITH ICOGRADA

Having created and run several global online creative collaboration projects since 1998, in 2005 Omnium began an exciting collaboration with the International Council of Graphic Design Associations (Icograda) by conceiving a series of free and voluntary online design projects for students and their teachers around the globe under the banner of *Creative Waves*. Three significant projects have taken place under this banner to date (Creative Waves '05, Creative Waves '07 and Collabor8) that collectively have involved approximately 500 individuals from over 50 countries worldwide. Notably, the second Creative Waves project, that took place over three months in 2007 called *Visualising Issues in Pharmacy [VIP]*, progressed the *Creative Waves* direction to align with Omnium's more recent research activities that encourage online collaboration on more socially-aware design projects to aid people in less fortunate locations around the world.

The initial *Creative Waves* project, titled *03>04>05* and held over a seven-week period during March and April in 2005 saw a cross-disciplinary e-learning project between graphic design and photo-media students. The Creative Waves '05 project linked over 100 art and design students and their teachers from member institutions of the worldwide Icograda Education Network (IEN) and was structured to examine new ways of working collaboratively online and the prospects these open up for communicating visually with people around the world who would most likely never ever meet. By doing so, it continued Omnium's existing research that challenges traditional paradigms of individual creative processes and their championing of exclusiveness, isolation and sole-ownership of creative outcomes.

Throughout the project, the volunteer participants formed strong creative and social bonds with partners in distant parts of the world, receiving regular feedback and support from not only the variety of teachers who volunteered to take part, but also established creative professionals using the Internet as their sole communication tool. An added complexity of the project was the introduction of official mentors housed within each of the small creative working teams and the inclusion of invited special guests to add expertise and excitement to the proceedings.

In hindsight, the first *Creative Waves* project received a significant amount of acclaim, however, the real success of the project was not so much the creative work that took place, or that resulted, but the interaction and socialisation between so many distanced people that occurred. One of the main aims we intended for the project was in fact to open up discussion about the process of designing and in particular the critique of visual communication processes – to this end the project was a great success. Too often perhaps, especially in areas of graphic design, visual end-results are left to be viewed in isolation and to explain themselves, whereas this project aimed to address the prospect of discussion about works in progress and to be able to view the entire process of so many young designers around the globe and not just be presented with their end results.

Following conclusion of the *Creative Waves* '05 project, the processes involved and the outcomes produced by the many participants were, as mentioned earlier, presented at numerous design and education conferences in many countries; including the 2005 Ascilite (Australasian Society of Computers in Learning in Tertiary Education) Conference in Brisbane, Australia. During this conference Omnium was awarded the 2005 Ascilite President's Award for the inaugural Creative Waves initiative as well as for the Omnium® Software used to host the entire event. Additionally though, the conference was to have a more important part to play in the next few years for Omnium's research. Following the presentation of the *Creative Waves* '05 project at the conference, Omnium was approached by

Figure 2. The visual progression of one team's work process from the first Creative Waves project

staff from the University of Auckland's School of Pharmacy who were interested in discussing some sort of collaboration to progress teaching and learning strategies for their undergraduate pharmacists. Like many other disciplines outside of the visual arts and design, pharmacy curricula increasingly are able to include more and more visual and digital materials available to students and teachers.

Many of the more traditional scientific diagrams and tables used in previous texts are now being produced in highly graphic formats including movie files and 3D animations. In addition, students have a vastly increased resource of materials through the many avenues offered by the web. It was a suggested collaboration that seemed highly appropriate and an opportunity for Omnium to try to improve the opportunities for a completely 'new' discipline, in the same way that it had been doing for the visual arts for nearly a decade.

Around the same time, Omnium and Icograda were already in discussions again for a follow-up to the initial *Creative Waves '05* project; one that again could be offered to students and teachers globally. Omnium's intentions with a subsequent

Creative Waves project was to include its new direction of offering a project that had more of a purpose and real brief; one that would align itself with the aims to help less fortunate people in remote parts of the world by connecting like-minded creative folk who could offer their own time to help such a cause.

Creative Waves '07: Visualising Issues in Pharmacy [VIP]

Following nearly twelve months of planning and preparation, which included the design, program-ming and introduction of a brand new version (v4.0) of the Omnium® Software, the *Creative Waves '07* project, titled *Visualising Issues in Pharmacy [VIP]*, was ready to be launched. The new VIP project ultimately aimed to produce a series of visual campaigns to raise public aware-ness of six health issues that were chronically affecting small rural communities in Kenya, Af-rica. Through a combination of over one hundred pharmacy participants around the world, together with a similar number from design disciplines, the VIP project would attempt to produce campaigns to cover issues relating to:

- Malaria
- Tuberculosis
- Adherence (regarding the correct usage of medicines)
- Sexually Transmitted Infections (notably HIV/Aids)
- Chronic Disease
- Immunisation

As a result of a short promotional campaign, using a simple information website about the project built by the Omnium team, as well as announcements through both the Icograda and Icograda Education Network newsletters, hundreds of people had applied to take part in the *Creative Waves '07* project from over 35 countries worldwide. The combined project participants were split into four user-types: students; teachers acting as free-roaming mentors; invited special guests; and the six pharmacy and four design co-ordinators with the overall project was convened by the Omnium Research Group. In addition, the entire project was formally endorsed by, and offered as a collaboration between the worldwide professional governing bodies of Icograda (representing the graphic design side of the project) and the Federation Internationale Pharmaceutical - FIP (representing the pharmacy/health sciences side of the project).

When facilitating online projects on such a global scale, with clearly structured e-learning intentions, Omnium has for many years established and strongly recommended the need for two very inter-dependent foundations: a clear and well documented working process; and a highly user-friendly and technically proficient software platform. In regard to the technical platform (software), despite it being a crucial aspect to offering such projects and an aspect that has demanded huge amounts of time, expense and consideration over the last ten years, it is not the main focus of Omnium's projects or research, albeit a necessity. For the purposes of this paper, we will describe some of the software's features used as we detail

the progression of the work but mainly concentrate on how the VIP project was facilitated and structured around Omnium's five-stage creative process for online creative creativity. We should also explain that the VIP project was separated into two overlapping seven-week phases (pharmacy and design) which both applied the five-stage process equally efficiently, although again for the purposes of this paper, we will concentrate on the latter design phase.

Creative Waves '07: Design Phase

Following an initial seven week start to the VIP project that saw over one hundred students, teachers and special guests from various areas of the health sciences and pharmacy collaborate together to ultimately form six detailed research reports on each of the recognised health issues (identified above) that affect the specific rural community of Winam in Kenya, an equal number of design participants took over the project for a further seven weeks - interacting with the pharmacy participants who in many ways acted as the clients and advisors.

Of critical importance to the designers, who resided in numerous countries worldwide, was to have a base of advisors located in Kenya itself, who could relay information about the culture, traditions, behaviours, living conditions and even folklore of the people whom the project was intended to assist and help. Such an important resource to a project of this nature included students, teachers, health workers, renowned professionals in the field and non-profit organizations who were familiar with or directly located in the targeted area. Two of the most influential contributors to the project were George Onyango and Salim Opere from the Help Heal Organisation, located in the village of Winam, Kenya and directly assisting the villagers facing the daily difficulties caused by the six identified health concerns. A highly evocative, frank and influential lecture written by George Onyango, could be argued as the catalyst to the

entire project and a series of accompanying photographs, made available through the Omnium®
Software galleries pages, gave participants the
instant reality of the problems being faced.

Of the many discussions that occurred throughout the three-month Creative Waves VIP project,
two discussion threads in particular generation an
enormous amount of interaction and direct information from the location itself. The two threads,
facilitated by George and Salim, along with many
other Kenyan participants, together generated over
20,000 words of text in a series of questions and
answers from participants to those able to advise
from the location.

Following a highly structured format of progression through Omnium's five-stage working
process, including daily news announcements,
weekly lectures written by project coordinators
and invited guests, live online chat sessions with
luminaries in the field of design and health sciences, and progressive design briefs to facilitate the
process of designing public awareness campaigns
about eh six identified health issues, the project
began to hone down a wide variety of suggested
creative approaches until several focused studies
were formed. It was interesting, as well as somewhat frustrating to observe, that the designers in
their smaller design teams were arguably selecting
specific ideas to work on too early in the process
without fully investigating the scope of ideas that
could be potentially created.

During the third *identify* stage of the project,
the design convenors introduced the notion of
"worldstorming" where each of the 100 design
participants were asked to come up with ten quick
ideas for campaigns that could promote awareness
of the six health issues. Within a very short time,
over six-hundred ideas were suggested which were
in turn sent to the Help Heal workers in Kenya
for their opinion and feedback. As a result it was
decided that three sets of suggestions would be
taken through stages four and five of Omnium's
OCC working process—a game for school children
to play with their teachers, peers and families; a

series of stickers that conveyed simple messages
about prevention and adherence; and designs for s
set of soccer uniforms to be worn by both formal
teams of young local footballers as well as the
average kid in the street who would be wearing
the outfits as simply trendy street wear as opposed
to formal uniforms.

The designs for each set of campaigns were
themselves taken through the five-stage process
by students and mentors who had been arranged
into new working teams until final solutions were
presented at the end of the seven week design
phase. Each of the final designs were versatile
enough to be able to be adjusted and amended to
deal with any one of the health issues and to date
Omnium is in a stage where it is seeking sponsorship and/or assistance to have the design realised.
On completion of the final designs being produced,
each of the public awareness campaigns is to be
sent to the village of Winam to be facilitated to
the community by the volunteers in location.

All of the process work from both the pharmacy
and design phases of the project can be viewed at
the archive of the Creative Waves project inter-

*Figure 3. One of the outcomes of the Creative
Waves VIP Project was a set of soccer kits with
slogans about the dangers of HIV to engage the
young men of Winam who play soccer a great
deal. Here are the packages of the shirts being
sent off to Kenya.*

face – creativewaves.omnium.net.au – within the Galleries area, along with every other facet of the project including lectures, discussions, team work, transcripts of the live chat sessions and profiles of every participant who took part.

The third in the series of Creative Waves projects, titled *Collabor8* – creativewaves.omnium. net.au/c8 – was recently run in 2008 and saw students from art & design colleges in Australia and China link together online to examine specific cultural, visual and language differences that affect creative work taking place between the two countries. For details of all the projects and to view the archives since 1998, visit the Omnium website: www.omnium.net.au

REFERENCES

Bennett, R. (2000). Om'nium [vds]: Presenting an On-Line Future for Tertiary [Design] Education. *Outline 9*, (winter 9), 17-24.

Bennett, R., Chan, L. K., & Polaine, A. (2004). *The Future Has Already Happened: Dispelling some myths of online education.* Proceedings of the Australian Council of University Art and Design Schools Annual Conference 2004, Canberra, Australia. Retrieved from http://www.acuads.com.au/conf2004/conf2004.htm.

Castells, M. (2000). *The Rise of the Network Society: The Information Age: Economy, Society and Culture Vol 1 (The Information Age).* London: Blackwell Publishers.

Coates, T. (2006). *Greater than the sum of its parts.* Paper presented at the Future of Web Apps, San Francisco.

Gillingson, S., & O'Leary, D. (2006). *Working progress: how to reconnect young people and organisations.* London: Demos.

Green, H., & Hannon, C. (2007). *Their Space: Education for a Digital Generation.* London: Demos.

Holden, J. (2007). *Logging On: Culture, Participation and the Web.* London: Demos.

Johnson, S. (2001). *Emergence: the connected lives of ants, brains, cities, and software.* London: Scribner.

Leadbeater, C. (2008). *We-think: The Power of Mass Creativity.* London: Profile Books Ltd.

Leadbeater, C., & Miller, P. (2004). *The pro-am revolution: how enthusiasts are changing our society and economy.* London: Demos.

Lenhart, A., Madden, M., & Hitlin, P. (2005). *Teens and Technology: Youth are leading the transition to a fully wired and mobile nation.* Washington, DC: Pew Internet & American Life.

McDonough, W., & Braungart, M. (2002). *Cradle to Cradle: Remaking the Way We Make Things.* New York: North Point Press.

McMillan, S. J., & Morrison, M. (2006). Coming of age with the internet: A qualitative exploration of how the internet has become an integral part of young people's lives. *New Media & Society, 8*(1), 73–95. doi:10.1177/1461444806059871

O'Reilly, T. (2005). *What Is Web 2.0: Design Patterns and Business Models for the Next Generation of Software.* Retrieved October 8, 2007, from http://www.oreillynet.com/pub/a/oreilly/tim/news/2005/09/30/what-is-web-20.html

Patrick, C. (1937). Creative Thought in Artists. *The Journal of Psychology, 4.*

Rheingold, H. (2003). *Smart Mobs: The Next Social Revolution.* New York: Perseus Books, U.S.

Salmon, G. K. (2000). *E-moderating the Key to Teaching & Learning Online.* London: RoutledgeFarmer.

Sifry, D. (2007). *State of the Live Web*, April 2007. Retrieved November 3rd, 2007, from http://www.sifry.com/alerts/archives/000493.html

Wallas, G. (1926). *The Art of Thought.* San Diego, CA: Harcourt Brace Jovanovich, Inc.

Weinberger, D. (2007). *Everything Is Miscellaneous: The Power of the New Digital Disorder.* New York: Times Books.

YouTube. (2006). *YouTube Fact Sheet.* Retrieved 8th October, 2006, from http://www.youtube.com/t/fact_sheet/

Chapter 4

Enhancing University Students' Interaction and Learning through Formative Peer–Assessment Online

Monica Liljeström
Umeå University, Sweden

ABSTRACT

This chapter draws upon data collected from a Swedish project with the aim to implement and evaluate peer assessment/peer review in online and distance education in the context of higher education. Previous studies of peer assessment in on-campus settings are discussed with a focus on what impact these findings had on the design of the peer assessment element. Findings from a distance course with 60 students, in which peer assessment and peer assessment preparation was carried out trough asynchronous text based communication in FirstClass, are reported. Data are collected from multiple sources and analyzed with the aim to find out how peer assessment element worked in this asynchronous text based environment. The results indicate that the students' engagement and collaborative efforts in general was high. The overall conclusion is that peer assessment could be worth exploring further as a tool to enhance student collaboration and learning in courses based on asynchronous text based communication.

INTRODUCTION

In this chapter I will share some experiences from a joint project between the Departments of Education at Umeå University, Mitthögskolan and Luleå University, Sweden. The aim of the project was to implement and explore what peer assessment in the form of peer review contributes to enhancing the students' learning in online and distance courses.

Assessment in this article is understood as described by Sadler (2008, p 2) as: "...the process of forming a judgement about the quality and extent of student achievement or performance, and therefore by inference a judgement about the learning that has taken place". Although peer assessment/peer review has been researched by many others in on-campus environments there seem to be fewer studies on how this element works in an online and distance education setting.

DOI: 10.4018/978-1-60566-727-0.ch004

Our first step towards understanding how peer assessment could be organised in this context was to design a peer assessment element based on ideas gained from previous studies of peer assessment and peer assessment preparation, which we tried to fit into our existing online and distance courses. An important key to enhancing the quality of peer assessment/peer review, as will be further presented in this chapter, seems to be the opportunity for students to share, interpret and discuss criteria in order to gain a deeper understanding of their tacit dimensions.

The common means for communication in our online and distance education courses are postings on asynchronous message boards. But how would this method of communication work in the context of peer assessment?

In this chapter I will present some of the background studies we carried out before we designed and implemented the peer assessment element in a course within a special needs teacher training programme and also report some early findings from the project.

- Are there any signs that the interaction with other students had any impact on the students' understanding of criteria?
- Did the students value the peer assessment element and consider it to be of any importance for their learning process?
- How did the students judge that the text-based communication worked for negotiating meaning? What strengths and limitations can be identified?

Current Challenges in University Education

Recent developments in information and communication technology (ICT) have literally brought the University into our homes. For example, figures from 2005 show that 17 percent of all American students in higher education, or more than 3, 2 million persons, took at least one online course at a degree granting institution during the autumn 2005 (Allen & Seaman, 2006). The Open University in the United Kingdom provides online and distance education for around 150,000 undergraduate students and more than 20,000 postgraduate students (QS Top Universities, 2008).

The same trend is visible in Sweden, where all universities provide distance and online courses and programs through the Swedish Net University (Swedish Agency for Networks and cooperation in Higher Education (NSHU). Statistics from 2006 show that as many as every fifth student in higher education, which means around 77 000 Swedish students, were registered on courses at the Swedish Net University (NSHU, 2008).

Courses and programmes offered partly or entirely through ICT create flexible opportunities for students to conduct higher studies at the location and the times which are best suited to fit with other commitments in their lives. Students of today are expected to become autonomous, independent and self-directed learners who take responsibility for their own personal and professional development (e.g. Stefani, 1998; Sainsbury & Walker, 2007), thus changing the educator's role from expert to coach and facilitator.

Sociocultural and constructivist theories of learning are often consulted when setting the scene for the active learner with their situated approach to learning and emphasis on learning as a collective activity in a cultural context. Simultaneously, we are experiencing a trend towards extremely fine-grained approaches to measuring student achievements (e.g. Sadler, 2005). This may seem paradoxical as the idea of being able to find methods to make an absolute valid judgement about the level of someone's knowledge and skills derives from positivist theories and as such is questionable in this context (Orr, 2007).

This means that teachers in online and distance education are facing a challenging task to meet the demand to provide high quality education for highly heterogeneous groups of students by means of fairly new technical solutions, whose strengths and limitations have not yet been fully explored.

Assessment and Examination as Central Elements in Online and Distance Education

The scenario described above may be one of the explanations for the results of previous Swedish studies by Hult (2005, 2007), in which assessments in 50 net-based courses, varying in discipline, length and level, were collected and analysed. One of the most striking results in these studies was that students on these courses had to go through a great number of different assessments spread out over time during the course. Interviews with teachers confirmed that the courses to a great extent are built around the assessments, in effect they serve the purpose of building the content of the course.

The continuous assessments also frame the students' course work in a way which forces them to stay active throughout the whole course, thus providing support to enable them to complete the course. Assessments in this perspective seem very central to building both the form and the content of net-based courses. This trend is also visible outside the Swedish context. Gibbs and Simpson (2005) report that an Open University student in United Kingdom may receive up to fifty times as much feedback on assignments over the course of an entire degree programme as students at conventional universities!

Becker et al (1968), Snyder (1971) and Miller & Parlett (1974) have all in different ways shown how examination and examination tasks in higher education tends to have a steering effect on student learning. This means that assessment and examination tasks must be designed to correlate with the idea of independence and critical thinking in learners if we want to enhance the students' possibilities to develop these types of skills.

The Tacit Dimensions of Standards and Criteria

In this article it is assumed that all criteria and standards have a tacit dimension; they are imbued with an implicit meaning that is not always visible to the students (e.g. O'Donovan et al. 2004). This specific meaning could be described as a result of the traditions, methods, and theories used and negotiated within the 'communities of practice' of the overall academic context. This includes the idea that the students should develop abilities of a generic nature, for example ethical and social responsibility, communication and information literacy, problem-solving, critical thinking, reflection and self-direction in learning (Sainsbury & Walker, 2007).

However, there are also specific traditions within the particular institutions where the students conduct their studies which are implicitly embedded in the text of the steering documents. Access to the implicit meanings in these documents is gained within these communities' through negotiations, interactions between the members of the staff and through the practical use of assessments. Full understanding of the community's shared meaning of how a student product should be constructed in order to correspond to what these communities regard as "the correct way" is hard to put into explicit words without reducing it to simple statements. Because of the complexity of verbalising the shared meaning it is easier to gain an understanding of it through interaction and practical experience.

When the students enter their studies they may not be familiar with the ideas within the academy and accordingly the meaning inscribed in standards and criteria may not be clear to them. This could trigger some students to become what Miller and Parlett (1974) referred to as 'cue-seekers'; students who orientate towards cues that provide information about what is rewarded in the assessment system and thereby result in successful strategies to pass their exams. Other students (with Miller and Parrett's words 'cue deaf') may not be as aware that there are specific meanings imbued in the criteria and standards which they need to grasp and orient towards when being assessed, thus being more likely to experience examination failures than 'cue seekers'.

In that sense the conclusion can be drawn that frequent assessment and feedback from the teacher in net-based courses could be one way to support both 'cue seekers' and 'cue deaf' students to gain a better awareness of what's expected of them and may help them to direct their learning to meet the requirements for successful study outcomes. The many assessments throughout the course with rich feedback from the teacher could transmit the implicit meaning or the "hidden curriculum" and make it more explicit to the students. Nevertheless, it must be questioned if frequent comments in assessments by the teacher really support the idea of autonomous, independent and self-directed learners, or if it creates more teacher dependent students than ever (Torrance, 2007).

The frequent assessments could also limit the students engagement in the course materials by triggering them to focus only on what they believe will be rewarded when assessed: "They are strategic in their use of time and 'selectively negligent' in avoiding content that they believe is not likely to be assessed (Gibbs & Simpson, 2004).

The time spent on constant production of assessment products to be sent for feedback to the tutor could also be restraining when it comes to interactions with peers. This could especially be an issue since distance and online studies are often conducted parallel with other commitments, for example work or/and family life, which gives some students little room for engagement in the role of co-constructor of knowledge.

One could also assume that the frequent need to write feedback to the students results in a heavy work load for the teacher when dealing with large study groups online. As the teacher usually does not have unlimited time to invest in a course one could also suspect that this frequent assessment

pattern leaves very little room for teachers to support their students' learning by other means than commenting their assessment products.

Could Peer Assessment be the Solution?

This background made us interested in exploring peer assessment further. Could this be a way of making it possible for students to be actively involved in assessing each other, adding something to their learning process? Could peer assessment support the idea of students as co-constructors of knowledge and open up for more student autonomy? What challenges would we face if we were to introduce peer assessment in the online setting?

Interest in formative assessment as a possible way to support students' learning seems to be increasing at the moment. However, as pointed out by for example Gibbs & Simpson (2004), Torrance (2007) and Sadler (2008), even the best intentions with using assessment to enhance student learning, could have the opposite effect. As Torrance (2007) points out, there is a risk that some uses of more formal assessment result in learning being displaced by procedural compliance. In such cases the students may learn how to produce a product which is likely to pass examination, but the grade will be achieved despite the fact that the student hasn't developed a deeper understanding of the subject as intended. Thus the underlying risk of formative assessment could be to produce reductionist learning and instrumental accountability rather than meaningful empowerment.

Of course, we don't want to replace learning with procedural compliance; we want our students to truly engage in the course materials. We want them to develop their understanding of the subject in a rich and deep way including what different theories contribute when it comes to understanding the world and its phenomenon, and be able to apply their understanding in other contexts than in the course and assessment situation.

This raised several questions about peer assessment, which build on an arrangement in which individuals consider the amount, level, value, worth, quality, or success of the product or outcomes of learning of peers of similar status (Definition by Topping, K, 1998). Could peer assessment procedures be a good strategy to reduce this risk for instrumental and reductive learning? Or could it even have the opposite effect? After all, the teacher can be assumed to have more experiences of the subject and the course content than the students, as well as of the community of practice from which criteria and standards derive. Thus teachers could be expected to have the ability to prevent instrumental learning by challenging students to engage further with the course content through their assessment comments, besides more general feedback on disposition and other formalities. These less complex criteria, such as disposition and general structure and other formalities, are fairly easy to make explicit and could therefore be what the students have gained most understanding of, and perhaps therefore are more likely to apply when peer assessing each other. This makes it important to ensure that peer assessment truly supports the intended enhancement of the students' learning rather than becoming a support for the instrumental learning that it is intended to prevent.

Several research studies on (formative) peer assessment, most of them carried out in on-campus settings indicate that this element contributes to the students' learning and development of critical appraisal skills. Macpherson (1999) found growth in the students' reflective and critical thinking skills after participating in a peer/tutor arrangement in which the students were to give oral feedback on each other's literature reviews. Anderson et al (1999) found evidence that students participating in peer assessment developed their skill of making reasoned justification of arguments.

According to Macdonald (2002) viewing other students' strategies to approach the assessment task seems to support an awareness of weaknesses in their own approaches. It could also be possible that the students gain a deeper understanding of the standards and criteria used by being exposed to a variety of strategies to solve the task than if they were only to receive feedback from the teacher on their own product.

The overall conclusion, drawn from many research studies on peer assessment in both face to face environments as well in an online context,, (e.g. Stefani, 1998, Boud, 2002; Higgins et al, 2002; Bloxham & West, 2004; McLuckie, & Topping, 2004, Sainsbury & Walker, 2007, Prince & Dominique, 2007) is that engaging students in deep collaboration, as in-depth collaboration rich enough to develop a collective understanding or 'shared meaning' (e.g. Head, 2003), through peer assessment indeed seems a promising method to try if one wants to support the idea of students as autonomous, independent and self-directed learners who take responsibility for their own personal and professional development.

PEER ASSESSMENT PREPARATION

A key issue in previous research on formative peer assessment is the need to prepare the students before they take part in peer assessment. If this is going to serve as a tool for learning it is important that the students develop an understanding of the inscribed meaning of standards and criteria in use, and how to apply them in practice. They must also gain awareness of how to use peer assessment as guidance for directing and supporting their learning during the learning process, rather than seeing it primarily as a tool for judging the total quality of the examination product, as this is the teachers' responsibility and area of knowledge.

Creating a common understanding of criteria between students and tutors seems a challenging task because of the tacit dimension. Previous research indicates that even if the criteria were presented in both written and verbal form, the understanding of some criteria differs among students and their tutors (e.g. Orsmond et al 1996, 1997, O'Donovan et al., 2004). As O'Donovan etal. (2004) points out this tacit knowledge about criteria is obtained from the shared experience of the staff when using the criteria for marking and feedback. Their conclusion is that the best way to create meaningful knowledge of assessment and standards is through both explicit communication and tacit transfer processes. Supervising and engaging the students in interpretation and negotiation of criteria as preparation for peer assessment activities could be a method of mediating this meaning and contributing to a deeper learning through the peer assessment process. It is important not to be too detailed when explaining criteria as this could reduce them to a list to be followed precisely in an instrumental way in the hands of the students.

The idea that students should actively be engaged in negotiating criteria is supported in a meta-analysis of 48 quantitative peer assessment studies by Falchikov & Goldfinch (2000). When comparing peer and teacher marks they found results which indicated that criteria derived from students, or when the students have agreed on the existing ones, give a better teacher-peer agreement in marking than if the criteria were only supplied by the teacher. Results from the same study also indicate that the use of well understood and explicit criteria give more accurate judgements than when students are left with little or no guidance on how to interpret the criteria. Furthermore the use of global judgements instead of assessing several individual dimensions seems to be an important factor in the success of peer-reviews. Overall the study indicates that students in fact *can* make reasonably reliable judgements.

Our Conditions When Trying out Peer Assessment in a Distance Course

Guided by the findings from previous research on peer assessment the project participants at each university selected a few courses in which peer assessment was implemented. The data in this chapter derives from a 10 week long course within a programme for special needs teacher training. The duration of most courses within this programme, as well as the majority of our online and distance courses, is five weeks followed by the final examination procedure. The reason why this particular course was chosen is because of the richness of data accumulated due to the length of the course. However, similar results have emerged to various degrees in courses of shorter length, and in courses which are not part of a programme and with an even more heterogeneous mixture of students than in the course where data for this chapter was collected.

The special needs teacher programme is carried out as a distance course with obligatory on-campus meetings every fifth week. The first part of the on-campus week is usually devoted to final examinations of the current course, while the second part is used for the introduction of a new course and introductory lectures.

The students on this programme can on one level be described a homogenised group, since a teaching certificate is a prerequisite for the programme. The students vary in age between participants in their late twenties up to age fifty plus students, and their teaching background varies from preschool teachers to college teachers and everything in-between. The course is taken by students from all over the country, which means that many of them have conducted their previous studies at other universities. It also means that there is a great variety in students' backgrounds when it comes to length of previous academic studies as well as in the content and design of those studies.

This may explain our previous experiences of students attending this programme. Some students already seem to have a basic understanding of the academic culture and what they are expected to perform when assessed while others tend to be very unsure of how to tackle the assessments and therefore are at risk to fail. As this course was conducted in mid-programme we found data which confirmed that some students had severe problems to pass the examinations in previous courses and that some had a hard time grasping what they were meant to perform. Therefore we found it highly interesting to find out if peer assessment could become a sufficient support for these students.

The course platform used was FirstClass, which enables both teachers and students to create their own topic threads for asynchronous discussions. It also enables synchronized communication through chat. We decided to use this platform mainly because it was familiar to all of the students since it is the standard platform for all teacher-training at the university where they conducted their studies. Some of the students were not very familiar with using a computer or communicating online when they entered the programme, so we did not want to confuse them by using a platform that they were new to.

The 60 students were divided into six smaller study groups and given their own area in FirstClass. In this area they had access to a message board for general discussions, one message board for course related issues, and a special message board for workshop activities related to the peer assessment element. In addition there was an area where all 60 students could interact, including a virtual café forum. The structure in FirstClass had already been designed by the teachers in the course and our only interference was to ask that our workshop forum be added to this structure.

Asynchronous text messaging was the main tool for communication for both pedagogical and practical reasons. One important pedagogical issue is that asynchronous communication supports the flexibility that may be the only way for students to fit their studies in with other life commitments, and the fact that it can be a democratic aspect as it allows everyone to make an utterance. The fact that some of the students were still new to using computers and communication through ICT was

also of importance for choosing to carry out this element through text based communication.

The written form in itself promotes a more systematic use of words than oral communication in order to compensate for the lack of attributes such as gesturing, mimic and tone of the voice (Ong, 1982, Olson, 1994). This need to use more specified words to clarify meaning to a reader could possibly support the students' understanding of forms of communication within the academic tradition and the specific discipline where they are conducting their studies. Black (2005, p9) goes as far as to draw the conclusion that:

Asynchronous discussion allows for reflective thought and "talk," components valued in effective discussion. These same components make asynchronous discussion more viable than synchronous discussion in fostering higher order thinking, social construction of meaning, and reflection.

But asynchronous, written communication could also be restraining. The intended rich and deep communication in online text based forums sometimes came to be dominated by a few active students while others remain noiseless "lurkers". One reason for this may be that some of the students prioritise their limited time to reading postings by others rather than spending time expressing their own views (Fung, 2004). Therefore we don't want to close any doors to other means of communication and plan to further our experiences by adding audio-visual techniques for communication in future courses to see what these means of communication could offer.

Designing the Peer Assessment Element

The course set up for the students in the special needs teacher programme included two final examination products which they were meant to work on during the off-campus weeks. One was a portfolio directed towards their professional development in which the course literature and lectures were processed in the form of lecture and literature comments. The other task was to outline a pedagogical issue of interest for their future profession, and to plan and conduct a field study on this matter to be presented in the form of a written 10-page research report.

No pre-planned activities were cancelled due to the implementation of the peer assessment element; the overall structure was left unchanged. We created our workshop area in FirstClass in addition to the pre-planned course message boards where both the peer assessment preparation and the peer assessment procedure were to take place. The students were to work through five workshops during the course. Since the number of participants on this course was quite large (60 students) they were assigned to smaller study groups of 7-8 participants and each group had their own discussion forum for the workshop activities.

The workshop element was designed with an initial focus on making the students more aware of implicit dimensions of the course criteria as a stepping stone for peer reviewing each other's course work later on in the course. There were no set rules for how often and to what degree the students had to participate in the workshop and the students were informed that their postings would not be assessed for grading purposes. We took a risk here that the students would choose to devote a minimum amount of time to engage in the peer assessment process. For example Prins et al. (2005) points out that limited participation by students in peer assessment assignments is a risk in the online environment. We decided that we wanted to see if the design and content of the peer assessment element would be enough to trigger the students' willingness to devote time to this. As extra motivation for participation we also included a self and peer evaluation task to be included in the portfolio, in which the students were asked to refer to their own and other's postings in the workshops while reflecting on what

value this had during the learning process.

Each workshop was open for postings on the discussion board for about five days to enable all students to find time to participate. The peer assessment task was designed as five steps in the form of workshops.

- In *Workshop I* the students were introduced to the idea of peer assessment. They were asked to reflect upon course criteria in the light of the Higher Education Act and the Higher Education Ordinance and discuss what these overarching steering documents meant for an understanding of the course criteria. The aim of the workshop was to establish some kind of consensus about criteria.

- In *Workshop II* the students were to apply their shared understanding of course criteria by assessing two example texts. They were then to present the results of their review of the texts and discuss and motivate their judgements. The students were tutored by questions aimed to stimulate further reflection over how the criteria were to be understood and how to use them in practice. They were also asked to try to identify similarities and differences in their individual understandings, and discuss eventual refinements in how the criteria could be understood and put into practise. At the end of workshop II the students were to draw conclusions from each other's experiences and their discussions and decide upon what criteria to use for peer assessing each other during the process of completing their final examination products.

- In *Workshop III* the students were each to publish a first draft of a literature comment to be assessed by the rest of their study group and by this means be provided with comments from their peers upon strengths and areas in need of improvement.

- In *Workshop IV* the students presented their

research plan for the examination task to plan, conduct and report a field study, and were to receive constructive feedback on this by their peers.

- In *Workshop V* the students presented the draft for the final report for peer review.

RESEARCH FOCUS AND METHODS

To answer the research questions addressed in this chapter, data were collected from multiple sources to gain a holistic view of how the peer assessment element worked in the text-based environment. Some data derives from the students' answers on to an online questionnaire, which they answered during the last day of the course in June 2008. The questionnaire was answered by 51 students (n=92% of the student group). Those who did not answer were students who did not participate in the on-campus meeting, where time was devoted to this evaluation.

Additional data was collected from their discussions of the topics in the workshop forums as well as from spontaneous comments (related to the research questions in this chapter) made in their workshop forums and other online discussion boards provided for the course.

Henri (1992) offers an analytic framework to deal with "the 'product' of learning (p 124)". Five dimensions of interaction are suggested; participative, social, interactive, cognitive and metacognitive, as important tools to identify the learning processes and strategies selected by online learners. At this stage of the evaluation of the peer assessment implementation, it is too early to see definite results of the quantification of data in accordance with Henries' model, due to the enormous mass of data generated by the students' postings. However it has been found useful to use these categories as reference points when examining samples of data when trying to get an overall view of participation.

The data collection and analysis focused on:

1. The reflections the students expressed about what impact postings from others had on their own understanding of standards and criteria and academic knowledge building in general
2. Reflections on the peer assessment/peer review element
3. Posts which indicated a change of mind when presenting their understanding of standards and criteria
4. Reflections on text-based communication.

FINDINGS

Initially the students seemed very confused by the peer assessment element. Some found it unrelated to the course and complained that it took valuable time from working on the examination tasks, despite the fact that we had tried to introduce them to the ideas behind peer assessment at the on-campus meeting at the beginning of the course. One of the students who answered the online questionnaire wrote this comment:

At the beginning of the course it felt like a side track, but as the course progressed the meaning of the workshop became clearer to me. I developed a new understanding of earlier activities in the workshop. But as I said, it took a while before the knowledge and understanding became visible and obvious to me (in translation).

Despite the initial confusion, the students started to make their initial postings in their workshops, and as it turned out they became truly engaged in the workshop discussions. The study group with highest activity made 432 postings and the group with lowest activity made 173 postings. Some of the difference in amount of postings between the group with highest and lowest activity is that there was a greater number of off topic postings in the high activity group than in the lower activity group. Another reason for the difference in amount of postings could be that the members of those groups carried out some of their discussions through physical meetings, which is indicated in their postings in the workshop forum.

Many students made their postings in the form of word documents posted as attachments, perhaps because writing their postings this way allowed more space to outline their thoughts and made possible spell-checking etc. It could also be a strategy to separate social comments from on-topic remarks as many of the messages with word document attachments contained some kind of social comment.

Activity in all of the groups seems rather stable over time. Data samples from the workshops in all of the study groups indicates the dimension "participative" (see Henri, p 125ff) since all students (in the sampled data) received at least one comment on on-topic postings by all group members, although some participants seems to have contributed with more postings than others.

The social dimension was also present in all of the groups, through small comments about life and personal thoughts. The discussions in all groups also showed interactive dimensions as the students sometimes referred to messages made by others as a starting point for their own argumentation. It is also possible to find cognitive and metacognitive dimensions in the postings. A lot of the students made spontaneous postings in the workshop, in which they reflected over their learning process and that they found the peer assessment element intriguing because it challenged their understanding. Metacognitive reflections like these were also found in data collected from their comments when they answered the online questionnaire.

Deep Collaboration for Cracking the Academic Code

When working with interpretation criteria in workshop I, the students were asked to discuss what it could mean to be "critical", "independent" and "reflective" in a scientific context. Many students answered these questions with comments like "this has to do with "trusting one's own judgements", it is when one is using 'common sense' and similar comments. There were however others, who for example said that it has to do with how to read, interpret and view a text or a situation with critical eyes, and draw conclusions.

In most of the groups differences in opinions were not further interpreted at this stage of the peer assessment preparation. Only a couple of students made references to scientific literature as a strategy to add some weight to their opinion. Although it is visible in the postings that they took great interest in each other's point of view they didn't challenge each other's understandings in any visible way. There are thus not many signs in the data that any student changed their original view of criteria in the data from workshop I, although different opinions were aired.

In *workshop II* the students were supposed to put the criteria they had agreed upon into action by assessing two example texts. These example texts were written to correspond with the instructions these students had when writing their own papers or reports, but the subject was something other than the course content. We hoped that this would make it easier for them to identify some general ideas in academic reasoning and reporting if the content wasn't as close at heart as a study in their own field might be.

Text one was authored in a purely referential style with a weak 'author voice', while *text two* was written in argumentative style in which the 'author voice' was present. Example text one only referred to studies already conducted on the research subject but with no clear purpose as to why this was referred. Text two referred to previous studies already conducted on the research subject but connected it to issues such as general trends in society and some comparisons with studies made in other fields were also mentioned as a part of the argumentation chain.

Initially the most common pattern in all study

groups was the approach where many students pointed out easily identifiable issues in the example texts, such as the amount of references to literature or the fact that example text two referred to an article in a newspaper which many found decreased the scientific value of the text. Many drew the conclusion that text one had a higher scientific value than text two, because all references used were from previous studies on the same topic as discussed in the text, which they found more relevant than the approach in text two where other sources had been used, including a newspaper article!

However, there were also other students in all of the groups that stated that they somehow thought that text two was the better one, although they didn't manage to express many arguments for why they made this conclusion. Some said that it had a better flow than the referential text or that they had the feeling it was a better text than the other.

There are many visible signs in the remarks the students made to each other's postings that they took a great interest in other's point of view. A few students managed to identify differences in opinion while most seemed to settle for identifying similarities with their own ideas.

At this point the students were tutored by being asked questions if they could identify any 'signs of scientific knowledge building' when studying how the texts were written. What conclusions could they make when looking at how the two authors had constructed their texts? Did they find that one or the other was showing more signs of independent and critical thinking? Did they manage to identify an author voice?

These were questions that seemed to trigger the students to engage further in collaborative analyse of the texts. The general opinion about the texts in all groups started to turn in favour of expressing the opinion that text two was of higher scientific value since the authors referred to other studies to put weight behind their own argumentation, thus creating new knowledge rather than just referring

to findings already made in the field of research. One of the students wrote that:

At first I thought that text one was more trustworthy, now I can see that text two is written in a more critical, argumentative and independent style, which adds to the trustworthiness. (in translation).

Similar comments were also found in all the other study groups, although some students also wrote that they still felt unsure if they had come up with the right answers or not but that they had started to understand that there might not be any simple answers to these questions.

However, it wasn't just the tutored peer assessment activities that seem to have had an impact on the students' learning and understanding. Data from the online questionnaire shows that as many as 84 percent of the students marked that they agreed in fully or to a high degree with the statement that participating in peer assessment/ review enhanced their learning. Interestingly enough there were more comments on what they had learned from assessing their peers than what they had learnt from being peer assessed. One of the values of assessing their peers, which was pointed out by several students, was the fact that it became obvious to them that the examination tasks could be tackled in a variety of ways. One student wrote in a comment that:

It was time consuming but gave me an enormous amount. To see how one could think in different ways made me see different aspects of the texts and how you can formulate and structure the presentation of reflections on a subject (in translation).

When we presented the results from the online questionnaire to these students we were given even more feedback. The students told us that they had found peer assessment/peer review rather time consuming but that they also felt that it was time well invested since they believed it had helped them to direct their learning and guided their work with the examination tasks.

One of the students stated that he actually thought he had saved some time by participating in peer assessment, since it made him understand what he was meant to perform so he didn't have to waste a lot of time figuring that out.

To summarise the findings from this course it is clear that almost all of the students came to find great value in participating in the peer assessment activities. It is also clear that students found that the rich collaboration with their peers enhanced their learning.

Transmitting Meaning through Text

According to the students' responses in the online questionnaire, most of them found a value in conducting their discussions through text based means. Some mentioned the flexibility which had enabled them to participate in the discussions when they found a gap between other life commitments. Others pointed out that it gave them time to reflect on the topic discussed and enabled them to go back and view earlier posts. One student wrote that:

It suited me perfectly. I can reflect whenever I want to, with anyone in the group. I can take my time and consider my own opinions. I also can go back and see how I thought before. I know that everyone in the group can read my reflections at any time.

One student mentioned that she thought text based discussions gave her a space she didn't find as easily in face to face communication for expressing her thoughts and opinions. There are several posts in the message boards (including the workshop forums) which also indicate that students reflected thoroughly upon each other's postings before responding to it by adding their own thoughts about other's comments. There are

also comments in which the student points out that a remark from a fellow student has made them think in a different way than before.

Other signs however indicate that it wasn't uncomplicated to conduct the whole process of meaning making through text. Study groups in which the students lived within close range of each other decided to further their discussions in physical meetings. Students in groups where participants lived further away from each other made plans to further the discussions during upcoming on campus meetings. There were also a few students who expressed in the online questionnaire that they found the text based discussion restraining and that they sometimes found it hard to express their thoughts in a way that could be understood in the way they intended.

CONCLUSION

An overall conclusion from the students' reactions to the peer assessment/peer review element is that this strategy to enhance students' learning seems well worth exploring further. As shown, a majority of the students were actively involved in the discussions despite the fact that participating in peer assessment was not a graded performance and no rules were set up for acceptable minimum participation.

It would be naïve to believe that it is possible for the students to gain a full understanding of the implicit meaning of standards and criteria just by participating in peer assessment processes in just one course. The teacher will always be the most knowledgeable member of 'a learning community' when it comes to assessment of student products, since they are full time members of the academic community in contrast to the students who are there for a shorter period of time when conducting their studies. Despite these reservations the high level of engagement in discussing criteria and assessing each other combined with their comments in the online questionnaire shows that the students clearly found value in this experience.

A first step towards understanding the deeper meaning of the criteria, and thereby empowering the students to direct their studies in relation to this, could be to understand that there are deeper meanings behind the explicit criteria, and it seems that these students became aware of this while interacting in the workshops. This could be a starting point for them to develop more and deeper understanding about the world views within the academy throughout the rest of the programme, which would consequently provide them with effective tools to conduct their studies successfully. The results clearly indicate that peer assessment in online and distance education could promote the same growth in the students' reflective and critical thinking skills as has been found in previous studies on peer assessment in face to face environments. It also seems to trigger the students to devote time and engagement to interaction and collaboration.

It seems that tutoring and adding challenges to the students' initial understanding of the criteria is valuable to help them gain access to the implicit dimensions of criteria to be used when assessing each other during the learning process. The idea of peer assessment preparation is to share the underlying ideas behind criteria, which means that the students should not be left alone when trying to gain this understanding. It was easy enough to provide such tutoring during this particular course as additional teacher resources were added since it was a development project. However this could become a time consuming element for the teacher to handle once it is implemented in courses with no extra resources. On the other hand, much of the feedback the teacher would have to write to individuals is handled by the students, and the final examination products are well processed before the students hand them in. If the students become more familiar with the ideas within the academic culture it could result in improved chances to pass the final examination. This would cut down much of the effort the teacher has to make to instruct these students about what they must improve in order to pass the examination.

How the preparation for peer assessment, as well as the peer assessment procedure best should be designed and carried out in the online environment seems to be a dilemma. As we still have a lot of data to analyse and also intend to try other variations of the assessment design presented in this article in future courses we are still far from being able to point to a 'best practice'.

To stay with text based communication could mean that all students have an equal chance to make their voice heard and more time to reflect and formulate their thoughts. But at the same time some of the data indicates that the students experienced some limitations in the 'text talk' and wanted to clear things up in face to face communication. A possible solution which we will try is to combine text discussions with a conclusive seminar facilitated through audiovisual techniques. This would give the students both the time for deep reflection and the possibility to clear up misunderstandings and tie up loose ends.

Using FirstClass as a platform for communication must be considered to have worked well in this course, since the students managed to collaborate by means of it with such engagement. This can probably partly be explained by the fact that the students were already familiar with this platform. It shows that it might be wise to stick to the communication tools the students are used to when implementing a new element such as peer assessment. Even so, it would be interesting to investigate if other platforms with better options for integrating chat functions, audio visual technique and asynchronous text communication in the same interface could be even more effective as a scene for the peer assessment element.

This study was carried out in a course within a distance education programme, which means that the students already knew each other and also had the possibility to meet each other on a regular basis in a physical environment. It was also beneficial that the course duration was as long as ten weeks which made it easy for them to devote time to engaging in peer assessment. All of them had some previous experience of academic studies. Yet many of our students are new to academic studies and conduct their studies entirely online in courses that are only five weeks. Could the peer assessment element also be introduced in this type of course?

Some promising results from our implementation of peer assessment in one of our online courses shows the same engagement in these students' approach to the peer assessment activities as in the case of the special needs teacher training programme students. Some of the statements from an evaluation questionnaire in this five week long course show that many of these students believed that their participation in peer assessment had helped them crack some of the academic codes and thereby enhanced their learning. We believe that adding audiovisual techniques to enable the students to participate in conclusive discussions would be especially valuable in these types of shorter non-programme courses, but what type and to what amount is yet to be tried. All in all, our experiences of peer assessment in online and distance education shows promising signs of being valuable for stimulating deep collaboration and enhancement of the students' learning.

REFERENCES

Anderson, T., Howe, C., Soden, R., Halliday, J., & Low, J. (2001). Peer interaction and the learning of critical thinking skills in further education students . *Instructional Science, 29*, 1–32. doi:10.1023/A:1026471702353

Becker, H. S., Geer, B., & Hughes, E. C. (1968). *Making the grade: the academic side of college life.* New York: Wiley

Black, A. (2005). The use of asynchronous discussion: Creating a text of talk. *Contemporary Issues in Technology & Teacher Education, 5*(1), 5–24.

Boud, D. (2000). Sustainable Assessment: Rethinking assessment for the learning society . *Studies in Continuing Education, 22*(2), 151–167. doi:10.1080/713695728

Falchikov, N., & Goldfinch, J. (2000). Student Peer Assessment in Higher Education: A Meta-Analysis Comparing Peer and Teacher Marks. *Review of Educational Research, 70*(3), 287–322.

Fung, Y. (2004). Collaborative online learning: interaction patterns and limiting factors. *Open Learning, 19*(2), 135–149. doi:10.1080/0268051042000224743

Gibbs, G., & Simpson, C. (2004). Does your assessment support your students learning? *Learning and Teaching in Higher Education, 1*(1), 3–31.

Gibbs, G., & Simpson, C. (2004-05). Conditions under which Assessment Supports Students' Learning. *Learning and Teaching in Higher Education, 1*, 1–29.

Head, G. (2003). Effective collaboration: deep collaboration as an essential element of the learning process. *Journal of Educational Enquiry, 4*(2), 47–62.

Henri, F. (1991). Computer Conferencing and Content Analysis. In A.R. Kaye (Ed.) *Collaborative Learning Through Computer Conferencing. The Najaden Papers.* Berlin: Springer Verlag.

Hult, A. (2005). *Examination över nätet - en studie av 10 nätuniversitetskurser.* Umea, Sweden: UCER/ Umea Centre for Evaluation Research.

Hult, A. (2007). *Examinationen är kursen - En analys av examination i kurser över nätet.* Swedish Agency for Networks and cooperation in Higher Education.

Macdonald, J. (2002). Exploiting Online Interactivity to Enhance Assignment Development and Feedback in Distance Education, Open Learning. *The Journal of Open and Distance Learning, 16*(2), 179–189.

Macpherson, K. (1999). The Development of Critical Thinking Skills in Undergraduate Supervisory Management Units: efficacy of student peer assessment. *Assessment & Evaluation in Higher Education, 24*(3), 273–284. doi:10.1080/0260293990240302

Miller, C. M. L., & Parlett, M. (1974). *Up to the mark: a study of the examination game.* London: SRHE.

O'Donovan, B., Price, M., & Rust, C. (2004). Know what I mean? Enhancing student understanding of assessment standards and criteria. *Teaching in Higher Education, 9*(3), 325–335. doi:10.1080/1356251042000216642

Olson, D. R. (1994), *The world on paper.* Cambridge, UK: Cambridge University press.

Ong, W. J. (1982) *Orality and literacy: The Technologizing of the Word.* New York: Methuen.

Orsmond, P., Merry, S., & Reiling, K. (1996). The importance of marking criteria in peer assessment . *Assessment & Evaluation in Higher Education, 21*(3), 239–249. doi:10.1080/0260293960210304

Orsmond, P., Merry, S., & Reiling, K. (1997). A study in self-assessment; tutor and students' perceptions of performance criteria. *Assessment & Evaluation in Higher Education, 22*(4), 357–369. doi:10.1080/0260293970220401

Prins, F. J., Sluijsmans, D., Kirschner, P. A., & Strijbos, J.-W. (2005). Formative peer assessment in a CSCL environment: a case study. *Assessment & Evaluation in Higher Education, 30*(4), 417–444. doi:10.1080/02602930500099219

Sadler, R. D. (2005). Interpretations of criteria-based assessment and grading in higher education . *Assessment & Evaluation in Higher Education, 30*(2), 175–194. doi:10.1080/0260293042000264262

Sadler, R. D. (2008). Indeterminacy in the use of preset criteria for assessment and grading. *Assessment & Evaluation in Higher Education, iFirst Article*, April 2008, 1-20.

Sainsbury, E. J., & Walker, R. A. (2008). Assessment as a vehicle for learning: extending collaboration into testing. *Assessment & Evaluation in Higher Education, 33*(2), 103–117. doi:10.1080/02602930601127844

Snyder, B. R. (1971). *The hidden curriculum.* New York: Knopf.

Stefani, L. (1998). Assessment in Partnership with Learners. *Assessment & Evaluation in Higher Education, 23*(4), 339–350. doi:10.1080/0260293980230402

Swedish Agency for Networks and cooperation in Higher Education, homepage. The Swedish Higher Education act (n.d.). Retrieved January 7, 2009 from http://www.sweden.gov.se/sb/d/3288/a/19574

Swedish Higher Education Ordinance (n.d.). Retrieved January 7, 2009 from http://www.sweden.gov.se/sb/d/3288/a/19574

Topping, K. (1998). Peer-assessment between students in colleges and universities. *Review of Educational Research*, (68): 249–276.

Torrance, H. (2007). Assessment as learning? How the use of explicit learning objectives, assessment criteria and feedback in post-secondary education and training can come to dominate learning. *Assessment in Education: Principles . Policy & Practice, 14*(3), 281–294.

Chapter 5
Preparing the Next Generation of Innovators through Collaboration

Marjorie Darrah
West Virginia University, USA

Angela Dowling
Suncrest Middle School, USA

ABSTRACT

Every country is challenged to stay competitive in the new global economy. The education system within a country must play a pivotal role in ensuring the next generation is prepared to meet the challenges of the 21st Century workplace. Companies have realized that collaboration is a key competency that will bring success in the global economy. It is necessary that teachers understand the needs of our changing economy and incorporate methods to facilitate collaboration, communication, creativity, leadership, responsibility, self-direction, and people skills. This challenge is a global issue and this chapter discusses the steps the US is taking to ensure that its citizenry remains innovative, how the business community is using collaboration to be competitive, the issues encountered in schools to meet challenges of the 21st Century, and positive evidence that the landscape of education is changing in response to the desperate need to produce the next generation of innovators.

INTRODUCTION

Innovation will be the single most important factor in determining America's success through the 21st century. (Council on Competitiveness, 2005, p. 7)

Science and technology careers are the fastest grow-ing career areas in the United States today and are

DOI: 10.4018/978-1-60566-727-0.ch005

projected to continue to grow throughout the next ten years at a record setting pace. Of the ten occupa-tions expected to have double-digit growth before 2014, five of these include science and technology: network systems and data communications analysts, database administrator, computer software engineer and applications, medical scientist, and network and computer systems administrators (Owens, 2006). According to Thomas Owens (2006), editor of Busi-ness 2.0 Magazine, the bad news about outsourcing does not apply to the most creative and difficult technical work, which is likely to remain here in the US. Adding to our nation's need for technical workers is the retirement of the baby boomer generation, whose absence will quickly deplete the ranks of experienced technology workers, leaving openings for younger recruits. To fill this desperate need for science and technical workers in the US, students, even as young as middle school, should be encouraged to think about choosing a career in science and technology. Not only should these students be encouraged to consider these career options, but they should be prepared to be the innovators our nation will need to fill these high level positions of the future.

Meeting the US future demand for highly qualified science and technology workers entails a challenge for both primary and secondary teachers. Teachers must become fluent in the requirements of these industries (i.e., tools, capabilities, and resources) as well as the ability to translate these requirements into actionable and stimulating learning experiences. Teacher training and professional development needs to include the introduction of pedagogical strategies for preparing students for the 21st Century workplace and integrating technology-related competencies seamlessly into the current science and mathematics core curriculum.

There is an abundance of research that focuses on the need for more science, technology, engineering and mathematics (STEM) workers now and in the future. According to one recent estimate, while only five percent of the U.S. workforce is employed in STEM fields, the STEM workforce accounts for more than fifty percent of the nation's sustained growth (Babco, 2004). In a document titled *The Knowledge Economy: Is the United States Losing Its Competitive Edge?* (Task Force, 2005), several serious signs of trouble were pointed out. The most significant sign is that the US is not awarding STEM degrees at the same rate as other countries. Undergraduate science and engineering (S&E) degrees within the US are being awarded less frequently than in other coun-

tries. For example, only 5.7% of first university degrees in the US are in the natural sciences and engineering, while in some European countries, including Spain, Ireland, Sweden, the United Kingdom, France and Finland, this percentage is between 8 and 13. In Japan Natural Science and Engineering awards make up 8%, and Taiwan and South Korea each award about 11%. In 2000, Asian universities accounted for almost 1.2 million of the world's S&E degrees and European universities (including Russia and Eastern Europe) accounted for about 850,000 S&E degrees, while North American universities accounted for only about 500,000 degrees. In 2000, about 78% of doctoral degrees (89,000 of the approximately 114,000) earned worldwide in S&E were earned outside the United States (The Task Force on American Innovation, 2005).

Our nation is facing a serious future shortage of STEM professionals, and such shortages could put the US at risk in both the economic and security sectors since it would require dependence on engineers from other countries in high technology jobs in the future. The US congress responded to these needs by passing the The National Innovation Act of 2005 (109th Congress, 2005). This bill responded to the report published by the Council on Competitiveness (Council on Competitiveness, 2005), by focusing on three primary areas of importance for improving the US innovation in the 21st Century: (1) research investment, (2) increasing science and technology talent, and (3) developing an innovation infrastructure. This bill also established a President's Council on Innovation to develop a comprehensive agenda to promote innovation in both the public and private sectors. It also expanded existing educational programs in physical science and engineering and considerably increased the funding for basic research, nearly doubling research funding for the National Science Foundation by 2011.

In 2006, President Bush unveiled his American Competitiveness Initiative (ACI) (White House Office of Communications, 2006), a strategy to keep the US the most innovative country in the world. The ACI committed $5.9 billion in FY 2007 and more than $136 billion over 10 years to increase investments in research and development (R&D), strengthen education, and encourage entrepreneurship and innovation. The ACI asserts that education is the gateway to opportunity and the foundation of a knowledge-based, innovation-driven economy. To prepare Americans to compete more effectively in the global marketplace, the ACI committed $380 million in new Federal support to improve the quality of math, science, and technological education in K-12 schools and engage every child in rigorous courses that teach important analytical, technical, and problem-solving skills.

In order to both motivate and prepare today's students for careers in the technology STEM fields, efforts need to be made to ensure that students are given multiple opportunities to explore technical concepts. In conventional science and mathematics education, many K-12 students do not have the opportunity to learn about technical careers until they attend college and are faced with choosing a major they know little about. Foundational technological concepts must be introduced to students, and students need to communicate with technical professionals who can inspire them to consider technology and engineering-related fields as a viable career path.

This chapter seeks to explain how students need to be prepared through innovative teaching practices to begin developing the necessary skills to enter the ever changing workplace of the global economy. It also focuses on how classrooms must change to cultivate the acquisition of such skills as collaboration, creativity, communication, leadership, responsibility, self-direction, and the ability to interact with people.

THE 21ST CENTURY WORKPLACE EMPHASIZES COLLABORATION

One vital competency in the new global economy is the ability to successfully collaborate with peers. A company's competitive edge is intrinsically tied to the ability to quickly collaborate with co-workers, partners and customers. This can be seen clearly in the responses to a recent survey in which the majority of respondents verified that on-demand collaborative tools can accelerate business processes and help employees work better, faster and cheaper. IDG Research Services (CXO CIO Media Custom Solutions Group, 2007) recently surveyed 144 CIO Magazine subscribers to gain insight into how and why collaboration technology is creating competitive advantage. The key findings from the survey include:

- The most innovative companies are leveraging collaboration technology to accelerate business processes inside and outside the firewall.
- Supporting knowledge workers and interacting with external audiences is highly important to the majority of respondents.
- Companies using on-demand software are indisputably experiencing its many benefits (CXO CIO Media Custom Solutions Group, 2007).

According to MacCormack (2007) of Harvard Business School and his colleagues in a white paper titled *Innovation Through Global Collaboration: A New Source Of Competitive Advantage*, companies need to invest in building collaborative processes to equip their employees for the challenge. This white paper discusses the need to rethink the way companies manage innovation. The traditional approaches seek to accomplish innovation by a centralized and collocated R&D team. This is rapidly becoming outdated; and instead, innovations are now being brought to market by diverse networks of firms who have unique capabilities and can collaborate to meet a common goal. This new model requires that employees of these firms develop different skills, in particular, the ability to *collaborate* with colleagues across a wide variety of circumstances to achieve innovation. The authors point out that "despite this need, there is little guidance on how to develop or deploy this ability" (MacCormack, 2007, p. i).

One document from km Sciences, Inc. (2006) for project managers shows how this company focuses on collaboration as a method for increasing the value of their knowledge. The authors point out the problem today with too much information, people not being able to get the information they need, people not being able to find an expert, and the explosion of new media tools. They focus on "knowledge collaboration" as a vital solution to these problems. The document explains this concept in the following paragraph:

Why focus on Knowledge Collaboration? Who can assign a value to knowledge that is sitting static in a repository? However, the minute a worker is seeking knowledge, as soon as two workers are sharing knowledge, whenever several workers are debating and presenting; knowledge quickly attains value. Therefore, we see that the crucial element to defining value in knowledge is when it is in action, used by people. We see the value magnified when it can be utilized by a group in dynamic ways. This is what we would call collaboration. (km Sciences, Inc., 2006, p. 1)

Many companies do some form of sales and operations planning to synchronize market data with production output. Their planning, in the past has often been insular and static, resulting in the sales and operations planning becoming almost dysfunctional, lacking the communication and the insight into market demands (Wells, 2007). Today, companies are taking a more strategic approach through the collaboration of key departments. As the company's marketing, finance, sales, and operations departments collaborate to continuously

monitor and meet customer demand, they create business plans with the latest and most accurate data and begin to develop and measure a common set of metrics. With integrated processes, companies are better able to synchronize supply and demand, improve revenue, decrease costs, and increase customer satisfaction (Wells, 2007).

Even in the construction industry, which tends to adopt a conservative stance towards technological change, they are realizing that a wide range of operational and competitive advantages can be gained from implementing innovative collaborative technologies (Micheletti, 2007). A construction industry brief shows the importance of transactional networks and IT networking services that promote internal integration of company workflows while improving external collaborative processes in order to coordinate activities with third-party stakeholders and agents around construction projects. These techniques can successfully address most of the challenges affecting the construction industry today, such as its geographic dispersion, demanding communication requirements, and complex project management needs. Electronic collaboration tools (such as email, group calendaring and scheduling, etc.) can increase the productivity of the construction employees and effectively change the way in which construction projects are managed and implemented (Micheletti, 2007).

How are students being prepared to make the transition to this 21st Century workplace with the demands of constant collaboration and other skills that were not readily observed in the classrooms over the last 10 years? The Partnership for the 21st Century has outlined the skill sets that today's students need to be successful in the 21st century (Partnership for 21st Century Skills, 2004). They believe that educators must go beyond the usual basic academics and intertwine these skills into all of the content areas. In order for students to be successful in the 21st Century workplace, they need to master three main sets of skills; creativity and innovation, critical thinking and problem solving, and communication and collaboration. If students can master these skills and incorporate them into their everyday thinking, they will be more successful in the 21st century workplace.

The case study referenced later in this chapter utilized and the cognitive apprenticeship strategy to enable students to acquire authentic workplace skills within a real-world context. In situated learning, "knowledge needs to be presented in authentic contexts — settings and situations that would normally involve that knowledge. Social interaction and collaboration are essential components of situated learning — learners become involved in a 'community of practice' which embodies certain beliefs and behaviors to be acquired (Lave and Wegner, 1990)." Likewise, the cognitive apprenticeship strategy (Collins, Brown, and Newman, 1987), allows for a master of a skill to teach an apprentice the skill.

In the past many classroom learning activities have emphasized learning of abstract concepts out of context. The case study shows how learners were better able to internalize and utilize the concepts presented because they were involved in a "community of practice" where they were able to use the knowledge in a situation that was realistic and within context. Some of the learners also became the masters of the skills and were able to pass them on to their peers in a way that no teacher would have been able to accomplish alone.

Today's students are the citizens of tomorrow. We now live in a world where rapidly changing technology infuses every part of our environment and daily lives. Our citizens of tomorrow need to be literate in many areas of technology in order to be effective in everything that they do. This next generation also needs to be able to learn quickly from others in real-world workplace settings. They need to develop skills of communication and collaboration which facilitate conveying information and skills to others. The schools and teachers that educate this generation must change to meet this challenge.

MEETING THE CHALLENGE THROUGH THE CHANGING EDUCATION LANDSCAPE

Issues and Concerns

To succeed in today's world, it is not enough that students know their content and be able to think critically. They must be flexible and adaptable. They must be able to accept varying roles in the workplace that are constantly changing. Students must learn to take initiative and be self-directed. They must be able to use what they know and reach beyond just a basic understanding to complete ever-changing tasks that must be handled in a very efficient manner. It is vital that our students be comfortable with working collaboratively in teams with people from a wide range of social and cultural areas. They must be able to set high standards independently for themselves and develop an excellent work ethic in order to be innovative and produce high quality work. If our students can learn to incorporate these skills and take leadership and responsibility in everything that they do, then they will be effective citizens of the 21st century.

The rate of change in technology for communication and information has increased at an astonishing speed (Mehlman, 2003). It is highly likely that we will see more change in the near future than we ever did during the 20th century. Information and communications technologies are significantly changing which skills will be required to be successful in the 21st century. Already businesses that are successfully integrating these skills are being more productive and surpassing the competition. Three main beliefs should guide our use of these technologies. First, we need to recognize that these technologies can only benefit us if they are used wisely. They can be used to make our world a better place or they can aggravate the problems. Second, digital literacy is not about only accessing the internet or using technology proficiently; respecting copyright and valuing privacy should be of utmost importance. Last, we need to remember that the success of a network increases exponentially the more that it is used. We will all benefit as citizens of the 21st century if we understand how to use and value communication and information technologies.

Most educators would agree that traditional education practices used in the last century will not prepare students for the 21st Century workplace. Before the turn of the century, the National Academy of Sciences concluded that the education that many students were receiving in science, mathematics, and technology was not adequate for a world that was quickly being transformed by scientific and technological advances (NAS, 1997). Their report indicated that an understanding of science, mathematics, and technology is very important in the current workplace. As routine tasks become computerized, more and more jobs require high-level skills that involve critical thinking, problem-solving, communicating ideas to others, and collaborating effectively. The US is likely to loose its competitive edge without a better-educated workforce.

Daggett (2005), in his presentation at the Model Schools Conference, calls attention to the fact that education is integral to maintaining the cultural and structural stability of our society, which is changing at the global level.

... it is imperative for the U.S. to consider which actions we must take to remain a viable world presence. More and more, the American public points to education as the answer . . . or part of the problem. The Trends in International Math and Science Study (TIMSS) has shown American students to be quite average among the participating nations. The gap between technology and education continues to widen in America (Moore's Law is a sobering reminder of just how great the disparity is) because, as a nation of educators, we are not adapting to changes in society. Perhaps the added scrutiny on education in the end will help create the spark that ignites a renaissance

for America – just as it did over a century ago when the U.S. was beginning its march to world prominence. (Daggett, 2005, p. 1)

Although much attention has recently been given to guarantee that the education community adapts so that students will be prepared to compete in the new global economy, there are many obstacles to overcome. With an aging teaching population in the US, there are challenges to meet the needs of preparing students for the 21st Century workplace. In A Statistical Profile of the Teaching Profession, Siniscalco (2002) indicates that for countries with large numbers of teachers in their forties or fifties, there are implications not only for future teacher shortages, but questions of how to adapt teacher qualifications to meet the demands in the rapidly changing area of information and communications technology (ICT). Over the past twenty years, the median age of primary and secondary school teachers in the US has increased from 36 to 43. In 2000 census statistics, teachers ages 40 and over accounted for 60% of the workforce (Population Reference Bureau, 2002). Coupled with the aging teaching population is the increase in student enrollment. In recent years, the enrollment in primary and secondary schools has reached over 48 million, the highest since the early 1970's during the peak enrollment of the baby boomers. This trend has a significant affect on the student-teacher ratio and school resources, and in many cases has led to teacher shortages in many areas.

Today's students are known as "digital natives"- they have grown up using technology such as computers, video games, cell phones, Internet, etc. (Prensky 2001a). Because of this, they learn in a much different way. What does this mean for us as educators? Our current educational system was not designed to teach these types of students. With our aging teaching population, the majority of the teachers today are "digital immigrants." They were not raised in this digital world and at some point have adapted (to varying degrees) to using these types of technology. If we think of the digital natives as speaking a "language" then the digital immigrants are generally speaking a language that the native may not understand. Today's students are used to receiving information very quickly. They can multi-task much more efficiently. They prefer to work randomly, want to see pictures before the text, and function best when they can network with others. They prefer instant gratification, regular rewards and playing games. This creates a struggle for today's teacher to reach students who have different outlooks and think in an entirely different way.

What this means for today's educators is that our students are fundamentally different than what we have ever experienced because they think differently. Research has shown that their brains may even be "wired" differently. It is highly unlikely that today's students will adapt to traditional teaching methods so it will need to be the education system that changes. Just because today's teachers need to start "speaking" the students' language does not mean that the content needs to be altered. The content needs to be presented in a different way. This can be done through using software, computer programming, robotics, etc. This cannot be done without also teaching the ethics that goes along with it (Prensky, 2001a).

It is widely believed that today's students' brains are not exactly wired differently but that they have more "connections" (Prensky, 2001). This is due to the fact that they have been raised in a digital age where they are more likely to have been playing videos games, watching TV or talking on cell phones instead of speaking face to face or reading books. This observation has brought about a new concept called "Neuroplasticity". The idea behind this concept is that as a result of the different types of stimulation the brain has received, it does not necessarily "re-wire" but reorganizes itself. Our brains are compared to plastic. It has also been shown that different life experiences can change thinking patterns. This has great significance when looking at the

current generation. They have grown up playing video games and using computers. Their minds jump around; they do not think sequentially but in parallel. Researchers believe that today's students' brains are psychologically different (Prensky, 2001b).

Since today's students are accustomed to interactivity, they seem to have short attention spans. It's not that they cannot pay attention to traditional teaching practices; they are most likely choosing not to. Unfortunately it appears that a sacrifice has been made because of this. It is difficult for students to reflect and create "mental models". The biggest challenge facing educators is to find a way to present the content in such a way that reflection and critical thinking skills are built in to their lessons. Educators of today can do one of two things. They can either pretend that the new type of student is not learning in a different way and persist in presenting material in traditional ways; or they can adapt their teaching methods and be more creative in how content is presented by finding other ways to present the material (Prensky, 2001b).

Examples of Innovative Instruction

Theories that emphasize the importance of social interaction in cognitive growth (Vygotskii, 1978) suggest that successful collaboration involves learning that is contextualized in a social setting. This learning may involve verbal interaction, collective decision making, conflict resolutions, peer teaching, and other group learning situations that are characteristic of a classroom setting.

The NICE (Narrative Immersive Constructionist /Collaborative Virtual Environment) Project provides opportunities for very young students to learn collaboration in a unique way through some very sophisticated technology. NICE implements a persistent virtual garden in which children may collaboratively plant and harvest fruits and vegetables, cull weeds, and position light and water sources to differentially affect the growth rate of plants. This activity takes place in a highly graphical immersive VR system called a CAVE. The project combines immersion, telepresence, immediate visual feedback, and interactivity (Rousses, 1999). The children in the case studies displayed excellent collaboration and no competition. In most cases, on-task communication was observed and there was general agreement on actions. Based on these observations, issues regarding the selection and number of members in a group of second-graders must be taken into account for a successful collaborative combination.

Many researchers and educators have seen the value of using 3-D graphics to motivate students. Kid's Programming Language, or KPL, is a greatly simplified integrated development environment and programming language which emphasizes graphics programming, including 2D and 3D graphics. KPL is educational freeware targeted at the 10-14 age group. The KPL developers are trying to address the issue of declining computer science interest and enrollment by capturing and holding beginners' interest through emphasis on graphics and games programming (Schwartz 2006).

Another project in São Paulo used the synergy of interactive technologies, computer graphics and collaborative learning to improve educators and students' knowledge. The project was carried out at Ernani Silva Bruno Municipal School environment, situated in Parada de Taipas, in the suburbs of the city of São Paulo. This project used accessible Web standard languages, such as Hyper Text Markup Language (HTML) and Virtual Reality Modeling Language (VRML), to enhance children's interest in studying and collaborating to author content related to subjects such as Mathematics, Geography, Geometry, Languages and Arts. (VRML is a computer language that can be used to render three-dimensional graphics. It can be viewed by several free browser plug-ins.) This initiative, implemented in a socioeconomically disadvantaged area, supported collaborative work and improved communication between students and educators. Some of the outcomes noted in this project were: increase in students' digital literacy skills; increase in social inclusion; enhanced student self-esteem; and increased community collaborative work engagement inside and outside the school environment. This project demonstrated the importance of providing opportunities for children and educators' to use state-of-the-art technology and brought about increased motivation and self investment in their lifelong education (Franco, 2006).

A different idea that has been given importance in the education community is teaching across the curriculum or interdisciplinary approaches to curriculum. Collaboration is the key to accomplishing this type of instruction. The challenge with interdisciplinary approaches has been the struggle to integrate teachers of academic subjects with the projects that technology educators are accomplishing in classrooms. One suggestion that has been made by the ITEA (ITEA 2000/2002) is the use of communication technology to deliver content and more specifically, a video production technology course serving as the vehicle to integrate teacher collaboration among the variety of academic subject areas.

Loveland and Harrison in Technology Teacher (Loveland, 2006) discuss how television production can be used in middle and high school curriculum to integrate many subject areas and enhance collaboration between students and teachers. Many schools now have facilities where students can design, produce, and broadcast news programs, special events, and television shows. These types of video production courses have many benefits. Technology teachers develop collegiality with the academic teachers within the school. Schools report enrollment declines being reversed in technology education, leading to full technology education programs. The courses can motivate students to study and prepare them for the 21st Century workplace by allowing them to develop skills in collaboration and effective communication (Loveland, 2006).

Open source is also taking a huge role in revitalizing education. Cottenham Village College in Cambridge, UK, now runs its entire online teaching, learning and home community, which consists of about 1,500-1,600 users, on a completely open source system. Google and Moodle provide email and the virtual learning environment (John, 2008). All of the Information and Communication Technology curriculum is entirely online with all lessons and learning activities completed at school and at home. Moodle is used to direct the students through the learning objectives. Google not only provides quick, efficient and easy-to-use email and calendar but also the capabilities for sharing documents online through Google Apps. In preparation, students are brought in over the summer for a week to acclimate themselves to the web site and software. They get their own Google Apps accounts and then communicate with each other over the summer (John, 2008).

Wikis have recently come to the forefront in education as a form of software allowing a wide range of collaborative learning activities. Grant (2008) discusses the potential uses of wikis in relation to collaborative learning communities and networked groups and briefly addresses the use of other types of social software such as internet discussion forums, social networking sites and social bookmarking. The study examines classes of 13-14 year olds in Information Communication and Technology at a specialist secondary school in Gloucestershire, UK. The teachers assigned the students to random groups of six and nine, each group having its own separate wiki, which was to address a three week history-based project about "Innovations in Technology Since 1950." Students were given latitude to present their research any way that they wanted in the context of their wiki and could work on it during class time and at home. The students worked collaboratively, individually or in pairs on a particular topic within the project scope. While the students understood that they were publishing their content online, they were more concerned with editing their own pages than

someone else's. They took ownership in their work and treated it as they would have any other project to be worked on for class that would use traditional methods (Grant, 2008). Grant (2008) concludes that wikis have enormous potential for learning both in and out of the classroom and different types of social software can very likely support learning communities and group networks in education.

In a project called "Teaching with Games," over one-thousand teachers and students (made up of 10 case studies in four schools with over 300 students ranging in ages 11 to 13 years) used commercial over the shelf games to teach content, teamwork, and problem solving (Ulicsak, 2007). Games such as, The Sims 2, Roller Coaster Tycoon 3, and Knights of Honor were used in traditional settings with content-based curriculum. A key result was that teachers who focused on competency skills such as teamwork and problem solving were more likely to use the game as it was meant to be used. Teachers who were more interested in developing content knowledge were more likely to change the intended usage of the game for their purposes. The researchers suggest that, in order that the games can be more easily used in an educational setting, that it would be helpful to have other resources available related to different uses of the game. It was found that teachers only need the game to be accurate to a certain degree in order to be useful in the classroom. In general, teachers take what they need from the game to accomplish their educational needs (Ulicsak, 2007).

In-Depth Case Study at One US Middle School

This case study demonstrates how situated learning and cognitive apprenticeship ideas can play out in a formal learning setting to foster 21st Century Skills in students. The case study involves a computer graphics elective for 7th and 8th grade students at Suncrest Middle School in Morgan-

Figure 1. Model of Suncrest Middle School built in VRML by students

town, West Virginia. As part of this elective, various technology skills were taught including Photoshop, Microsoft Publisher, Dreamweaver, HTML and VRML. Because the school webpage was also authored by the students in this elective, all technology skills needed to be taught during the first semester. The second semester was devoted to completing a new school web page.

The teacher involved in the study acted as a facilitator with students being self-directed for the most part. Since the students had learned a new skill via VRML programming, they wanted to include it as part of their web page design. The web page required skills with Photoshop, Dreamweaver/HTML and VRML. The students were tested to ascertain their strongest skill sets; they were then organized into teams according to their proficiencies. Students who were more adept at using Dreamweaver/HTML were placed in charge of constructing the web page and the students who had expertise in VRML were charged with brainstorming a VRML project to include with the web page design. The two teams were then given a specific area of the lab to complete their assignments.

Because there is a recognized need for students to be prepared for the 21st Century workplace, the teacher treated the two teams as research/development teams. Discussions were held with the class as a whole and with individual teams to clarify what was to be done. Students were to choose their leaders and assign jobs to individuals. For the purposes of this chapter, we will be focusing on the VRML group. This group brainstormed ideas about possible projects and decided that they would like to make a 3D scale model of the school. Realizing the complexity of the project and the time constraints, they set deadlines for themselves, divided up the different sections of the school for different individuals and chose a project manager. The team chose their project manager considering expertise in programming with VRML. The project manager was not in charge of completing a specific area or region of the school. The manager was in charge of trouble-shooting difficulties that arose and combining team members' work (individual notepad files with the programming) into one large file. The end product was a 3D scale model of the school constructed entirely using VRML programming language (Figure 1). This model can now be accessed via the homepage of the school's webpage (http://boe.mono.k12.wv.us/SuncrestMiddle/).

21st Century Workplace Skills

This case study highlights how one teacher simulated the workplace for her students and facilitated the learning of many of the essential 21st Century Skills (collaboration, communication, creativity, leadership, responsibility, self-direction, and people skills). This project also used exciting technology to motivate students to develop the skills necessary to succeed in today's workplace and to

Figure 2. Left: Photograph of Suncrest Middle School. Right: Virtual Model of Suncrest Middle School built in VRML by students.

compete in a global economy. Direct instruction, modeling, cognitive apprenticeship and situated learning are learning theories which were incorporated into the context of this project. The 21st Century workplace requires that students be able to work collaboratively and successfully in finding solutions to problems in a modern context.

Communication and Collaboration

During this study there was ample opportunity for the students to exercise their communication skills while working collaboratively in their design teams. Students came to class everyday knowing exactly what they needed to do. Each student immediately would sit down at a computer and open their file to get started. They were very willing to help each other if troubleshooting was involved. If there was a difficulty that could not be solved with peer to peer interaction, they would then consult with the project manager. Again, the teacher was utilized as a guide and was not part of any individual team.

The project members were a diverse group of students and yet they collaborated very well. They constantly checked in with their project manager and the project manager, in turn, would circulate around the room to gauge the team members' progress. All of the students realized that they were working towards a common goal, and given their timeline, they accepted equal responsibilities

and efficiently met their deadlines.

Creativity and Innovation

For this project, students demonstrated skills of innovative thinking by choosing their own design project and collaborating to creatively develop a 3-D virtual model of their school building. They brainstormed their ideas and even though the project they chose seemed to be daunting at first, they utilized deadlines and teamwork to complete the task on time. Their model was added to the school home page on the last day of the school year.

Team members showed self-direction and creativity by using digital photographs of the actual brick of the building in their model, floor plans of the school, measurements of building features and student designed logos. Students continually were walking around the school during class time to check their measurements, etc. They even enlisted the help of the school janitor to climb up on top of the school and measure how far the roof was recessed from the edge wall. By utilizing these different aspects, they created a very accurate virtual representation of their school (see Figure 2).

Critical Thinking and Problem Solving Skills

A great many difficulties arose during this project. All troubleshooting was handled within student teams; the project manager also acted as liaison between the teams and the teacher. Whenever difficulties were encountered, the problems were solved via troubleshooting and consultation with the project manager.

Since all VRML code was to be their own, team members were not permitted to copy and paste any code. The only exception was the code for the trees which surround the school in the virtual model. Students were able to find a free code available online for these trees. This, however, presented a major difficulty when the project manager added these trees to the model because the leaves were not constrained to individual trees, but spread across the entire model. This situation afforded the students the opportunity to problem solve and think creatively as a collaborative team when they all worked together to find the computer code which would constrain the leaves to the individual trees. This information was then given to the project manager who then added it to each individual tree in the program.

Life and Workplace Skills

This study was an exceptional opportunity to observe how students (even at the level of middle school) could function in a real-world type of situation. In the 21st Century workplace, the skills of collaboration, communication, creativity, etc. are necessary. In this project, students were able to effectively work together and collaborate to complete an innovative design project. They monitored their own progress, set their own deadlines and met them efficiently. They were flexible and adapted to any difficulties encountered on the project and adjusted their priorities as needed.

Students were able to demonstrate that they had mastered the skills being taught by applying these skills in a simulation setting. They set high standards for themselves and met them. Leadership skills were demonstrated not only by the project manager, but by individual team members in completion of the project. The students were able to utilize the strengths of all of the students

involved to complete a creative and innovative project.

The following year, the same teacher again presented a different group of students with the responsibility of choosing an additional VRML project to add to the school's webpage. After discussion and voting amongst themselves, they decided that they wanted to make a virtual model of their hometown of Morgantown, West Virginia. Knowing that this was quite an ambitious project, even more so than making a virtual model of the school, the teacher discussed the inherent difficulties involved. The students decided to stay with their project and proceeded to divide themselves into groups that would be in charge of different areas and well-known sections of the city.

For the Morgantown virtual model, the students were again innovative and creative in their project. As a group, they decided the scale. One of the students constructed a conversion formula for everyone to use. To get a better idea of where everything was situated in the area, students used Google Earth to study various sections of the city and to scale their distances. The students also used online search engines to find pictures of the buildings so that they could make more accurate models. All troubleshooting was handled within groups and with a project manager. Unfortunately, because of the size of the project only a few of the structures were completed. However, the students learned as much and worked as hard doing this project as they had the year before. The teacher learned that letting students choose the project, although motivating for them, can lead to a scoping problem due to their lack of experience. Students can learn a valuable real-world skill of being able to properly access what can be accomplished in a given time frame with given resources (one of the most important ideas in the business world).

Through teamwork and collaboration, the students involved in this project created a very accurate virtual representation of their school. They used higher order thinking skills and sound reasoning in their self-organization. They used innovative troubleshooting to solve problems as they occurred. The students also effectively used authentic workplace tools to prioritize, plan and execute their design project and produced a relevant, high quality model. Students effectively simulated a real world scenario similar to that of a software development team and utilized skills that will be required of them in order to effectively function in the work force they will be entering in a few short years.

To further engage students with 21st Century Skills, this teacher has branched out into using more Web 2.0 tools. Most recently, students contributed to a classroom science wiki and collaborated on a project to produce a wiki about various genetic disorders.

CONCLUSION

The US is facing the challenge to stay competitive in the new global economy. The education system must play a pivotal role in ensuring that the next generation is prepared to meet the challenges that lie ahead. Traditional educational techniques, although effective in the past, are not sufficient to prepare students for the 21st Century workplace. The US has recognized the desperate need to stay competitive and has passed legislation related to encouraging innovation.

Companies have realized that collaboration is a key competency that will bring success in the global economy. Many techniques are being employed to ensure that collaboration happens within the organization and between organizations. Teachers need to understand the needs of our changing economy and need to incorporate methods that will facilitate the use of 21st Century skills such as collaboration, communication, creativity, leadership, responsibility, self-direction, and people skills. Students need to be learning and practicing these skills during their formative years along with their content knowledge in the

core subject areas.

Many educational researchers and teachers are developing techniques that will encourage the use of these important 21st Century skills in the classroom. Teachers are using cutting-edge technologies and innovative ideas to revitalize the classroom. Students are beginning to learn in environments that simulate or at least have a number of components that they will encounter when they enter the workplace. This will ensure that tomorrow's students will be prepared to become the innovators of the future that will guarantee our country remains competitive in this ever changing global economy.

REFERENCES

109th Congress. (2005). *The National Innovation Act of 2005*.

Babco, E. (2004). *Skills for the Innovation Economy: What the 21st Century Workforce Needs and How to Provide It*. Washington, DC: Commission on Professionals in Science and Technology.

Collins, A., Brown, J. S., & Newman, S. E. (1987, January). *Cognitive apprenticeship: Teaching the craft of reading, writing and mathematics* (Technical Report No. 403). BBN Laboratories, Cambridge, MA & Centre for the Study of Reading, University of Illinois.

Council on Competitiveness. (2005). *National Innovation Initiative (NII) Final Report - Innovate America: Thriving in a World of Challenge and Change*.

CXO CIO Media Custom Solutions Group. (2007, February 13). *Collaborative Efforts: Survey Reveals Clear Business Acceleration Using On-demand Collaboration Technology*.

Daggett, W. R. (2005, June). *Preparing Students for Their Future*. Presented at June 2005 Model Schools Conference

Franco, J. F., Sandra Regina da Cruz, S. R., & de Deus Lopes, R. (2006). *Computer Graphics, Interactive Technologies and Collaborative Learning Synergy Supporting Individuals' Skills Development.* Paper presented at ACM SIGRAPH2006, Boston, MA.

Grant, L. (2006). Using Wikis in Schools: A Case Study. *Futurelab-Innovation in Education,* Retrieved August 23, 2008, from http://www.futurelab.org.uk/resources/documents/discussion_papers/Wikis_in_Schools.pdf

International Technology Education Association. (2000/2002). *Standards for technological literacy: Content for the study of technology.* Reston, VA: Author.

James Rhem & Associates, LLC., (1996-2003). *Active Learning: Creating Excitement in the Classroom, The National Teaching & Learning Forum.* Retrieved August 11, 2008, from http://www.ntlf.com/html/lib/bib/91-9dig.htm

John, M. (2008). Mind the Gap-Open Source is a Player. *Futurelab-Innovation in Education.* Retrieved August 23, 2008, from http://www.futurelab.org.uk/resources/publications_reports_articles/web_articles/Web_Article1065

km Sciences, Inc. (2006). *Knowledge and Collaboration for Project Managers.* Retrieved August 1, 2008 from http://whitepapers.itbusinessnet.com/whitepaper812/

Lave, J., & Wenger, E. (1990). *Situated Learning: Legitimate Periperal Participation.* Cambridge, UK: Cambridge University Press.

Loveland, T., & Harrison, H. L. (2006). Video Production: A New Technological Curricula. Preview. *Technology Teacher, 66*(3), 7–13.

MacCormack, A., Forbath, T., Brooks, P., & Kalaher, P. (2007). *Innovation through Global Collaboration: A New Source of Competitive Advantage.* Cambridge, MA: Harvard Business School. Retrieved August 1, 2008 from http://hbswk.hbs.edu/item/5760.html

Mehlman, B. P. (2003). *ICT Literacy: Preparing the Digital Generation for the Age of Innovation.* Retrieved August 11, 2008, from http://www.technology.gov/Speeches/p_BPM_030124-DigGen.htm

Micheletti, G., Manenti, P., & Eibisch, J. (2007). *A Construction Industry Brief. Benefiting the Bottom Line: Collaboration and Collaborative Technologies.* IDC Executive Brief, IDC EMEA. Retrieved August 1, 2008 from http://www.idc.com

National Academy of Sciences. (1997). *Preparing for the 21st Century: The Education Imperative.*

Owens, T., & Kelley, R. (2006). The Next Job Boom: The 10 fastest-growing jobs. *Business 2.0 Magazine.* Retrieved August 22, 2008 from http://money.cnn.com/2006/05/02/technology/business2_nextjobboom_hotjobs/index.htm

Partnership for 21st Century Skills (2004). *Framework for 21st Century Learning.* Retrieved August 11, 2008 from http://www.21stcenturyskills.org/

Pausch, R. (1995). A Brief Architectural Overview of Alice, a Rapid Prototyping System for Virtual Reality. *IEEE Computer Graphics and Applications.* Retrieved August 11, 2008, from http://www.cs.cmu.edu/~stage3/publications/95/journals/IEEEcomputer/CGandA/paper.html

Population Reference Bureau. (2002). *The Changing Age Structure of U.S. Teachers.* Retrieved on August 15, 2008 from http://www.prb.org/Articles/2002/TheChangingAgeStructureofUS-Teachers.aspx

Prensky, M. (2001a). Do They Really Think Differently? *Horizon, 9*(6).

Prensky, M. (2001b). Digital Natives, Digital Immigrants. *Horizon, 9*(5).

Prensky, M. (2008). *Programming: The New Literacy*. Retrieved August 13, 2008, from Edutopia website: http://www.edutopia.org/programming

Route 21 (2007). *21ˢᵗ Century Skills in West Virginia*. Retrieved August 12, 2008, from Welcome to Route 21: Retrieved August 11, 2008, from http://www.21stcenturyskills.org/documents/p21_wv2008.pdf

Schwartz, J., Stagner, J., & Morrison, W. (2006). *Kid's Programming Language (KPL)*. Presented at ACM SIGRAPH2006, Boston, MA.

Siniscalco, M. T. (2002). *A Statistical Profile of the Teaching Profession*. International Labour Organization and United Nations Educational, Scientific and Cultural Organization.

Task Force on the Future of American Innovation. (2005, February 16). *The Knowledge Economy: Is the United States Losing Its Competitive Edge?* Retrieved August 22, 2008 from www.future-ofinnovation.org.

Texas Instruments (2003). *Engineering and Education Statistics: Fact Sheet*. Retrieved December 19, 2006 from http://www.ti.com/corp/docs/press/company/2003/c03033.shtml

Ulicsak, M., Facer, K., & Sandford, R. (2007). Issues impacting games-based learning in formal secondary education. *International Journal on Advanced Technology for Learning (IJATL)*.

Vygotskii, L. (1978). *Mind in Society: The Development of Higher Psychological Processes*. Cambridge, MA: Harvard University Press.

Wells, A. M., & Schorr, J. (2007). *Sales and Operations Planning: The Key to Continuous Demand Satisfaction. SAP Insight Business Process Innovations*. Retrieved August 1, 2008 from http://www.sap.com

White House Office of Communications. (2006). *The American Competitiveness Initiative: Encouraging Innovation*, April 18, 2006.

Chapter 6
Social Networking Sites (SNS) and the 'Narcissistic Turn'
The Politics of Self–Exposure

Yasmin Ibrahim
University of Brighton, UK

ABSTRACT

The advent of the Internet hailed the ability of users to transform their identity and expression and articulation of the 'self' through their digital interactions. The Internet in its early days enabled the user to re-define identity through the text-based environment of the internet without declaring their offline persona or identity. In comparison new social software like Facebook have brought about a narcissistic turn where private details are placed on a global arena for public spectacle creating new ways of connecting and gazing into the lives of the others. It raises new social issues for societies including the rise of identity fraud, infringement of privacy, the seeking of private pleasures through public spectacle as well as the validation of one's identity through peer recognition and consumption.

INTRODUCTION

The Internet in its early days signified the re-birthing of the individual and most prominently the 'self' as technology enabled the user to re-mediate identity through a text-based environment. Anonymity and virtuality constituted a form of 'avatarism' where individuals could re-invent their presence online without declaring their offline persona or identity (See Donath 1998; Froomkin 1995). In comparison, new social networking sites (SNS), such as Facebook, signify a 'narcissistic turn' where offline identities are publicized online and constructed through a multimedia platform to create new forms of self-expression, gaze, spectacle, and sociabilities. Equally, social networking is embedded within a new economy of sharing and exchanging personal information between friends and strangers. The sharing and communication of personal details have reached unprecedented levels with the proliferation of e-commerce and social networking sites in recent years (See Szomsor et al. 2008; Geyer et al. 2008; Strater & Richter 2007; Stefanone 2008; Lampe et al. 2006; Joinson 2008).

DOI: 10.4018/978-1-60566-727-0.ch006

This marks a shift from the earlier 'virtuality' discourses of the Internet which perceived anonymity and the ability to transform identities online as a form of empowerment whilst raising the tenuous issues of trust, intimacy and deception. The increasing popularity of social networking sites, on the other hand, emphasizes the narcissistic tendency in the human condition manifested through an exhibition of the self through photos and other multimedia content. The publicizing of personal details on a global arena for public spectacle creates new ways of connecting and gazing into the lives of others. It raises new social issues for societies, including the rise of identity fraud, infringement of privacy, the seeking of private pleasures through public spectacle, as well as the validation of one's identity through peer recognition, connection and consumption online. The ability to connect with offline networks through online self-profiles and content and additionally the possibility of inviting audiences to be part of the 'friends' list celebrates the declaration of offline identities.

The politics of self-revelation on the Internet creates the need to understand new forms of computer-mediated behavior which are emerging and may have implications for the ways in which users construct and express their identities. The creation of profiles and the ability to make connections through these constructs indicate how these become a form of social capital in forming connections and communion with a wider imagined community offline and online. This chapter examines the phenomenon of self-exposure through social networking sites on the Internet and discusses how the emergence and popularity of these sites reflects a shift in debates about identity discourses on the Internet on a theoretical and societal level. The chapter also delves into the social and legal implications of self-revelation and, more specifically, how social networking sites create risk communities where an awareness of risks exists along with the urge to reveal in order to make contact and connections with others. Social networking sites function through complicit risk communities which highlights both the narcissistic strand as well as the postmodern hazards that lurk in the online environment.

THE EARLY DISCOURSES OF THE INTERNET

The term *cyberspace* was coined by science fiction writer William Gibson in 1982 to capture the nature of a space both real and illusory. This duality is one of the fundamental reasons why investigations of online spaces are complex and multi-dimensional. Early writings on the Internet portrayed the new medium as constituting a virtual space which was divorced from offline existence (Miller and Slater, 2000: 4). Miller and Slater (2000) define *virtuality* as the capacity of communicative technologies to constitute, rather than mediate, realities and to form relatively bounded spheres of interaction. These discourses often portrayed the emergence of new forms of society and identity (Rheingold, 2000) in which the 'virtual was often disembodied from the real' (Miller and Slater, 2000: 4). This disembodiment represented a form of escapism from real society where individuals could invent, deconstruct, and re-invent their identities. As such, cyberspace created fluidity in terms of identity as well as a form of release from the confines of the real world.

From this perspective Computer Mediated Communication (CMC) represents an unusual form of communication, as it does not fit into the conventional distinctions between public and private, and direct and mediated communication. (Diani, 2000: 386). CMC stands in a somewhat ambiguous relationship to other forms of communication. Its private and public nature is unclear. In line with the nature of communications on the Internet, there is also the question of how people establish identities in cyberspace. Because of the fact that we are not physically present on the Internet and because we can present many different personas there, the individual voices that make up a cyber community are often referred to as 'avatars' (Jordan, 1999: 59, 67). The irrelevance of geographical location with regard to CMC contributes to the phenomenon known as *disembedding*: that is, enabling users to transcend their immediate surroundings and communicate on a global platform (Giddens, 1990). Besides this feature of 'disembedding', the online environment prior to Web 2.0 was defined by the use of discursive form (textuality) and the ability to communicate anonymously. These features are seen as empowering since users are not constrained by both time and space and are at liberty to recreate and deconstruct their identities online.

The 'avatar' culture may offer people a degree of freedom to conceal identity and to approach taboo topics without the constraints of the real world. It can help forge new identities as well as new relationships. As the 'virtual' world is mediated through technology, the user may be bound by a new set of rules to negotiate this realm. Nevertheless, this hybrid form of communication does not exist in a vacuum. Discourses in the Internet can interact with happenings in other media and reflect one's physical context of existence. As such various online interactions can be embedded in disparate ways into larger social structures, such as professions and social movements. The dynamics of online interactions may be difficult to comprehend except through this physical embedding (Friedland, 1996; Miller and Slater, 2000; Slevin, 2000; Wynn & Katz, 1997; Slater, 2002). In this sense, the culture of the physical world can invariably transcend into cyberspace, thus further altering the pattern of mediated communications.

Early discourses of the Internet and present debates about the web indicate that identity is a contentious and fragmented construct in view of the absence of physical cues in a discursive and subsequently a multimedia environment (Stefanone et al. 2008:107). Compared to the earlier Internet environment which leveraged on

experimentation with identity, today's computer-mediated communication aligns the users closer to their offline selves. The increasing emphasis on existing offline identities and relationships as well as physical and non-verbal communication cues and manipulation defines the nature of computer-mediated communication today (Stefanone et al. 2008).

THE PROLIFERATION OF NETWORKING SITES

The shift in the discourses of empowerment and increasing need to declare and share identities may also be attributed to the technological advancements inherent in the new social web. Web 2.0 encapsulates a plethora of tools - including wikis, blogs, and folksonomies - which promote creativity, collaboration, and sharing between users (Szomszor et al. 2008:33). The multimedia experience and social communication platforms thus equally characterise the Web 2.0 user culture. From a technical and social perspective, Web 2.0, in comparison to its earlier manifestation, refers to improved applications, increased utilization of applications by users, and the incorporation of content generative technologies into everyday life by those who can afford and access such technologies. Anderson (2007) identifies the Web 2.0 environment as a new and improved second version and particularly a user-generated web which is characterised by blogs, video sharing, social networking, and podcasting - delineating both the production and consumption of the web environment where both activities can be seamless. Beyond its technical capacities, the term is a convenient social construct to analyze new forms of processes, activities, and behaviors - both individual and collective as well as public and commercial - that have emerged from the Internet environment.

Unlike earlier websites which thrived on the notion of anonymity and virtuality, these new platforms for social communion emphasise the declaration of real offline identities to participate in the networking phenomenon. While the forerunners of social networking sites in the 1990s included sites such as Classmates.com, the advent of the new millennium heralded a new generation of websites which celebrated the creation of self-profiles with the launch of Friendster in 2002 which attracted over 5 million registered users in a span of a few months (See Rosen, 2007; Mika 2004; Mislove et al. 2007; DiMicco & Millen 2007). Friendster was soon followed by MySpace, Livejournal.com, and Facebook; these sites convened around existing offline communities such as college students. In the case of MySpace the site was originally launched by musicians to upload and share videos while Facebook initially catered to college students but is presently open to anyone who wants to network socially online. Some of these sites have witnessed phenomenal growth since their inception. MySpace, for example, has grown from 1 million accounts to 250 million in 2008 (Caverlee et al. 2008: 1163). Additionally, several of the top ten most visited sites on the web are social networking sites (cf. Golbeck & Wasser 2007: 2381).

The creation and exhibition of self-profiles can be historically located and is not unique to the new media environment. Christine Rosen (2007) points out that historically the rich and powerful documented their existence and their status through painted portraits. In contemporary culture, using a social networking site is akin to having one's portrait painted, although the comparative costs make social networking sites much more egalitarian. She contends that these digital 'self-portraits' signify both the need to re-create identity through the online platform as well as to form social connections. Invariably images play a role in the representation of self and in fostering communication (See Froehlich et al.2002; Schiano et al. 2004Bentley et al. 2006). For Rosen (2007: 15), the resonant strand that emerges is the 'timeless human desire for attention'.

Undoubtedly, users join such sites with their friends and use the various messaging tools to socialize, share cultural artefacts and ideas, and communicate with one another (Boyd, 2007). As such, these sites thrive on a sense of immediacy and community (Barnes, 2006). With social networking sites there is a shift in the re-making of identity. While social connection sites in the 1990s illuminated the sense of place with home pages, global villages, and cities, with social networking sites there has been an emphasis on the creation of the 'self' through hobbies, interests, interactions, and a display of users' contacts through multimedia formats (Rosen, 2007). According to Boyd and Heer (2006: 2), 'the performance of social identity and relationships through profiles has shifted these from being a static representation of self to a communicative body in conversation with other represented bodies.' The emphasis of self-expression, through the creation of profiles, anchors publicity, play, and performance at the core of identity formation and communication. As such, identity is mutable online and not embodied by the body, and often the need to disclose real-life identities is intimately tied to this community's code of authenticity in making identity claims where friends and peers can verify claims made in the profiles (Donath & Boyd, 2004).

Social networking sites can support a variety of shared multimedia content beyond photos to include video and music, can be constitutive of self-identity and representation, and can become a playground for the creativity of millions (Geyer et al. 2008:1545). Geyer et al. (2008) point out that while such sites connect people with each other through content and profile sharing, some sites focus on a single content type as in the case of Flickr and YouTube when communities form through the sharing of photos or videos. Other sites may entail the sharing of many types of content.

In assessing SNS's, Boyd and Ellison (2007) highlight three distinctive features: the user's ability to construct a public profile, articulate a list of other users with whom they share a connection, and view and traverse their list of connections and those made by others within the system. According to Ralph Gross and Alessandro Acquisti (2005), such sites, through the emphasis on personal profiles, offer a representation of users for others to peruse with the intention of contacting or being contacted by others to meet new friends or dates, find new jobs, receive or provide recommendations, and much more.

Dana Boyd (2006) postulates that while the meanings of practices and features can differ across sites and individuals the notion of sharing is intrinsic to these sites. Personal information and private comments on a public platform then become a form of social capital which people trade and exchange to build new ties and to invite different types of gaze and spectatorship. Chapman and Lahav (2008) point out that while there is a novelty surrounding social networking behavior from the perspective of researchers, this behavior will become increasingly integrated with other forms of communication as social networking becomes increasingly incorporated into one's everyday routines. This means that social networking behavior will function in conjunction with other communication options including email, instant messaging, and mobile devices.

The need to attract public attention in some way through daily interactions and to seek familiar and unknown audiences characterizes social networking sites. Stefanone et al. (2008) maintain that this behavior is linked to the 'celebrity culture' that is evident in mainstream media and particularly in television genres such as reality TV (See Stefanone et al 2008). With user-generated content and the ability to host profiles on interactive sites, the Web 2.0 environment enables users to participate in celebrity culture by constructing themselves as active personas online. Stefanone et al. (2008: 107) contend that new multimedia technologies erode 'the behavioural and normative distinctions between the celebrity world and the mundane everyday lives of the users.' They argue that the

dissolution of this boundary is discernible in two resonant strands: the popularization of the reality television genre and the proliferation of social networking sites which hinge on the revelation of offline identities. They identify these two trends as reconfiguring the media environment where audiences are more than the recipients of media messages. Audiences as users and consumers can become 'protagonists of media narratives and can integrate themselves into a complex media ecosystem' (Stefanone et al. 2008: 107). They argue that platforms, such as social networking sites, emphasize aspects of human interaction that have been traditionally associated with celebrities, including the primacy of image and appearance in social interaction. This may have social implications, such as 'promiscuous friending,' where the network is both a collection of known relationships as well as people with whom users may have never met. Beyond enabling social connections, this could lead to fame-seeking or the desire to be 'popular' through the social imaginary of the multimedia environment.

The popularity of such sites may also be explained by the need of some people to look into other peoples' lives or to increase awareness of others within their physical and virtual communities (Strater & Richter 2007: 157). Inherent to such a landscape is the ability to track other members of the community where the 'surveillance' functions allow an individual to track the actions and beliefs of the larger groups to which they belong (Lampe et al. 2006: 167). Lampe et al. (2006) define this as social searching or social browsing where it enables users to investigate specific people with whom they share an offline connection. Lampe et al. (2006:167) take the relationship between social networking and social browsing further by asserting that 'users largely use social networking to learn more about people they meet offline and are less likely to use the site to initiate new connections.'

IDENTITY AND SOCIAL NETWORKS

The identities established in social networking sites function to enable offline and online networks. Often, the identity that is constructed online reflects the complex entwining of computer-mediated communications on the one hand and offline social networks on the other. Jon Kleinberg (2006: 5) contends that 'distributed computing systems have incessantly been entwined with social networks that fuse user populations' in the online and offline environments. The growth of activities such as blogging, social network services, and other forms of social media on the Internet has made large-scale networks more evident and visible to the general public. As Adam Joinson (2008: 1027) points out, websites, such as Facebook, were originally built around existing geographical networks of student communities. This meant that offline communities were reflected in the online environment; such communities function in a number of ways: for example, as a means of sustaining relationships by providing social and emotional support; as an information repository; and, as offering the potential to expand one's offline and online networks. In view of this, on-line settings beyond being rich data on the construction of identity by users have also become rich sources of data for large-scale studies of social networks (See Backstorm et al. 2007; Caverlee et al. 2008; Mislove 2007; Mori 2005; Goussevskaia 2007; Joinson 2007).

Wellman (cf. Lange, 2007: 2) defines *social networks* as 'relations among people who deem other network members to be important or relevant to them in some way, with media often used to maintain such networks.' Another essential component of such sites is that user profile information involves some element of 'publicness' (Preibusch et al,. 2007) and it is the consumption of private details which sustains the culture of gaze and the curiosity of the invisible audience. Communication technologies, such as the Internet with its global platform where data can be end-lessly circulated and anyone can leave electronic footprints, 'erode the boundaries between 'publicity' and 'privacy'(Weintraub & Kumar, 1997). Lange (2007), explains that social network sites are websites that allow users to create a public or semi-public profile within the system and one that explicitly displays their relationship to other users in a way that is visible to anyone who can access their profile. Consequently, Boyd (2007) considers SNS's as the latest generation of 'mediated publics' where people can gather publicly through mediated technology. She points out that features (such as persistence - i.e. the permanence of a profile and its circulation in cyberspace - searchability, replicability, and invisible audiences) constitute the key elements of this environment. Users' behavior may be mediated by these features without necessarily integrating the underlying immediate and future consequences or risks embedded in these technologies or their actions.

The ability to tag photos to profiles and the presence of photo recognition software means that there is a loss of visual anonymity which can be complemented by new forms of gaze (Montgomery, 2007). Equally, the semantic nature of the web can simplify or reduce 'web-based communications to the descriptive and may unconsciously ascribe social values by describing these relationships as 'friends' or 'acquaintances.' According to a study done by Sheffield Hallam University, while the number of friends people can have on such sites is massive, the actual number of close friends is approximately the same in the face-to-face real world (Randerson, 2007). Mori et al. (2005: 82) point out that semantic web-based ontologies deliberately simplify such relationships. Danah Boyd (2004:1280), in her enthnographic study of the Friendster site, found 'people are indicated as friends even though the user does not particularly know or trust the person.' In this sense, the semantic web flattens the complexity of relationships and falsely assumes that publicly visible or articulated social networks and relationships can be conflated with private relationships.

As such, publicity (and public labels such as 'friends'), exchange, and sharing are integral and definitive parts of the SNS culture where the emphasis is not entirely on the authenticity of the information but the elements of connection and connectivity it can create (Nardi, 2005). Social networking sites can also capture the shift in identities of users when they transition from one life phase into another. Such transitions can include progress from school to workplace where the social connections and identity of the user can shift. In tandem with this, DiMicco and Millen (2007:383) argue that these platforms are complex as such sites can reflect the fact that users have 'transitioned between life stages and expanded their number of social connections, and these sites can assist users in maintaining social networks and diverse social relations.' This then entails a degree of managing self-identity on such spaces and perhaps the creation of multiple identities through multiple profiles to delineate a distinction between corporate and non-coporate identites, for example, or between formal and professional relationships compared to long-term friendships. DiMicco and Millen's (2007:386) research reveals that multiple identities can nevertheless be burdensome where users may require more technical knowledge to navigate access control mechanisms which may deny access to one set of users while allowing a target audience to view selected profiles.

Gross & Acquisti (2005), point out that the most common model of the SNS is the presentation of the participant's profile and the visualization of his or her network of relations to others. Such sites can encourage the presentation of a member's profile (including their hobbies and interests and the publication of personal and identifiable photos) to the rest of the community through technical specifications, while visibility of information can be highly variable amongst such sites. Most networking sites make it easy for third parties, from hackers to government agencies, to access participants' data without the site's direct collaboration, thereby exposing users to risks ranging from identity theft to online and physical stalking and blackmailing (Gross & Acquisti, 2005).

Additionally users browse neighbouring regions of their social network as they are likely to find content that is of interest to them. Thus search engines may use social networks to rank Internet search results relative to the interests of users' neighbourhoods in the social network.

RISKS

The casualness with which people reveal personal details online is related to the different norms people apply to online and offline situations where these variant norms have implications for notions of privacy, authenticity, community, and identity. Research conducted by Mislove et al. (2007:41) on sites such as Flickr, LiveJournal, Orkut and YouTube reveals that these sites are the portals of entry into the Internet for millions of users. Equally, they invite advertisements as well as the pursuit of commercial interest; this means users in these networks tend to trust each other having been brought together through common interests. *Trust* has been defined in various ways in sociological literature. Golbeck et al. (2003) define it as credibility or reliability in human interaction where it can entail the according of a degree of credence to a person through interpersonal communication. With specific reference to information sharing, Mori et al. (2005:83) infer that trust could relate to reliability with regard to how a person handles information that has been shared or reciprocated. Gips et al. 2005 argue that the 'social' aspect of these networks is self-reinforcing; this means to be trusted one must make many 'friends' and create many links that will slowly pull the user into the core of activities.

Barnes (2006), in citing Benniger, postulates that electronic forms of communication are gradually replacing traditional modes of interpersonal communication as a socializing force, mediating and at times displacing social norms in different contexts. In the interactive spaces of the Internet, there may be a disconnect between the way users say they feel about the privacy settings of their blogs and how they react once they have experienced the unanticipated consequences of a breach of privacy (cf. Barnes, 2006; Gibson 2007; Mannan & Oorschot 2008). The issue of privacy setting can be problematic on social networking sites for users since a default privacy setting can constrain a user's need to meet and network with more people beyond their offline network (Joinson 2008: 1035). Mannan & Oorschot (2008: 487) concur that there is a tendency to overlook privacy implications in the current rush to join others in 'lifecasting' and users may work on the false impression that only friends and family are consuming the personal content.

Gross & Acquisti's (2005) anecdotal evidence suggests that participants are happy to disclose as much information as possible to as many people as possible, thus highlighting the design and architecture of sites which hinge on the ease with which personal information is volunteered and the willingness of users to disclose such information. The perceived benefits of selectively revealing data to strangers may appear larger than the perceived costs of possible privacy invasions. Other factors (such as peer pressure and herding behavior, relaxed attitudes towards or lack of interest in personal privacy, incomplete information about the possible privacy implications of information revelation, faith in the networking service or trust in its members, and the myopic evaluation of privacy risks of the service's own user interface) may drive the unchallenged acceptance by users of compromises to their safety (Gross & Acquisti 2005; Strater & Richter 2007; Gibson 2007), thus sealing the role of SNS's as complicit risk communities. Strater & Richter (2007) point out that large-scale analyses of Facebook have revealed that a majority (87% on average) of students have default or permissive settings. While a significant

majority have an awareness of privacy options, less than half ever alter their default setting. This means that while users do not underestimate the privacy threats of online disclosure, they can nevertheless misjudge the 'extent, activity and accessibility of their social networks' (Strater & Richter 2007: 158).

According to a 2008 study by Ofcom, over one fifth of UK adults have at least one online community profile (cf. Szomszor et al. 2008). Caverlee at al (2008: 1163) nevertheless point out that the growth of social networking sites has come with a huge cost as these sites have been subject to threats such as specialised phishing attacks, the impersonation of profiles, spam, and targeted malware dissemination. Unanticipated new threats, they state, are also bound to emerge. They identify three resonant vulnerabilities which plague social network users: malicious infiltration, nearby threats, and limited network view. Malicious infiltration covers the illusion of such networks being secure through the provision of requiring a valid email address or a registration form when in effect malicious participants can still gain access. Similarly, nearby threats allude to the nearness of malicious users who can be a 'few hops away' despite users believing they have a tight control over their direct friends. Lastly, a limited network view describes the fact that users have a myopic perspective on the entire network as they may not be privy to information about the vast majority of participants in the entire network. The Facebook site for example maintains over 18 million user profiles with 80% to 90% of college undergraduates as users where users are allowed to disclose more varied information fields on the site (cf. Strater & Richter 2007: 157). Strater and Richter's (2007) research on Facebook also reveals that users were unaware of the ability of others to remove, delete, and in other ways control tagged photographs and wall posts from their profiles, thereby consigning such personal images and information to a life of permanent circulation and consumption on the web.

Barnes (2006), in citing Katz and Rice (2000), describes the Internet as a 'Panopticon where surveillance is part of the architecture'. There are a myriad of risks lurking in the trails of data people leave in SNS sites and in the ways it is mined for commercial, legal, and criminal purposes. SNSs such as LiveJournal.com, Facebook, Myspace, Friendster, and Google's Orkut.com have been a source of concern in the US, initiating federal laws that require most schools and libraries to render such web spaces inaccessible to minors in order to protect them from harm (McCullagh, 2006). Similarly, in the UK, the House of Lords Science and Technology select committee has suggested that both private and public sectors need more effective ways to deal with the rise of online fraud and hacking and have recommended the formation of a new national police squad charged with reducing online crime (Johnson, 2007). The Information Commissioner's Office (ICO) in the UK has also drawn up official guidelines for the millions of people who use such sites, offering warnings such as 'a blog is for life' and 'reputation is everything'. People are also advised that entries can leave an 'electronic footprint' and that the lives of people can be put at risk by the reckless disclosure of information (Hough, 2007). The notion of data and profiles having a permanence and circulation in unexpected ways is something the ICO wants to impress on people in terms of potential harm and transgression of privacy.

Early discourses of the Internet celebrated not only the ability to re-invent identity online but also the concept of 'avatarism' where a user can have multiple identities. But although this can certainly be empowering, it can also enable new forms of deception. New forms of narcissism enabled by SNS's, however, celebrate the notion of constructing one's offline profile online and inviting others to start friendships through such representations of self. Users may not then think beyond the cultural ethos of these spaces. Additionally, in tandem with the declaration of real identities online, deception and faking are also

part of the terrain. Dana Boyd (2004), in observing the Fakesters in Friendsters website, notes that users' appropriation of well-known celebrity and media profiles, or the invention of their own, 'exercises a certain creativity and introduces playful expression' which draws an audience that wishes to engage with these users. She asserts that 'fakesters' were a means of 'hacking the system to introduce missing social texture'. Boyd's argument is that the phenomenon of the Fakesters reflects the fundamental weakness of trust in the network (in this particular instance the reference was to Friendsters) where there is an ambiguity between the real and the parody.

Beyond the personal information posted by social networkers, there are also worries about privacy after Facebook's secret operational code was published on the Internet. The Facebook site in the UK has 3.5 million users and about 30 million users worldwide. The company blamed the leaked code on a 'bug' which meant that it was published accidentally (Johnson, 2007). While such glitches may not necessarily allow hackers to access private information directly, they could nevertheless help criminals close in on personal data. While some personal information listed on the site is semi-private, government and quasi-government agencies, such as Get Safe Online in the UK, are worried that criminals who become friends with other users have the potential to find out much more information about them (Johnson, 2007). Research by Websense supports the idea that criminals 'work as an underground community, sharing information on what tools and methods work when it comes to tricking consumers on SNS and hackers have realized that they need to become discreet when it comes to social networking since they need to blend in with the crowd where links can be added to sites, such as Wikipedia, to lure users onto corrupt sites' (Vassou, 2006; Newman 2006). There have also been numerous incidents of spyware and spamming being employed on such sites (Rosen, 2007).

The constant demand to make these sites attractive to advertisers means that privacy of users can be compromised in other ways. Wendlandt (2007) notes that online advertising is the fastest growing segment of the advertising industry, currently accounting for more than 25% of advertising growth per year, translating to more than five times the recent average annual growth of other types of media with about 6-7% spent on Internet advertising globally. Recently, 13,000 Facebook users signed a petition protesting against the networking site's new advertising system which alerts members of friends' purchases online. Some Facebook members have even threatened to leave due to the fact that the new system allowed their friends to find out what they were planning to give them for Christmas (Wendlandt, 2007). Preibusch et al. (2007) point out that popular SNS sites, such as MySpace.com, collect data for e-commerce purposes. User profiles are important for data mining in such websites. Data that accrues on the web is not only used for communicating but also for secondary purposes that may be covered in the SNS's terms of use. Such data can be acquired by marketing agencies for targeted marketing or by law enforcement agencies and secret services, etc (Preibusch et al, 2007).

FUTURE TRENDS

With the increasing popularity of social networking sites, the incorporation of various multimedia formats and functions in these platforms, the supplanting of actual offline networks through social networks on the internet construct social networking sites as viable spaces for the movement of new forms of both social and financial capital (i.e. advertising, e-commerce and data mining). Here the act of connecting with larger user communities present challenges and risks for users, social software designers, commercial organizations and government bodies. The increasing appropriation of social networking sites into our everyday lives (through mobile technologies)

and everyday engagements mean that visibility and non-visibility of social and personal networks will construct online identities as a vital part of a data economy. The need to reveal and to limit information flows and to enact a secure environment for users whilst enforcing users to comply with data management protocols on such sites will enact these as a contested space of new forms of sociability and social deviance. The users' notion of security, privacy and the human need for communion will continue to temper the social networks as complex and complicit risk communities.

CONCLUSION

The narcissistic streak in social networking sites that is evident through the creation of self- profiles hinges on the disclosure of offline identities where public spectacle and gaze repoliticize the construction of self. The notion of self in social networking sites is both imagined through self-description and crafted through textual and multimedia environments but equally through its articulation and display of contacts and its ability to invite or deny communion with other users. In this sense, the concept of self is anchored through both individual agency and imagination as well as other users' gaze and consumption of these profiles. This explicit ethos of exposure, display, and spectacle define the cultural ethos of social networking sites. This phenomenon again ignites debates about the issues of identity formation on the Internet where identity can be created and defined in multiple ways and is amenable to deception and inauthenticity. In the process, it highlights the complex nature of the Internet environment which can demand different cultural responses from different online spaces and communities of users. Self-exposure and narcissism gives a platform for re-definition of offline identities and new sociabilities which can in turn reconfigure and redefine the notion of friendship and community in these spaces. SNS's also herald the emergence of complicit risk communities where personal information becomes social capital which is traded and exchanged and where the concept of public or private can be defined through the nature of users' access, gaze, and the transactions and interactions they permit.

The culture of social networking sites thrives on the narcissistic and the performative, on one hand, and reciprocity and exchange, on the other. Hence the potential dangers and risks of willingly disclosing and displaying personal details become part of the architecture or code of these sites. The appropriation of new technologies by individuals in order to communicate, form new communities, and maintain existing relationships signifies new ways in which risk becomes embedded and encoded into our social practices, posing new ethical and legal challenges which inadvertently expand the landscape of risk.

REFERENCES

Anderson, P. (2007). What is Web 2.0? Ideas, technologies and implications for education. *JISC Technology & Standards Watch*. Retrieved, July 19, 2008, from http://www.jisc.ac.uk/media/documents/techwatch/tsw0701b.pdf

Backstrom, L., Cynthia, D., & Kleinberg, J. (2007). Wherefore art thou R3579X? Anonymized social networks, hidden patterns, and structural steganography. *Proceedings of the WWW 2007 conference*, May 8-12, 2007, Alberta, Canada.

Barnes, S. B. (2006). A privacy paradox: Social networking in the United States. *First Monday, 1*(9). Retrieved July 19, 2008, from http://firstmonday.org/issues/issue11_9/barnes/index.html

Bentley, F., Metcalf, C., & Harboe, G. (2006). Personal vs. commercial content: The similarities between consumer use of photos and music. *Proceedings of the SIGCHI conference on Human Factors in computing systems*, April 22-27, 2006, Montréal, Québec, Canada

Boyd, D. (2004). Friendster and publicly articulated social networking. *CHI 2004,* April 24-29, 2004, Vienna, Austria.

Boyd, D. (2007). Social network sites: public, private or what? *Knowledge Tree*, 13, Retrieved Dec 12, 2007, from http://kt.flexibelearning.net.au/tkt2007/?page_id=28

Boyd, D., & Ellison, N. B. (2007). Social networking sites: Definition, history and scholarship. *Journal of Computer Mediated Communication, 13*(1), 11. Retrieved Dec 12, 2007, from http://jcmc.indiana.edu/vol13/issue1/boyd.ellison.html

Boyd, D., & Heer, J. (2006). Profiles as conversation: Networked identity performance on friendster. *Proceedings of the Hawaii International Conference on System Sciences (HICSS-39)*, January 4-7, Persistent Conversation Track, Kauai, Hawaii.

Caverlee, J., Liu, L., & Webb, S. (2008). Towards robust trust establishment in web-based social networks with social trust. [Beijing, China.]. *WWW, 2008*(April).

Chapman, C., & Lahav, M. (2008). International ethnographic observation of social networking sites. *Proceedings of the CHI 2008 conference on Human Factors in Computing Systems*, April 5-10, 2008, Florence, Italy.

Diani, M. (2000). Social movement networks: Virtual and real. *Information Communication and Society, 3*(3), 386–401. doi:10.1080/13691180051033333

DiMicco, J., & Millen, D. (2007). Identity management: multiple presentations of self in facebook. *Group '07, Conference on Supporting Group Work*, November 4-7, 2007, Sannibel Island, Florida, USA.

Donath, J. (1998). Identity and deception in the virtual community. In P. Kollock, & M. Smith (Eds.), *Communities in cyberspace* (29-59). London: Routledge.

Donath, J., & Boyd, D. (2004). Public displays of connection. *BT Technology Journal, 22*(4), 71–81. doi:10.1023/B:BTTJ.0000047585.06264.cc

Friedland, L. A. (1996). Electronic democracy and the new citizenship. *Media Culture & Society, 18*, 185–212. doi:10.1177/016344396018002002

Froehlich, D., Kuchinsky, A., Pering, C., Don, A., & Ariss, S. (2002). Requirements for photoware. *Proceedings from the Conference on Computer Supported Cooperative Work: CSCW 2002*. New Orleans, LA.

Froomkin, A. (1995). Anonymity and its enmities. *Journal of Online Law*, 4. Retrieved Dec 12, 2007 from http://www.wm.edu/law/publications/jol/95_96/froomkin.html

Geyer, W., Dugan, C., DiMicco, J., Millen., D., et al. (2008). Use and reuse of shared Lists as a social Content Type. *Proceedings of the CHI 2008, conference on Human Factors in Computing Systems*, April 5-10, 2008, Florence, Italy.

Gibs, J., Fields, N., Liang, P., & Plipre, A. (2005). SNIF: Social networking in Fur. *Proceedings of the CHI 2005 conference on Human Factors in Computing Systems*, April 2-7, 2005, Portland, Oregon, USA.

Gibson, R. (2007). Who's really in your top 8: Networking security in the age of social networking. *Proceedings of the SIGUCCS' 07, conference on user services*, October 7-10, 2007, Orlando, FL.

Gibson, W. (1984). *Neuromancer*. New York: Ace Books.

Giddens, A. (1990). *The Consequences of modernity*. Stanford, CA: Stanford University Press.

Golbeck, J., Hendler, J., & Parsia, B. (2003). Trust networks on the semantic web. *Proceedings from Agents 2003, conference on cooperative information agents*, August 27-29, Helsinki, Finland.

Golbeck, J., & Wasser, M. (2007). Social browsing: Integrating social networks and web browsing. *Proceedings from CHI 2007, conference on Human Factors in Computing Systems*, April 28 – May 34, San Jose, CA.

Goussevskaia, O. Kuhn. M., & Wattenhofer, R. (2007). Layers and hierarchies in real virtual networks. In *proceedings of IEEE/WIC/ACM International Conference on Web Intelligence* (pp 89-94). IEEE Computer Society: Washington, DC.

Gross, R., & Acquisti, A. (2005). Information revelation and privacy in online social networks. *Workshop on Privacy in the Electronic Society* (WPES). Retrieved from Dec 4, 2007 from http://privacy.cs.cmu.edu/dataprivacy/projects/facebook/facebook1.html

Horst, S. A., & Miller, D. (2006). *The Cell Phone: An Anthropology of Communication*. Oxform, UK: Berg.

Hough, A. (2007, November 23). Fraud warning for users of social networking sites. *Reuters*. Retrieved Dec 4, 2007, from http:today.reuters.co.uk/misc/

Johnson, B. (2007, Aug 13). Facebook's Code Leak Raises Fears of Fraud. *Guardian Unlimited*. Retrieved April 12, 2007, from http://www.guardian.co.uk/technology/2007/aug/13/internet

Joinson, A. (2008). 'Looking at,' 'looking up' or 'keeping up with people?' motives and uses of facebook. *Proceedings from CHI 2008, conference on human factors in computing systems*, April 5-10, Florence, Italy.

Jordan, T. (1999). *Cyberpower: the culture and politics of cyberspace and the internet*. London: Routledge.

Kendall, L. (2002). *Hanging out in the virtual pub: identity, masculinities, and relationships online*. Berkeley, CA: University of California Press.

Kleinberg, J. (2006). Distributed social systems. *Proceedings from PODC '06, conference on principles of distributed computing*, July 22-26, Denver, CO.

Lampe, C., Ellison, N., & Steinfield, C. A. (2006). Face(book) in the crowd: Social searching vs. social browsing. *Proceedings of the CSCW '06, Conference on Computer Supported Cooperative Work*, November 4-8, Banff, Alberta, Canada.

Lange, P. (2007). Publicly private and privately public: Social networking on YouTube. *Journal of Computer-Mediated Communication, 13*(1), 18. Retrieved December 4, 2007, from http://jcmc.indianna.edu/vol113/issue1/lange/html

Mannan, M., & Oorschot, P. (2008). Privacy-enhanced sharing of personal content on the web. *WWW '08*, April 21-25, 2008, Beijing, China.

Mika, P. (2004). Social networks and the semantic web. *Proceedings of the IEEE/WIC/ACM International Conference on Web Intelligence*, 20-24 September, Beijing, China.

Miller, D., & Slater, D. (2000). *Internet: An Ethnographic Approach*. London: Berg.

Mislove, A., Marcon, M., & Gummadi, K. (2007). Measurement and analysis of online social networks. *Internet Measurement Conference '07*, October 24-26, San Diego, CA.

Montgomery, E. (2007). Facebook: Fraudsters' Paradise? *Money.UK.MSN.com*, November 20, 2007. Retrieved December 4, from http://money.uk.msn.com/banking/id-fraud/article.aspx?cp-documentid=5481130

Mori, J., Sugiyama, T., & Matsuo, Y. (2007). Real-world oriented information sharing using social Networks. *Proceedings from SIGGROUP '07 conference on supporting group work*, Sannibel Island, FL.

Nardi, B. A. (2005). Beyond bandwidth: Dimensions of connection in interpersonal communication. *Computer Supported Cooperative Work, 14*, 91–130. doi:10.1007/s10606-004-8127-9

Newman, R. (2006). Cybercrime, identity theft and fraud: practicing safe internet – Nework security threats and vulnerabilities. *InfoSecCD Conference '06*, September 22-23, 2006, Kennesaw, GA.

Preibusch, S., Hoser, B., Gurses, S., & Berebdt, B. (2007, June). Ubiquitous social networks – opportunities and challenges for Privacy-aware user modelling. *Proceedings of the Data Modelling Workshop*, Corfu, Greece. Retrieved December 4, 2007, from http://vasarely.wiwi.hu-berlin.de/DM.UM07/Proceedings/05-Preibusch.pdf

Randerson, J. (2007). Social network sites do not deepen friendships. *The Guardian*, September 10. Retrieved December 4, 2007, from http://guardian.co.uk/science/2007/sep/10/socialnetwork/print

Rheingold, H. (2000). *The Virtual Community*. New York: Harper Collins.

Rosen, C. (2007). Virtual friendship and the new narcissism. *New Atlantis (Washington, D.C.), 17*, 15–31.

Schiano, D., Nardi, B., Gumbrecht, M., & Swartz, L. (2004). Blogging by the rest of us. *Proceedings in CHI 2004, Conference on Human Factors in Computing Systems*, April 2004, Vienna, Austria.

Slater, D. (2002). Social relationships and identity on/off-line. In L. Lievrouw & S. Livingstone (Eds.), *Handbook of New Media: Social Shaping and Consequences of ICTs*. London: Sage.

Slevin, J. (2000). *The Internet and Society*. Cambridge, UK: Polity Press.

Stefanone, M., Lackoff, D., & Rosen, D. (2008). We're all stars now: Reality television, web 2.0, and mediated identities. *HT'08*, June 19-21, Pittsburgh, PA.

Strater, K., & Richter, H. (2007). Examining Privacy and Disclosure in a Social Networking Community. *Symposium on Usable Privacy and Security* (SOUPS) 2007, July 18-20, 2007, Pittsburgh, PA.

Szomszor, M. (2008). Correlating user profiles from multiple folksonomies. *HT '08 Conference on Hypertext and Hypermedia*, June 19-21, 2008, Pittsburgh, PA.

Vassou, A. (2006). Social networking sites driving new wave of security. *Computeractive*, December 13, 2006. Retrieved Dec 4, 2007, from http://www.computeractive.co.uk/articles/print2170872

Weintraub, J., & Kumar, K. (Eds.). (1997). *Public and private in thought and practice*. Chicago: University of Chicago Press.

Wendlandt, A. (2007). Web advertising to come under EU scrutiny. *Reuters*, November 23. Retrieved Dec 4, 2007, from http://www.reuters.com/articlePrint?articleId=USL229260820071123

Wynn, E., & Katz, J. E. (1997). Hyperbole over cyberspace: Self-presentation and social boundaries in internet home pages and discourse. *The Information Society*, *13*(4), 297–327. doi:10.1080/019722497129043

Section 2
Interactive Tools for Collaboration

Chapter 7
Wikis for Collaboration & Knowledge Management
Current Practices & Future Directions

Clif Kussmaul
Muhlenberg College, USA; Elegance Technologies, Inc., USA

ABSTRACT

This chapter examines how collaboration and knowledge management (KM) can be supported using wikis and related tools. A wiki is a web site that makes it easy for users to create, edit, and link pages without specialized tools. The chapter seeks to help readers understand what KM and wikis are, and when and why wikis can support collaboration and KM. The chapter identifies associated challenges and best practices. Organizations should assess cultural factors, recognize the differences between top-down and bottom-up approaches, and leverage the KM "market". Projects should be iterative, focus on either mapping or capture, start with pilot projects and simple structures, and focus on key users and roles. Systems should be off-the-shelf, avoid "either-or" conflicts, and provide structures to facilitate common tasks. The chapter also discusses future directions and implications in these rapidly changing areas.

INTRODUCTION

This chapter examines how collaboration and knowledge management (KM) can be supported using wikis and related tools. A wiki is a web site that makes it easy for users to create, edit, and link pages without specialized tools. Knowledge management (KM) is "the leveraging of collective wisdom to increase responsiveness and innovation" (Frappaolo, 2006, p. 8). The chapter seeks to help

readers understand what KM and wikis are, and when and why wikis can support collaboration and KM. It identifies associated challenges and best practices, and reviews complementary tools and techniques. It emphasizes the flexibility of wikis, including the ease with which they can be used to prototype and refine user interfaces for KM tasks and activities. It also discusses future directions and implications in these rapidly changing areas.

The chapter provides a multidisciplinary perspective, since effective collaboration involves a variety of disciplines, including business, soft-

DOI: 10.4018/978-1-60566-727-0.ch007

ware development, psychology, and sociology. Throughout this chapter, "platform" refers to the underlying tool, which could be used in many settings, and "system" refers to an actual instance, with content that is specific to an organization.

The chapter draws on the author's experiences using and contributing to several wiki platforms, teaching with wikis, and consulting for business, educational, and governmental organizations seeking to use wikis for KM, as well as experiences working in global organizations and managing global virtual teams. In particular, many of the examples are based on consulting projects. In the first, referred to below as SalesCom, the author worked with sales and marketing staff in a international company to develop a wiki KM system for product information and marketing materials, so that SalesCom staff could make better use of existing materials based on product line, customer, or geographic region. In the second, referred to below as EnginCom, a group of engineers created a wiki for their own use that gradually spread across the engineering department, and the author reviewed the resulting KM system and recommended next steps. In the third example, referred to as ResourceOrg, a group of faculty (including the author) started a public web site to share teaching materials.

The remainder of this chapter is organized as follows. The Background section provides relevant background on KM, wiki characteristics in general, and uses of wikis for collaboration and KM. The Challenges section presents some of the key challenges in using wikis for collaboration and KM, grouped into several categories. The Best Practices section identifies and discusses best practices for initiating and sustaining wiki-based systems for collaboration and KM, organized into several groups. The Future Directions section describes future directions in wikis and their use in collaboration and knowledge management, as well as some implications. The Conclusions section is followed by lists of references and additional reading.

BACKGROUND

This section provides relevant background on knowledge management (KM), wiki characteristics in general, and uses of wikis for collaboration and KM.

Knowledge Management

Making better and more efficient use of the knowledge of people in an organization can have enormous benefits (e.g. O'Dell & Grayson, 1998, p. 8-9), particularly for knowledge-intensive work, where professionals often spend 20-25% of their time trying to find needed information (Koenig, 2001). Our main focus is on collaboration for knowledge management and information sharing, either within an organization or in a (usually virtual) community. However, there are other forms of collaboration, such as collaboration within a team with a specific objective (usually project-based).

O'Dell and Grayson (1998) describe how KM can provide business value in three main areas: customer relationships, best practices to improve internal operations, and new product development. At SalesCom, customer relationships were a major goal, while EnginCom's KM system supported engineering operations and new product development. The author worked with a third organization to develop a wiki to manage and review proposals for internal development projects in order to allocate resources more effectively.

Views of KM have changed and evolved over time (e.g. Snowden, 2002; Figallo & Rhine, 2002). Initially, KM focused on supporting decision making and business process reengineering by treating knowledge as a collection of objects that could be gathered and organized. However, in the mid-1990s, the emphasis shifted to describing and sharing knowledge, recognizing an important distinction between *explicit knowledge*, which is easily codified, and *tacit knowledge*, which is more difficult to articulate, but often more valuable. For example, product specifications and pricing are explicit, while skills to identify prospects, develop relationships, and make sales are largely tacit. The relationships between explicit and tacit knowledge led to the "SECI" model (Nonaka, 1991; Nonaka & Takeuchi, 1995):

- Socialization: Tacit → Tacit
- Externalization (or articulation): Tacit → Explicit
- Combination: Explicit → Explicit
- Internalization: Explicit → Tacit

Despite this shift in emphasis, over half of KM systems failed to meet expectations, often due to problems with user training and education (KPMG, 2000; summarized in Koenig, 2001). More recently, KM has shifted to focus on collaboration and interaction, since it is often easier and cheaper to help individuals and groups quickly locate others with relevant knowledge, rather than attempting to codify and catalog knowledge that may not be needed or used. Thus, Frappaolo (2006) identifies four ways to use or apply knowledge:

1. **Intermediation:** connect knowledge seekers with providers
2. **Externalization:** capture knowledge in external repository
3. **Internalization:** extract knowledge from external repository
4. **Cognition:** apply knowledge to make decisions

For example, at SalesCom knowledge is externalized when a sales representative adds notes from a sales call to a KM system, and internalized when another rep accesses those notes. Intermediation occurs when the second rep contacts the first to learn more, and cognition occurs when the reps change their tactics based on this knowledge.

KM projects that require significant up-front investments are usually initiated top-down, which also provides higher visibility, access to resources, and high-level champions, although it may be harder to convince people to invest the time and energy in a system when the individual benefits are not yet clear. As KM priorities have shifted and the cost of supporting IT systems has decreased, it has become easier and more common to start bottom-up, using small, self-selected pilot projects in which small groups address problems or opportunities that matter to them. Such projects generally require fewer resources, can start quietly, and can be extended once they have proven themselves. The author has worked with multiple organizations (including both SalesCom and EnginCom) where a wiki-based KM platform was installed on an extra desktop or laptop in a few days. After the system is properly configured, adding additional groups or projects is simple. Once the value of the system is clear, it is much easier to obtain resources and other support to expand and improve the system.

KM can be distinguished from other management trends by three characteristics (Snowden, 2006). First, KM has origins in several different domains. Second, KM focuses more on improving productivity. Third, KM encourages distributed collaboration rather than centralized control and IT systems. However, Snowden also argues that technology and other standards have been emphasized prematurely, and that the SECI is not a good general model for KM.

Wikis

A *wiki* is a web site with several distinctive features. (To distinguish the site from the supporting software, the latter is referred to as the *wiki platform*.) First, and most notably, wiki pages (also called topics) can be created, edited, and linked together using a standard web browser, with little or no specialized knowledge or experience. Initially, most wiki platforms used plain text or simplified markup conventions, but increasingly they include or support graphical text editors. Second, wikis store all previous versions of each page, including

Table 1. Some popular wiki platforms

Wiki	URL	Open Source?	Notes
DokuWiki	docuwiki.org	Y	PHP
FosWiki	foswiki.org	Y	Perl
MediaWiki	mediawiki.org	Y	PHP, used by Wikipedia
MoinMoin	moinmo.in	Y	Python
PmWiki	pmwiki.org	Y	PHP
TikiWiki	tikiwiki.org	Y	PHP
TWiki	twiki.org	Y	Perl
Confluence	atlassian.com	N	hosted or installed
PBwiki	pbwiki.com	N	hosted
SocialText	socialtext.com	N	hosted
WikiSpaces	wikispaces.com	N	hosted

the author and time of the change. This enables users to review the page's history and evolution, and to easily undo accidental or malicious changes, which is particularly important for wikis (such as WikiPedia, described below) with a culture of open access. Third, wikis try to separate the content of a specific page from the visual appearance of the overall site. Thus, users can focus on putting the right content in each page, while graphic designers and the wiki platform provide consistent headers, footers, menus, color, fonts, and other details, so that the wiki looks like a coherent site, not a random assortment of pages. The first wiki was developed in 1994-1995 by Ward Cunningham (Leuf & Cunningham, 2002); "wiki" is a Hawaiian word for "quick". Currently there are over 100 wiki platforms, with a wide variety of characteristics and features (CosmoCode, 2008). Most wiki platforms are open source but there are also commercial platforms (see table 1).

Unlike other web sites or documents which are often controlled by a few gatekeepers, wikis make it easy to create, edit, and link content, so wikis can be used for personnel directories, scheduling, and other dynamic applications. For example, the author often uses wikis to collaborate on grant proposals or other writing projects, since all authors have access to the most current

version. At the same time, the wiki version history enables people to see who made specific changes, and view or reinstate previous versions of a page if necessary. Wikis also make it easy for people to progress gradually from adding comments and making minor changes to more complex formatting and larger restructuring. Wikis impose relatively little structure on content, so it is easy to adjust the site's navigational structure, or provide multiple parallel structures for different uses. This flexibility can also lead to confusion, particularly for newly created wikis; it helps to have designated facilitators, and adopt patterns, practices, and structures that have worked well elsewhere (Mader, 2008).

Probably the best known wiki is Wikipedia, "the free encyclopedia that anyone can edit" with over 2.5 million articles in English. People unfamiliar with wikis often assume incorrectly that Wikipedia is a typical wiki (Mader, 2008, p. 25), but there are important differences. For example, Wikipedia allows anonymous editing of most pages, while many wikis restrict access to members of a particular community, or are only available via an institutional intranet. Wikipedia is primarily an encyclopedia (although it also has areas for discussion, and to describe its internal processes), but wikis can support collaborative editing, discussion, and other uses. Wikipedia entries have been proposed as conceptual identifiers for KM (Hepp, Siorpaes, & Bachlechner, 2007), and their history provides rich data for models of collaborative editing (e.g. Priedhorsky, Chen, Lam, Panciera, Terveen, & Reidl, 2007; Viégas, Wattenberg, & Dave, 2004; Viégas, Wattenberg, & McKeon, 2007).

Nearly all wiki platforms provide keyword searching, and can allow users to attach images or other (formatted) documents to wiki pages. Most platforms also support authentication and authorization to determine who can access which pages, and what actions they can perform. However, many wikis, including Wikipedia, have a strong tradition of minimizing restrictions, and using community norms and the page history to prevent or correct problems. Finally, many platforms also make it easy to add new capabilities to the wiki without a detailed knowledge of the internal workings. "It's impossible for a software vendor to please everybody, and it's not a good business decision to do so, because the vendor should be focused on building an amazing, high-quality core product" (Mader, 2008, p. 54). As a result, the more popular wiki platforms have rich collections of extensions and customizations; MediaWiki, the platform used by Wikipedia, has over 1000 extensions. For example, the author has developed several extensions to support KM, including a TWiki module to help manage bibliographic entries, and other TWiki enhancements to allow users to weight search results.

Wikis for Collaboration & Knowledge Management

Wikis have a variety of uses in KM, and their potential has been described in the popular press (e.g. Hof, 2004; Swisher, 2004). Wikis are particularly well suited for collaboration and interactive information design; "the chief difference between the wiki and more traditional content management (CM) or knowledge management (KM) systems is

structure. … the wiki starts off with the minimum possible structure and grows a custom structure based on how each person, team, or project uses it" (Mader, 2008, p. 41). Wikis can help to codify explicit knowledge and map tacit knowledge, since content, pages, sections, and navigational schemes can easily be added or modified. For example, in ResourceOrg, resources were organized in three parallel ways: by discipline, by depth of knowledge (e.g. basic, intermediate, and advanced); and by when in the project lifecycle the resources are most relevant. This allowed users to browse the content in a variety of ways depending on their perspective and needs.

Wikis are used for KM in a variety of settings, including university courses and libraries (e.g. Blake, 2006; Fichter, 2006; Glogowski & Steiner, 2008; Raman, Ryan, & Olfman, 2005), sales and marketing, and engineering. Chau and Maurer (2005) describe a case study of a software company that used a wiki to exchange ideas, document decisions and rationales, share social information, identify experts, and coordinate project tasks and collaboration. Users were motivated by the presence of needed information, ease of use, desire to help others, as well as encouragement from management. Most of the top contributors were developers, and none were managers, suggesting that the wiki was mostly self-organized. 58% of the content was in unstructured formats, demonstrating the roles of both tacit and explicit knowledge. 80% of read-accesses were to just over 20% of the pages, and 25% were to the top 10 pages. Similarly, 10 users made 75% of contributions, and 5 made 55%. This pattern of wiki use and users is typical.

Majchrzak, Wagner, and Yates (2006) surveyed 168 wiki users to understand why and how wikis are used in corporate settings. Most are used for KM in areas ranging from software development and project management to technical support, sales and marketing, and research and development. The median respondents use wikis that are 12-24 months old, with an average of 12 contributors and

25 other users, suggesting that most wikis are used within groups rather than across organizations. Older wikis tend to have more accesses and more participants, suggesting that wikis are sustainable beyond short-term projects. For contributors, the wiki makes their own work easier; improves knowledge reuse, collaboration, and process improvement; and enhances their reputation.

KM can benefit from other features and capabilities, which can be provided by wikis or other tools (see Figallo & Rhine, 2002, ch 7; Wagner, 2004). In some cases a wiki platform may provide enough functionality to obviate the need for other tools, simplifying the environment for users and IT staff. In other situations, a wiki can be the portal that accesses other tools which provide benefits that justify additional integration and learning. For example, the Trac project management system includes a wiki component which can automatically link to tasks in the task tracking component and to files in the source code control system component. More structured information can be stored in traditional databases or in appropriate wiki pages; for example, TWiki enables users to define specific fields in a form, which can then be associated with pages; this is used in workflow applications such as document management and tracking tasks, defects, and features, including TWiki's own defect tracking system. Blogging can be useful for unstructured KM (Cayzer, 2000), particularly if supported by tagging and search capabilities. Threaded discussion forums are useful for archiving conversations; for example, every article in Wikipedia has a corresponding "talk" page for discussion about the article. Blogs and discussion forums make it easy to share thoughts and best practices, but they tend to focus on the process of collaboration rather than the result, and so they may be less effective at summarizing best practices and other knowledge in ways that facilitate reuse.

The design and implementation of a system and its underlying platform, and the resulting user experience, can also facilitate (or discourage) participation and collaboration. Wikis allow users to focus more on content and less on the overall appearance of a page, which can be customized by a graphic designer. The wiki's version history makes it easy to view or restore previous versions of a page, so that fewer security restrictions are necessary. Many wiki platforms allow users to create and continually refine templates for new pages. Increasingly, wikis provide ways to define and use more structured data, allowing further customization by users.

Thus, the net effect of these wiki features (templates, structured data, ease of search and navigation) is that non-technical users can quickly prototype and iteratively refine customized user interfaces for their KM tasks, without specialized tools and with limited support. As specific areas or tasks within the system become popular or important, they can be refined and improved incrementally.

CHALLENGES

Using wikis for collaboration and KM presents a number of challenges, which can be grouped into three categories, discussed in the following sections: organizational issues, tool and platform tradeoffs, and larger trends.

Organizational Issues

A first set of challenges involve organizational issues, including barriers to the spread of best practices, and incentives for participation.

KM systems are usually intended to help share best practices. However, Szulanski (1994) reports that best practices can take over two years to spread across an organization, and identifies several barriers. People might not know that needed information is available within the organization, or might not appreciate its benefits. Furthermore, they might lack the time, resources, or existing relationships needed to utilize available information. O'Dell and Grayson (1998, pp. 18ff) identify five similar barriers: organizational silos, reluctance to use ideas developed elsewhere, lack of common perspectives and terminology, focusing on explicit rather than tacit knowledge, and a lack of time or other resources. KM initiatives and systems are intended to help overcome such barriers. Furthermore, note that the effective use of a KM system entails additional best practices involving the KM process.

A variety of techniques can be used to address these challenges. Creating glossary pages can help to bridge terminology problems. Initially, it may help to focus on specific groups or sub-organizations, where people have shared perspectives and mutual trust. For example, at EnginCom, one engineering group developed a KM system, and other related groups found it useful, which led to broader adoption. Another useful technique is to identify common document types or actions and develop corresponding tools, to make it easier for people to contribute to the KM system. Most wiki platforms allow users to create templates that are used for new pages, and some support fields for multiple-choice, numeric, or other data. For example, SalesCom defined templates for sales call reports and for monthly status reports. The author helped another organization to develop forms to help people submit and review project proposals.

Participation is critical to system success. People must be confident that collaborating and using the KM system will help them find needed knowledge. Furthermore, they must be willing to contribute their own knowledge. However, "people rarely give away valuable possessions (including knowledge) without expecting something in return" (Davenport & Prusak, 2000, p. 26). Thus, it is important to understand both the roles and incentives of people who use the system.

In most KM systems, the vast majority of the content is contributed by a few people, and most people contribute rarely (if ever), although they may well use knowledge in the system; this is il-

Figure 1. Model of KM contributors

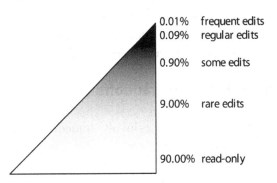

lustrated in figure 1. According to Nielsen (2006), in most online communities 1% of participants contribute most of the content; 9% contribute occasionally, and 90% read but never contribute, while for Wikipedia the frequencies are closer to 0.003%, 0.2%, and 99.8% - i.e., 1000 users contribute 2/3 of the content. Nielsen observes that it is impossible to overcome this inequality, but suggests some ways to encourage broader participation. A particular KM system probably has an optimal distribution, even if it cannot be calculated. If too few people contribute, they may become overwhelmed, or the system may not be useful. On the other hand, in some situations a KM system run by a few knowledgeable or well-connected brokers might function quite well. At the other extreme, if too many people contribute, it may be difficult to find the truly useful knowledge. Some online communities find that modest barriers result in higher quality (e.g. Taylor, 2007); this may also be true for KM projects.

There are many ways to encourage participation, although they can have unexpected drawbacks. Organizations can hire or assign staff to create content, in order to help bootstrap the KM system so that it contains more information. However, this may lead other users to assume that contributing content is the sole responsibility of those assigned staff. Organizations can provide explicit incentives, although these may decrease intrinsic motivation, or be manipulated. Often, a more productive tactic is to find ways for the

KM system to simplify or streamline work that is already being done. For example, regular reports can be entered directly into the system rather than being sent to a manager for review.

Tool & Platform Tradeoffs

A second set of challenges involve tradeoffs in the design of the wiki platform (or other KM tools) and in the design of a particular KM system.

The KM system should be easy to use. Since (as described above) most people use it rarely and briefly, the system should not require experience or training in order to start seeking or contributing content. It should also be easy to add new content or structures to the system. At the same time, a smaller group of people contributes most of the content and does most of the editing and organizing. These users expect (and may be more willing to invest time learning) powerful tools to search, format, categorize, and restructure content. Some of these users will evolve gradually from the first group, so the system should support and encourage a gradual transition between these groups. Similarly, larger organizations need systems that scale well to hundreds or thousands of users, with different needs and in different locations; a tool intended for small groups may have trouble scaling to enterprise uses. For example, TWiki's default search engine searches every page and returns an alphabetical list of pages containing given keywords. This may be sufficient for a small system, but is inadequate for a system with thousands of pages. Fortunately, TWiki has extensions to create search indexes, and to weight results by importance. Another example of this tradeoff is the use of formatting in wikis. Initially, most wikis supported only plain text, with a limited set of formatting options using special conventions (e.g. "*bold*" or "_underlined_"). This made it simple to edit, search, and format content, and many early wiki users were technical users who were already familiar with using such conventions. Over time, wikis added more formatting options,

and attracted users who were less comfortable with such conventions, and more accustomed to WYSIWYG word processing tools. As a result, wikis began to support WYSIWYG editors, although most still convert text into a different markup format for storage, which presents other problems. (Such editors were rare when wikis were first developed, so perhaps the emphasis on plain text was at least partly a rationalization of technical limitations.) There is a clear trend toward more complete (and complex) formatting options, in the near future, this should be the default for most major wiki platforms.

There are also tradeoffs between flexibility and structure. Although ease of creating and editing content is a great advantage, a wiki system can start to resemble a used bookstore with an enormous inventory but no way to locate specific items, or even know if a particular item exists. Some structure can help to avoid such problems, but too much can discourage users. Similarly, although most wikis encourage a flexible security model where anyone can edit any content, in many cases a more restricted model is necessary because of organizational politics, legal requirements (such as non-disclosure agreements), or other reasons.

Finally, there are tradeoffs between an emphasis on adding new content and an emphasis on refining existing content. A system focused on adding new content might emphasize features to support threaded discussion, comments on existing content, and attaching files. However, searching through pages of discussion or attachments in a variety of formats can be inefficient and frustrating. In contrast, a system focused on refining existing content might discourage such features, and emphasize tagging, indexing, and collaborative editing to produce fewer but more reliable and more usable resources. However, this emphasis also requires more effort on the part of contributors. Of course, these tradeoffs also depend on organization culture and incentives, as discussed above.

Larger Trends

A third and final set of challenges involve larger trends that affect collaboration and KM.

The rapid pace of change in information technology presents both benefits and challenges. Some of today's technical limitations (such as processing speed, disk space, and network bandwidth) may disappear within a few years. At the same time, there will be new challenges and limitations as systems strive to incorporate more and larger data objects, including images, audio, and video. It is difficult to predict what new applications and opportunities will appear, even in the next few years, which makes it difficult to design current platforms and systems to address future needs. For example, the Semantic Web (Antoniou & van Harmelen, 2004; Berners-Lee, Fensel, Hendler, Lieberman, & Wahlster, 2005) will annotate content using standardized taxonomies to make it easier for computers to perform search and analysis tasks currently done by humans. Some experimental wikis and related tools incorporate semantic concepts (e.g. Cayzer, 2004; Schaffert, 2006).

There are also challenges from the increasing role of collaboration (particularly virtual collaboration) in peoples' lives. As described above, KM systems have evolved from archival databases designed to support executive decision making to systems which support continual collaboration across and between organizations. It is increasingly common to work in virtual teams that span locations, organization, time zones, and national boundaries (e.g. Duarte & Snyder, 2000; Pinsonneault & Caya, 2005; Powell, Piccoli, & Ives, 2004). People are increasingly comfortable socializing, networking, and collaborating with people they have never met face to face. As a result, tools for collaboration and KM are used by a wider variety of people for a wider variety of tasks. Popular conceptions of how systems should work and what they should be able to do are increasingly driven by a few major providers.

Thus, people expect every search tool to work as well as Google and every text editor to work as well as Microsoft Word or Open Office, which presents daunting challenges for other vendors and products.

BEST PRACTICES

The following sections identify and discuss best practices for initiating and sustaining wiki-based systems for collaboration and KM, organized into three groups: organizational factors, project factors, and tool and platform factors.

Organizational Factors

Assess Organizational Culture

Organizational culture has a strong impact on KM projects, and particularly on wiki-based projects that depend on a variety of people contributing, editing, and maintaining. DeMarco and Lister (1999, p. 4) remind software developers that "the major problems of our work are not so much *technological* as *sociological* in nature" (original emphasis). Thus, organizations should address cultural issues before focusing on technical details, particularly for a wiki, which "cannot function without a community and should not be considered separately from it" (Blake, 2006). For KM systems to be effective, the organizational culture must value sharing over hording; this can be a challenge when the organization is facing rapid change, when employees compete with each other, or when they worry about job security. People must believe that they (as well as others) will benefit from contributing knowledge, and that their contributions will not be exploited, used against them, or attacked unfairly (Figallo & Rhine, 2002, p. 114). It is difficult for other factors to overcome cultural problems; "if the process of sharing and transfer is not inherently rewarding, celebrated, and supported by the culture, then artificial rewards won't have much effect and can make people feel cynical" (O'Dell & Grayson, 1998, p. 82).

At SalesCom, sharing product information helps sales and marketing staff work more effectively. Similarly, materials developed for one client can be adapted for other clients, as long as the original author is confident that their generosity will be reciprocated. Closely knit engineering groups at EnginCom may be eager to share within the group, but more wary of sharing knowledge with other groups that compete for internal resources. Conversely, it is very difficult to create effect KM in broader, less cohesive groups. Many public KM sites, including ResourceOrg, fail to reach critical mass; visitors don't see enough useful content, and so are reluctant to invest energy to contribute content of their own.

Top-Down or Bottom Up?

It is important to determine whether a specific KM project is being initiated top-down or bottom-up, and plan accordingly. Particularly with wikis, both approaches are feasible. As discussed above, in the 1990s KM projects often needed a top-down mandate to obtain required resources for technology, integration, and training. A high-level champion can help provide resources and support, and help to align personal and business incentives. Even if participation is mandated, a champion should model participation and continually remind others to participate (Charman, 2006). However, Charman also points out that top-down approaches can stall when the mandate changes or priorities shift, and that bottom-up approaches are preferable because they are more likely to become self-sustaining. A wiki's low cost, ease of use, and general flexibility make it possible for KM projects to start within small groups and gradually grow in size and scope. Thus, in most situations, a bottom-up approach is preferable, and most of the project factors discussed below focus on bottom-up projects.

A bottom-up approach worked well at Engin-Com, although it led to problems later when the engineering groups were reluctant to switch from their organic KM system to a different system deployed by the organizational IT department. It also worked at SalesCom, where the project's original sponsors could demonstrate a working system before requested high-level support for broader deployment.

Understand & Manage the KM Market

Recognize that the KM system is a market (in the economic sense). There are *sellers* who provide or offer knowledge, and *buyers* who need or want knowledge. There are also *brokers* who try to bring buyers and sellers together. A factor analysis of wiki contributions (Majchrzak, Wagner, & Yates, 2006, see above) identifies a fourth role: *editors* who integrate and (re-)organize existing content. People and organizations perform these roles, but so do systems and tools – the system is a broker, and improvements to its user interface (particularly its search, navigation, and authoring functions) can enhance the efficiency of the market. Mader (2008, p. 12) identifies additional roles in wiki, including some roles which make the system less efficient or less productive. Although most markets assume that buyers and sellers exchange goods directly, markets such as KM systems where this does not occur can be understand using "balanced value flows" (Ghosh, 2005).

People and organizations perform the roles of seller, buyer, broker, and editor for a variety of reasons. Clearly, a buyer hopes to obtain useful knowledge from the system; but the incentives for sellers, brokers, and editors are less obvious, and thus more important to understand. "One of the challenges of knowledge management is to ensure that knowledge sharing is rewarded more than knowledge hoarding" (Davenport & Prusak, 2000, p. 29). Incentives can be considered from several perspectives. Davenport and Prusak (2000, p. 31-34) identify three categories. *Reciprocity* is usually the most important - people give because they expect to receive. Next is *repute*; having a reputation for being knowledgeable can lead to greater reciprocity, job security, and other indirect benefits. Finally, there is *altruism,* where people don't care about immediate benefits; this may depend on organizational culture. Figallo and Rhine (2002, p. 217) identify four categories of incentives. Some are purely *personal*, such as a desire to help, learn, or achieve respect. Others are *cultural*, based on organizational norms. A third group of incentives are *goal-oriented*, such as a desire to get work done faster or to save money. Finally, some are *compensatory*; people may receive salary or bonuses for participating, or when their contributions benefit others.

At both SalesCom and EnginCom, many users are both sellers and buyers, so reciprocity and repute are key incentives. At EnginCom, the system is organized as a set of largely separate wikis for individual groups, so that each group can effectively edit its own content. Conversely, SalesCom has one system for the entire sales organization, so that standards are most difficult to establish, and over time there is likely to be a greater need for editors. This is a clear problem on public wikis used for technical support – there can be multiple pages chronicling attempts to answer similar questions, making it more difficult for users to find the best answers efficiently. Note that compensatory incentives must be chosen carefully, however; SalesCom offered a bonus for employees who made the most contributions to a new KM system; as a result, some employees uploaded large collections of documents without really considering or appreciating how useful they would be for others.

Project Factors

Test Fast, Fail Fast, Adjust Fast

This slogan is attributed to Tom Peters, and rapid iteration is also central to many software devel-opment methodologies; it is probably the most important advice for any new project. Try the simplest thing that seems likely to work, check to see how well it works, and then decide what to do next. More structured "waterfall"-style processes may be necessary when deploying large enterprise systems, but wikis are so flexible that a more agile, iterative approach is generally more successful. Problems can be detected and correctly quickly, and once a few groups are using the system suc-cessfully, they provide good models for other groups to follow.

At SalesCom, search capabilities were en-hanced using this approach. Initially, searching the system produced a list of all pages that matched the search string, listed alphabetically. People quickly noticed (and complained) when results near the top of the list were less useful than results further down. The search system was modified to count the number of matches, and display pages with the most matches first. This was a clear im-provement, but some users suggested that pages which had the search term in the title or section headings should appear earlier in the list, prompt-ing more changes.

Mapping or Capture?

Decide whether the goal is to *map* the location of knowledge that exists in people, organizations, or other IT system, or to *capture* knowledge in the system where other people can access it. Hansen, Nohria, and Tierney (1999) review approaches to KM, and conclude that organizations need to decide strategically whether to emphasize explicit or tacit knowledge, because this decision has far-reaching implications. Those that emphasize explicit knowledge should try to capture knowl-edge in materials that can easily be reused or customized for different purposes; this requires a larger investment for infrastructure, creating, and disseminating, but once materials are developed they can be reused very efficiently. On the other hand, organizations that emphasize tacit knowledge should try to create maps to make it easy to identify and connect with experts; this is easier to create, but there is less potential for reuse. Wikis can be adapted to either strategy, or to a combination. The collaborative editing capabilities allow experts to contribute more explicit knowledge to the system, while the wiki version history can help to identify experts in particular topics so that they can be contacted directly.

In the author's experiences, most wiki KM systems begin by capturing explicit knowledge, usually by uploading or copying and pasting content that already exists within the organization. Common mapping techniques include departmental directories, user home pages that describe responsibilities and interests, and links to external resources. However, it is common for mapping to gradually emerge in the KM system, particularly when the system uses social networking features, such as comments, discussion forums, frequently asked questions, and ways to rate the quality of information in the system. People can then identify experts from the frequency and reliability of their contributions to related topics in the wiki. Researchers are investigating ways to assess the reliability of wiki content and authors (e.g. Priedhorsky Chen, Lam, Panciera, Terveen, & Riedl, 2007; Viégas, Wattenberg, & Dave, 2004; Viégas, Wattenberg, & McKeon, 2007); in the near future, wikis should incorporate tools for automatic assessment.

Pilot Projects

Appropriate pilot projects are important to get collaboration and KM started in safe, supported environments, with supporting structures and examples that will help the system expand in the future (Mader, 2008, p. 63). Initially, pilots should be small enough to be manageable; it's better to do one thing well than many things poorly. At the same time, pilots need to be big enough to illustrate the system's value; it might be unnecessary if all of the participants work in the same office and can speak to each other directly. The people involved in the pilot should be open to new approaches, focused enough to be successful, but diverse enough to be representative of the roles and attitudes across the organization.

Pilot projects worked well at SalesCom and EnginCom – in both cases, wikis were initially developed by small groups who could experiment freely and adjust as needed. In contrast, ResourceOrg started by designing high-level structures and supporting tools, some of which were never used.

Simple but Representative Structures

Albert Einstein is quoted as saying "Make everything as simple as possible, but not simpler." This is certainly true of wikis for collaboration and KM. Keep the initial structure simple so that users can understand it and so that it can adapt as the KM system evolves. At the same time, make the structure complete enough that users can see how the larger system will work (Blake, 2006). Remember that "all models are wrong, but some are useful" (Box & Draper, 1987, p. 424); provide structure to help people be productive, rather than trying to address all possible problems in a comprehensive structure that isn't relevant to immediate needs. Also, match parts of the wiki structure to the organizational structure. Conway (1968) famously observed that system designs (particularly in software) mirror the structures of the organizations that produce them. Ensure that each team, department, or division using the system has a home page, with links to parent, child, and sibling units. Fortunately, in a wiki it is easy to maintain multiple navigation structures, so knowledge can also be accessed in other ways.

SalesCom developed templates for the most common pages; periodic reviews of new pages will help to identify opportunities for more templates. Initially, SalesCom imposed very little structure, although this may present challenges as the system grows. Conversely, EnginCom chose to create a separate structure for each engineering group, which makes it easier for people to find content from their own group, but may inhibit the sharing of information across groups.

Identify Key Users & Roles

Identify key groups of users in the organization, and then identify and work to understand the key users and roles within those groups. Help each group learn to adapt the wiki to its needs. Work to convert key users into project *evangelists* who can engage others, and work to convert evangelists into *trainers*, since they have valuable insight into how others in their group work and how they could benefit from the project (Charman, 2006). Look for emerging patterns or needs that can be leveraged to help the rest of the organization. For example, Mader (2008, p. 12) describes a variety of common user roles as patterns to be sought out and developed, as well as some "anti-patterns" to be avoided.

At both SalesCom and EnginCom, the wiki KM systems were initiated by typical users (sales and marketing staff, and engineers, respectively), with technical support from external consultants. However, both organizations may encounter problems when they expand their KM systems to organizational units that were not involved in the initial pilot.

System & Platform Factors

Buy or Borrow, Don't Build

Use existing platforms and tools whenever possible, and build or extend them in house only as a last resort. It is generally more cost effective to use mature open source projects or commercial products. Such platforms provide a variety of benefits that many not be apparent initially. Because they have survived in a competitive marketplace, they are more likely to be well designed, with robust architectures and usable interfaces. They

have larger user bases, so it is more likely that problems have been identified and corrected, and that expert consultants are available to assist with configuration and customization. The major open source wikis, for example, have many extension modules to address specific problems, and maintain lists of people and organizations that provide consulting services. At the same time, O'Dell and Grayson (1998, pp. 88-89) recommend spending less than 1/3 of project resources on IT, and argue that more valuable knowledge, including tacit knowledge, should often use simple solutions. As discussed above, it is better to start simply, and add complexity only as needed.

Both SalesCom and EnginCom started with a mature wiki platform that provided most key features. At EnginCom in-house staff installed and maintained the system, and an external consultant was hired to review the system and recommend improvements. SalesCom invested in several days of consulting to install and configure the system and provide informal training to a few lead users, with additional consulting to review and enhance the system. At SalesCom, the KM system contains many attached files in a variety of formats; rather than paying consultants to enhance the wiki platform to search these files, SalesCom will probably purchase a commercial search appliance.

"Both-And" not "Either-Or"

Some of the challenges discussed above were presented as tradeoffs between options that appear mutually exclusive, but at times it is possible to achieve "both-and" rather than "either-or". Thus, user interfaces can be both easy to use and powerful. For example, advanced features can be hidden from novice users, and then gradually revealed over time (through a "tip of the day" feature), via user preferences, or by monitoring user activity to predict likely next steps (e.g. Borges & Levene, 1999; Perkowitz & Etzioni, 2000). Achieving "both-and" is often the result of extensive experimentation and testing, which is yet more justification for using existing platforms and tools.

In the wiki KM system at SalesCom, users can sign up to receive email notifications when particular pages are modified. The wiki syntax used to specify these notifications is flexible and powerful, but confusing to novice or occasional users. Thus, the system was modified so that each pages includes a simple subscribe/unsubscribe button; this is much easier to use, but advanced users still have access to the underlying syntax.

Develop Supporting Structures

One the platform and system are in place, look for ways to facilitate common tasks. For example, create templates for common page types; most wikis can do this easily, and a template makes it easier to create new pages quickly and consistently. For example, it is often useful to have templates for individuals, departments or other organizational groups, cross-functional project teams, competitors, clients, and key products or product lines. Some wikis (e.g. TWiki) support user-defined *forms* for more structured data. Some wikis also support *tagging*, where pages can be annotated with user-selected keywords, which can then be used to organize and visualize pages in ways not anticipated by the original navigational structure. Such features should become more common and mature as wikis and other content management platforms continue to converge. Most of the popular wikis encourage the development of extension modules; this requires more time, expertise, or consulting support, but may be appropriate for tasks with special requirements. Finally, recognize that platforms provide a framework that imposes structure and good practices, but most of this can be changed as the real needs of the system become more apparent.

As described above, SalesCom developed templates for common documents. As people become more comfortable using the KM system to access explicit knowledge, they may become more will-

ing to use other parts of the system, particularly some of the social networking features that can facilitate access to tacit knowledge.

FUTURE DIRECTIONS

This section describes future directions in wikis and their use in collaboration and knowledge management, as well as some implications.

KM will continue to develop as a source of competitive advantage, as will the best practices for how to manage (or enable) knowledge. As organizational structures become flatter, more collaborative, and more interconnected, KM systems will becomes more common, more connected, and more distributed, which will require "federated" tools to integrate and connect knowledge across and even between enterprises. More people will need or want to use KM systems, and they will have a wider variety of backgrounds, attitudes, and expertise. As a result, businesses and academic institutions will face new challenges and opportunities in helping people learn to use such tools quickly while at the same time develop deeper mastery when appropriate.

Wikis will continue their rapid evolution. Increasing numbers of occasional and non-technical users will make ease of use even more important. Thus, more wikis may include features to support usability testing. Wikis will provide better support for formatted and structured text, and for non-text data, such as graphics, pictures, audio, and video. The increasing volume of content will drive more sophisticated search and navigation tools, including formal taxonomies and user-generated tags for semantic analysis, and adaptive or predictive navigation (e.g. (e.g. Borges & Levene, 1999; Perkowitz & Etzioni, 2000). As wikis are used by larger and more traditional organizations, their security and permissions will become more sophisticated, which may lead to tension with the historically open wiki culture. Wikis and other content management platforms will overlap and converge. There will be fewer, more capable, and more differentiated platforms; others will fail to maintain a critical mass of users and developers. This consolidation will be difficult, but ultimately beneficial.

Wikis will continue to be valuable for collaboration and KM, particularly in areas and organizations with extensive tacit knowledge, or explicit knowledge which evolves quickly and is this not conducive to more structured KM systems. As wiki-based KM systems grow in scope and are used in larger organizations, they will need to strike a balance between consistency, for enhanced efficiency, and customization, to adapt to the ever changing knowledge landscape.

In addition to the organizational and technical opportunities described above, there will be other research opportunities, particularly in the social sciences. Collaboration tools, such as wikis, discussion forums, task tracking systems, and version control systems, provide a rich data source which can be mined in a variety of ways (e.g. Borges & Levene, 1999; Jensen & Scacchi, 2007). In addition to studies focused on how people use specific tools, such data could also support studies of how people learn and different styles of learning, particularly for adult learners. There are also opportunities to study how KM systems and other virtual communities grow and evolve over time, including their norms and expectations for participation (e.g. O'Mahony & Ferraro, 2007).

CONCLUSION

This chapter examines the uses of wikis and related tools for collaboration and knowledge management. Using wikis for collaboration and KM presents challenges involving organizational issues, tool and platform tradeoffs, and larger trends in technology and society. The chapter identifies and discusses best practices involving organizational factors, project factors, and tool and platform factors. The chapter also reviews complementary tools and techniques. It emphasizes the flexibility of wikis, including the ease with which they can be used to prototype and refine user interfaces for KM tasks and activities. The chapter also discusses future directions and implications in these rapidly changing areas. It is clear that wikis and related tools will continue to evolve rapidly, supporting knowledge management and information sharing within and between organizations, and providing opportunities for scholarship and innovation in a variety of related disciplines.

REFERENCES

Antoniou, G., & van Harmelen, F. (2004). *A Semantic Web Primer*. Cambridge, MA: The MIT Press.

Berners-Lee, T., Fensel, D., Hendler, J. A., Lieberman, H., & Wahlster, W. (2005). *Spinning the Semantic Web: Bringing the World Wide Web to Its Full Potential*. Cambridge, MA: The MIT Press.

Blake, P. (2006). Using a wiki for information services: Principles and practicalities. In *Proceedings of New Librarians Symposium*. Sydney: Australian Library and Information Association.

Borges, J., & Levene, M. (1999). Data mining of user navigation patterns. In *Revised Papers from the International Workshop on Web Usage Analysis and User Profiling*, (pp. 92-111). Berlin: Springer.

Box, G. E. P., & Draper, N. R. (1987). *Empirical Model-Building and Response Surfaces*. Hoboken, NJ: Wiley.

Cayzer, S. (2004). Semantic blogging and decentralized knowledge management. *Communications of the ACM, 47*(12), 47–52. doi:10.1145/1035134.1035164

Charman, S. (2006). An adoption strategy for social software in the enterprise. *Corante*. Retrieved May 13, 2008, from http://strange.corante.com/archives/2006/03/05/an_adoption_strategy_for_social_software_in_enterprise.php

Chau, T., & Maurer, F. (2005). A case study of wiki-based experience repository at a medium-sized software company. In *Proceedings of the 3rd International Conference on Knowledge Capture* (pp 185-186), Banff, Alberta, Canada.

Conway, M. E. (1968). How do committees invent? *Datamation, 14*(4), 28–31.

CosmoCode. (2008). *WikiMatrix: Compare them all*. Retrieved May 10, 2008, from http://www.wikimatrix.org

Davenport, T. H., & Prusak, L. (2000). *Working Knowledge*, (2nd Ed.). Boston: Harvard Business School Press.

DeMarco, T., & Lister, T. (1999). *Peopleware: Productive Projects and Teams*. New York: Dorset House.

Duarte, D., & Snyder, N. (2000). *Mastering Virtual Teams: Strategies, Tools, and Techniques that Succeed*, (2nd Ed.). Hoboken, NJ: Jossey-Bass.

Fichter, D. (2006). Using wikis to support online collaboration in libraries. *Information Outlook, 10*(1), 30–31.

Figallo, C., & Rhine, N. (2002) *Building the Knowledge Management Network: Best Practices, Tools, and Techniques for Putting Conversation to Work*. Hoboken, NJ: Wiley.

Frappaolo, C. (2006). *Knowledge Management*, (2nd Ed.). Mankato, MN: Capstone Press.

Ghosh, R. A. (2005). Cooking-pot markets and balanced value flows. In *CODE: Collaborative Ownership and the Digital Economy*, (pp. 153-168). Cambridge, MA: The MIT Press.

Glogowski, J., & Steiner, S. (2008). The life of a wiki: How Georgia State University Library's wiki enhances content currency and employee collaboration. *Internet Reference Services Quarterly, 13*(1). doi:10.1300/J136v13n01_05

Hansen, M. T., Nohria, N., & Tierney, T. (1999). What's your strategy for managing knowledge? *Harvard Business Review, 77*(2), 106–116.

Hepp, M., Siorpaes, K., & Bachlechner, D. (2007). Harvesting wiki consensus: Using Wikipedia entries as vocabulary for knowledge management. *IEEE Internet Computing, 11*(5), 54–65. doi:10.1109/MIC.2007.110

Hof, R. D. (2004). Something wiki this way comes. *Business Week*, (June): 7.

Jensen, C., & Scacchi, W. (2007). Role migration and advancement processes in OSSD projects: A comparative case study. In *Proceedings of the 29th International Conference on Software Engineering*, (pp 364-374). Washington, DC: IEEE Computer Society.

Koenig, M. (2001). User education for KM: The problem we won't recognize. *KM World*, December.

KPMG Consulting (2000). *Knowledge Management Research Report*. London: KPMG Consulting.

Leuf, B., & Cunningham, W. (2001). *The Wiki Way: Quick Collaboration on the Web*. Boston: Addison-Wesley Professional.

Mader, S. (2008) *Wikipatterns: A practical guide to improving productivity and collaboration in your organization*. Hoboken, NJ: Wiley.

Majchrzak, A., Wagner, C., & Yates, D. (2006). Corporate wiki users: Results of a survey. In *Proceedings of the 2006 International Symposium on Wikis*, (pp 99-104), Odense, Denmark: ACM Press.

Nielsen, J. (2006). Participation inequality: Lurkers vs. contributors in internet communities. *Jakob Nielsen's Alertbox*. Retrieved May 2008 from http://www.useit.com/alertbox/participation_inequality.html.

Nonaka, I. (1991). The knowledge-creating company. *Harvard Business Review, 69*(6), 96–104.

Nonaka, I., & Takeuchi, H. (1995) *The Knowledge-Creating Company: How Japanese Companies Create the Dynamics of Innovation*. Oxford, UK: Oxford University Press.

O'Dell, C., & Grayson, C. J. (1998) *If Only We Knew What We Know: The Transfer of Internal Knowledge and Best Practice* (1st Ed). New York: Free Press.

O'Mahony, S., & Ferraro, F. (2007). The emergence of governance in an open source community. *Academy of Management Journal, 50*(5), 1079–1106.

Perkowitz, M., & Etzioni, O. (2000). Towards adaptive web sites: Conceptual framework and case study. *Artificial Intelligence, 118*(1-2), 245–275. doi:10.1016/S0004-3702(99)00098-3

Pinsonneault, A., & Caya, O. (2005). Virtual teams: What we know, what we don't know. *International Journal of e-Collaboration, 1*(3), 1–16.

Powell, A., Piccoli, G., & Ives, B. (2004). Virtual teams: A review of current literature and directions for future research. *ACM SIGMIS Database, 35*(1), 6–36. doi:10.1145/968464.968467

Priedhorsky, R., Chen, J., Lam, S. K., Panciera, K., Terveen, L., & Riedl, J. (2007). Creating, destroying, and restoring value in Wikipedia. In *Proceedings of the 2007 International ACM Conference on Supporting Group Work* (GROUP 2007), Sanibel Island, FL.

Raman, M., Ryan, T., & Olfman, L. (2005). Designing knowledge management systems for teaching and learning with wiki technology. *Journal of Information Systems Education, 16*(3), 311–320.

Schaffert, S. (2006). IkeWiki: A semantic wiki for collaborative knowledge management. *1st International Workshop on Semantic Technologies in Collaborative Applications (STIC'06)*, Manchester, UK.

Snowden, D. (2002). Complex acts of knowing: Paradox and descriptive self-awareness. *Journal of Knowledge Management, 6*(2), 100–111. doi:10.1108/13673270210424639

Snowden, D. (2006). Whence goeth KM? *Cognitive Edge*. Retrieved May 12, 2008, from http://www.cognitive-edge.com/2006/11/whence_goeth_km.php

Swisher, K. (2004). 'Wiki' may alter how employees work together. *The Wall Street Journal*, July 29.

Szulanski, G. (1994). *Intra-Firm Transfer of Best Practices Project*. Houston, TX: American Productivity and Quality Center.

Taylor, C. (2007) Why commercial Wikis don't work. *CNN Money Business 2.0*. Retrieved May 12, 2008 from http://money.cnn.com/2007/02/21/magazines/business2/walledgardens.biz2/index.htm

Viégas, F., Wattenberg, M., & Dave, K. (2004). Studying cooperation and conflict between authors with history flow visualizations. In *Proceedings of the SIGCHI Conference on Human Factors in Computing Systems*, (pp. 575-582). Vienna, Austria.

Viégas, F., Wattenberg, M., & McKeon, M. (2007). The hidden order of Wikipedia. In *Proceedings of the 12th International Conference on Human-Computer Interaction*, Beijing, P.R. China.

Wagner, C. (2004). Wiki: A technology for conversation knowledge management and group collaboration. *Communications of the Association for Information Systems*, *13*, 265–289.

ADDITIONAL READING

Alavi, M., & Leidner, D. E. (2001). Review: Knowledge management and knowledge management systems: Conceptual foundations and research issues. *MIS Quarterly*, *25*(1), 107–136. doi:10.2307/3250961

Ambrozek, J., & Cothrel, J. (2004). Online communities in business: Past progress, future directions. In *Proceedings of the 7th International Conference on Virtual Communities*. The Hague, Netherlands.

Burnett, G., & Buerkle, H. (2004). Information exchange in virtual communities: A comparative study. *Journal of Computer-Mediated Communication*, *9*(2).

Chauvel, D., & Despres, C. (2002). A review of survey research in knowledge management: 1997-2001. *Journal of Knowledge Management*, *6*(3), 207–223. doi:10.1108/13673270210434322

de Vries, S., & Kommers, P. (2004). Online knowledge communities: Future trends and research issues. *International Journal of Web Based Communities*, *1*(1), 115–123.

Drucker, P. F., Garvin, D., Leonard, D., Straus, S., & Brown, J. S. (1998) *Harvard Business Review on Knowledge Management*. 6th ed. Boston, MA: Harvard Business School Press.

Ebersbach, A., Glaser, M., & Heigl, R. (2005). *Wiki: Web Collaboration*. Berlin, Germany: Springer.

Fenstermacher, K. D. (2005). Revealed processes in knowledge management. In *Professional Knowledge Management: Third Biennial Conference*. Berlin, Germany: Springer.

Fuchs-Kittowski, F., & Köhler, A. (2005). Wiki communities in the context of work processes. In *Proceedings of the 2005 International Symposium on Wikis, San Diego, CA* (pp 33-39). New York, NY: ACM Press.

Fitzgerald, R. (2007). Wikis as an exemplary model of open source learning. In *Handbook of Research in Open Source Software*, (pp. 681-689), Hershey, PA: IGI Global.

Ghosh, R. A. (Ed.). (2005). *CODE: Collaborative Ownership and the Digital Economy*. Cambridge, MA: MIT Press.

Gonzolez-Reinhart, J. (2005). *Wiki and the wiki way: Beyond a knowledge management system.* C. T. Bauer College of Business, University of Houston. Retrieved May 10, 2008 from http://www.uhisrc.com/FTB/Wiki/wiki_way_brief[1]-Jennifer%2005.pdf

Grudin, J. (2006). Enterprise knowledge management and emerging technologies. In *Proceedings of the 39th Annual Hawaii International Conference on System Sciences*, (track 3, p 57a). University of Hawaii at Manoa.

Hann, I. H., Roberts, J. A., Slaughter, S. A., & Fielding, R. (2002) Why do developers contribute to open source projects? First evidence of economic incentives. In *Proceedings of the 2nd Workshop on Open Source Software Engineering, The 24th International Conference on Software Engineering, Orlando, FL*. New York, NY: ACM Press.

Holsapple, C. W., & Joshi, K. D. (2000). An investigation of factors that influence the management of knowledge in organizations. *The Journal of Strategic Information Systems*, *9*(2-3), 235–261. doi:10.1016/S0963-8687(00)00046-9

King, W. R., Marks, P. V. Jr, & McCoy, S. (2002). The most important issues in knowledge management. *Communications of the ACM, 45*(9), 93–97. doi:10.1145/567498.567505

Korfiatis, N., & Naeve, A. (2005). Evaluating wiki contributions using social networks: A case study on Wikipedia. In *Proceedings of the First Online Conference on Metadata and Semantics Research.* Association for Information Systems.

Koh, J., Kim, Y.-G., Butler, B., & Bock, G.-W. (2007). Encouraging participation in virtual communities. *Communications of the ACM, 50*(2), 68–73. doi:10.1145/1216016.1216023

Kollock, P. (1999). The production of trust in online markets. *Advances in Group Processes, 16*(1), 99–123.

Kussmaul, C., & Jack, R. (2009) Wikis for knowledge management: Business cases, best practices, promises, & pitfalls. *Web 2.0: The Business Model,* Lytras, M. D., Damiani, E. and Ordóñez de Pablos, P., editors. Berlin: Springer.

Louridas, P. (2006). Using wikis in software development. *IEEE Software, 23*(2), 88–91. doi:10.1109/MS.2006.62

Lueg, C. (2003). Knowledge sharing in online communities and its relevance to knowledge management in the e-business era. *International Journal of Electronic Business, 1*(2), 140–151. doi:10.1504/IJEB.2003.002170

MacInnes, I., & Hu, L. (2005). Business models for online communities: The case of the virtual worlds industry in China. In *Proceedings of the Proceedings of the 38th Annual Hawaii International Conference on System Sciences,* (track 7, volume 07). University of Hawaii at Manoa.

Mason, D., & Pauleen, D. J. (2003). Perceptions of knowledge management: A qualitative analysis. *Journal of Knowledge Management, 7*(4), 38–48. doi:10.1108/13673270310492930

Sawyer, K. (2007). *Group Genius: The Creative Power of Collaboration.* New York, NY: Perseus Books Group.

Sundstrom, E., & Associates. (1998). *Supporting Work Team Effectiveness: Best Management Practices for Fostering High Performance.* Hoboken, NJ: Jossey-Bass.

Tapscott, D., & Williams, A. (2006). *Wikinomics: How Mass Collaboration Changes Everything.* New York, NY: Portfolio Hardcover.

Usoro, A., Sharratt, M., Tsui, E., & Shekhar, S. (2007). Trust as an antecedent to knowledge sharing in virtual communities of practice. *Knowledge Management Research & Practice, 5,* 199–212. doi:10.1057/palgrave.kmrp.8500143

von Krogh, G., Ichijo, K., & Nonaka, I. (2000) *Enabling Knowledge Creation: How to Unlock the Mystery of Tacit Knowledge and Release the Power of Innovation.* Oxford, UK: Oxford University Press.

Wong, K. Y., & Aspinwall, E. (2005). An empirical study of the important factors for knowledge-management adoption in the SME sector. *Journal of Knowledge Management, 9*(3), 64–82. doi:10.1108/13673270510602773

Zhu, Z. (2004). Knowledge management: Towards a universal concept or cross-cultural contexts? *Knowledge Management Research & Practice, 2*(2), 67–79. doi:10.1057/palgrave.kmrp.8500032

Chapter 8
Maximize Collaboration Using Topic Maps–Based Ontology

Myongho Yi
Texas Woman's University, USA

ABSTRACT

Enhanced information organization is more critical than ever in the digital world where ill-structured information is increasing because of the rapid growth of intranets, the Internet, and user-created content. This chapter discusses limitations of current information organization approaches in the digital age and incorporating ontology into information organizations, thus enhancing collaboration possibilities. This chapter compares the two ontology languages, RDF and Topic Maps, addresses the selection guidelines between the two ontology languages, and then presents user performance using a Topic Maps-based ontology.

INTRODUCTION

Through both voluntary and enforced means, massive and varied types of information have been created and used in the digital space. Web 2.0 innovations allow people to be more productive than ever before. According to a study by Miniwatts Marketing Group (2008), the Internet usage growth between 2000-2008 was 305%. If we can effectively search and reuse or share this massive quantity of information, we can save our resources to reinvent wheels. However, the problem lies with searching.

The enormous amount of information available on the Internet is mainly searched using search engines; however, search engines often return irrelevant and lengthy information. In order to find relevant information, users evaluate a lengthy list of irrelevant results, often resulting in information anxiety (Wurman, 1989) and cognitive overload. Cognitive overload occurs when users feel the burden of having to make decisions as to which links to follow and which to abandon (Conklin, 1987).

Even though users spend their resources to filter massive amount of irrelevant information, they agree that collaboration is inevitable in the digital space.

DOI: 10.4018/978-1-60566-727-0.ch008

Due to the main activities of collaboration, reusing and sharing digital resources over the World Wide Web, effective information retrieval must be an imperative part of collaboration.

As an effort to improve information retrieval, researchers have endeavored to find more efficient information organization methods. Their efforts can be summarized into three major categories of methods: term lists, classification/categorization, and relationship groups (Zeng, 2005). With the realization that these three groups of information organization methods did not significantly improve information retrieval (Smeaton & Berrut, 1996; Voorhees, 1994), a few newer information organization methods that focus more on relationships among the information units have been recently studied.

One noticeable method is the Semantic Web. The Semantic Web emerged as a dynamic web for sharing data on the current static web in 1998 (Berners-Lee, 1998). The Semantic Web Architecture was released in 2000; however, there is little penetration into current web and information systems. There are criticisms (Ian Horrocks, Bijan Parsia, Peter Patel-Schneider, & Hendler, 2005; Patel-Schneider, 2005) of the Semantic Web, and those problems will be examined in this chapter.

This chapter introduces an alternative data model to cope with some criticisms of the current Semantic Web Architecture and presents a study that explored the alternative data model to measure user performance.

This chapter is organized as follows: In Section 2.1, we address criticisms of two Semantic Web Architectures and describe the two data models. In Section 2.2, we discuss the differences between the two data models. In Section 2.3 we provide guidelines for choosing appropriate data models. Section 2.4 presents user performance using a Topic Maps-based ontology system; Section 2.5 concludes with future directions in the context of collaboration.

TWO SEMANTIC WEB ARCHITECTURES AND TWO DATA MODELS

Problems of the First Semantic Web Architecture

According to Patel-Schneider (2005), the current architecture (See the left-hand side of Figure 1) for the Semantic Web has problems when expressive Semantic Web languages such as RDF are integrated. The Resource Description Framework (RDF) is a language for representing information about resources in the World Wide Web. World Wide Web Consortium supports RDF; however, RDF is not suitable for the Semantic Web (Patel-Schneider, 2005). Patel-Schneider criticizes that RDF is not sufficient to encode complex syntactic information in triple form.

Due to the limitations of RDF and first-order logic, ontology engineers and domain experts are concerned about the difference between users and domain experts. There is a similar issue between users and indexers. When an indexer chooses a term that a user does not utilize, the user has a hard time finding relevant resources.

The burden of knowing what could link to what information should be removed from both domain experts and users (Holm, 2001). The system must present and process the information without requiring it know the complicate and non-agreed relationships between the data. Instead, the system can show built-in relationships to users and let them navigate and decide the relevance of information. Topic Maps (TM) explicitly show the structure and relationships among digital resources.

In order to resolve the issue of RDF triple for the current Semantic Web Architecture, different data models such as Topic Maps can be used. Topic Maps do not have triple issues or rules issues. Users can see explicit relationships among resources. Recent change of the first Semantic Web Architecture (the right-hand side of Figure

Figure 1. Initial and new Semantic Web architectures

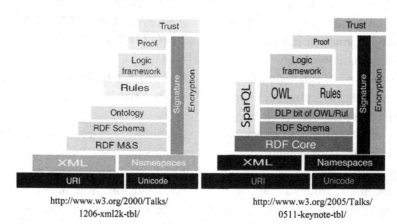

http://www.w3.org/2000/Talks/
1206-xml2k-tbl/

http://www.w3.org/2005/Talks/
0511-keynote-tbl/

1) may be achieved using Topic Maps.

Two Data Models; RDF and Topic Maps

With the support from the World Wide Web Consortium, Resource Description Framework (RDF) and the Web Ontology Language (OWL) have been used to implement ontology-based information systems. Unfortunately, RDF is simply not adequate in the Semantic Web architecture. In other words, RDF is not suitable as a basis for both the syntax and semantics of the Semantic Web (Patel-Schneider, 2005). The necessity of expressive Semantic Web languages is demanding (Patel-Schneider, 2005). Even though there are two ontology languages, RDF and Topic Maps (TM), most Semantic Web Architecture-related researchers have focused on RDF. In addition, there is a lack of guidelines to aide in choosing between TM and RDF.

THREE DIFFERENT PERSPECTIVES ON TOPIC MAPS AND RDF

The goal of Topic Maps and RDF is similar, and some efforts to make these two data models interoperable have also been conducted. The World

Wide Web Consortium (W3C) and ISO have set up a task force to make these two standards interoperable. The Semantic Web Best Practices and Deployment (SWBPD) Working Group supports the RDF/Topic Map Interoperability Task Force (RDFTM) to help users who want to combine data from W3C RDF/OWL and ISO topic maps. However, there are some differences when it comes to choosing the right data models.

The topics, associations, and occurrences that comprise Topic Maps allow users to describe ontologies. Each data element in a Topic Map is called a topic. Any term in a thesaurus can be seen as a topic in Topic Maps. Each topic can be given multiple names, and it is not necessary to distinguish between topics with the same names. This means that the topic Tim Berners-Lee can be entered as "Tim BL," "TBL," or the "Inventor of World Wide Web," resulting in the same information, thus solving the synonym problem (Pepper, 2002a, 2002b) This parallel is an equivalence relationship in a thesaurus (UF and USE). Associations express relationships between topics, e.g. "Tim Berners-Lee" made "http://www.w3.org/RDF." Associations are inherently multidirectional. The statement Tim Berners-Lee made http://www.w3.org/RDF automatically implies the statement http://www.w3.org/RDF was made by Tim Berners-Lee (see Table 1). Occurrences

Table 1. Data model in topic maps

Statement: The author of http://www.w3.org/RDF is Tim Berners-Lee		
Topic	Association	Topic/Type
Tim Berners-Lee	Creates	http://www.w3.org/RDF

show where information about a topic can be found (similar to an index). Occurrences can also have types, such as user-created content (UCC), podcasts, wikis, music videos, blogs, tutorials, etc. about http://www.w3.org/RDF.

Topic Maps and RDF are two available data models in the Semantic Web. As illustrated in Table 2, Topic Maps and RDF are different from user, information, and system perspectives.

Both Topic Maps and RDF use URI as an identifier. When systems use the same URI to refer to different resources, it creates confusion. For example, system A uses http://www.ibm.com/company to refer to IBM's home page, while system B uses the same URI to refer to IBM. When these two systems try to exchange data, they cannot because of their different usages of the same URI (Pepper & Schwab, 2003). While RDF does not have a mechanism to cope with this confusion, Topic Maps provide a subject identifier and subject indicator to resolve this confusion. Users cannot

rely on names because of synonym, homonym, and multiple language problems. To resolve these issues, users need to use identifiers that are clear both to humans and machines. A subject identifier is an URI used by a machine to identify a subject, and a subject indicator is information used by humans to identify a subject. The topic "apple" can be identified by a machine using http://psi.fruit.org/#apple. A subject indicator about "apple" can be used for a human to identify it. Both subject identifier and indicator refer to the same subject in the real world.

Topic Maps provide rich representations of a topic by using three different kinds of topic characteristics: topics, associations, and occurrences. RDF has only one way to make assertions about things: triple (subject, predicate, object), and triplet notation is not expressive enough (Schaffert, 2001).

One of the main differences between Topic Maps and RDF is the structure of the representation

Table 2. Differences between topic maps and RDF

		Topic Maps	RDF
User		Search and Browse based on explicitly shown semantic relationships	Search based on implicit semantic relationships
Information	Thing	Subject	Resource
	Symbol	Topic	Node
	Structure	Topic, Association, Occurrence	Subject, Predicate, Object
System	Syntaxes	XTM, HyTM, LTM	RDF/XML,N3
	Data Models	Topic Maps	RDF
	Constraints	TMCL	RDF Schema, DAML+OIL, OWL

Note: XTM (XML Topic Maps), HyTM (HyTime Topic Maps), LTM (Linear Topic Map Notation), N3 (Notation 3)

Figure 2. Topic maps-based ontology modeling

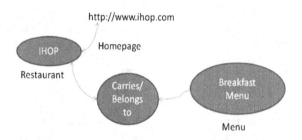

(Garshol, 2002). Garshol asserts that RDF only relates one thing to another, while Topic Maps can relate any number of things. In Topic Maps, users can discern between the relationships that are represented which makes it easier to build complex relationships. Figure 2 and Figure 3 illustrate the different structures of the representation in Topic Maps and RDF.

MIGRATION SELECTION GUIDELINES

Topic Maps and RDF have many similarities. They both have data models and their syntaxes are based on XML. Topic Maps are subject-centric whereas RDF is resource-centric (Pepper, 2002b). In other words, Topic Maps mainly focus on the subjects

that the information is "about"; whereas RDF defines information resources and attaches a metadata structure to them. The Library of Congress Subject Headings (LCSH) in the domain of library sciences are an example of a subject language that is used for creating Topic Maps (Pepper, 2002b). The Anglo-American Cataloguing Rules (AACR) is an example of a document language used for creating RDF (Pepper, 2002b).

One of the important guidelines to consider when choosing between Topic Maps and RDF is whether the subjects are addressable or non-addressable. The subject of every assertion in an RDF model is a resource, identified by a URI. The subject of every assertion in a Topic Map is a topic, representing a subject, which may be addressable or non-addressable (Pepper, 2002b). Addressable subjects are identified by their URIs (as in RDF); non-addressable subjects are identified by the URIs of one or more subject indicators. This important distinction is not present in RDF.

In RDF, assertions have a direction (Garshol, 2002). The direction of the statement "John ordered the Belgian Waffles—ordered (John, the Belgian Waffles)" (1) is different from the direction of the statement "The Belgian Waffles ordered John—ordered (The Belgian Waffles, John)" (2), which in turn is different from "The Belgian

Figure 3. RDF-based ontology modeling

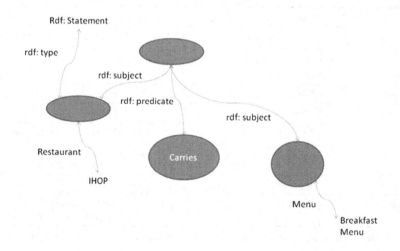

Waffles were ordered by John—was-ordered-by (the Belgian Waffles, John)" (3). This leads to the tendency in RDF to create redundant, inverse relationships (of which (1) and (3) are examples). Yet, the ability (provided by DAML-OIL) to state explicitly that "ordered" and "was-ordered-by" are inverse relationships does not completely solve the redundancy problem. In Topic Maps, it is not possible to assert that "John ordered the Belgian Waffles" without also asserting that "The Belgian Waffles were ordered by John"; they are one and the same association (Pepper, 2002b).

This additional expressivity is made possible by the notion of association roles, which make clear the kind of role played by each participant in a relationship. The association role can illustrate more than binary relationships (Pepper, 2002b). In RDF, assertions are always binary. An RDF statement, consisting of a subject, a predicate, and an object, expresses a relationship between subject and object, for example, "John ordered the Belgian Waffles—ordered (John, the Belgian Waffles)." In Topic Maps, assertions are n-ary (Pepper, 2002b). An association may have any number of roles and can thus represent more complex relationships (Pepper, 2002b), for example, "John ordered the Belgian Waffles with maple syrup—ordered (John, the Belgian Waffles, maple syrup)." Understanding the differences between Topic Maps and RDF allows information professionals to choose either Topic Maps or RDF for their metadata migration. Specifically, if data has more than binary relationships, Topic Maps will be a better choice to migrate data.

USER PERFORMANCE USING TOPIC MAPS-BASED ONTOLOGY INFORMATION RETRIEVAL SYSTEM

The recent study by Yi (2008b) shows user performance using a Topic Maps-based ontology information retrieval system. Forty subjects participated in a task-based evaluation where two dependent variables, recall and search time, were measured. The findings of this study show that a Topic Maps-based ontology information retrieval (TMIR) system has a significant effect on both recall and search time, compared to a thesaurus-based information retrieval (TIR) system.

The experiment purposely examined associative relationships between resources belonging to different hierarchies that are explicitly provided and could be recognized as better candidates for improved recall and shorter search time. This study demonstrates that relationship-based query searches using this TMIR system resulted in improved recall and shorter search times than fact-based query searches. The results of this study demonstrate the possibility of Topic Maps-based ontology to enhance information retrieval system performance through better support for associative relationships between resources belonging to different hierarchies by providing explicit relationships among resources.

Significant difference in recall and search time was found between the experimental group performing fact-based queries and the control group performing fact-based queries. As illustrated in Figure 4, the average recall percentage for the experimental group performing fact-based queries was 83%, and the average recall percentage in the control group performing fact-based queries was 85%. The average search time for the experimental group performing fact-based queries was 91 seconds, and the average search time for the control group performing fact-based queries was 86 seconds (See Figure 5).

One of the most significant findings of this study was the substantial difference in search time and recall between the performance of relationship-based queries using a TMIR and the performance of relationship-based queries using a TIR system. There was a significant mean difference in recall and search time between the experimental group performing relationship-based queries and the control group performing relationship-based queries. As illustrated in Figure 6, the average

Figure 4. Recall for fact-based query (Yi, 2008a)

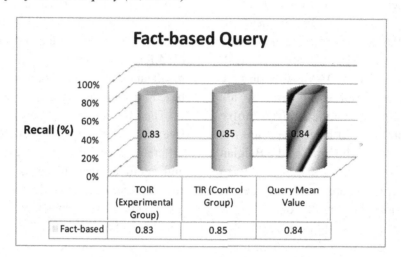

recall percentage for the experimental group performing relationship-based queries was 76%, and the average recall percentage for the control group performing relationship-based queries was 43%. The average search time for the experimental group performing relationship-based queries was 89 seconds, and the average search time for the control group performing relationship-based queries was 191 seconds (See Figure 7).

An unanticipated result was the short amount of time taken to conduct fact-based queries in the control group where the thesaurus-based informa-

tion retrieval system was in use (See Figure 8). A possible reason for this result is that the subjects were more familiar with this search manner and therefore did not need any supplementary time to gain knowledge of the search method or the system. In contrast, the nature of the TOIR system required additional time for users to become familiar with the system.

Figure 5. Search Time for fact-based query (Yi, 2008a)

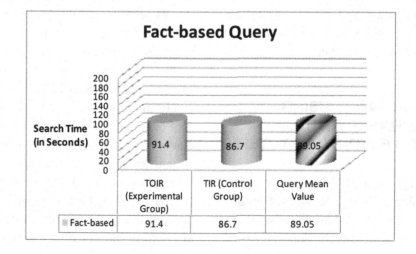

Figure 6. Recall for relationship-based query (Yi, 2008a)

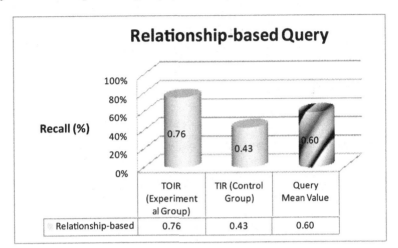

CONCLUSION AND FUTURE RESEARCH DIRECTIONS

This chapter explored critical components, ontology, of the current Semantic Web Architecture. Topic Maps and RDF, ontology languages or data models, have similar goals; however, each has unique advantages. This chapter addresses the issues of the current Semantic Web Architecture, three differences between RDF and Topic Maps, and selection guidelines between two data models. This chapter also presents a study which measures user performance using a Topic Maps-based ontology information retrieval system. Although the results of user performance using Topic Maps have improved, more research is needed in the following areas to maximize the collaboration. First, it will be necessary to conduct a user study to evaluate different aspects of Topic Maps, such as internal and external occurrences. Second, further research should be directed at migration of existing metadata. Sufficient metadata already exists to further collaboration in libraries and information agencies.

Figure 7. Search time for relationship-based query (Yi, 2008a)

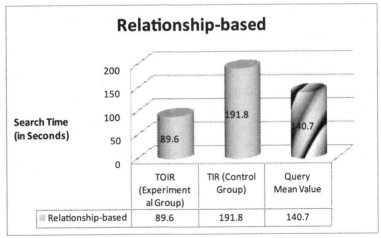

Figure 8. Search time for fact-based query (Yi, 2008a)

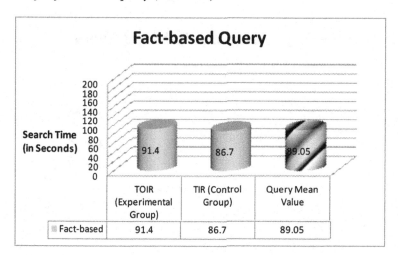

Many standards and technologies are necessary to enhance collaboration in the digital age. Social tagging is an interesting research agenda. Tagging is an activity of individual effort to label resources. Building relationships among user-created tagging and retrieval of those tags might be a very interesting research direction. Ontology merging is another research area that needs to be explored. For a decade, many ontologies have been created but the research on integration or sharing ontology has received little attention. Trust is an imperative factor for information reuse and sharing. When a user collaborates with others, trust plays a significant role. Without trust in each other, there is no open collaboration among users. Both technical and non-technical aspects of security must be considered to provide trust for collaboration. A good example of a technical approach for collaboration is a Public Key Infrastructure (PKI). One of the PKI features is non-repudiation, and this feature allows users to ensure who edits and is responsible for digital resources. Without having the mechanism that verifies who sends/receives/modifies information resources, collaboration is discouraged.

REFERENCES

Berners-Lee, T. (1998). *Semantic Web Road map*, January 14, 2004. Retrieved from http://www.w3.org/DesignIssues/Semantic.html

Conklin, J. (1987). Hypertext: An Introduction and Survey. *IEEE Computer, 20*(9), 17–41.

Cutter, C. A. (1875). *Rules for a printed dictionary catalogue*. Washington, DC: Government Printing Office.

Garshol, L. (2002). *Topic maps, RDF, DAML, OIL*. Retrieved March 14, 2007, from http://www.ontopia.net/topicmaps/materials/tmrdfoildaml.html

Holm, J. (2001). *Real World Applications of Topic Maps*. Paper presented at the XML 2001, Florida, USA.

Horrocks, I., Parsia, B., Patel-Schneider, P., & Hendler, J. (2005). Semantic Web Architecture: Stack or Two Towers? In F. Fages & S. Soliman (Eds.), *Principles and Practice of Semantic Web Reasoning* (pp. 37-41). Dagstuhl Castle, Germany: Springer.

Miniwatts Marketing Group. (2008). *World Internet Users and Population Stats*. Retrieved August 1, 2008, from http://www.internetworldstats.com/stats.htm

Patel-Schneider, P. F. (2005). A Revised Architecture for Semantic Web Reasoning. In F. Fages & S. Soliman (Eds.), *Principles and Practice of Semantic Web Reasoning* (pp. 32-36). Dagstuhl Castle, Germany: Springer.

Pepper, S. (2002a). *The TAO of Topic Maps*. Retrieved January 12, 2006, from http://www.ontopia.net/topicmaps/materials/tao.html

Pepper, S. (2002b). *Ten Theses on Topic Maps and RDF*. Retrieved March 23, 2007, from http://www.ontopia.net/topicmaps/materials/rdf.html

Pepper, S., & Schwab, S. (2003). *Curing the Web's Identity Crisis*. Retrieved November 23, 2004, from http://www.ontopia.net/topicmaps/materials/identitycrisis.html#Pepper2003

Schaffert, S. (2001). *RDF and RDF Schema: An Overview*. Retrieved October 3, 2006, from http://www.schaffert.eu/download/slides/rdf_overview.pdf

Smeaton, A. F., & Berrut, C. (1996). *Thresholding postings lists, query expansion by word-word distances and POS tagging of Spanish text*. Paper presented at the fourth text retrieval conferences, Gaithersburg, MD.

Voorhees, E. M. (1994). *Query expansion using lexical-semantic relations*. Paper presented at the 17th ACM SIGIR conference on research and development in information retrieval.

Wurman, R. S. (1989). *Information Anxiety*. New York: Doubleday.

Yi, M. (2008a). Information organization and retrieval using a topic maps-based ontology: Results of a task-based evaluation. *Journal of the American Society for Information Science and Technology, 59*(12), 1898–1911. doi:10.1002/asi.20899

Yi, M. (2008b). *Topic Maps-based Ontology and Semantic Web - Ontology-Driven Information Retrieval System*. Saarbrücken, Germany: VDM Verlag.

Zeng, M. L. (2005). Using software to teach thesaurus development and indexing in graduate programs of LIS and IAKM. *Bulletin of the American Society for Information Science and Technology*, (pp. 11-13).

Chapter 9

Collaborative Retrieval Systems
Reusable Information Quests

Ying Sun
SUNY at Buffalo, USA

ABSTRACT

Collaborative search generally uses previously collected search sessions as a resource to help future users to improve their searching by query modification. The recommendation or automatic extension of the query is generally based on the content of the old sessions, or purely the sequence/order of queries/ texts in a session, or a combination. However, users with the same expressed query may need different information. The difference may not be topic related. This chapter proposes to enrich the context of query representation to incorporate non-topical properties of user information needs, which the authors believe will improve the results of collaborative search.

INTRODUCTION: HOW MANY QUESTS ARE THERE?

In support of collaboration among individuals whose work involves exploration of data networks (such as the World Wide Web, or sets of intelligence information, or more detailed databases of scientific information), some researchers are examining a problem that I will call "quest reuse". The central idea is that a person doing such research is on a quest that has specific goals. Those goals are reflected in the search moves and value judgments made

by the investigator. This chapter will research the problem of storing in compact form those moves and judgments so that later investigators may exploit them to speed and increase the effectiveness of their own research.

Anyone who puts down a task, and resumes it some time later makes use of the associating powers of the brain, and of various support systems, to get the human mind back in context. The same individual, even when working with the same set of data, might have several possible contexts, and, indeed might have several contexts simultaneously latent in mind while scanning or browsing. We know that the human mind is superb at this scanning and

DOI: 10.4018/978-1-60566-727-0.ch009

associating activity, and do not envision taking the mind out of the loop. We are looking for ways to increase the power and the ease of that mental work. People often say that there are "innumerable contexts." We know that the exabytes of data flow are quite numerable -- there are simply too many of them. But the number of contexts is some reasonably finite multiple of the number of people that a system would support. In the whole world this is perhaps thousands of billions. Surely many of them are so similar that sharing and reuse would be really worth aiming for.

In an agency or corporate context, there are perhaps thousands of searchers who might form a pool, and they may each have no more than a few hundred contexts that would be of interest to us. These contexts would have enormous overlap. All the people tracking developments in Iran's nuclear program have only a few contexts: scientific; political; warning analysis; background analysis, etc. The key idea of "Quest Reuse" (QR) is to store and reuse pools of "quest profiles" that are effectively labeled by context, retrievable by others with closely related contexts, and that contain parameter settings which help a support system (a hypothesis testing tool, a search engine, a report generator, etc.) to refine, disambiguate and prioritize what it seeks and what it finds. To give the familiar trivial example, the word "bank" in the aviation context loads more heavily on "change direction" than it does on "financial institution".

The chapter will address researches at finding out how to represent and store these profiles, and how to retrieve them by *similarity* rather than simply by *name*. That is, QR is valuable if I can know that Larry often works on the same problems as I do, and I tell the machine 'Please load context "Larry 23".' But it is priceless if, by the very actions I take, the system can recognize that I would benefit from the context "Abigail 19", when I have never heard of Abigail. In a sense this is the familiar theme of "finding experts". But the experts are to be labeled automatically by

analysis of what they look for, what they study hard, and what they mark as "worth keeping" [a crucial part of the model], as well as "what they say they are up to". We believe this is a worth developing area, so that the many minds working on crucial problems can be working more effectively together, communicating through the perfect memories of the not-very-smart systems that they use.

This same problem, in the specific application to counterterrorism intelligence, is known as "shoebox sharing." The name is a holdover from the days when an analyst would maintain a shoebox containing 3x5 cards or 5x8 cards summarizing interesting bits of information that he or she found during research. Now that such information is stored on the computer, it could in principle be available to other analysts, but it would be simply a waste of their time unless they can make targeted forays into the material to retrieve that which is most relevant to their own present quests.

BACKGROUND

In any model of information retrieval, an information retrieval process is divided into three basic parts: collections of information objects, users, and searching techniques. Developments in information technology, especially the personal computer and the Internet, have brought significant changes to the user and the information collection components. However, the techniques do not change much of the fundamental mechanism that represents and matches user needs and information objects much. With the successful application of information retrieval techniques in web searching since early 90's, the searching techniques have improved greatly, prompted by the huge business interest of searching market. However, the advances were mainly focused on developing ways of improving existing indexing and ranking techniques. For example, PageRank, the successful Google technology, uses the vast link structure of the Web as a valuable source of ranking web pages.

The user group of current information retrieval systems has been exploding and becoming more and more varied. It is much easier for any person to access a huge amount of information from various sources. The vast number of users is not a challenge for searching systems with the development of fast processor and cheap storage space. However, as a result of large number of non-expert searchers, the poor quality of queries remains a major challenge for most retrieval systems. Though baring the quality problem, the vast size of accumulated query pool, provides possible candidate contexts, which, while properly indexed, can be used to facilitate later searches.

The vague query problem is not new. It has been proved by many researches that most web queries are short—2 to 3 terms, and most search sessions include little query modification and are generally 2-3 queries in length (Croft and Thompson, 1987; Spink, 1997). As summarized by Barouni-Ebrahimi and Ghorbani (2008), researchers work in three directions to help to improve query quality:

(1) Query Recommendation will provide a list of old queries (or search sessions) that are ranked by their similarities to the new submitted query (Raghavan and Sever 1995; Kantor, et al., 1999; Glance, 2001; Baeza-Yates, Hurtado, and Mendoza, 2004; Zhang and Nasraoui, 2006). Generally, an old query and corresponding information with it (result pages, followed links, etc.) are used to calculate the similarities between the submitted query and the saved search sessions. In other words, the similarity is based on the text of the query and the retrieved and/or clicked pages.

(2) Query expansion is a method to add some suggested terms or phrases to a new submitted query to solve the short query problem.

The suggested terms may come from previous search sessions' top ranked documents (Fitzpatrick and Dent, 1997), or from previous users' modification of their queries (Cui et al., 2002), or from a knowledge base (Liu and Chu, 2007).

(3) Query Completion refers to the method that while a user is typing a query, the system will automatically suggest some frequent words for the last incomplete word in the query. Google's suggestion service is an example of query completion. White and Marchionini (2007) prove the importance of such function.

All three mechanisms need a similarity measure to link a new query with saved query session. The similarity measure can be divided into two groups: the traditional IR bag-of word measure, which looks at the term appearance and frequency in the saved queries and retrieved/clicked results; and the behavior based measure, which uses the sequence of previous searches as a indicator to identify the importance of some terms or queries. A query context, or Quest, as we proposed, should go beyond topicality of the old queries and documents.

The third part of a standard information retrieval model is information collection. As we have discussed above, part of the collection (retrieved/clicked previously) is an important source in representing a Quest. With the development of free Web, especially the recent development of social networks, the formats and genres of information have been enriched considerably. Both business and end users have noticed the importance of this new type of information. As a result, the new challenge to IR systems is not only about how to represent this new collection, but also to verify the possibility of using this user-contributed information to enrich the Quest representation, and how.

Figure 1. Text properties

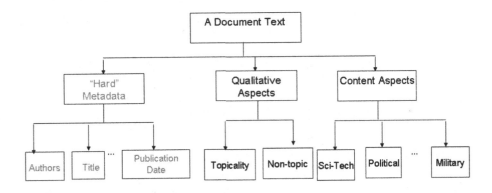

QUEST REPRESENTATION

What to Represent

As shown in Figure 1, a collection of texts can be represented in many ways in an information system. Generally these ways include metadata, which are "externally known" properties of texts, and the topic or content of texts. In current systems, topical relevance is basically the only text property that is used to retrieve and rank texts. However, the differences between texts are not only topical. Studies of users' information need or relevance judgments (Barry 1994; Bruce 1994; Saracevic 1975, 1996; Vickery, et al 1987) have shown that users distinguish between texts on the same topic, and such non-topical differences are also crucial to the selection of relevant texts. For example, considering a query about the "North Korea Nuclear weapons problem", different users will require texts that assume different levels of expertise, depending on the users' backgrounds. Many basic introductory texts should not be delivered to an intelligence analyst who tracks information about this problem daily. Meanwhile, depending on the tasks at hand, the analyst may require objective texts that represent the latest news about the issue, or subjective texts that contain the opinions about the problem.

We call these properties of text, such as level of difficulty, reliability of the sources of information, authoritativeness of content, etc., **Qualitative Aspects (QAs)** for two reasons. First, these properties are usually associated with the "quality" of a text. Second, these properties do not have generally accepted quantitative methods by which to represent them, yet. (Ng, et al, 2003, Tang, et al, 2003)

Content aspects are other dimensions by which texts about same topics can be differentiated. We use the concept of Content Aspects (CAs) to refer to some broad perspectives in the texts of the problem. To give an immediate example, a discussion of "Syrian military capability" might appear in an article that is primarily concerned with technology issues, primarily concerned simply with comparison of military forces, or primarily concerned with an assessment of an overall political situation. Depending on the nature of an analyst's request the distinction between these three might, or might not, be of great importance in deciding which quests should be reused.

We propose a collaborative search system (Figure 2) taking the existing framework of AntWorld system, an example of query recommendation system). In AntWorld, when a new user of the system, represented as "You" in the diagram, begins a quest, you examine documents

Figure 2. Collaborative search system

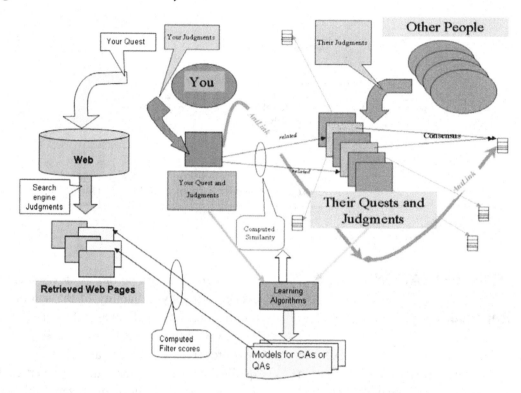

and make your judgments about them. The system accumulates these into a description of your quest and your judgments, and adaptively develops a model by which it computes similarity between your quest and stored profiles of quests that have been conducted earlier by other people. When it identifies similar quests, it then looks at materials that had been found useful by the owners of those quests, and computes some kind of consensus, judgment or ranking. The system then provides an "Ant-link" which carries you directly from your present search point to those materials that had been judged relevant by the other users. Different from other recommendation systems, which use implicit indicators of relevance (topic similarity of old search sessions), AntWorld needs users' active contribution about the relevance of retrieved results, which may put extra requirement on the user side.

However, we don't believe that should be a concern based on two observations. First, it will

not be a problem in any system targeting an intranet environment. In such situation, searching and judging is part of the information seekers job. Second, we believe that with the development of social networks, the new generation of web users may be more willing to contribute.

Add to the old model of AntWorld is the learning algorithms. These learning algorithms work with your quest and judgments, and your responses to suggestions made. These are integrated with the present models of content aspects and quality aspects, to improve the rule by which stored quests are matched to your present quest. This will involve looking at the retrieved web pages from your quest in much more sophisticated ways than was done in the AntWorld System (which simply used term frequencies). Details are discussed below.

The key is that three things will change: we will move to a larger class of representation methods; we will consider a large range of matching methods and, most significantly, we will work with state of the art learning methods to optimize the matching of a present quest to one or more of the existing quests.

How to Represent Quests

Bag of Words

Even though many researchers have pointed out dimensions other than the topic in users' information needs, a general, task-independent representation of text contents still is the primary representation in all information retrieval systems. This representation is based on the occurrence and/or frequency of words, phrases. The basic assumption is that the presence or absence of words in a text is an indication of topic.

Frames

We use concept of frames as described by the builders of the HITIQA system (Small teal. 2004). A frame is an event or relation expressed in a piece of text. Entities involved in the event or relation make up the frame's attributes, such as location, person, organization, date, etc. The HITIQA system uses BBN's Identifinder to extract attributes from text passages. The central verb or noun phrase of the passage is put in the TOPIC attribute of the frame, which indicates the event or relation, such as accident, trade, etc. Some extension of the basic frame concept generates specialized typed frames. For example a *transfer* frame must have three attributes; TO, FROM and OBJECT.

In other words, a frame is a partially structured representation of text. It gives a deeper understanding of a text than what can be expressed by a bag of words, by making use of the semantic functions of words.

Qualitative Aspects (QAs)

Since qualitative aspects are, in principle, content-independent, content-independent features should be used to represent them. Luckily, a document is more than a bag of words. Some natural language features are promising candidates.

Using language features to differentiate documents on dimensions other than topic has long been the focus in computational stylistic studies. The assumption of stylistics research is that the style of any text implies the choice of words and the choices of arrangement and punctuation of words that are actually used in a document. In turn, identifying the "style markers" (words and patterns) supports categorizing or identifying documents with particular styles. Various types of computable linguistic features have been proposed as such markers.

In an early review of the analysis of literary style, Holmes (1985) lists a number of possible features that can be used in analysis of authorship. These include:

- Word-length: frequency, distributions
- Syllables: average syllables per word, distribution of syllables per word
- Sentence-length
- Distribution of parts of speech
- Function words

According to Rudman, over 1,000 linguistic features have been proposed (Rudman, 1997). Tweedie et al. also list a variety of linguistic features that can be used as style markers (Tweedie et al, 1998). Chaski's work includes word length, vocabulary richness, frequency of function words, punctuation marks etc as common "style markers" (Chaski, 2001). Argamon has applied such features to identify the sex of authors, and has compiled a very extensive classification of stylistic features. (Argamon, 2003).

The variety of features described above indicates that there is some success but there is no consensus on which features are best. The separation of non-topical document qualitative aspects from topicality is essentially similar to the separation of "style" and content in the context of computational stylistic studies. Therefore stylistic studies form a reasonable starting point to identify possible qualitative aspects indicators from the sets of "style markers". Our work has shown that some of the "style markers" are promising indicators of document qualitative aspects (Sun, Dissertation, Fall 2005).

As mentioned above, we will use GATE to obtain the Part Of Speech frequencies. We will also use GATE's extensible Gazetteer function to count the frequencies of lists of words (entities and declarative words). GATE itself has some default entity lists, such as *person, location, date*, etc. We also can create our own expanded entity lists. We will use WordNet to find all hypernyms of all words in one GATE default list. Then we combine the two sets of words together and remove duplicates to form our expended entity list. WordNet is a lexical reference system that organizes English nouns, verbs, adjectives, and adverbs into synonym sets (Fellbaum 1998). It is developed and maintained by the Cognitive Science Laboratory at Princeton University.

We will also use WordNet to obtain various declarative word lists. The general method, used in our earlier work, starts from a list created by a human expert, who examines pieces of texts which are saved as evidence in support of user judgments about qualitative or content aspects. We call these "Revealed Indicators", represented as a list R. We then use WordNet to get all ancestors of the words in the original list. Those words that appear in both the original list and the ancestor list form a list called R^+. Those words that show up only in the ancestor list, and not in the original list form a list called R^-.

For other features, we use Perl Scripts to calculate the location and frequency of the features. This work will build on an extensive library of scripts developed in the HITIQA project, over the past three years (Ng, et al, 2003; Bai, et al, 2004; Rittman, et al 2004).

Content Aspects (CAs)

Content aspects are different from document topics. However their relationships with documents contents are not quite as "orthogonal" as are qualitative aspects. In the proposed research we will build on techniques developed in the HITIQA project.

We propose to identify indicators from four sources: **Naïve Word Lists.** We are presently creating lists of words for each of several content aspects (military, scientific-technical, biographical, etc.). The words in each list must satisfy the condition that they represent the corresponding content aspect and discriminate it from other aspects. **Named Identities.** The assumption is that the frequencies of some types of named identities may vary a lot among different aspects. **Adjective Classes.** In our previous work, we have accumulated several classes of adjectives. The categories of these classes are related with content aspects. **Style Markers.** A particular content aspect may be associated with a particular style. For example, a text with science-technology perspective is more likely to be objective. We propose that some style markers may be good indicators of CAs. In all of this we will build on knowledge gained in the work with the HITIQA system.

HOW TO ASSESS SIMILARITY

The vector space model is used when documents are represented as a bag of words. In the vector space model, each document in the collection is represented as a vector with components labeled by terms. Each term in the vector has its own weight to reflect how important it is in describing the content of the document. If the collection contains T index terms, each document will be a T-dimensional vector. The element $w_{i,j}$ in the vector is the weight of term i in document j. If there are D documents in the collection, a $T \times D$ term-by-document matrix will represent the whole collection. The columns of this matrix are vectors representing the documents, in terms of their composition by terms. Every document's position in the term-document space represents the content of the document.

In information retrieval systems, geometric relationships between document vectors are used to calculate the similarities of document vectors in content. The most commonly used measure of similarity is the cosine of the angle between the two document vectors.

When a user inputs a query, the query is treated just like another document and is represented as a vector too. So the similarity between the query and any document can be calculated the same way as between two documents. Documents will be ranked according to their similarity to the query.

We propose to represent QAs and CAs by several groups of linguistic features. In contrast to the concept of bag of word representation of document topic, each linguistic feature itself may not represent a dimension in the space of QAs or CAs. How to calculate the similarity of two documents on QA or CA will depend on the models learned.

For a linear model, each QA must be reduced to a number. The angle between two documents' QA scores can be used as similarity measure.

For rule-based models, each document will be classified into a definite group of QA or CA. The similarity assessment problem then turns into binary classification problem.

MACHINE LEARNING ISSUES

Machine learning is a key component to quest presentation and similarity measurement. The first machine learning issue is classification of quests based on their QAs or CAs. A growing number of statistical classification and machine learning techniques have been applied to text categorization. Most of these applications are based on document content. Our work has proved that multiple learning methods can be used to classify documents based on their QA or CA features.

Classification is the process of trying to predict the category for unknown data, given existing classified data. Typically the data set is divided into a training data set and a test data set. Elements of a training data set are described by a set of independent features and a target variable whose value is available. A machine learning algorithm is applied to the training data set iteratively to identify patterns of features in the training data set. This is usually repeated many times until the error is reduced below some threshold. The patterns might include many features in the set or only a few of them. The produced pattern must be represented in some type of model, such as a decision tree. Once a pattern is chosen, the test data (unknown to the algorithm) are run through the pattern, and the error rate is recorded. Again, this is usually repeated several times with different test sets, to get an average error rate. With a collection of hand-tagged texts on QAs and CAs, a supervised learning method will build classifiers, and then the resulting models will be evaluated on new test cases.

The second issue of machine learning is that the system must learn how to represent and match users' quests to stored quests. This is similar to the adaptive filtering problem, where incoming messages are represented, typically, by very large vectors, and the underlying assumption is that some connected and "well shaped" subset of these vectors are the ones that should be transmitted for further human review. (This problem is dual to the increasingly common Spam problem.) However, there is a cost associated with verifying that a specific message should indeed have been transmitted. At any moment in time, the sensor module has a "current belief" about which messages should be transmitted. But strictly following this rule precludes any exploration, and is sub-optimal. Indeed, initially, a priori probability that any message should be transmitted is too low to justify transmitting it. Therefore there must be some period of exploratory transmission to establish a rule. Heuristics of the form: "explore until some criterion C is met, and do not explore thereafter" have, with various escape clauses, produced the best performance in the TREC2004 evaluation (CAS 2004). The effect of variation in the learning model itself is given by (Fradkin and Kantor, 2004, 2005). Models that concentrate on the conditional posterior probabilities that a message should be transmitted have been explored by (Elovici, Shapira, Kantor; 2003, 2005).

CONCLUSION

Collaborative search, or social search, has been predicted to be the next big thing on the Internet. Both Yahoo! and Microsoft have released their collaborating search tools. It is easy to see that there are many issues involved in the collaborative searching system design. The focus of the technology development, as well as research, is mainly on the design of interface to facilitate the collaboration of searching. In this chapter we limited our discussion from a different perspective: quest representation and matching. We proposed the idea of construction of a richer query profile (Quest) above and beyond the topicality feature of the user's information need which is currently in common use. Quests will be shared by searchers and will be simply picked up by a future user if the Quest is similar enough to his/her information need context.

To make the proposed idea practical, much research is needed to, first, identify a set of characterizes that are important to be involved in Quest (query profile), we proposed two sets such properties in this chapter based on previous works, a study with current web users, especially social network frequent users will be helpful to update the proposed categories; second, improve the learning models for automatically access information objects against those categories; last, design and conduct evaluation of the impact of the system on the work product of user groups.

REFERENCES

Argamon, S., Koppel, M., Fine, J., & Shimoni, A. R. (2003). Gender, Genre, and Writing Style in Formal Written Texts. *Text*, *23*(3). doi:10.1515/text.2003.014

Bai, B., Ng, K. B., Sun, Y., Kantor, P., & Strzalkowski, T. (2004). The institutional dimension of document quality judgments. *In the Proceedings of the 2004 Annual Meeting of American Society for Information Science and Technology.*

Barouni-Ebrahimi, M., & Ghorbani, A. A. (2008). An interactive search assistant architecture based on intrinsic query stream characteristics. *Computational Intelligence*, *24*(2), 158–190. doi:10.1111/j.1467-8640.2008.00326.x

Barry, C. L. (1994). User-defined relevance criteria: An exploratory study. *Journal of the American Society for Information Science American Society for Information Science*, *45*(3), 149–159. doi:10.1002/(SICI)1097-4571(199404)45:3<149::AID-ASI5>3.0.CO;2-J

Bruce, H. W. (1994). A cognitive view of the situational dynamism of user-centered relevance estimation. *Journal of the American Society for Information Science American Society for Information Science*, *45*(3), 142–148. doi:10.1002/(SICI)1097-4571(199404)45:3<142::AID-ASI4>3.0.CO;2-6

Chaski, C. (2001). Empirical evaluations of language-based Author identification techniques. *Forensic Linguistics* . *The International Journal of Speech Language and the Law*, *8*(1).

De Vel, O., & Nesbitt, S. (1997). A Collaborative Filtering Agent System for Dynamic Virtual Communities on the Web. *Working notes of Learning from Text and the Web, Conference on Automated Learning and Discovery CONALD-98,* Carnegie Mellon University, Pittsburgh, 1998.

Elovici, Y., & Kantor, P. B. (2003). Using the Information Structure Model to Compare Profile-Based Information Filtering Systems. *Information Retrieval, 6*(1), 75–97. doi:10.1023/A:1022952531694

Fellbaum, C. (Ed.). (1998). *WordNet: An Electronic Lexical Database.* Cambridge, MA: The MIT Press.

Fradkin, D., & Kantor, P. B. (2004). A Design Space Approach to Analysis of Information Retrieval Adaptive Filtering Systems. *The 13th ACM Conference on Information and Knowledge Management* (CIKM). November 2004.

Fradkin, D., & Kantor, P. B. (2005). Methods for Learning Classifier Combinations: No Clear Winner. *Proceedings of ACM Symposium on Applied Computing 2005, Information Access and Retrieval Track.*

Holmes, D. (1985). The Analysis of Literary Style – A Review. *Journal of the Royal Statistical Society. Series A (General), 148*(4), 328–341. doi:10.2307/2981893

Kantor, P. B. (1989). Scholars Cross Reference System. In *Annual Research Report of OCLC,* OCLC, Dublin, OH (pp. 26-27).

Kantor, P. B. (1993). The Adaptive Library Network Interface: A Historical Overview and Interim Report. *Library Hi Tech, 11,* 81–92. doi:10.1108/eb047897

Kantor, P. B. Melamed, B., Boros, E., & Menkov, V. (1999). The Information Quest: A Dynamic Model of User's Information Needs. In L. Woods, (Ed.) *Proceedings of the 62nd Annual Meeting of the American Society for Information Science,* (pp. 536-545).

Kantor, P. B., Boros, E., Melamed, B., Meñkov, V., & Shapira, B. (2000). ANTWORLD: Capturing Human Intelligence in the Net. *Communications of the ACM, 43*(8), 112–115. doi:10.1145/345124.345162

Karamuftuoglu, M. (1998). Collaborative information retrieval: Toward a social informatics view of IR interaction. *Journal of the American Society for Information Science and Technology, 49*(12), 1070–1080. doi:10.1002/(SICI)1097-4571(1998)49:12<1070::AID-ASI3>3.0.CO;2-S

Kushner, H., & Pacut, A. (1982). A Simulation Study of Decentralized Detection Problem. *IEEE Trans. On Automatic Control, 27*(5), 1116–1119. doi:10.1109/TAC.1982.1103071

Ng, K. B., Kantor, P., Tang, R., Rittman, R., Small, S., Song, P., & Strzalkowski, T. Sun, Y. & Wacholder, N. (2003). Identification of Effective Predictive Variables for Document Qualities. *Annual Meeting of the American Society for Information Science and Technology,* ASIST2003.

O'Conner, M., & Herlocker, J. (1999). Clustering Items for Collaborative Filtering. In *Proceedings of the ACM SIGIR Workshop on Recommender Systems.*

Pennock, D., Horvitz, E., Lawrence, S. C., & Giles, L. (2000). Collaborative Filtering by Personality Diagnosis: A Hybrid Memory- and Model-Based Approach. *Proceedings of the 16th Conference on Uncertainty in Artificial Intelligence,* UAI 2000.

Rittman, R., Wacholder, N., Kantor, P., Ng, K. B., Strzalkowski, T., & Sun, Y. (2004). Adjectives as indicators of subjectivity in documents. *Proceedings of the 67th Annual Meeting of the American Society for Information Science and Technology*, (pp. 349-359).

Rudman, J. (1997). The state of authorship attribution studies: Some problems and solutions. *Computers and the Humanities, 31*(4), 351–365. doi:10.1023/A:1001018624850

Saracevic, T. (1975). Relevance: A Review of and a framework for the thinking on the notion in information science. *Journal of the American Society for Information Science American Society for Information Science, 26*(6), 321–343. doi:10.1002/asi.4630260604

Saracevic, T. (1996). Relevance reconsidered. Information science: Integration in perspectives. *Proceedings of the Second Conference on Conceptions of Library and Information Science,* Copenhagen, Denmark, (pp. 201-218).

Small, S., et al. (2004). HITIQA: Towards Analytical Question Answering. In *the Proceedings of The 20th International Conference on Computational Linguistics (Coling 2004)*, Geneva, Switzerland, August 2004.

Smyth, B., et al. (2003). I-SPY -- Anonymous, Community-Based Personalization by Collaborative Meta-Search. In *Proceedings of the 23rd SGAI International Conference on Innovative Techniques and Applications of Artificial Intelligence, 2003.*

Smyth, B. (2004). Exploiting Query Repetition and Regularity in an Adaptive Community-Based Web Search Engine . *User Modeling and User-Adapted Interaction, 14*(5), 383–423. doi:10.1007/s11257-004-5270-4

Sun, Y. (2005). *An Investigation of Using Natural Language Features as Indicators for Automatic Document Classification on Non-Topical Properties – through Machine Learning Methods.* Unpublished doctoral dissertation, Rutgers University, New Brunswick, NJ.

Tang, R., Ng, K.B., Strzalkowski, T., & Kantor, P. (2003) Automatically Predicting Information Quality. *HLT/NACCL '03.*

Tweedie, F., & Baayen, R. (1998). How variable may a constant be? Measure of lexical richness in perspective. *Computers and the Humanities, 32*(5), 323–352. doi:10.1023/A:1001749303137

Vickery, A., Brooks, H. M., Robinson, B., & Vickery, B. C. (1987). A Reference and Referral System Using Expert System Techniques. *The Journal of Documentation, 43*, 1–23. doi:10.1108/eb026798

Chapter 10
Automatically Evaluating the Quality of Contents Created by Open Collaborative Knowledge Building

Kwong Bor Ng
Queens College, CUNY, USA

ABSTRACT

Using wikis, with minimum planning, significant projects can be accomplished almost effortlessly by collaborative knowledge building through continuous contributions from caring community members. Since any registered member can change the content of a wiki page at any time, how to enhance the quality of a wiki becomes a pressing issue. This paper reports a pilot study of identifying factors that can enhance the quality of contents built by open collaborative knowledge building. Using stepwise discriminant analysis and logistic regression, several variables were successfully identified that could contribute positively to the high quality of wiki pages. The result was analyzed using Receiver Operating Characteristic (ROC) curves from signal detection theory. The predictor worked remarkably well and was promising, with a high detection rate and a low false-alarm rate. The finding can help programmers and architects of open collaborative knowledge building systems to design and implement mechanisms that will facilitate high quality content creations.

INTRODUCTION: THE QUALITY OF WIKI CONTENT

The first wiki, with the name WikiWikiWeb (also known as WardsWiki, see Figure 1), was invented by Ward Cunningham in 1994 in order to make the exchange of ideas between programmers easier ("WikiWikiWeb History").

WikiWikiWeb was then installed in an Internet domain (i.e., URL: http://c2.com) in 1995. Since it was basically used by a small group of computer programmers, quality control of individual wiki page was not an issue. Until the end of the last century, not too much people know about wikis. Wiki became very popular primarily due to the success of Wikipedia (http://www.wikipedia.org, see also Ebersbach *et al* 2008) which was launched

DOI: 10.4018/978-1-60566-727-0.ch010

Figure 1. The original WikiWikiWeb, the first wiki in the world. Its appearance is not that fancy, but it initiated a wiki revolution

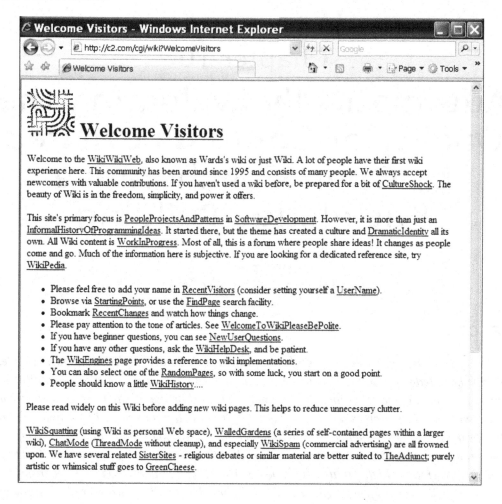

in 2001.

Wiki provides a simple platform for accumulating, sharing and structuring information where community members can contribute freely. Because of the appearance of Wiki, Collaborative Knowledge Building becomes a popular practice for many knowledge-based organizations to deliver documentation, to replace their FAQs, and to offer help-pages to their members, especially for the institutions and organizations who encourage the constitution and maintenance of self-organizing social networks of users (Wasko & Faraj 2005, Lin *et al* 2006, Moore & Serva 2007), and for the companies who have a customer-centric

philosophy (Wagner & Majchrzak 2007).

As a collaborative writing environment, the power of a wiki rests on its essential characteristic, i.e., there is no ultimate authority and no final definite wiki page. There may be a general direction or theme, but the actual content of a wiki is molded and manifested by contribution made by individual members and accumulated through community collaboration. In other words, any member of the community can affect its quality. While wiki becomes increasingly popular, involving all kinds of content contributors, the question of how to enhance or ensure its quality also becomes more and more pressing (Lih 2004,

Figure 2. The main page of the experimental wiki. It was the only page when the pilot study started. All other pages and categories were added and modified by students.

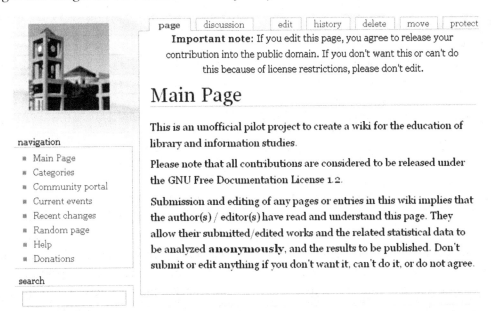

Desilets 2005, Kohl 2008). Collaborative knowledge building using wiki always comes with the problematic dimension of quality.

Information and data quality is not a new topic. The term "Quality" is defined by International Organization of Standards (1986) as "the totality of characteristics of an entity that bear on its ability to satisfy stated and implied need" (Standard 8402, 3.1). There has been considerable research on information quality (e.g., see Wang and Strong 1996, Eppler & Wittig 2000, Helfert 2001, and Naumann 2002). We can also implement automatic mechanisms to estimate the quality of a document created in a static and non-collaborative environment (e.g., see Ng *et al* 2003, Tang *et al* 2003 and Ng *et al* 2006). The advance of open collaborative knowledge building systems posts new questions in this area: what affects the quality of an information product when it is produced collaboratively in a distributed environment? Can we also estimate the quality of content built in this kind of collaborative writing environment using automatic means? In this paper, we report a pilot study that was designed to answer these questions,

discuss and analyze its very promising results.

EXPERIMENTAL SETUP AND METHOD OF INQUIRY

The appearance of Wiki provides new opportunities for learning more of the collaborative knowledge building process (Cress & Kimmerle 2008). In this pilot study, a MediaWiki clone was installed in a Linux server. Students in five master level courses would use this wiki as a learning tool to foster their understanding of key concepts and topics covered in the class.

In the beginning, there was only one page in the wiki (i.e. the main entrance page, see Figure 2). After introducing to students about the wiki and how to contribute content, students were encouraged to create, edit, modify, categorize and link wiki pages collaboratively.

All contributed pages must be about topics covered in the classes. Only registered member could contribute contents, but users could register under usernames and participate anonymously.

Table 1. Basic descriptive statistic of the wiki

Number of registered members who contributed content to the wiki at least once	59
Number of wiki pages created	143
Average number of contribution per page	3.7
Median of the number of contribution	4
Maximum number of contribution to a wiki page	18
Minimum number of contribution to a wiki page	1
Length of the shortest page (in number of words)	38
Length of the longest page (in number of words)	431

There was no way to tell whether a student has registered and contributed contents to the wiki or not. Participation was voluntary and would have no effect on students' grades. Students could also use the wiki without participation (i.e., as a non-member who can view and search and read, but cannot change the content.)

The pilot project was ended after five months. About one third of the students (59 out of 153) contributed contents to the wiki. When the project ended, there were 143 wiki pages. All pages were created by students (except the main entrance page). Most of them were create collaboratively in the sensed that they have been added and edited by multiple members across time. Table 1 summarizes the statistics of this wiki.

After the semester, students who have received A+ grade were invited to judge the quality of the wiki pages. Eight students participated. Each wiki page was examined by two students who have received A+ in the corresponding course (corresponding to the subject area of the page). All wiki log information and statistics, including username, were not given to the judges. The judges only had the contents of the pages and nothing else to make the judgment. The judgments were based on seven quality criteria whenever applicable (see table 2, which is a modification based on Ng *et al* 2006).

If a page was judged as a good quality page, it would receive a quality score 1, otherwise, it would receive a quality score 0. It is understandable that sometimes students would not agree with each other in their quality judgment (Lee *et al*, 2006). If the judgments of the two judges were not the same, the instructor of the class would decide the final score. Table 3 summarizes the results of the quality judgments.

With the quality judgments available, we would investigate whether a statistical relation-

Table 2. Criteria of quality of wiki pages created by collaborative knowledge building.

Quality Aspect	Definition
Accuracy	The extent to which information is precise and free from known errors.
Objectivity	The extent to which information is free from personal biases or personal preference.
Depth	The extent to which the coverage and analysis of information is detailed.
Reference Authority	The extent to which information is based on authoritative references.
Readability	The extent to which information is presented with clarity and is easily understood.
Conciseness	The extent to which information is well-structured and compactly represented.
Grammatical Correctness	The extent to which the text is free from syntactic problems.

Table 3. Statistics of quality judgments

Number of pages judged	143
Number of pages judged to be good quality pages by both 2 judges	53
Number of pages judged to be good quality pages by one judge but not the other	11
Number of pages judged to be good quality after instructor examination to resolve the difference between two judges	5
Final number of good quality pages in the wiki	58
Final number of ordinary pages (i.e., wiki pages that did not receive "good quality" status.)	85

ship existed between:

1. The quality of the wiki pages, and
2. (A) The http access data recorded in the http log file accessing the wiki pages; (B) the collaborative statistics recorded in the wiki log file, and (C) the textual features of the wiki pages.

The objective was to identify variables that were highly correlated with the quality of contents created by open collaborative knowledge building, and then use the variables to help to create automatic mechanism that can locate contents that might have low quality. Table 3 listed the categories of variables used in the correlation.

We applied various advanced statistical methods to analyze the data and identify factors that would affect the quality of a wiki page. Based on the analysis, machine learning method was applied to construct an automatic quality predictor. The following sections report the findings.

DATA ANALYSIS AND RESULTS

At the exploratory stage of data analysis, we started with parametric statistical methods to understand the relationship of the possible predictive features (as summarized in Table 3) and the quality of a wiki page (as summarized in Table 4) based on a normal distribution assumption. The goal was to determine which technique would be most effective in classifying the pages correctly into two groups: high quality pages and ordinary pages. From the many techniques we used, we found that linear discriminant analysis (Klecka 1980) gave us a clear picture of the effectiveness of using the predictive variables to estimate the quality of the pages.

Discriminant Analysis and Stepwise Variables Selection

In discriminant analysis, we sought a linear combination of the frequencies of all the variables summarized in Table 3 (denoted by v_i in the following equation) as the basis for assigning pages into the two groups (high quality pages vs ordinary pages):

$$S = b_0 + S b_i v_i$$

where S is the discriminant score. Beta was chosen in such a way that the ratio of between-group sum of squares to the within-group sum of squares would be maximum, i.e.,:

$$\frac{(\frac{\sum_{i \in high} S_i}{N_{High}} - \frac{\sum_{k=1}^{N_{all}} S_k}{N_{all}})^2 + (\frac{\sum_{j \in Low} S_j}{N_{Low}} - \frac{\sum_{k=1}^{N_{all}} S_k}{N_{all}})^2}{\sum_{i \in High}(S_i - \frac{\sum_{i \in High} S_i}{N_{High}})^2 + \sum_{j \in Low}(S_j - \frac{\sum_{j \in Low} S_j}{N_{Low}})^2}$$

Table 4. Categories and examples of features of wiki pages used in data analysis

Feature Categories	Examples
Punctuation	Number of periods, question marks, exclamation marks, commas, semicolons, colons, dash, ellipsis, parentheses, brackets, quotation marks, forward slides, apostrophes, hyphens
Length	Average length of words in characters, sentence in words, paragraph in words. Length of title, subtitle, leading paragraph, and document
Unique words	Number of unique words; number of unique words excluding stop words
Entities	Number of persons, locations, organizations, and dates
Request activities	Number of time the pages has received a request from a registered member (e.g., "peer review" request, "clean up request", "page needing attention" request, etc.)
View activities	Number of time the wiki page has been viewed by users; Number of time the wiki page has been viewed by registered members
Page categories	Number of categories a page belongs to
Links	Number of outward http links; number of internal wiki links (link that points to another wiki page in the same wiki) in a wiki page
Collaborative activities	Number of comments and exchanges in the "article talk page"; Number of modification or addition
Intensity of Collaboration	Number of active registered members contributed to the page; Number of times a page received revision and modification by a contributor who was not the same contributor of the immediate previous edition of the same page; Time span counted from the new addition of the page to the final modification of the page measured in number of hours) divided by the number of modification.
Age	The age of a page measured in number of hours
Part of Speech	Number of tokens, proper nouns, personal pronouns, possessive pronouns, determiners, preposition, verbs in base form, verbs in past tense, verbs in present participle, verbs in past participle, verbs in present tense, verbs in ing form

where *High* denotes high quality pages, *Low* denotes ordinary pages, and *N* is the number of pages.

The result of the discriminant analysis is summarized in Table 5 as a confusion matrix (Kohavi and Provost, 1998), which contains information about actual and predicted class memberships done by a classification system. In our case here, the classification system classified the wiki pages into two classes: high quality pages and ordinary pages.

As indicated in Table 4, there were many predictive variables used in the analysis, some of them could be redundant, in the sense that their contribution to the overall predictive power could not ignored. To eliminate redundant variables in order to save administrative works as well as computing resources, we used stepwise discriminant analysis algorithm (Huberty 1994) to reduce the number of predictive variables. Mathematically speaking, stepwise method cannot give a better result, but it can decrease the number of predictive variables dramatically.

In our stepwise approach, the first variable included has the largest value for the selection criterion, then the value of the criterion is re-evaluated for all variables not in the model. The remaining variable with the largest criterion value is entered next. At this point, the variable which was entered first is re-evaluated to determine whether it meets the removal criterion. If it does, it is removed from the model. Next, all variables not in the equation are examined for entry, followed by an examination of the variables in the equation for removal. Variables were removed until none remain that meet the removal criterion. Variable selection terminates when no more variables meet entry or removal criteria. Using this approach, we reduced the number of predictive variables from more than one hundred to only a few with only

Table 5. Confusion matrix of the exploratory study using linear discriminant analysis

Actual Group	No. of Cases	Predicted Group Membership	
		High Quality Pages	Ordinary Pages
High Quality Pages	58	54	4
		93.1%	6.9%
Ordinary Pages	85	13	72
		15.3%	84.7%
Percent of "grouped" cases correctly classified: 88.1%			

4% decrease in the correct classification rate. The remaining variables were:

- **Sum of request:** The sum of all kinds of requests (e.g., "peer review request", "clean up request", "page needing attention" request, etc.) placed by registered users either to the author or to the others.
- **Interaction frequency:** The number of time a page received revision and modification by a contributor who was not the same contributor of the immediate previous edition of the same page.
- **Active-member involved:** The number of active members contributed to a page (an active contributor is defined as a registered member who contributes more than 4 times to the wiki, where 4 is median of the number of contributions per contributor)
- **Average length of paragraph:** Number of words divided by number of paragraph
- **Use frequency of active talk pages:** The number of "article talk page" used by contributors
- **Personal names and Organizational name:** The frequencies of personal names and organizational names appear in a page.

Logistic Regression

There are some inherent limitations associated with discriminant analysis. For example, it as-
sumes a multivariate Gaussian distribution of the predictive variables, and that may not be valid for the array of variables based on textual characteristics and collaborative frequencies. Therefore we supplemented discriminant analysis with logistic regression.

We constructed the following equation: $\frac{P}{1-P} = e^y$ where p is the probability for a wiki page to have high quality, and y is a linear combination of the predictor variables: $y = \alpha_0 + S\alpha_i v_i$. The ratio between p and $1 - p$ should be greater than one for high quality pages, and less than one for ordinary wiki pages. Alpha was chosen to maximize the correct prediction rate (Menard, 1995).

Applying the same step-wise selection algorithm mentioned in the previous section to the logistic regression, we retrieved a slightly different set of good predictive variables: the **Average length of paragraph** (in number of words) was gone, instead, the logistic regression picked up **Length of leading paragraph** (in number of words). The correct classification rate is slightly better than the discrimination analysis: 90.1% of the wiki pages were correctly classified.

We continued our investigation using some other non-parametric approaches, including decision tree method, local weighted regression, and support vector machine method. They all had similar performance, and no one bit the performance of logistic regression.

The best way to understand the power of the

Figure 3. ROC curves of the training data set (the upper curve) and the testing data set (the lower curve)

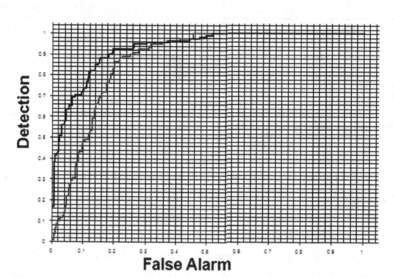

method is to use a machine learning approach, that is, to see if the predictive variables extracted and their parameters estimated from one set of data and then apply the result to another set of data.

We randomly divided the wiki pages into two data sets, each set consists of half of the high quality pages and half of the ordinary wiki pages, then used one set (we call it the training data set) to estimate the parameters of the logistic regression equation, and applied the result to predict the quality of the wiki pages in the second set (we call it the testing data set). In the following section, we report the result of this application.

Receiver Operating Characteristic (ROC) Curve

ROC (receiver operating characteristic) curve is a tool from signal detection theory (Egan 1975, Swets 1996). It is a graphical plot for a binary classifier system as its discrimination threshold is varied. It shows the chance of correct detection as a function of the number of false alarms.

If we consider classifying high quality pages correctly as "detection" and incorrectly classify-

ing ordinary pages as high quality pages as "false alarm", we can plot a ROC (Receiver Operating Characteristic, see Egan 1975 and Swets 1996) curve by sorting the odd of being a high quality page for each and every wiki page in the testing data set. The odd was calculated using the stepwise logistic regression equation constructed from the testing data set.

In Figure 3, the upper curve is from the training data set and the lower curve is from the testing data set. Every point along the curves represents a possible cutoff point to discriminate between high quality pages and ordinary pages. The associated detection rate of a point is the ratio of the number of high quality pages that would be correctly classified using that point as a cutoff to the total number of high quality pages in the testing data set. The associated false alarm rate of a point is the ratio of the number of ordinary pages that would be incorrectly classified as high quality pages using that point as a cutoff to the total number of ordinary pages in the testing data set.

As we can see from the graph, the predictive power of the ROC curves are pretty good. When detection rate of the training data set is as high as

80%, the false alarm rate is just about 12%. The predictive power of the ROC curve on the testing data set is lower than for the training set, but still powerful. For example, using the same cutoff point, when the detection rate is 80%, the false alarm rate is 20%. In other words, the machine can predict 80% of the high quality pages correctly if we allow 20% of the ordinary pages to be incorrectly classified as high quality pages.

CONCLUSION

The importance of the above ROC curves lies in two facts:

1. It permits system architects to select thresholds for classification that are appropriate to their own assessments of the relative cost of misclassifying good quality pages and ordinary pages.
2. The relative strength of different predicting algorithms (e.g, the odd estimated by stepwise logistic regression reported above) can be read easily from the ROC, since a prediction algorithm whose ROC curve lies always above that of another algorithm will be superior to it no matter what the user's specific estimates of costs and values may be. In other words, we can use this study as a baseline for further investigation of other predictive algorithm and compare their performance using the ROC.

In this study, we proved that one could use log data and textual features to automatically estimate the quality of contents built by collaborative knowledge building. This is a very important and necessary mechanism for a collaborative knowledge building system when its size becomes so large and its grow rate becomes so fast that no one can catch up with all the addition and modification, and to keep the overall quality of the contents to be satisfactory.

We were far from exhausting all the possible use of the predictive variables in this pilot study, for examples, we did not use any normalization techniques, and we did not apply techniques like principal component analysis to form composite variables. More importantly, we only have an intuitive understanding, but not a solid theory, to explain the predictive power of the variables. With a good theory, not only we can identify hidden predictive variables more easily, we can also create new composite variables to improve prediction power. This will be the next step of this study.

REFERENCES

Cress, U., & Kimmerle, J. (2008). A systemic and cognitive view on collaborative knowledge building with wiki. In *Computer-Supported Collaborative Learning (3)*, (pp. 105-122). Berlin: Springer.

Desilets, A., Paquet, S., & Vinson, N. G. (2005). Are wiki usable? *WikiSym 2005 – Conference Proceedings of the 2005 International Symposium on Wikis*, (pp 3-15).

Ebersbach, A., Glaser, M., Heigl, R., & Warta, A. (2008). *Wiki Web Collaboration, 2 Ed.* Berlin: Springer-Verlag.

Egan, J. P. (1975). *Signal detection theory and ROC analysis*. New York: Academic Press.

Eppler, M. J., & Wittig, D. (2000). Conceptualizing information quality: A review of information quality frameworks from the last ten years. In B. D. Klein, D. F. Rossin, (Ed.), *Proceedings of the 2000 conference on information quality*, (pp. 83-96). Cambridge, MA: Massachusetts Institute of Technology.

Helfert, M. (2001). Managing and Measuring Data Quality in Data Warehousing. *Proceedings of the World Multiconference on Systemics, Cybernetics and Informatics*, (pp. 55-65).

Huberty, C. J. (1994). *Applied Discriminant Analysis*. Hoboken, NJ: Wiley-Interscience.

Klecka, W. R. (1980) *Discriminant analysis*. Sage University Paper series on quantitative applications in the social sciences, series no. 07-019. Thousand Oaks, CA: Sage.

Kohavi, R., & Provost, F. (1998). Special issue on Applications of Machine Learning and the Knowledge Discovery Process. *Machine Learning, 30*(2-3).

Kohl, D. F. (2008). From the editor: Sacajawea, wikis and trusted guides. *Journal of Academic Librarianship, 34*(5), 387-388.

Lee, E. Y. C., Chan, C. K. K., & Van Aalst, J. (2006). Students assessing their own collaborative knowledge building. *International Journal of Computer-Supported Collaborative Learning, 1*, 57–58. doi:10.1007/s11412-006-6844-4

Lih, A. (2004). Wikipedia as participatory journalism: Reliable sources? Metrics for evaluating collaborative media as a news resource. In *Proceedings of the Internal Symposium on Online Journalism*.

Lin, S. C., Chen, Y. C., & Yu, C. Y. (2006). Application of wiki collaboration system for value adding and knowledge aggregation in a digital archive project. *Journal of Educational Media and Library Science, 43*, 285–307.

Menard, S. (1995) *Applied logistic regression analysis*. Sage University Paper series on quantitative applications in the social sciences, series no. 07-106. Thousand Oaks, CA: Sage.

Moore, T. D., & Serva, M. A. (2007). Understanding member motivation for contributin to different types of virtual communities: A proposed framework. In *Proceedings of the 2007 ACM SIG-MIS Computer Personnel Research Conference: The Global Information Technology Workforce, SIGMIS-CPR 2007*, (pp. 153-157).

Naumann, F. (2002). *Quality-driven Query Answering for Integrated Information Systems*. Berlin: Springer-Verlag. Retrieved on November 9, 2002 from http://link.springer.de/link/service/series/0558/tocs/t2261.htm

Ng, K. B., Kantor, P., Strzalkowski, T., Wacholder, N., Tang, R., & Bai, B. (2006). Automated Judgment of Document Qualities. [JASIS]. *Journal of the American Society for Information Science and Technology, 57*(9), 1155–1164. doi:10.1002/asi.20393

Ng, K. B., Kantor, P., Tang, R., Rittman, R., Small, S., Song, P., et al. (2003). Identification of effective predictive variables for document qualities. In R. J. Todd (Ed.) *Proceedings of 2003 Annual Meeting of American Society for Information Science and Technology* (pp. 221-229.) Medford, NJ: Information Today, Inc.

Swets, J. A. (1996). *Signal Detection Theory & ROC Analysis in Psychology & Diagnostics: Collected Papers*. Mahwah, NJ: Lawrence Erlbaum Associates, Inc.

Tang, R., Ng, K. B., Strzalkowski, T., & Kantor, P. (2003). Automatically predicting information quality. In D. Radev & S. Abney (Eds.), *Proceedings of Human Language Technology Conference of the North American Chapter of the Association for Computational Linguistics, Companion Volume* (pp. 97-99). East Stroudsburg, PA: Association for Computational Linguistics.

Wagner, C., & Majchrzak, A. (2007). Enabling customer-centricity using wikis and the wiki way. *Journal of Management Information Systems, 23,* 17–43. doi:10.2753/MIS0742-1222230302

Wang, R. Y., & Strong, D. M. (1996). Beyond accuracy: What data quality means to data consumers. *Journal of Management Information Systems, 12*(4), 5–34.

Wasko, M. M., & Faraj, S. (2005). Why should I share? Examining knowledge contribution in networks of practice. *MIS Quarterly, 29,* 25–58.

WikiWikiWeb History. (2009). Cunningham & Cunningham, Inc. Retrieved from http://c2.com/cgi/wiki?WikiHistory

Section 3
The Design of Information Spaces for Next–Generation Collaboration

Chapter 11
Speak First, Then What?

Jay Heuer
SarJay GmbH, USA

ABSTRACT

In a world of information overload, digital collaboration provides the means to spew out more and more content. Mass does not equal class. Simply adding data to a "knowledge base" does not make it better, just as adding "eyeballs" to a web site does not make it more significant. In this chapter, Dr. Heuer explores how to unleash the undernourished "dark side" of collaboration: Listening. As a seasoned practitioner of online collaboration, he argues from the lead user's perspective. His objective: to propose enhancements to a hypothetical system, increasing the amount of "Listening" (that is content consumption rather than production) in online collaboration. This should help transform a band of content junkies into true participants in a discussion rather than folks on soapboxes.

INTRODUCTION

In a world where content is created and published at the drop of a hat (and a very small one for all that matters), digital collaboration has become a quest for relevance. How many times have you started a new knowledge base for a project with high hopes, only to see it decay into a cluttered mess of unrelated pontifications, untraceable decisions, and irrelevance? Why is that so? Can it be avoided? Potentially, answers wait at the fundamental levels

of interaction: Listening, Talking, and Observing.

In the age of Twitter, Facebook, and Microsoft SharePoint, "Talking" is available in abundance. Since "Observing" (including facial expressions, body language, etc.) is rather difficult to achieve in the asynchronous, dispersed, and overloaded context of today's workplace, the key to improving collaborative systems could be "Listening".

Listening is in short supply. Experience shows that the more folks listen to each other, the better the results. "Listen before you Speak" is true in the world of online work, even more so than in the real world, as the online medium is less forgiving,

DOI: 10.4018/978-1-60566-727-0.ch011

Figure 1.

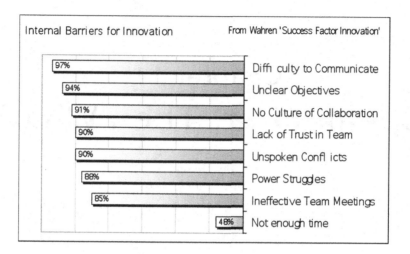

does not forget easily, and lowers the barriers of talking.

In this article, we will explore some of the basic tenants of system-supported collaboration, especially the encouragement of listening to others. We envision the necessary expansions to the available toolsets to increase relevance, to reduce re-work and throw away, and to make working together remotely more fun than fad.

BACKGROUND

Online collaboration has come a long way. Starting with simple email and chat, we soon matured into document sharing (remember when Netscape added the [input type="file"] capability in 1995 in Navigator 2.0). From there, we moved on to the world of Content Management Systems, including Wikis and other publishing approaches. The journey has taken us now to Web2.0- style "collaborative" systems like YouTube, where users add content and then respond to it.

In his book *"Success Factor Innovation"*, Wahren published the list of "Internal Barriers to Innovation" (Figure 1) (Wahren 2003). Communication-related issues are at the core of many of the issues. In the corporate world, online

collaboration has become increasingly important, bridging the divides of space (geography) and time (availability of data or talent). Not surprisingly, systems managing basic ingredients of collaboration like documents, calendars, and task lists receive a lot of attention, though the initial forays have been disappointing from a usability standpoint. Enhanced tools for online collaboration will receive a warm welcome if they drive simplicity and reduce the load.

In short: **better system design is not optional, it is essential for corporate success.**

The Economist Intelligence Unit conducted a study in 2007 on the Risks and Opportunities of the Knowledge Worker (Economist 2007). It states the main issues around inadequate access to information are:

- **54%** experience lost productivity
- **47%** mention bad decision making
- **45%** observe a loss of agility or competitive responsiveness

Current systems are great soapboxes to speak from, but they lack mechanisms to draw a crowd of listeners. SharePoint, Media Wiki, Joomla and the likes are miles ahead of the crude beginnings in 1995. However, they still lack a compelling structure to drive "listening", this essential feature to entice and enforce true collaboration. These systems seem to consider "listening" as:

- **passive**: today's systems do not capture a true record of listening activities!
- **non-value add**: what is being visibly improved by listening?
- **dreary**: so much content, so little time!
- **expensive**: what does the individual gain from listening?

The Economist Study also finds:

- **57%** of the participants do not have ready access to the information needed to do their job
- **42%** claim they cannot find relevant information when it is needed
- Only **38%** state that email is not an effective communication tool

Further: "*While knowledge workers are satisfied with the quality and quantity of information available to them, they feel burdened and frustrated by the amount of time it takes to collect, analyze and process it.*", (Economist 2007), p 5. Yet 55% stated that their company is very significant or significant in obtaining the relevant data. As the report puts it: "*knowledge workers often resort to workarounds...*" ditto, p. 5.

The participants go on to list these challenges to do their job (incl. always-often-sometimes):

- **80%** claim the information is scattered across multiple systems
- **76%** state the information is poorly organized
- **73%** reformat the available information

In essence, the information is there, but it is hard to get at, digest and reuse.

Some may come to the defense of modern collaboration systems, pointing to the ***commenting capability*** as a solution. In my experience, that is a hollow argument. Commenting on posts is a disjointed, somewhat hidden affair between the poster and the commenter. Rarely have I seen actual discussions being conducted here, especially between several people. Often, after a few comments, this post occurs: "*why don't we discuss this in person?*" That is the end of the online repository of information, as most of the following discussion is offline. I*n effect, the commenting system does not allow for actual, natural, casual, and effectual interaction.*

What did the Economist survey respondents claim as the top challenges (excerpt)?

- Improved ability to integrate complex information from various sources: **46%**
- Easier access from your desktop: **42%**
- Analytical and reporting tools: **41%**

In short, what is needed are tools that ***use*** all the available information better.

What needs to change? I believe we need to think harder about enabling "Listening" as a key component to communication and collaboration. That will drive the use of information rather than the focus on simple availability.

TO LISTEN IS TO ADD VALUE

Why will online, collaborative "Listening" solve some problems in collaboration? Why not better tagging, better commenting tools, more slicing and dicing of content to make it easier to find. Here are some of the issues we can find in the way today's online collaboration concepts work. We will present them as actual episodes in a team's work.

Meet **Joe**, **Mary**, **Bazzar**, and **Mel**. All four are members of a New Product Development project totaling more than 50 team members. They are working together across several boundaries:

- *geographic*: Joe and Mary are co-located, Bazzar and Mel sit in their own locations
- *functional*: Joe works in marketing, Mary in design, Bazzar in technology, and Mel is the project leader
- *seniority*: Joe is the most senior of the bunch, Bazzar the youngest (he never worked on a project like this before)
- *language*: Joe and Mary are native English speakers, Bazzar and Mel are not

As "Lead Users", these four have demanding requirements.

There are demanding (and expensive) solutions such as co-location, cross-functional organizations, coaching, and language training to resolve these issues. These are typically not economically feasible. An appropriately designed collaboration system offers relief for some of these issues.

Issues, Controversies, Problems

In working with real life collaboration application, I came across several shortcomings. Below you will find an overview of the issues discussed in this text. This list does not claim completeness or a specific focus on the formally most important issues:

- **The "Tree falling in the Forest" Trouble**: so much content, so little time
- **The "Functional Fallacy"**: structuring content after functions
- **The "Post Partum" Phenomenon**: post and forget
- **The "Ignore the Ramblers" Idea**: ignoring commentators
- **The "Measure what I do" Malaise**: only what is measured can be improved
- **The "Pontification" Problem**: when people are too much involved
- **The "Content Generation Divide" Dysfunctionality**: more than words

- **The Sacred Cow Conundrum**: how dare you measure me!

The "Tree Falling in the Forest" Trouble

The "project vault", as the content repository and collaboration platform has become known as, now has more than 500 documents. When the project was started, the standard corporate structure was installed, based on the functions. There are separate folders for "Marketing", "Design", "Technology", "Project Management", "Sales" and the like. This greatly helped the team members to know where to post their documents. Some of them created sub directories inside their own. Mary added folders for "Prototyping", "External Consultants", and "Discards". Joe structured his folder after "Consumer Insights", "Advertising", and "Projections". Bazzar rarely uses the repository, as he relies on the Concurrent Versioning System that Technology has established. There are no folders in his directory, and only a few rather hefty documents. Mel has a folder structure that mimics the stage gates he has to lead the project through: "Concept", "Conversion", and "Execution".

Documents are spread all over these folders, some containing even more sub-folders, as their owner saw fit. Mary now adds a new design consultant, Des, to the team, and instructs him to "go understand the project by looking at the documents". After a day, Des returns to her in frustration. "I cannot make heads or tails from this. What is important, what do I need to read?" So Mary starts to look for herself, and is quickly overwhelmed. Where did all this stuff come from? She asks Mel: "Why are we using the repository thing when we don't find anything in there? I am posting my stuff like you asked us to do, but I cannot understand what everybody else is doing."

Figure 2.

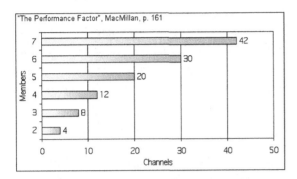

Mel advises her to make the content more dynamic, more relevant to her current work. Mary now starts to be serious about her own documents. She commits a large number of her "work-in-progress" to the repository, to make it more relevant and lively. And then she waits. Waits for comments, emails, anything. But nothing happens.

How much impact will adding a single document have when the repository is rather substantial? Any collaborator will inadvertently ponder this question. He or she reflects on her own behavior to judge others. Most folks do not use repositories extensively. They will go when they are told (mostly through an email notification), or when the process they execute demands it from them. Rarely do we see people "just browsing" the information.

Network effects play a role, too. Consider Figure 2 (MacMillan 2001): the number of communication channels grows exponentially with the team members. The more people work in a repository, the more overwhelming the communication task.

The **structure of single posts** is causing some of the behavior. Most repositories allow for the upload of documents, usually products out of Microsoft Office applications. They then ask for a description of the contents of the document, a bit on the author, maybe some keywords or tags, and that's it. The document ends up as an attach-

ment of a small description. That is what the user sees when they are looking for something. Opening attachments is a bore, since the browser will ask for permission to open or save, then the application handling the document starts, and then the document might not be what the description promised. After a few experiences like that, users quickly learn that leaving through the content is extremely tedious and to be avoided.

So what happens to all those documents published? They turn into gravestones, only read by the determined. **They turn into trees falling in the forest: does anybody hear them? The immediate effect is disillusionment, frustration and a deep distrust in the process forcing the tool upon the user.**

The "Functional Fallacy"

Mel is starting to wonder whether the corporate content structure is such a good thing. The functional content tree seemed to be such a good idea in the beginning, making it easy for everybody to find a place for their work products.

Now, that seems to be not such a good idea any more. The tree structure makes it hard to find something, unless you have a good idea what you are looking for. The functional top level does not help here, but makes people collaborate less cross-functionally. In addition, there is little tie to the process of the project itself, the stage gates. Content is somewhat unattached to the heartbeat of the project.

In a hierarchical repository, the author needs to make exclusive decisions on where to place the content. If the hierarchy is also functional, the flow of information through the project itself is very hard to follow. One would have to hop between different branches of the content tree to connect the individual content pieces to the whole.

The belief that functional considerations are more important than process flow drives many issues of buried content. Since the structures tend be imposed at high levels in the repository, cross-functional work is effectively discouraged or even stifled.

The "Post Partum" Phenomenon

Joe has been posting diligently to the repository. Every time he got a new report of a survey or a focus group, the data went straight into the collaborative space. He is really proud "playing it open", as he calls it, with all the data out there.

There is, however, a nagging feeling: nobody ever talks to him about these posts. In fact, he never touches them again himself, since all the relevant information is right there at his fingertips on his PC. All this effort seems to be rather a waste of his time. However, he soldiers on, believing in the power of sharing.

Another way a repository turns into a dump is users that diligently post absolutely everything, but never touching it again. The authors make their decisions offline. The repository is not relevant for work. It is just a way to leave a paper trail of finished work products.

Users quickly notice this kind of behavior. In order to get into the decision making loop, they take the discussion offline, effectively destroying the initial intention of the tool. The amount of posted documents is impressive, and very hard to critique. It is, however, counter-productive.

The "Ignore the Ramblers" Idea

Now that Mary started to use the vault in earnest, she starts to see comments on her documents. Some of them are useful in her mind, others not or just beside the point. Rather than to waste her time on the last two types, she concentrates her responses on the ones she sees to be important. All other comments she leaves dangling.

Out of fear that she might hurt the author's feelings, she also exercises restraint in the online commenting system herself. When she sees a document she does not agree with, Mary actually goes and talks to the poster herself in person. After the conversation, she feels stupid to still post the comment, as everything has been said already.

Commenting is a huge exposure. Saying one's opinion about somebody else's work is a daunting act. Using an asynchronous medium like a web site makes it even harder, since there is no way to interact directly with the person to spare their feelings or clarify points. Add the public nature of comments, and you can understand the stress and the amount of sheer courage it takes to add anything other than "Well Done".

Team culture plays a large role, affinity and trust being rather high on the list of drivers of success. Commenting can be a minefield, with mutual retaliation potential. It can be exhausting and distressing for a person with a Feeling Preference (on the Myers-Briggs Type Indicator™). Do not be surprised that comments have a **large no-mans-land** between strangers (where the cost of a "flame war" is low) and tight teams (where players understand each other very well).

The "Measure What I Do" Malaise

Mel is noticing a lack of participation in the vault as well. He wants to help the team to maximize the utility of the tool, and starts with the facts: the usage statistics.

He quickly finds that Joe is the top poster, with almost 40% of all new documents coming from him. He also notices that Bazzar is hardly posting at all. The system does not allow him to see the commenting activities, but a quick, random scan shows him that there are very few comments. The team seems to agree on most issues posted.

He presents his findings at the next Project Management Meeting, and is very surprised by the responses.

Bazzar tells him that he is posting every relevant bit of technical information on the CVS repository, where it belongs. He does not want to bore the other participants with drawings, source code listings and test results. All that information he compresses into a weekly report, which he posts every Friday afternoon. He also adds that he does not comment on some of the issues he sees, since his English is not good enough to express himself formally in a comment. Rather than alienating the author, he handles these things in person, when the opportunity arises.

Mary tells him that she does disagree with several of the documents, but that she resolved the issues with the authors directly, rather than posting an impersonal comment.

Mel simply does not have the data to manage his team's use of the repository. He does not know how many times they look at documents, and how long they spend on the document, reading it. He does not know about the need and reluctance to comment. He does not see the importance map of documents. He is flying blind.

The "Pontification" Problem

Now that Bazzar has gotten the direction to be more active in the repository, he starts to add serious amounts of content and comments. He quickly overtakes Joe as the main content source, and finds time to comment on at least half of all new documents.

The issue is: most of his documents are so technical in nature that nobody is reading them, and most of his comments are so long and opinionated that the others are starting to ignore them. Since he wants to be relevant, Bazzar starts to be even

more forceful in his comments, which turns the rest of even more. A vicious circle starts.

Some folks need more "airtime". That is perfectly normal. When this expression turns into pontification, especially in commenting systems or in document posts, it strains the fabric of a collaborative system. There are few mature defenses against the usurping of communication bandwidth.

The "Content Generation Divide" Dysfunctionality

The longer the project runs, the more content the team amasses in the vault, the more they are concerned about losing cohesion. More and more, the team makes decisions without leaving a direct trace in the repository. Sure, there are meeting protocols, but they do not capture the way the team reached the decisions. All those nuances are lost, all the deep reasoning is not part of the documentation. Mary said it the best: "We are using charcoal to draw a rainbow".

Since the commenting feature does not really work, and capturing the intricate ways of decision-making is so tedious and subjective, a lot of the deep reasoning of decision-making is lost. One of the main drivers for the repository is the ability to do meaningful post-mortems. Without the details, such an analysis can only scratch the surface. Conversations, meetings, conference phone calls, all this unstructured and non-Microsoft-Office content dissipates into thin air. They are vital, though, as studies have shown as depicted in Figure 3. (MacMillan 2001).

Words only convey 10% of the meaning. Text is important to make content searchable / findable, it is sometimes not enough to make content understandable. Here, a richer medium, e.g. captured audio or even video is important. The collaboration tool needs to be able to seamlessly integrate these content types without artificial

Figure 3.

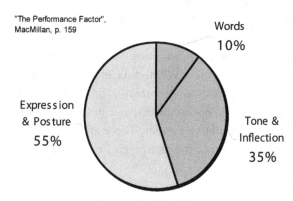

"The Performance Factor",
MacMillan, p. 159

Words
10%

Tone &
Inflection
35%

Expression
& Posture
55%

barriers ("click here to watch" links really do break the flow or reading).

The Sacred Cow Conundrum

Mel is still frustrated about the lack of hard statistics about the work of his team. The repository should be able to tell him where folks place their emphasis, what is working, where decisions are hanging. He cannot get at this information without talking to individuals, with all the subjectivity that entails. He is looking to make a bold move: measure what is being done.

When he suggests this at the next team meeting, he receives a surprising backlash. "I am a designer, not a stock picker. This is creative work. There is no way you can and should measure that", says Mary. Bazzar adds: "How can you reduce is to a set of a numbers? How can you? Anything you do will be a gross misrepresentation of our work".

A hard truth about knowledge workers is that they are rather reluctant to be measured doing their work on knowledge. The more creative the work is, either in design, artistic expression, or engineering, the harder the resistance will be. Professionals support the need for data, but they are very leery of attempts to take their freedom of creativity away. Finding a set of statistics that will achieve the purpose of managing knowledge

better while getting the support from the participants is tricky.

Solutions and Recommendations

To address these issues and shortcomings, we recommend:

- **Record "Listening" Activity**: basic relevant data capture
- **Extractors and Converters**: beyond ASCII text
- **Deep Versions**: multiple drafts and traces
- **Expires By**: forced content expiration
- **Deeper User Profiles**: a mix of observation and configuration
- **Beyond Commenting**: capturing all data streams around content
- **"Tres Facet Auditorium"**: require reviewers to complete content
- **"Content Rating"**: find the outliers
- **Front Pages for Topics**: content at a glance
- **Follow the Flow**: content mapped onto the work process

In Figure 4, we have created a mockup for a possible document screen, which could be the centerpiece of the content management system.

Record "Listening" Activity

On a basic level, each document in the system will **capture and show its interactions with users**. This includes:

- how many times a user went straight to the document,
- how many times the document came up as part of a search,
- how many times it was shown in the front page,
- how many times a user clicked to see it,
- how long the user spent reviewing the

Figure 4. The "Document" system

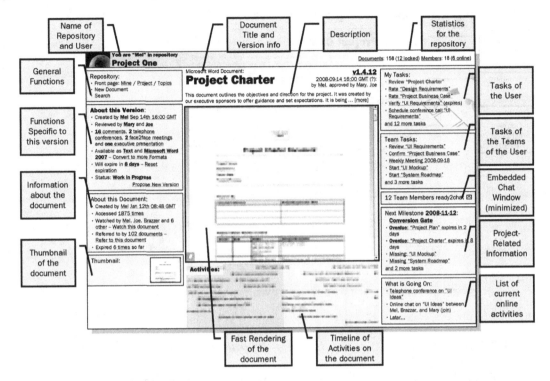

document,
- what activities the user performed, and
- where the user went after interacting with the document.

This data should be captured in addition to the times and durations for editing the document. All this information will add greatly to the understanding of the flow of activities and the importance of the document to users.

The system should aggregate the information from both the documents and the user's viewpoint. For **management purposes**, the user's listening activities are now much more transparent, as we can now see how many times he used search, how often he looked at the repository, and how long it took him to interact with a document. The reporting either should occur anonymously or named, based on the company's culture. In the case of anonymity, management will at least have an idea of how much time is spent actually using the repository. Targets would be tricky to set, but there is a minimum threshold of activity below which measures need to be taken.

This information needs to be **visible to the user**, to prevent it from becoming a bogeyman or a source of feeling betrayed. A good tool to show all the interactions is a graphical timeline, very much like the one used by the SIMILE project. Using AJAX, the client device can assemble the timeline rather than the server. As a result, the download of information will be much faster and the resulting "widget" of information much more interactive than a simple image. The system can display versioning and other advanced features in a user-friendly manner. See the mockup screen (Figure 5).

For all users, **a list of their most active documents** should also be available. Here is a list of the reports possibly displayed on the user's activity profile screen:

Figure 5. The "History of a Document" screen

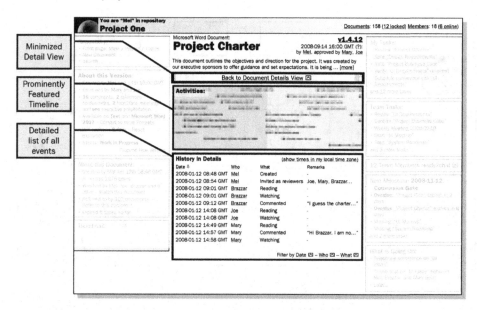

- Most accessed document
- Most edited document
- Most commented document
- Document with the most review cycles
- Abandoned documents
- Most searched documents
- Most linked-to documents
- Most important documents from the user's point of view
- Documents the user is currently working on

Mary can now see that Des did not spend a lot of time looking for documents. He gave up rather quickly, after only browsing the files in the "Design" folder. Looking at her own documents, she also noticed that several of those she considered important were in effect dormant. She quickly adds reviewers to them to attract work to them.

She also adds a few documents to her "Important to me" list, which is part of her online profile. The system aggregates the "Important to the Team" list, displayed in each of the front pages of the

repository, from those individual lists.

Extractors and Converters

When browsing the repository, the document could be displayed right there in the browser window, without the need of starting the content application. The system should actually converts all documents into a common, simple format that does not require a large application to start. This should *not* be Adobe Acrobat, as its format is geared towards printed media, making it unsuitable for presentations with animations, videos etc. A more appropriate format could be Adobe Flash or Microsoft Silverlight.

The system could store all documents in four "rendering versions":

1) the **original binary format**, used to work with the document on future versions
2) the **visual presentation format**, used to quickly browse through the document
3) the **text format**, used to quickly scan and search the content

4) a **thumbnail** to be used in lists and timelines

All four should be available to the user directly on one page, and she does not have to worry about conversion: the system will handle that in the background. It should retain the different rendering versions even when the document is versioned up to ensure that prior versions remain easily accessible.

Joe was looking for a specific presentation the team gave to executive management. He did not remember the name, but he remembered the title of one slide: "How to make it happen". He types this text into the repository's search engine, and selects "Advanced Search". This allows him to specify more information about the search. He selects "Headline" and "Exact Phrase" from the menu. The system now looks for headlines in documents that contain this phrase. The meaning of "Headline" is defined specifically for each application type: word documents have headlines directly; in PowerPoint, it means titles in slides; in Excel, headlines are the names of worksheets, and so on.

The system now searches for those documents that match the criteria. Surprisingly enough, several documents match. Joe switches the view of the results from simple list (a list of all the documents, their author, creation and last-edit dates, maturity level and status) to "Thumbnails". Here, the list also contains the visual presentation format of the first page. Still not satisfied, Joe switches to "Timeline View", where he quickly finds the presentation he remembers by glancing at those thumbnail pictures.

Clicking on the thumbnail, Joe navigates to the document itself, which opens right in front of him immediately. If the document had been wrong, it would have taken him only a few seconds to navigate to the next one.

Deep Versions

The repository should track all committed changes to each document as the backbone of its sub-content structures. It should attach all comments, discussions etc. to a specific version of the document to ensure consistency and further the understanding of the maturation process.

Versioning should be clearly visible in the document screen, with a current version number prominently displayed. The user could expand this version information to a time line of the events around this and prior versions. The timeline should show all activities, including sub-content, around the document, versioning steps and leaps, and the differences in the document. The user could literally trace changes back in time by walking down the time line.

The system should consider each document "draft" until it receives a new version number by peer review and agreement. The system could even maintain several versions of a draft to facilitate multiple proposals. In the end, only one of these drafts should be "promoted" to a version.

Depending on other features discussed below (see "Tres Facet Auditorium"), the number of peers required to attach a version number to a document might depend on the version itself. Traditionally, version numbers consist of three segments: "version.subversion.build". An example: version "2.1.231" identifies a document in version "2", subversion "1", and build "231". Version changes indicate major changes, usually departures from large parts of the document, from the prior version. Subversions indicate smaller changes, and builds usually contain error fixes and clarifications. The repository might accept build commits by one person, require a review of 2 peers for a new subversion, and a consensus of the whole peer group for a version change.

Mary was hesitant at first to post a document she considered half-finished to the repository. When she heard Brazzer laude this feature, she took up the courage to confront him in the meeting. "How is this going to help?" she asked. "I know my work is not done, why does it make sense to show something not yet done?" Brazzer told her about the software development concept of "Agile Development", which states "Commit Early, Commit Often". In essence, by posting her content as a "Beta Version", she allows interested peers to interact with it before proposing it as the next version. This interaction, he claims, will make her work better.

Mary tries it. She posts her initial draft to the repository, marking it as "Open for comments". Within a few hours, her rather daring thoughts attract several readers that add their perspective and thoughts to her work. Mary is not affronted by their thoughts, because she has not yet finalized hers either. Rapid discussions occur which drive the content to a much higher quality that previously expected.

Expires By

Preventing content from becoming stale is another huge task. Generating lots of content is good, though the sheer mass immediately puts large amounts of it in danger of becoming obsolete or irrelevant. A collaborative system that is concerned about more listening also needs to drive "listening to yourself". In essence, somebody needs to check content regularly to ensure it is still consistent and relevant. We need to create a permanent "nudge" connection between the author and her work. There are two ways to achieve that: reminders for the author to go check on her work, and the ability to challenge the validity and relevance of material through a peer review process.

The first alternative is rather easy to establish. All contents could receive an expiration date, which is set/reset at each creation/edit event. The system might even suggest a new date, depending on the type of content and its maturity. Then, when the "end is near", the author could be made

aware of the pending expiration and can evaluate whether the information in the document is still relevant and valid. If so, she can either reset the clock or mark the document as "settled", meaning the document is not longer maintained and no more changes will occur. The only actions available for a "settled" document are "superseded by a successor" and "deprecated".

The second alternative of a peer challenge is harder to implement, and more interesting. Being able to challenge content's validity and relevance with regard to its freshness through the system is potentially powerful. In essence, this is a miniature workflow through which a reader can get one more peer to agree the content needs checking and updating. In the first alternative, the user flags the document as outdated, which makes it appear in the list of outdated documents, highlights it, and informs the author of the flag. The other approach would allow the user to send a request to one or more peers directly. If one of the peers agrees with the request, the system would flag the document as expired and asks the author to trigger a refresh.

Mel uploaded the Project Charter at the beginning of the project. After several stage gates have passed, the project morphed somewhat under the influence of new market and technology insights. The stored charter does not reflect these changes.

Mary notices this in her follow-up work for Des, but is not sure whether the changes are really that pressing. Using the system's "This is outdated" function, she asks Joe to read the charter quickly and make a decision on the matter, listing the concerns she has. The system asks her during this step whether it should notify Mel of her concern as well. She declines.

When Joe receives her email, he quickly scans the document and agrees with Mary, adding comments of his own to her notice. This triggers a status change for the document, making it "Potentially Expired", which in turn sends an update to Mel that changes are needed. This update includes the reasoning Mary and Joe have written down in the previous steps. Mel receives an email and updates the charter document. Mary and Joe have been added as the peer reviewers of the change automatically.

Deeper User Profiles

To turn strangers in a project to people knowing each other is a daunting task. The system could help by providing in-depth, activity-based information about each user. What is she interested in, what are her areas of expertise, what is she responsible for, where do people trust her judgment? What are her thoughts on the project and needed decisions. Whose postings does she follow? Where is she most active? The answers to these questions can help her collaborators to understand her better.

The user needs to drive this profiling; the system would only collect, collate, and aggregate it. An easy way to achieve that could be to make the user's start page in part visible to others. In effect, her start page becomes her profile page. Here, she could:

- **register standing searches** for content activities, including date/time, location, sub team, author, keywords, content, most-published, most-commented, most urgently needed peer review
- list her **areas of interest** and view the activities in those
- list her **areas of expertise** (required reviewer), and view her activities in those areas
- list her **areas of responsibility**, and view her activities (decisions) in those
- list her **personal project blog**
- **make personal comments**, more like notes, that allow her to collect her thoughts on a specific topic in private before posting

content publicly
- **post more personal, non-transactional information** such as photos, interests etc. (think MySpace page)

Now a user's activities in the repository would have a known focal point. Her collaborators could steer to that page to understand what is happening in the user's life.

Des started to work with the team and quickly became active in the vault. When he started to comment and suggest changes, the already established team members wanted to know more about him. Des' system profile became a quick way to understand his thinking.

His profile showed the documents he authored and reviewed, his topics of interest, the areas where his suggestions were received favorably (his expertise), and the work products he was responsible for. The most insightful information came from his personal blog, where he shared his experiences in joining the team and his expectations for the project.

Beyond Commenting

The repository lives through the interaction of its members. They form opinions; they make decisions through interactions. Interactions should come in different forms, going far beyond simple comments:

- Online real-time chats, both text and voice
- Online asynchronous news groups
- Formal peer reviews, including formal status change requests
- Telephone Conferences
- Face2face meetings

The modern repository could handle all these interactions and present them in a unified way to the users. Look at the mockup (Figure 6).

Figure 6. "Beyond Commenting"

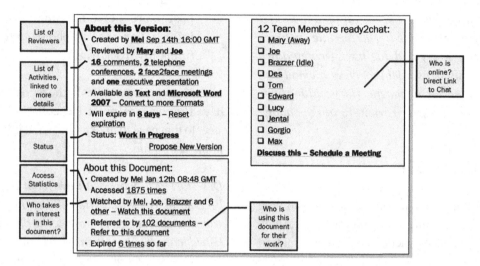

From a document, the users could quickly start and online chat with the author and other interested peers. Clicking on "Discuss this" would show the chat-system status of the author and all the users that have interacted with the document, grouped by the level of interaction. The user could now select which of those people need to be part of the discussion. If one of them is offline, the user would have the option to issue a meeting request for an online or offline meeting, or she could make sure the missing user gets an emailed transcript of the discussion. She could then start the chat with all the available parties. The contents of the chat would become part of the documents profile, adding to the richness of its context.

The user could also use **offline means** to discuss the document, by subscribing to a NEWS: newsgroup specifically for the document. From that moment on, her newsreader (e.g. Outlook Express) would receive all information updates pertaining to this document. She could also post comments offline; the system would merge them at the appropriate time and place into the discussions.

When the user would schedule a meeting, the system would create a placeholder for the document that will contain the meeting minutes of the conversation. The user could attach audio protocol files, which the system would automatically convert to text (see more info in "Non-Structured Content" below). The system would remind the user to post the results of the meeting after a certain grace period.

Mel started to use the repository to capture the decision making process extensively. Per his request, the call provider recorded the weekly project teleconference call to MP3. He posted the results protocol together with the recording to the repository. The system-generated transcript proved invaluable in later discussion. The system did not yet recognize different voices and tied them to people, but it did show the discussions in a searchable way.

"Tres Facet Auditorium"

A particular feature of a modern repository should be the inability of the original author to declare a document "completed". This effectively prevents content dumping, since peers would need to review and accept all new content before it is considered completed. To prevent abuse, at least two peers would need to agree on the maturity of the content.

This "Three is Company" approach would encourage authors to have engaged listeners to keep their content out of limbo. Content nobody reads and cares about is clutter or "toxic". This feature would also drive a sense of responsibility, ownership, and quality through the community.

The system could directly support working on the maturity of a document, preferably in the versioning subsystem. Each version of the document would be the base for all the sub-content like comments, discussion etc).

Bazzar was rather upset that he now needed to spend time with his peers talking about the content he posted. He quickly became rather adept in presenting his technical content in a way that made it easier for his peers to understand and review it.

"This makes me think, rather than just copy & paste the data," he agreed in a team meeting. "Since the data turns into information by you guys understanding it, the real value is not in me posting but in you reading and 'getting' it."

"Content Rating"

Allowing peers to rate content is a way to let the repository help identify "excellence in the craft". Allowing peers to vote on the quality of work is one way to collect credible information about the author's capabilities in a modified 360° feedback.

This feature is rather challenging to some team cultures. Anonymous feedback could pose a challenge, as it opens the door for toxic remarks without consequences. The author would need to have a systematic way to challenge ratings, with the system capturing the resulting argumentations.

Content rating would allow for the selection of "Best in Class" documents, a further way to acquire prestige and status in the author's community of practice. Just like "LinkedIn Answers",

the various front pages of the repository could display such prominently. They could be used a submissions into a "Benchmark of Excellence" repository, collecting examples of the "shared art" of the Community of Practice.

Initially, Mary was uncomfortable by the thought that she could rate somebody's work, and that others would rate her work as well. This struck her as rather dangerous to the team cohesion. After the feature had been around for a time, she quickly noticed that only the "outliers" actually received ratings: the outstanding and the obviously bad.

This really helped her accept the feature and participate. She liked praising people, so rating exceptional content highly was pleasant. Mary also realized that it was in her best interest to rectify quality issues within the team quickly, and there was no better way to get a potential issue looked after than through a bad rating. She realized that she swung a big stick here, used it with care and measure, and had some successes. When the first low rating arrived for her work, she looked at the reasoning and decided that the rating was fair. This had not been her best work, and she had hated the topic. Maybe somebody else would be better suited for the task, or maybe she really needed to grow up and deliver solid work. Overall, this was an unexpectedly healthy experience.

Front Pages for Topics

Front pages are compelling collections of information. They would present the documents of a specific topic in a way that makes navigation easier and drives a deeper understanding of the health and vitality of the repository. Front pages could consist of:

- **list of documents** resulting from different searches (most recently changed, most recently posted, most reviewed, orphaned, in need for review, most commented on, most active, required to complete the process step / topic, close to expiration etc.)

- **timeline of current documents** on the topic, displaying the latest document activities, with different color codes for the kind and status of documents
- **highlighted single documents**, usually with a short description and their thumbnail
- **highlighted users** with a short summary of their profile
- **statistics** in numeric and graphical form
- an **online forum** in which the topic itself can be discussed
- **RSS links** to all these elements and the forum page itself (the RSS subsystem generates a snapshot of the front page one a day at a defined time and converts it into a RSS post)
- additionally, the front page contains somewhat static information about the topic, e.g. the process step, its definition and training material

Topics would provide a way to slice and dice the document cloud with sensitivity to a specific perspective. Topics could include "user testing", "use cases", "executive communication" etc. Typically, a tag or keyword subsystem implements topics.

Figure 7 is a mockup of a possible front page for the topic "*Project Management*":

Des is in need of understanding all existing work on use cases. The front page of the repository provides him with a dropdown list of the most popular topics. "Use Cases" is not one of them, so he navigates to the "List of Topics", where he quickly finds what he is looking for.

Navigating to the front page for the "Use Cases" topic, he is presented a typical portal page showing a list of the most recently changed use cases, those that are not completed, a list of all docu-

ments marked "Completed" that are use cases or reference use cases. He can also see who posted the most use cases, who performed the most peer reviews, and who is an expert on use cases. This collection allows Des to dive into the topic content and the human aspects quickly. There even is a forum specifically for this topic where he can post questions.

Follow the Flow

An enhanced repository should offer a greater flexibility in structuring the document cloud. Typically, documents are stored in the hierarchical tree structure known from most file systems: files and folders. Users are familiar with the concept, and know how to navigate it. Users also know that in large repositories, finding the right information is a formidable task.

A different way of storing documents is by tags. Authors can use and define tags freely, in essence flattening the document cloud into a collection of top-level folders (the tags). As appealing as this approach is, it does not really help, since now finding the right tag becomes critical.

A robust alternative approach could be to map the project process onto the repository. The process could become the backbone of the repository. It would be aware of where in the process the project is, and automatically suggests that step as the home of the current version of the document. A document's context would be the basis for the search. Each process step would have required and optional documents, which could be hard wired into the repository. When a user is looking for a document, she could step along the process map, accessing the list of documents the process requests. Here, she could find relevant information much faster than through a tree structure. This approach would also facilitate automated completeness checks.

Each process step would have a front page containing an excerpt from the project plan as a time line, displaying major activities and associ-

Figure 7. The "Front Page" screen

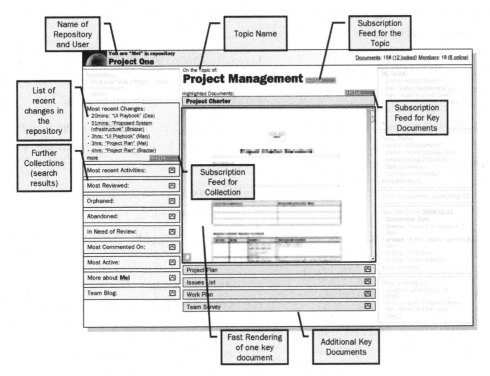

ated documents. This would allow the authors to understand the context of their work. The default front page of the repository would be the one of the current process step.

It is important to understand that this is not proposing to map the process onto a tree structure directly. The process map itself is the starting point for the navigation. Here, the user could move back and forth along the process and deeper into the work performed for each of the process steps. Keywords could help this "diving into the data space" by outlining desired customers or other "perspective" of the document cloud. Documents could span the entire process with their versions (consider the project plan and its revisions, for instance).

Mel is very interested in the state of the project documentation. Using the process map structure, he quickly assembles the vital information about the state of the required and optional documents

from the repository front page. Especially the statistics portion offers him vital insights, as well as the list of outstanding reviews and unfinished documents.

Mel uses this information to post the weekly update to the project, defined as one of the key documents for the front page. The front page displays such documents prominently.

CONCLUSION

- **Encourage Listening** by means of tracking of listeners, listening behaviors, and listening rewards; adding more focus on collaborating than posting
- **Reduce Noise and Waste** by means of system-supported active and passive filtering, automatic recasting into different media, powerful yet intuitive search and

embedded messaging (instant messages, discussions, etc.); allow and differentiate between *opinionated* (one author), *controversial* (multiple authors) and consented (accepted by multiple authors) content

- **Deal with diverse usage goals** (browsing, searching, tracking, understanding etc.) by means of flexible repository structures, multiple presentation modes for content sets and applications to generate & maintain content meta-structures

FUTURE RESEARCH DIRECTION

In this chapter, we emphasized some of the challenges in interaction design that modern collaboration systems face. We envisioned a future release of such a system with features addressing these challenges. There is only anecdotal evidence about the effect such enhancements will have. Using an existing system as a control, we would like to add the new features and observe the impact: more commenting, less zombie documents, more online decision making and recording. If one of the CMS providers is interested taking that step, we would be delighted to further the research with concrete observations.

REFERENCES

DeGraff, J., et al. (2002). *Creativity at Work*. New York: Wiley & Sons.

Duarte, D. L., et al. (2006). *Mastering Virtual Teams*. New York: Wiley & Sons.

Economist Intelligence Unit (2007). Enterprise Knowledge Workers: Understanding Risks and Opportunities.

Hamel, G., et al. (2007). *The Future of Management*. Cambridge, MA: Harvard Business School Press.

Hayes, C. (2006). *Position Paper: Collaboration Challenges in Distributed Engineering Design Projects*. University of Minnesota.

IBM & Cisco (2007). *Enhancing the Way People Work Through Unified Communication*, [White paper].

LinkedIn Answers (n.d.). Retrieved from http://www.linkedin.com

Logan, D., et al. (2008). *Tribal Leadership*. New York: Collins.

MacMillan, P. (2001). *The Performance Factor*. Nashville, TN: Broadman & Holman Publishers.

Maxwell, J. C. (2003). *Relationships 101: what every leader needs to know.*

Microsoft & Verizon (2006). *Meetings Around the World: The Impact of Collaboration on Business Performance,* [White paper].

The SIMILE Project Timeline Tool (n.d.). Retrieved from http://simile.mit.edu/timeline/

Vanderbilt, T. (2008). *Traffic – Why we drive the way we do*. New York: Knopf.

Wahren, H.-K. (2003). *Success Factor Innovation.* [trans. Erfolgsfaktor Innovation. Ideen systematisch generieren, bewerten und umsetzen]. Berlin: Springer.

Wenger, E., et al. (2002). *Cultivating Communities of Practice*. Cambridge, MA: HBS Press.

Chapter 12
Collaboration in Open Source Domains
A Perspective on Usability

Görkem Çetin
Gebze Institute of Technology, Turkey

Mehmet Göktürk
Gebze Institute of Technology, Turkey

ABSTRACT

Free and open source software (F/OSS) developers have a tendency to build feature-centric projects rather than following a user-centered design, ignoring the necessity of usability in the resulting product. While there are many reasons behind this, the main cause can be stated as the lack of awareness of usability from developers' point of view and little interaction of project stakeholders with Human-Computer Interaction (HCI) studies. This chapter examines different types of collaboration methods of usability experts and developers focusing particularly on open source projects, together with potential issues envisaged during the communication phases. The chapter also focuses on the collaboration trends and patterns of HCI experts, developers and users with an emphasis on concerns related to inefficient exploitation of current tools and technologies and provides an open usability engineering method which could be exploited in distributed projects.

INTRODUCTION

Free/Open Source Software (F/OSS) is a generic term that is used for software developed under a license, which allows the use, modification and distribution of the software without claiming a fee for it. There are other terms, like "open source", which describe a slightly different version of the F/OSS term; however the basic idea is the same in terms of usage, distribution and modification. A surprising fact with F/OSS development is that while this model does not pose an in-line methodology with traditional software development models, there's a growing interest in F/OSS products showing an effective, rapid and reliable software development process. As of this writing, there are more than 1.5 million registered users in Sourceforge with more than 150.000 projects and Apache is the clear market leader with 53% market share according to Netcraft statistics.

DOI: 10.4018/978-1-60566-727-0.ch012

Over the last 20 years, we have seen an abundance of literature on how usability can be used to leverage the return of investment, increase end user satisfaction and lower the training budget. Setting interface standards, providing usability requirements before a software project begins, heuristic evaluations and usability tests have been conducted in order to evaluate and improve an application or a series of web pages in order to increase the performance of the end user.

On the other hand, little attention has been paid to the usability of end user applications in F/OSS projects, although it is widely acknowledged as a success factor of desktop applications developed on the Internet. Lack of common usability design guidelines and methods of communication between usability experts and F/OSS developers resulted in F/OSS software with relatively low level of usability. While there are counterexamples of this, it's worth investigating the main factors of lack of F/OSS application usability and concentrate on how to improve the user centric design experience of voluntary projects, since usability can be integrated into current open source development processes.

As such, F/OSS usability is an important phenomenon deserving a study in itself. User centric design has not been the first priority of open source projects developed by people geographically distributed in all parts of the world. Thus, it can be argued that usability awareness and representation has been neglected for a long time. Traditionally, F/OSS has been successful in server products (Apache, MySQL, etc), libraries and compilers (GNU C compiler, Glibc, Qt, GTK) and console-based applications (bash shell, pine, etc). These applications were used by experienced people in specific organizations like universities and research institutes and those who have used them demanded less training and usability criteria. Most of the users of these applications are relatively technically sophisticated and the average desktop user is using standard commercial proprietary software (Lerner and Tirole, 2002).

Lack of clear usability requirements, awareness of user-centered design and a social collaborative tool to discuss usability issues usually result in a poor evaluation for F/OSS products. This is problem in ergonomic design and interface psychology, and hackers have historically been poor at it (Raymond, 1999). As F/OSS matures and enterprises start using F/OSS, it entered the mainstream area and enterprises started to demand not only reliability, security and efficiency, but usability, ergonomics and ease of use. As a result, in order to answer the demand from customers, some open source projects have tried to adopt techniques from previous proprietary work, such as explicit user interface guidelines for application developers (Benson, Adam, Nickell & Robertson, 2002).

On the other hand, there's a scarcity of published usability studies and test reports of F/OSS from academics. We are aware of studies on GNOME (Smith, et. al., 2001), Greenstone (Nichols, Thomson, Kirsten & Yeates, 2001), file browser screening test (Reitmayr, 2007), Linux desktop out of box experience (Göktürk & Çetin, 2007) and OpenOffice.org usability test (Çetin, Verzulli & Frings, 2006), to name a few. While there is little formal research on F/OSS usability, developers are well aware that F/OSS usability is a problem that should be solved and usability is a significant issue of unsuccessful F/OSS projects. According to Müehling (2004), "it becomes clear that F/OSS projects have a fundamental problem: they lack usability resources that help achieve better usable software for non-geek users".

Issues stemming from development paths affect the usability process of open source projects. Lack of developers also indirectly means lack of usability experts. Hierarchical models in which main decisions are taken by lead (core) developers with a lack of user interface design background affect the usability centeredness of F/OSS projects, hence the usability of the product. A developer working in a F/OSS project should have explicit rights and title, together with a strong technical

Figure 1. Sample tasks of potential usability experts and contributors

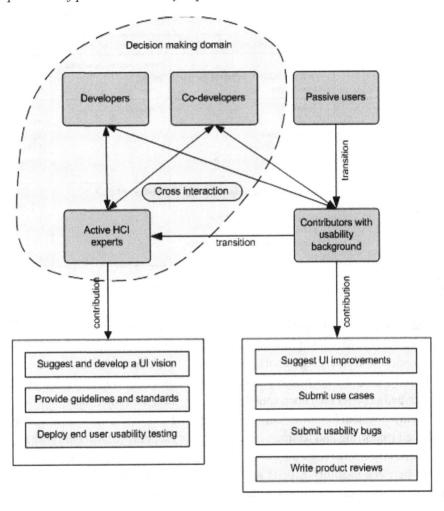

background in order to increase the usability of resulting product. Like Apache project, many open source projects are meritocracy, therefore usability experts need to provide a series of strong evidences to support their suggestions, otherwise developers do not tend to compare them with any other generic contributor with an opinion.

While there's little evidence that F/OSS projects are structured in terms of usability knowledge and expertise, there are both active (i.e., those who share their knowledge by sharing ideas, attending discussions and giving feedback) and passive HCI experts, for whom we need to identify the amount of contribution for each entity. We also do not have a measured relationship between

usability and F/OSS projects. Figure 1 gives a more detailed overview of a F/OSS project with developers and the process from a passive user to an active HCI expert. Potential tasks are also given in boxes.

Usability in open source community does exist but rather is considered as a matter of taste. Indeed, each developer has a personal way of implementing user interfaces. In Table 1, three criteria (employment of HCI experts, communication between HCI experts and project developers and reporting a testing process) are discussed between open source and closed source model, together with advantages and disadvantages. Since some of the arguments are subject to debate, these are

Table 1. Usability methods and models in distributed groups and closed groups

Criteria	Distributed Groups		Closed Groups	
	Structure	(Dis)advantages	Structure	(Dis)advantages
Employment	Weak	(+) fast (+) not subject to a technical barrier (-) low degree	Better than open source model	(+) well defined criteria (-) potentially undiscovered
Communication	Virtual	(-) informal (+-) online (-) asynchronous (-) usually limited vision (-) control of the software by programmers	Physical	(*) formal (*) well defined (+) direct communication (*) hierarchical, top-down approach
Reporting and testing	Emerging	(-) no well defined tasks and guidelines (-) no well defined templates (+-) less comprehensive (*) generally indirect communication	Well established	(+) direct communication of experts with users

(+) Advantage (-) Disadvantage (*) Neutral

enlisted as neutral. In summary, usability in open source model can be stated as weak (employment), virtual (communication) and emerging (reporting and testing). Similarly, usability in closed source model can be described as better than open source model (employment), physical (communication) and well established (reporting and testing).

There are issues and concerns regarding communication paths between usability experts and F/OSS developers, targeting cognitive and social norms:

1. Developers are uninformed about contextual inquiry and user centered requirements process, resulting in a lack of immediate experience of observing product use in the field.
2. Usability experts do not have a detailed understanding of how F/OSS projects work, usually coming on strongly as critics, rather than contributors, builders or problem solvers. While part of this is perception, another part is the tendency that usability experts lack the ability or willingness to develop software. In an open source world with a limited set of tools and immature development frameworks by means of quality and quantity compared to proprietary world, a minimum experience of the software development mental model is sought to build next generation user interfaces.
3. Developers do not have the benefits and outcomes of working with a usability expert. Personal contact between developer and usability expert is often ignored, leaving little or no space to get any form user feedback and to show that the product does actually not work the way the developers thought it would.
4. Lack of scientific research in this field results in a lack of respect in the validity of the field of usability by software developers, and use of scientific usability metrics the developers can relate to, in order to assess their applications' user interface.

USABILITY PROCESSES

Usability of computer applications is becoming more important with the increase of relatively uneducated people with less skill to cope with the complexity of user interfaces. Lately, it has been observed that users are unwilling to put up with uncomfortable or difficult since experience with some current interfaces has shown them that software can indeed be easy to learn and pleasant to use (Nielsen, 1994). Therefore, high usability is a must requirement of a software application, since there are an increasing number of mature and competing products in the market. However, without proper usability evaluation methods, it's not possible to measure the usability level of a particular application as all contemporary commercial products where product maturity and technical challenges are already left behind within/among competing products.

There are many usability evaluation methods for different domains, from mobile devices (Kjeldskov and Stage, 2004) to interactive TV sets (Pemberton and Griffiths, 2003; Daly-Jones, 2002; Gauntlett and Hill, 1999). These include expert evaluations like cognitive walkthroughs (Lewis, Polson, Wharton and Rieman, 1990; Wharton, Bradford, Jeffries and Franzke, 1992) or heuristic evaluations (Nielsen and Molich, 1990). We can classify usability evaluation methods into four, namely formal methods, automated methods, empirical methods and heuristics. A formal method (Card, Moran & Newell, 2003) benefits from formal and metric models to take usability measurements. Automatic method measures usability by measuring a user specification through an application. It stems from usability measures to describe the functioning of a system through the assessment of the software (Byrne et. al., 1994). An empirical method provides the most reliable methodology among all, since it incorporates a sample of real world users by examining the properties of usability and observing how a sizeable sample of real users uses the system (Butler, 1996). The inspection method is based on the heuristics and rules of functioning, and it includes a single assessor who carries out the inspection of the application (Nielsen, 1990). Other sub-types of evaluation methods include verbal protocols

(Ericsson and Simon, 1984), critical incident reporting (del Galdo, Williges, Williges and Wixon, 1987) and user satisfaction ratings (Chin, Diehl and Norman, 1988).

Usability processes produce competing products, by consistently evaluating the user interface using methods mentioned above. Obviously, coordinated and cooperative design has been an important task lately, with the introduction of Internet and internet-enabled software houses. In an open source world, there's a lack of understanding of "representative user", who will help assess the end product usability. Without this pool of users, developers can only imagine and develop according to their mental model, potentially ignoring end user tasks. According to Nielsen (1994), users should be involved in the design process through regular meetings between designers and users however this is often not possible when the software is developed internationally, speaking of thousands of kilometers between developers' country borders. Current attempts to gather developers and usability experts in regular meetings do not disperse the issue of "lack of interaction" with end users.

User contribution to product usability has been investigated in the literature for a long time. They are not designers, however can propose different interaction alternatives like designers when they are given enough time, support and environment. On the other hand, since reactions and critics to design could act as a barrier towards new incentives and building blocks for innovation. A communication channel is required, exploiting the advantages of the Internet, by guiding users to a productive discussion. In an internet-supported environment where software is developed in a free and unrestricted manner, a centralized, decision making authority is needed to focus the discussions not only for development, but also for usability merits. Both usability experts and end users expect to be encouraged to design smaller instances of a big picture so that these parts are regarded as design representatives or instances of illustration.

Table 2. Frequency of some keywords in KDE, GNOME and Mozilla bug database. Numbers given include only those found in open bugs.

Keyword	KDE bug database	GNOME bug database	Mozilla bug database
Total number of open bugs by 9/9/2008	32000+	37000+	44000+
Usability	1020	997	38
Usable	678	414	115
Interface design	111	71	6
Human interface guidelines	8	19	1
User centric (centered) design	1	5	0

During the discussions, a category-specific or product-specific user interface guideline could also be produced.

According to Nichols and Twidale (2006), main arguments for the proposition that usability may be an area of concern for OSS can be summarized as follows:

1. Developers are not typical end users.
2. Usability experts do not get involved in OSS projects.
3. Open source projects lack the resources to undertake high-quality usability work.
4. Interface (re)design may not be amenable to the same approaches as functionality (re) design.

In the absence of usability expertise, 'itch-based OSS design' will not necessarily succeed in improving ease of use for those users, such as novices, whose background differs from that of the developers (Nichols and Twidale, 2005). Still, a typical, basic search on KDE, GNOME and Mozilla bug database show that there are relatively less number of bugs containing the terms usability, usable, interface design, human interface guidelines and user centric design (Table 2). On the other hand, a study by Çetin, Verzulli and Frings (2007) reveals that one third of KDE bugs are usability bugs, the table shows that reporters do not refer to the aforementioned terms

while submitting a usability bug.

Nichols and Twidale (2006) outline some of the usability work in open source projects. Their observations derive from ethnographic study of the Mozilla and GNOME projects, following an observational approach based around bug repositories, mailing lists and blogs. Other interesting usability activities in F/OSS domain include usability sprints, usually held periodically. In a sprint, open source developers, usability practitioners, project managers, and users gather to discuss methodologies in order to improve the usability of F/OSS software and apply those processes towards specific projects. With the goal to catalyze a shared understanding and ongoing collaboration between the usability and open source communities, these physical meetings blur the distance among disconnected stakeholders of F/OSS community.

There are many published methodologies to ensure a user centered design process during the development of a product. All of these methodologies focus on the end users who will directly benefit from the product and the purpose for which they use. Among various usability methodologies, card sorting, usability testing and video screen capturing are the least used ones in open source domain since these require a systematic progress and relatively high degree of usability expertise.

Over years, researchers tried to align usability

Table 3.

Opened by Vinicius Depizzol (reporter)
2006-12-07 14:57
gnome-cups-manager should follow the GNOME Human Interface Guidelines.
Comment #1 from Christian Persch (developer)
2006-12-10 18:47
Thanks for the bug report.
Could you be more specific about where exactly gnome-cups-manager lacks HIG compliance?
Comment #2 from Vinicius Depizzol (reporter)
2006-12-11 14:50
The properties window of the printer (Edit > Properties) don't follow the Layout Specification [1] of GNOME HIG, as well information alerts (Printer >Print test page) [2].
Thank you.
[1] http://developer.gnome.org/projects/gup/hig/2.0/design-window.html#layout-callouts-figure
[2] http://developer.gnome.org/projects/gup/hig/2.0/windows-alert.html

engineering (UE) concepts and processes with that of software engineering (SE). It was a matter of seamless integration of UE within SE so that developers would be able to progress without waiting for, or get interrupted from usability engineers. Given that a graphical user interface comprises half of the development effort and code in modern applications (Myers and Rosson, 1992), there have been mathematical computations regarding costs of usability development in order to justify the development efforts. While both SE and UE both provide a wide range of process models, these have been seldom exploited mutually in order to build a systematic model with a focus and approach on user centered design (UCD). According to Hakiel (1997), "Although the emergence of human factors engineering predates that of software engineering, an integrated approach to the design of ease of use in human-computer systems is yet not routine in the software industry." There are many reasons behind this, namely i) current UE models differ much from SE models, ii) usability models are complex, iii) company managers do not believe that usability is cost justified, and iv) project managers, designers and developers see HCI as an academic subject (Granollers, Lorés, and Perdrix, 2003). The challenges have popped up within the integration models of SE and UE, and researchers have identified different SE process models with different abilities to create usable products,

assessing their UE absorption level.

This issue, by far, is not limited to uninstitutionalized UE methods. Distributed projects with a loose development process have far more issues than those developed under a controlled mechanism. The issues arise from different facts, mainly bug reporting systems and hierarchical decision paths. For example, deciding whether fixing a usability bug affects the issue itself, or should the developer work on other parts of the user interface to keep the coherence and satisfy compatibility (i.e within-application consistency) has been an issue. If the application is relatively small and has a few number of screens, the bug does not have a rolling effect. On the other hand, if the bug affects the whole desktop (i.e. changing a logo, modifying a help page, having a major update to the basic UI library), its implications should be analyzed deeper, potentially including other developers. Moreover, identifying whether a bug is really a usability bug has been an issue. Nichols and Twidale (2007) note that some usability bugs have been regarded as unneeded. This may stem from the fact that the compliance of a bug with the human interface guidelines (HIG) of the given product or project cannot be easily determined due to lack of adequate guidelines. As an example, Table 3 shows discussions which have been taken from GNOME bug reporting tool, Bugzilla.

Table 4.

Kmail
New Print | *Check Mail^ | *Reply^ *Forward^ | Previous Next | Trash | Spam Ham | [User-defined Tags]
Konqueror Web
Previous^ Next^ Refresh Stop | Home Bookmark [URL]

Open source development process is transparent. Developers work on the Internet, mostly in an asynchronous manner, in order to collaborate, communicate and cooperate with the help of a variety of tools with a basic complexity (i.e. instant messenger) to a greater complexity (i.e. a comprehensive document sharing system). These tools help projects define and enforce some rules as required in order to ensure a seamless teamwork. Likewise, much of the usability work is transparent to users, hence everyone is invited and encouraged to provide feedback to the HIG (Human Interface Guidelines) developed, which in turn will be populated in a Wiki like page for review process. For example, the following excerpt is from the weblog of a KDE (an open source desktop environment) developer.

This is obso1337.org's weblog. She posts toolbar guidelines for generic KDE4 applications. Rather than using graphical rich explanation of how to describe the toolbar contents, she uses text based rendering of Kmail (a web client for KDE) toolbar, giving examples from different distributions and focusing on less cluttered and less confusing configuration. Among 19 responses to her blog, there are questions and comments from developers of different applications, end users and other usability experts. The main debate focuses on the use and aim of Back and Up buttons.

In another blog, a developer gives a proposal regarding the toolbar icon organization of an open source e-mail client (Table 4). In her text base diagram, split buttons are denoted by ^, icon separators are denoted by | and notes are denoted by *. There have been more than 18 responses

to his proposal, and upon debating on the new interface design using a collaborative approach, mentioned improvements to the user interface are expected to be merged in the new human interface guidelines.

Another usability activity seen in distributed projects is bug-hunting seasons. For example, in the scope of KDE 4 usability review cycle, KDE HCI working group announced the HIG hunting season, which is an experiment to include the community into the search for obvious infringements of the KDE HIG. This procedure is also backed by the projects, and end users analyze applications, by reporting user interface and interaction issues that can be stated like bugs. Users are asked to find points which disturb a seamless use experience, such as inconsistencies among applications, incomplete keyboard access, missing feedback, or overloaded configuration dialogs, toolbars or menus. This way, applications can be transparently analyzed and tested by anyone using a given checklist early before the UI becomes mature. Usability bugs are reported directly in the bug tracking system tagged with the attribute "HIG", so that it could later be easy for developers to search and fix a list of tagged bugs during the review cycle. Table 5 shows a checklist from a bug-hunting season.

Nichols and Twidale (2002) give a comprehensive outlook on how usability experts and open source developers work in a distributed manner. In their paper, authors explain how design-by-blog works in a way to leverage the design the UI and wait for comments in order to let the design evolve by time using pure end user participatory design methods. Alternating screenshots, textual commentaries and rationales, often giving examples

Table 5.

Today's Checklist: Configuration Dialogs
Today's checklist is about Configuration Dialogs - we plan to announce more lists every three or four days, for example toolbars, menus, context menus, color settings, keyboard access, feedback dialogs, and more. The procedure for reviewers is pretty simple: 　　1. You pick an application that is already in trunk, but not yet reviewed by another person. See the Wiki page for reference. 　　2. You open a checklist - today's focus is Configuration Dialogs - and go through the checklist items. 　　3. For each infringement you find, post a bug. In the title, write "HIG" and the number of the checklist item that is not met (e.g. CL1/1.1). 　　4. On the Wiki page of checklists, add a section for the application you reviewed and link all bugs you have created. For developers, this will probably mean a lot of work. However, many of the "HIG" bugs can be fixed easily by referring to the checklist, others will be harder. Regarding configuration dialogs, bugs that concern the dialog navigation or size of dialogs can be fixed easily; problems concerning the categorization or grouping require further analysis.

from interface guidelines help reach a consensus among project stakeholders.

A DISTRIBUTED USABILITY PROCESS

Requirements gathering is the first and foremost step in usability design. Scacchi (2002) claims that requirements for open source projects seem to be asserted, rather than elicited. In his paper, Scacchi examines features of a major release of the Firefox web browser an attempt to understand how prevalent this phenomenon is. Using archives of mailing lists and issue tracking databases, features of Firefox were tracked from first mentioning to the release date, to determine how requirements are proposed, adopted and implemented. In open source projects, requirements are normally not aligned with usability requirements, but they are rather separate, and most of the time usability requirements (i.e. acceptable levels of user performance, effectiveness and satisfaction) are ignored, giving a higher priority to extracting functional requirements and data requirements, i.e. structure of the system or the necessary database model.

Field experts in software requirements engineering propose a set of activities (i.e. process items) which (Davis, 1990) do not necessarily characterize an order. A software development starts with identifying requirements analysis. In open source world, requirements analysis is usu-

ally neglected, or requirements are only partly and simply identified. Moreover, many projects lack the distinction between functional and non-functional requirements.

Participatory design is the most prevalent part of the open usability lifecycle. However, most distributed projects start with little or no end users. Therefore, projects initially lack user aid during the predesign and design stage, hence developers provide marketing requirements, derive product usability features and build user interfaces with the help of their previous own experiences, without access to a group of knowledgeable users. This results in a continuous re-design during the development phase, and even after the project maturity stage. However, the inclusion of end users does not mean that usability engineers should be omitted, and the UE processes are left to end users providing half understood checklists, unfinished usability tests and unclear results. As in institutionalized usability process, distributed projects should deploy HCI experts with a background in open source software processes, and preferably, knowledge in open source tools and applications.

Since not all software engineers have a knowledge about usability processes and rather they tend to stick with SE models, our diagram does not radically modify the SE lifecycle but rather extends it, so that usability processes are immersed within the SE processes. This is done in a way that, if a particular usability activity is

Figure 2. Points of interaction for usability experts in open source projects

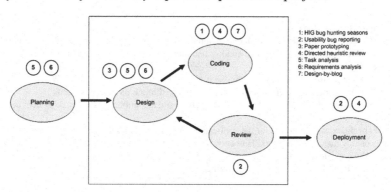

not seen in open source project domain, then it's automatically omitted so developers can focus on a potentially realizable method. Below is a graphical diagram showing what usability activities can be deployed during the production of an open source product where developers interact on a dispersed geographical location during an asynchronous time frame.

Figure 2 shows many advantages, giving a broad overview of when and which usability activities can be immersed in open source projects. The main differentiating point of this model is that, it provides additional activities and deletes those which cannot be realized in distributed, open source projects with little end user activity and budget. For example, usability tests are omitted while they are regarded as strong validators from end users' point of view.

Main features of this model are as follows:

1. Each stage is interconnected and related with at least one usability activity.
2. Usability starts early in planning stage; however it's a common way to increase the level of usability activities during the design and coding phases.
3. Each activity is used at least in one stage. The only point where the user is not involved is the planning stage.
4. Every activity can be tracked via the Internet, giving project stakeholders a controlling and

monitoring possibility.
5. It's a common sense to report usability bugs in the first review stage. As subsequent design > coding > review cycles occur, bug reports start to increase in design and coding stage also, with the help of increase in the number of end users.

CONCLUSION

In this chapter, we examined different types of collaboration methods of usability experts and developers working in a distributed domain, focusing particularly on open source projects. Given the limitations and features of usability processes in this approach, we proposed an "open usability engineering method" which could be exploited in distributed projects, which could assure the success of open source projects usability wise.

Just as the scarcity of well-defined usability processes, experts and users giving feedback in open source world, there's also lack of a structured approval system. Since developers are also users of the application, there's a self-approval method in terms of reliability, security, performance, and also usability, eliminating the need for 3rd party interaction. Instead of building a self-dependency framework, projects could be implementing an open, distributed usability approval methodology. A certification model could also be adopted in order to motivate developers and guide them through better understanding of usability principles.

REFERENCES

Benson, C., Adam, E., Nickell, S., & Robertson, C. Z. (2002). *GNOME Human Interface Guidelines 1.0*. Retrieved July 2, 2007 from http://developer.gnome.org/projects/gup/hig/1.0.

Butler, K. (1996). Usability engineering. *Interaction*, *3*(1), 58–75. doi:10.1145/223500.223513

Byrne, M. D., Wood, S. D., Foley, J. D., Kieras, D. E., & Sukaviriya, P. N. (1994). Automating interface evaluation. *CHI '94: Proceedings of the SIGCHI conference on Human factors in computing systems,* (New York, pp. 232–237 NY, USA)., New York: ACM, pp. 232–237.

Çetin, G., Verzulli, D., & Frings, S. (2007). An Analysis of Involvement of HCI Experts in Distributed Software Development: Practical Issues. *Online Communities and Social Comput., HCII 2007*, (LNCS 4564, pp. 32–40). Springer-Verlag Berlin: Springer-Verlag. Heidelberg

Chin, J. P., Diehl, V. A., & Norman, K. L. (1988). Development of an instrument measuring user satisfaction of the human-computer interface. *Proceedings of CHI Conference on Human Factors in Computing Systems* (pp. 213-218). New York: ACM, 213-218.

Davis, A. M. (1990). *Software Requirements: Analysis and Specification*. New York: Prentice-Hall.

Del Galdo, E. M., Williges, R. C., Williges, B. H., & Wixon, D. R. (1987). A critical incident evaluation tool for software documentation. In L. S. Mark, J. S. Warm, & R. L. Huston (Eds.), *Ergonomics and Human Factors*, (pp. 253-258). New York: Springer-Verlag, 253-258

Ericsson, A., & Simon, H. (1984). *Protocol analysis: verbal reports as data*. Boston: The MIT Press.

Gauntlett, D., & Hill, A. (1999). *TV Living: TV, Culture and Everyday Life*. London: Routledge.

Göktürk, M., & Çetin, G. (2007). Out of Box Experience Issues of Free and Open Source Software. *HCI International Proceedings,* (Volume 1), (LNCS_4550). ISBN: 978-3-540-73104-7

Granollers, T., Lorès, J., & Perdrix, F. 2002. Usability Engineering Process Model. – Integration with Software Engineering. *Proceedings of HCI International 2003*. Crete, Greece.

Hakiel, S. (1997). Delivering ease of use. *Computing & Control Engineering Journal*, April 1997.

Kjeldskov, J., & Stage, J. (2004). New Techniques for Usability Evaluation of Mobile Systems. *International Journal of Human-Computer Studies*, *60*(5-6): 599–620. doi:10.1016/j.ijhcs.2003.11.001

Lerner, J., & Tirole, J. (2002). Some Simple Economics of Open Source. *The Journal of Industrial Economics*, *46*(2), 125–156.

Myers, B. A., & Rosson, M. B. (1992). Survey on user interface programming. In *Proceedings of CHI'92,* Monterey, CA (pp. 195-202). New York: ACM, pp. 195-202.

Nichols, D. M., Thomson, A., Kirsten, T., & Yeates, S. (2001). Usability and open-source software development. In Elizabeth E. Kemp, Chris Phillips, Kinshuk, and & John J. Haynes, (Editors), *Symposium on Computer Human Interaction*, Palmerston North, New Zealand, (pp. 49–54). New York: ACM SIGCHI NZ.

Nichols, D. M., & Twidale, M. B. (2003). The usability of open source software. *First Monday* *8*(1). Retrieved September 15, 2005 from: http://firstmonday.org/issues/issue81/nichols/, 15 September 2005)

Nielsen, J. (1990). Big playbacks from discount usability. *IEEE Software, 3*, 107–108.

Nielsen, J., & Molich, R. (1990). Heuristic Evaluation of User Interfaces. *Proceedings of CHI Conference on Human Factors in Computing Systems,* (pp. 249-256). New York: ACM, 249-256.

Noll, J. (2008). Open Source Development, Communities and Quality. In Barbara Russo, Ernesto E. Damiani, Scott S. Hissam, Björn B. Lundell, Giancarlo G. Succi (Eds.), *IFIP International Federation for Information Processing*, (Volume 275, pp. 69–79). Boston: Springer.

Pemberton, L., & Griffiths, R. (2003). Usability evaluation techniques for interactive television. *Proc. HCI International*.

Raymond, E. (1999). *The revenge of the hackers.* In M. Stone, S. Ockman, and & C. DiBona (Editors), *Open Sources: Voices from the Open Source Revolution* (pp. 207-219). Sebastopol, Calif.: O'Reilly & Associates.

Scacchi, W. (2002). Understanding the Requirements for Developing Open Source Software Systems. *IEE Proceedings Software, 149*(1), pp. 24-39.

Smith, S., Engen, D., Mankoski, A., Frishberg, N., Pedersen, N., & Benson, C. (2001). GNOME Usability Study Report. *Sun GNOME Human Computer Interaction Laboratory*.

Wharton, C., Bradford, J., Jeffries, R., & Franzke, M. (1992). Applying Cognitive Walkthroughs to More Complex User Interfaces: Experiences, Issues, and Recommendations. *Proceedings of CHI Conference on Human Factors in Computing Systems,* (pp. 381-388). New York: ACM, 381-388.

Chapter 13
Lights, Cameras, Actions! Via Teacher Librarian Video Conferencing

Lesley Farmer
California State University, USA

ABSTRACT

How can professional organizations build an online community of practice that enables teacher librarians globally to connect meaningfully and make a difference locally—and beyond? Video conferencing is one solution. Using video conferencing, teacher librarians have a unique opportunity to help build a strong collaborative, professional network that will positively impact best practices while at the same time raise awareness of twenty-first century librarianship. Critical elements and practices are identified that facilitate communities of practice and support teacher librarian professional development. Aspects of video conferencing are detailed, and a case study on the use of video conferencing explains how to facilitate a nation-wide community of practice among teacher librarians.

INTRODUCTION

To become a proficient teacher librarian (TL) requires ongoing education and interaction with peers (Smith, 2003). Some school districts provide mechanisms for professional development: material and human resources, formal and information learning opportunities, and funding for participation in professional development venues. More recently, school districts and professional organizations have been experimenting with ways to build and maintain

communities of practice (CoP). For communities of practice to succeed, both social interaction and ongoing improvement must exist. Time constraints and transportation make face-to-face meetings increasingly problematic. In this interactive digital age, virtual social networking models need to be explored as an effective means of facilitating communities of practice, particularly if TLs are to expand their knowledge beyond local practice.

Video is making a comeback because of its multimedia and archival features. Particularly with the advent of digital camcorders and easy-to-use editing software, video has regained its reputation as a viable

DOI: 10.4018/978-1-60566-727-0.ch013

educational tool for professional development and management since video is an appropriate vehicle for training, knowledge management, systems analysis, and public relations.

This chapter explores the effectiveness of video conferencing as a mechanism for developing and maintaining a community of practice for learning leaders (such as teacher librarians). Using video conferencing, teacher librarians have a unique opportunity to help build a strong collaborative, professional network that will positively impact best practices while at the same time raise awareness of twenty-first century librarianship. This chapter examines the philosophy of communities of practice, the nature of video conferencing, and provides a case study on the use of video conferencing to facilitate a nation-wide community of practice among teacher librarians. Both general considerations and lessons learned from an extended case study are provided.

BACKGROUND

Teacher librarians (TLs) work in K-12 school settings, and have as their mission to ensure that students and staff become effective users of ideas and information. To carry out this charge, successful TLs:

- provide intellectual and physical access to materials in all formats;
- provide instruction to foster competence and stimulate interest in reading, viewing and using information and ideas;
- work with other educators to design learning strategies to meet the needs of individual students.

They need to develop and manage resource collections, serve as effective teachers as well as effective information specialists, and administrate a library program of services. The role of the TL requires multiple competencies (curriculum, media, administration, collaboration, professional development, etc.) and as a result of these efforts, TLs make positive advancements in multiple contexts.

The need to bring these multiple worlds together is becoming more critical because of the increasingly underestimated value of the TLs. In this digital age of easy access to online resources; who needs libraries? Can't online help take care of information questions? Yet, it is apparent that students usually are not efficient online searchers or critical thinkers. Who is best positioned to teach *all* students about how to access and process information in myriad forms for myriad purposes? TLs. They are truly resource persons, providing value-added physical and intellectual access to information and ideas. Not only do TLs know how information is created, disseminated, organized and used across the curriculum and beyond, but they know how to *teach* the entire school community how to be fluent and responsible users of these resources.

Using video conferencing, TLs have a unique opportunity to help build a strong collaborative, professional network that will provide ongoing professional improvement and facilitate collaboratively-created products (e.g., online bibliographies, web tutorials, library portals, digital learning objects) that can be shared with the rest of the education community.

Need for Professional Development

For K-12 teacher librarians (TL) to be effective in their work, they need to keep current in the field. Dall'Alba and Sandberg (2006) defined two dimensions of professional development: improved skills (the competency level) and embodied understanding of practice (the "big picture"); beginners tend to focus on the former, while experienced TLs may well stay at the competency level rather than continuing to seek challenges and take a longer-term perspective. Oberg (1995) found that expert TLs had stronger professional networks, and were committed to ongoing professional education, mentoring, advocacy, and policy development. The question arises: how can all ranges of TLs inform and support each other? How can local library programs and the profession as a whole advance?

Some school districts provide mechanisms for TL-domain professional development: district centers of professional materials, district telecommunications channels by job function, periodic meetings of all TLs, in-service workshops for TLs, on-site visits by district librarians, and money for individual conference attendance and online professional development. Professional associations also provide continuing education, which requires that TLs proactively join such groups and participate.

Several technology-based techniques have been used in these professional development avenues: special interest groups (SIG), listservs, online "chats," nings, blogs and wikis.

Need for Collaboration

Cunningham (1998) emphasized the effectiveness of workplace learning through interactions with other learners and experts, reinforcing social-interaction conceptualization. The TL is one person in the teaching profession that has the mantle of promoting and supporting meaningful collaboration among teachers. Paradoxically, collaboration among TLs is less frequent and more difficult to do. In most school settings, only one TL serves the school community. Particularly since school librarianship demands constant service and supervision, finding the time, the people, and the resources for professional development can be daunting.

Increasingly, school districts and professional organizations have advanced the use of communities of practice (CoP). Basically, a community of practice begins with members with common values and goals, a model that applies well to both face-to-face and online learning environments.

CoPs can be effective mechanism to accomplish a variety of activities:

- to inform: through email, discussion boards, blogs, wikis, online chat
- to gather data: through surveys, focus groups, discussion boards
- to assess: through peer review, joint rubric development, critical supervision
- to stimulate ideas: through discussion, dissemination of provocative readings, social networking tools
- to contribute knowledge: through discussion boards, web 2.0 applications, repositories

While CoPs have a social dimension that fosters interdependence, their chief raison-d'etre is organizational or professional improvement.

Usually, a CoP includes both new and veteran members, the idea being that each has unique perspectives and experiences; newer members may have current training or insights garnered from other organizations, and senior members bring a collective history and sagacity about organizational culture. In a virtual environment, CoPs start small because the contributions are limited to the number of people involved, but as the group grows, the impact correspondingly increases (Metcalfe's Law). For this reason, basing a virtual community on existing professional affiliations is a way to jump-start this impact. Critical features of a CoP include:

- A system of socializing new members to form a group identity
- a "flat" system so that everyone can learn from each other
- meaningful tasks that draw upon group wisdom and challenge members to learn more (Wenger, 1998).

Cox (2008) recommends the following actions as CoPs form:

- Emphasize outcomes about increased professional and student learning.
- Base actions on group needs.
- Cite research and literature that demonstrate the impact of CoPs.
- Select a reputable CoP leader and group facilitator.
- Develop an atmosphere of openness, respect, responsiveness, safety and trust.
- Design activities and recognitions that demonstrate the value of all participants; make CoP membership prestigious and powerful.
- Incorporate social opportunities in an invigorating environment.

CoPs also try to be sustainable, outlasting a single-goal task force mentality. For CoPs to be effective, there needs to be anticipated reciprocity (give-and-take of knowledge), increased recognition, and a sense of efficacy (Smith & Kollock, 1999). The group needs to develop a sense of trust and commitment that transcends possible conflicts, gain support from decision-makers, have sufficient resources to accomplish objectives, and experience public recognition.

Incorporating Technology

Increasingly, virtual communities of practice are being used to complement, supplement or replace face-to-face communities for several reasons: to overcome transportation and geographic problems, to provide a mechanism to communicate more often, to archive interactions and documents created by individuals and groups, to provide timely feedback, and to keep members active and engaged (Rheingold, 2000). However, virtual CoPs have disadvantages: sense of isolation, possibly less commitment and accountability, lack of nuanced communication cues (e.g., body language, tone), less spontaneity, technical limitations (e.g., cost of equipment, software, difficulty of learning the technology) (Lynch, 2002).

Several technology-based tools have been used to foster CoPs for TLs. Web 2.0 offers a variety of social networking tools to communicate and share documents; blogs, wikis, and social bookmarking provide asynchronous venues. Real-time online chat (e.g., http://www.tappedin.org), offers a way to provide guided group discussion; the chat is recorded and archived, and virtual offices store group documents. Virtual reality environments, such as Second Life, enable participants to synchronously chat and speak using avatars to represent themselves; documents may be stored in these environments. However, these virtual venues require current hardware and significant training time.

Longer-term CoPs sometimes use online course management systems (CMS) to provide a single-entry system that incorporates synchronous and asynchronous communication as well as archived documents. Both professional and higher education entities use this technology to facilitate threaded discussion and a federated building of knowledge. However, CMSs can be more complicated than participants want or need, and they are usually more costly or require additional technology expertise if they use an Open Source model.

Video conferencing (VC) as a collaborative tool for communities of practice provides a way to address some of the limitations of virtual communities. Using cameras, microphones, network connection and supporting hardware (e.g., a video conferencing terminal that includes a codec ("COmpressor/DECompressor") and a user interface) two or more parties can see and hear each other in real time. Current technologies make it possible for people to conference from their computer work stations for free with very little technical set-up. The Video Network Initiative gives good technical guidelines (http://www.vide.net/cookbook/). Video conferencing has been used by businesses for over two decades, mainly because its characteristics resemble a face-to-face experience more closely than other technologies.

The following features of VC make it a unique and beneficial conduit for CoPs:

- high-resolution video and audio that can accommodate groups of people
- real-time interaction without high transportation costs
- multi-location access
- ability to record sessions
- ability to incorporate external resources: computer, document stand, whiteboard, telephone link, dataconferencing link.

The Potential of Video Conferencing

On the whole, VCs offer a more personal, relational online learning environment for meaningful group interaction than other computer-mediated or audio medium. This form of communication also paves the way for TLs to work with their site teachers and administrators to organize VC collaboration opportunities with grade levels and departments outside their district or state. Typically, video conferencing has been used by librarians within large school districts, library consortia, and professional organizations. Recently, organizations are starting to talk with each other via video conferencing; when the American Library Association conference overlapped the National Educational Computing Conference, TLs from both organizations connected with each other virtually using a tabletop video set-up.

Video conferencing has several benefits that together uniquely facilitate CoPs:

- Participants feel included because they can experience everyone, including body language. Current technology provides high-resolution images with little if any time delay for voice synchronization, so that subtle expressions can be decoded accurately.
- Groups can access and consult with outside experts in their own environments (facilitating demonstrations and "field trip"

experiences) easily through this virtual medium.

- The live atmosphere is more relaxing than an audio or text-only setting, and encourages more conversation and better problem-solving (Sallnas, 2005).
- Live demonstrations, such as new products introduced by vendors, can simplify instructions, and questions can be handled immediately.
- Documents and realia can be shared more easily.
- Quick set-up time enables groups to share topics of immediate, timely interest
- Multiple sites can exchange the same information simultaneously, optimizing consistent messages (Higgs-Horwell & Schwelik, 2007; Townes-Young & Ewing, 2005).

Video conferencing also has drawbacks. Certainly, it works only as well as the equipment and the connectivity allow it to. Bandwidth capacity and workload (i.e., simultaneous use) are particularly important considerations, even with compressed video. Poorly managed video conferencing sessions can also lead to disappointing results. In their investigation of virtual teams, Anderson, McEwan and Carletta (2007) and Chakraborty and Victor (2004) noted these video conferencing issues:

- Remote sites tend to take on an us-them attitude, wherein each group tends to think more positively about themselves and downplays the remote groups.
- Talk is more task-oriented / less social, and bodies are more confined than in face-to-face meetings.
- The site which has the main event coordinator has higher status; other sites may feel less involved or at a disadvantage. Without a strong supervisor, the remote group may disengage. If two sites share the coordination, the lead people have to negotiate

communication. (It should be noted that leadership is more diffuse in video conferences than in face-to-face meetings.)

- When a large group uses video conferencing, the discussion becomes more formal and structured; communication tends to become lecture mode. People at the back of the room may feel less connected.
- Technical support is needed, at least for emergencies (which occur when it is least convenient).

Most of these issues relate to group dynamics that are impacted by spatial relations. The group facilitators at each location can optimize these dynamics, particularly over time. For instance, they can arrange each group in a semi-circle facing the camera to insure equitable distance from each other. Facilitators can remix seating for each video conference. Facilitators can mix cross-site questions and in-group discussion with summation to take advantage of different group dynamics (Green & Cifuentes, 2008).

In comparing different types of virtual collaboration, Weinfan and Davis (2004) found that video conferencing lends itself well to specific kinds of group outcomes and situations:

- when new work teams are being formed, but face-to-face meetings are not feasible
- when sharing information with knowledgeable members that cannot be accomplished by reading
- when brainstorming ideas with people who are not comfortable with online chat but cannot meet face-to-face
- when need to negotiate, influence, or decide a subjective issue that cannot be addressed face-to-face
- when sharing updates among cohesive groups
- when trying to resolve disputes when one member seems to dominate another.

Regardless, of the group's objective, several measures should be taken to ensure a positive video conferencing experience and foster positive group dynamics.

- Pre-test the equipment and connectivity.
- Set up the room to encourage easy eye contact and conversation. A semi-round table works well.
- Generally, small groups at a location work better than large ones, particularly if the video conference connects several sites. Smaller groups are also more effective for complex tasks and problem-solving.
- If a large group is participating, place microphones around the room to facilitate speaking; if possible, use a rotating camera, and orient the room so that it is wider rather than deeper.
- Take advantage of shared digital applications (e.g., whiteboard, concept-mapping tools) to accomplish tasks.
- Begin the section with socialization rituals (i.e., introductions, ice-breakers, fact-finding, overview).
- Check the group's commitment and alignment with expected outcomes.
- Check frequently for understanding, and summarize ideas along the way.
- Address us-them issues, and give credit for ideas.
- Try to relax time constraints.
- Set up a sequence of sub-tasks so groups can work within their sites as well as across sites during the video conferencing. For instance, each group might brainstorm ideas, and then share their top three choices with other groups. Each group might discuss one aspect or factor of an issue, and then synthesize their key points to the whole. As a whole, participants could identify several possible solutions, and then have each group investigate the implications of that solution and report back their findings

(Ertl, Fischer & Mandl, 2006; Weinfan & Davis, 2004).

Group facilitators should plan collaboratively ahead of each video conference session to balance presentations and active discussion. Providing reading material ahead of time, and complementing video conferencing with follow-up peer online postings also help individuals feel connected and empowered (Green & Cifuentes, 2008).

In their research on virtual communication, Weinfan and Davis (2004) found that video conferencing has greater impact when participants know each other, and are committed to a sustained professional relationship. Participants will work harder and accomplish more. In that respect, effective video conferencing and CoPs are mutually supportive. Both group dynamics and goals need to be positive and worthwhile. Video conferencing groups should get to know each other ahead of time, ideally face-to-face, but even a telephone conversation can frontload acquaintanceships. Additionally, video conferencing group roles and expectations need to be more explicit than for face-to-face groups. Nor should video conferencing constitute the sole means of interaction; ongoing communication to group members and ongoing work toward achieving goals is required. Particularly since most video conferencing sessions have time limits, continuous communication – be it traditional or digital – can lower stress and frustration.

CASE STUDIES IN TL TECHNOLOGY COLLABORATION AND VIDEO CONFERENCING

In the world of TLs, peer collaboration is most likely to occur within a large school district or professional association. A lonely elementary TL in Chicago met regularly with fifteen TLs in the district to review broad topics such as library technology, but the group didn't have enough

time to develop ideas. When a password-protected group electronic discussion list was established, members could input their ideas at any time between meetings. As a result of their long-standing collaboration, the group saved the district's TL positions (Riskin, 2005). That same process worked for the Long Beach Unified School District's TLs using a combination of face-to-face meetings, email, and listserv (Oehlman & Moore, 2007).

State agencies, universities, and professional entities have explored video conferencing as a way to provide professional development across a large geographic area. East Carolina University's Teaching Resources Center planned an implemented a Librarian to Librarian Networking Summit video conference. As a result of this venture, attendees collectively gained confidence and established networks in order to learn from each other on an ongoing basis. Their interaction has led to professional interdependence and mutual support (Bailey, Tell & Walker, 2007). Their success was due to thorough planning, relevancy of the content, using a roundtable format, making summit documentation available ahead of time, and following up the summit with more communication.

The INFOohio Instructional Development Task Force has used video conferencing since 2004 to provide statewide professional development and timely updates about Ohio's virtual library. This method allows local experts to give consistent and efficient, high-quality training from their site to the rest of the state as needs arise. Support materials are emailed in preparation of each training, and workshops are archived on the Internet for future reference (Higgs-Horwell & Schwelik, 2007).

The California Computer-Using Educators (CUE) Library Media Educators (LME) SIG exemplifies a state's professional organization effort to mission is to provide opportunities for professional development and collaboration. The SIG uses a number of collaborative tools to foster engagement and social networking: a web portal containing documents and announcements to keep the membership current, a monthly online chat session on technology and librarians, a synchronous online application (Elluminate) that enables participants to present and share documents, and a Ning to communicate with peers and to post multimedia documents. To provide a more personal, relational online learning environment, the latest CUE LME SIG venture is a teacher librarian video conferencing network (TVLN) that involves not only its members but school districts around the United States and other professional organization affiliates.

The project leveraged California's new K-12 high-speed network (K-12HSN), which offered free hardware and connectivity to offer a stable virtual environment. Interested partners were identified: Orange County Department of Education and the Los Angeles Unified School District (both which had video conferencing equipment and broadband lines, California State University Long Beach's librarianship program, the American Association of School Librarians (AASL), the Media Specialists SIG within the International Society for Technology in Education (ISTE), and the International Association for School Librarianship. An email invitation to existing educational and librarianship organizations to participate in the video network drew responses from five state educational entities. Interest has been instigated through human social networking: individuals talking with individuals, be it face-to-face, telephone, or digitally. The video experience makes TLVN "real."

The following structure for the TL Video Network captures the spirit of CoPs:

- TLVN cohorts are small groups (e.g., interest groups such as CyberSafety) who use video conferencing and other interactive technologies for open discussion and collaborative work.
- TLV Network focuses on information sharing and identification of TL needs for geographically diverse groups.

- The TLVN Ning (http://teacherlibrarians.ning.com/) serves as a communications gateway for TLVN.
- Elluminate (a web conferencing application) facilitates presentations.
- TappedIn (an online synchronous/asynchronous virtual community for K-16 educators, including TLS, that supports online chat, shared URL viewing, archived chats, uploaded files, and telecommunications) is used for TLV cohort work. TLVN has a virtual office at http://www.tappedin.org/.

What are the lessons learned from these TL CoPs who use video conferencing?

- Find partners who want to develop a CoP, and have a shared understanding of goals.
- Focus on individuals with passion and influence.
- Follow up quickly after first contacts.
- Plan each video conference carefully, particularly at the beginning, but allow for changes as needs emerge.
- Start by educating participants in the uses and benefits of video conferencing, with a focus on collaborative product development and program improvement.
- Give people something meaningful to do. Give them responsibility. Give them credit. Foster interdependence.
- Keep the structure simple and transparent.
- Be willing to change direction.
- Say "yes!" to opportunities.
- Provide technical support as needed.
- Build in administrative capacity to follow up registration requests, schedule video conference venues, train newcomers, and support TLV cohorts.
- Keep the faith, and keep preaching. And turn words into action.

FUTURE RESEARCH DIRECTIONS

This new iteration of video conferencing in the interactive Internet environment has not been researched systematically. Its specific purpose to support and advance CoPs is virgin research territory. Therefore, many factors may be investigated. Weinfam's and Davis's (2004) variable clusters provide a useful framework for posing viable research questions.

Contextual variables:

- What personal factors (motivation, experience, personality), if any, are predictors for success in using video conferencing in CoPs?
- At what stage of CoPs development is video conferencing most or least effective?
- How do existing social networks impact the effectiveness of video conferencing?
- What technological configurations and support are necessary or sufficient in using video conferencing in CoPs?
- How good of image resolution is adequate for group interaction?
- What kinds of tasks (e.g., complexity, uncertainty, content, importance/consequence) lend themselves to video conferencing for CoPs?
- What timeframes -- in terms of session length, task duration, group membership -- work best for video conferencing for CoPs?

Process variables:

- How does video conferencing impact CoP participation and decision-making? What processes can optimize these behaviors?
- How does the innate structure of video conferencing impact CoP processes?
- What kinds of cognitive support facilitate video conferencing task accomplishment?

- How does CoP group size impact video conferencing interaction and task accomplishment?
- To what degree do CoPs need to meet each other or get acquainted before using video conferencing?
- How does the novelty of video conferencing impact CoP group dynamics and task work? When novelty wears off, how do group dynamics and task work change, if at all?

Group outcomes:

- What kinds of video conferencing tasks are best served with different group structures?
- How do social and task agendas impact video conferencing?
- How important is administrative support in sustaining video conferencing?
- How does video conferencing impact groupthink?
- How do group dynamics and task work change as participants meet over time?

CONCLUSION

With today's level of technology and the impact of globalization, video conferencing has re-emerged as a viable communications vehicle for collaboration. When structured to support communities of practice, video conferencing offers a rich environment for complex discussion. Video conferencing, however, does not function best alone, but should be complemented by other communication methods: both one-way and interactive. At its best, video conferencing can motivate individuals to share ideas openly, and serve as a catalyst for CoPs to act purposefully.

REFERENCES

Anderson, A., McEwan, R., & Carletta, J. (2007). Virtual team meetings: An analysis of communication and context. *Computers in Human Behavior*, *23*, 2558–2580. doi:10.1016/j.chb.2007.01.001

Bailey, A., Tell, L., & Walker, H. (2007). Librarian to Librarian Networking Summit: Collaboratively providing professional development for school media personnel. *Southeastern Librarian*, *55*(1), 3–13.

Chatraborty, M., & Victor, S. (2004). Do's and don't's of simultaneous instruction to on-campus and distance students via video conferencing. *Journal of Library Administration*, *41*(1/2), 97–112.

Clagg, M. (2002). Why beginning teachers stay in the profession: Views in a Kansas school district, (Doctoral dissertation, Wichita State University, 2002). *Dissertation Abstracts International*, *63*(4), 1197.

Cox, M. (2008). Faculty learning communities: Recommendations for initiating and implementing an FLC at your campus. *Faculty Learning Communities*. Miami, OH: Miami University. http://www.units.muohio.edu/flc/recommendations.php

Cunningham, J. (1998, Feb.). *The workplace: A learning environment.* Paper delivered at the First Annual Conference of the Australian Vocational Education and Training Research Association, Sydney.

Dall'Alba, G., & Sandberg, J. (2006). Unveiling professional development: A critical review of stage models. *Review of Educational Research*, *76*(3), 383–412. doi:10.3102/00346543076003383

Ertl, B., Fischer, F., & Mandl, H. (2006). Conceptual and socio-cognitive support for collaborative learning in video conferencing environments. *Computers & Education*, *47*, 298–315. doi:10.1016/j.compedu.2004.11.001

Green, M., & Cifuentes, L. (2008). An exploration of online environments supporting follow-up to face-to-face professional development. *Journal of Technology and Teacher Education*, *16*(3), 283–306.

Higgs-Horwell, M., & Schwelik, J. (2007). I got by with a little help from my friends. *Library Media Connection* (Nov./Dec.), 36-38.

Lynch, M. (2002). *The online educator.* London: Routledge.

Oberg, D. (1995). *Sustaining the vision: A selection of conference papers.* 24th International Association of School Librarianship Conference July 1995, (pp. 17-25). Worcester, UK: Worcester College of Higher Education.

Oehlman, P., & Moore, R. (2007). Getting them to pay attention. *CSLA Journal*, *31*(1), 11–13.

Rheingold, H. (2000). *The virtual community.* Cambridge, MA: MIT Press.

Riskin, S. (2005). The Chicago Ninety. *School Library Journal*, *51*(11), 50–51.

Sallnas, E. (2005). Effects of communication mode on social presence, virtual presence, and performance in collaborative virtual environments. *Presence*, *14*(4), 434–449. doi:10.1162/105474605774785253

Smith, M., & Kollock, P. (Eds.). (1999). *Communities in cyberspace.* London: Routledge.

Townes-Young, K., & Ewing, V. (2005). NASA live: Creating a global classroom. *T.H.E. Journal* (Nov.), 43-45.

Weinfan, L., & Davis, P. (2004). *Challenges in virtual communication: Video conferencing, audioconferencing, and computer-mediated communications.* Santa Monica, CA: RAND Corporation.

Wenger, E. (1998). *Communities of practice.* Cambridge, UK: Cambridge University Press.

Chapter 14
Collaboration in Risk Markets

Scott Rummler
laserthread.com

ABSTRACT

Collaboration can be an effective tool for managing risk. A structured environment for sharing critical risk information can improve decision-making. The business environment currently in place makes it difficult to collaborate, due to complex and overlapping regulatory schemes. In addition, the computing framework used in risk-based sectors is not integrated, resulting in a patchwork of ad-hoc systems that make it difficult to collaborate in an efficient or transparent way. This chapter will present an example of a business framework in which organizations collaborate by trading risk-based products. This arrangement mitigates risk by allocating it to those organizations that can best handle it. A computing framework utilizing Web Services is presented that can help facilitate these types of transactions. Several challenges recur in knowledge management of risk, including trust, information filtering, connecting information ('connecting the dots'), and fluid information exchange. Examples from the insurance and financial industries are presented. Knowledge management of risk information can be facilitated by the development of an Ontology used to describe Web Semantics. A user interface for knowledge management that incorporates collaborative mapping, filtering, and community discussion is presented. Collaboration is being used more frequently to handle core business processes (deep collaboration) as opposed to generic communications such as Wikis (shallow collaboration). A structured environment for collaboration is risk environments can improve security, transparency, and effectiveness. This type of environment might have been used to mitigate the impact risk-based problems such as the current financial emergency. In conclusion, it is posited that a new type of product can emerge which incorporates the social-computing value of risk.

DOI: 10.4018/978-1-60566-727-0.ch014

INTRODUCTION

Collaboration can be an effective way to manage risk. Key information related to emerging trends and market risks, when made available in a collaborative system, can alert an organization earlier and improve decision-making. A number of tools have been developed which can help in this regard (Wikis, message boards, etc.). However, complex risk environments are usually not optimized for deeper forms of collaboration. A model in which market controls allow for the collaborative exchange of risk-based products and information can address this situation.

BACKGROUND

It has been demonstrated that collaboration can be an effective means to manage risk. Examples include processes, methods, and tools that allow users to share and process information related to risk in ways more effective than would be the case had they operated independently (van Grinsven, 2008). Decision networks of social agents can help build the confidence and cohesion required for successful action in an otherwise uncertain environment (Boff, 2007). Collaboration involving group decision support has been shown to increase productivity without information overload (Switzer, 2007).

The management of risk is becoming a most important part of the world economic scheme, as shown by recent financial market difficulties. Insurance and financial organizations must have sufficient funds to handle projected risk. Large corporations may have risk structures that are too complex to be transparent (Oster, 2002). This situation makes it difficult to implement a knowledge management program that could reduce risk.

While many organizations use Wikis and message boards to facilitate collaboration, these tools do not enable the rich interactions necessary to effect core business processes. As businesses move toward deep collaboration, the nature of the business interactions being done will change, and this will be reflected in the design of the resulting information systems.

COLLABORATIVE SYSTEMS FOR RISK ENVIRONMENTS

Organizational Framework

In order for collaboration to be practical in this context, various ways of looking at risk market organization should be considered. There are precedents for collaboration in risk management.

In the area of emission trading, the government assigns emission allowances for atmospheric pollutants produced in the U.S. on a yearly basis. Polluters that reduce their emissions can sell their pollution credits. Companies collaborate toward the most effective solution by buying and selling pollution credits. This is intended to encourage companies to make money by adopting new non-polluting processes. Those that do not will contribute to the cost of finding better alternatives.

In energy trading, power generators and users are never sure exactly how much power they will need in a given time frame, so they arrange for production based on estimates. They may buy or sell power to which they have already committed. This scheme will allow all parties to achieve the lowest marginal cost for power. The implementation of such a scheme is a large potential target of opportunity for the U.S. economy.

A related use is in the area of alternative fuels. If controls are used to create longer-term risk products, which can be fluidly traded, there is the potential for attracting a new large capital hedge market for investing in alternative energy, which is currently a major impediment to its development (Davis, 2008).

Figure 1. Core Layers of Collaboration

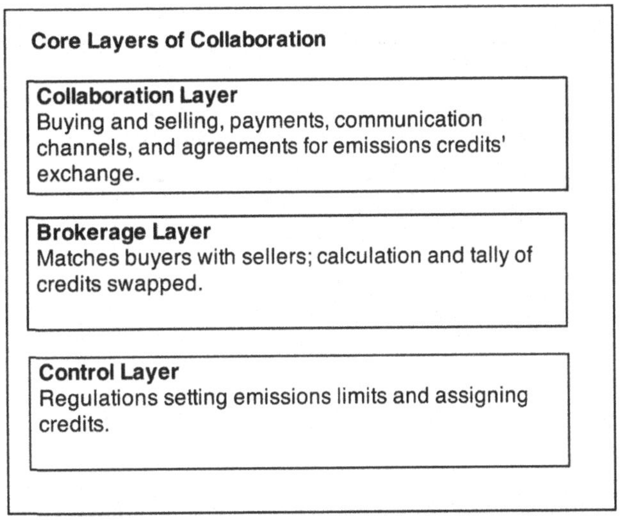

These approaches may be characterized by three layers of organization, which would form the basis for the core data model (Figure 1):

- A control layer, in which products are given time or quantity limits. An example is an insurance policy, which is purchased for one year, and is then placed into the risk market.
- A risk market ('broker mediated layer'), in which prices, purchases, and sales of risk products are maintained, and matches between buyers and sellers are found;
- A collaborative layer, in which groups are

free to form and to buy and sell risk products amongst themselves.

This scheme has the benefit of clarifying the underlying data model for the risk control environment. Each layer has clear entities in the form of organizations, roles, objects, and transactions (see Figure 2).

Disease and Demand Management Organizations

To take this model a step farther we can consider the case of health insurance. The health care system

Figure 2. High Level Data Model for Risk Collaboration

Layer	Actor	Role	Object	Action
Collaboration	Company	Buyer	Stock	Buy
	Individual	Seller	Energy	Sell
			Insurance	Search
Risk Market (Brokerage)				Find Matches
			Stock	Matches
			Energy	Transaction
			Insurance	Messaging
Control	Government	Legal	Stock	Policies
	Management	Administrator	Energy	Input
			Insurance	Output
				Certification
				Limits

Figure 3. Collaboration Model for Disease and Demand Management Organizations

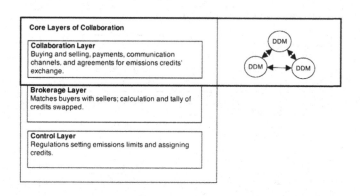

in England has shown that the successful design of financial incentives depends on understanding the complex interplay between central and local influences. In schemes where collaborative financing matches service goals with money, although groups complain they are being held back by joint restraints, in fact the end result can be an improvement over traditional financing and budgeting mechanisms (Wistow, 1990).

Health insurance is based on risk, as insurance companies charge premiums, which they must financially solve, for estimated claims. A large insurance company may have over a billion dollars of capital invested to improve shareholder value, ratings, and policy sales. Once risk is acquired, health insurance companies try to manage it by contracting with demand and disease management organizations.

Disease management companies attempt to determine the best course of treatment for conditions and populations based on outcomes relative to costs. Demand management is the adjustment of policyholder health choices and claims toward the most efficacious paths, presumably to the benefit of both parties.

Demand and disease management organizations can collaborate by trading risks. In an example scenario, a country adopts a single-payer system based on taxation and distributes the funds

through insurance companies into a risk pool of insurance policies, which are required to cover all people and conditions. Disease and demand management companies are expert at how to obtain the best outcome at the least cost, and would collaborate as independent agents. These groups would have access to an environment that would allow them to act collaboratively to buy or sell population or disease risk in a fluid way. This scheme has the potential to decrease costs and increase coverage and quality (see Figure 3).

Transactions

Risk-based industries such as insurance and finance require accountability, transparency, and compliance. These goals require standardized, universally adopted systems. The current ad-hoc and patchwork system is not robust enough to facilitate these types of complex transactions. In order to develop a unified, consistent, and efficient system for risk environments, it will be important to enable sophisticated transactions.

Many risk products are characterized by features (such as interest rate) and functional settings (when to send messages), which require high levels of openness, adoption, scalability, memory, integration, efficiency, and standardization of messaging. A Web Services model is strong in

Figure 4. Risk Reduction

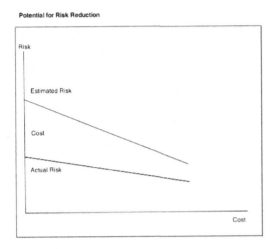

these areas. This model can use Web Services for program integration and Semantic Web for data integration and knowledge management.

A peer-to-peer model should be considered, as it has the following benefits (Androutsellis-Theotokis, 2004):

- Less cost and risk
- Better scalability and reliability
- Clearer trust relationships

While various profiles, specifications, and types of use may be desirable, the key aspects of these systems as they relate to a new high-level approach to interactive information designs for collaborative activity will be the focus of this article.

An overview of this scheme is presented in Figure 5.

Knowledge Management

A more fluid and rich collaborative knowledge management space would be required to effectively manage risk. An advantage of Web Services is that it can be used to encourage a standardized ontology, which will improve the knowledge management component.

We can support a clear data model by using Web Service Semantics to define Web Services properties. Semantics in the form of ontologies can be used to describe properties such as channels, constraints, actors, roles, objects, actions, and a product taxonomy (Dogac, 2006; 2008).

Example: General Web Services Properties Ontology

- Payments
- Constraints
- Channels
- Availability
- Security, trust, and rights
- Service quality
- Actors
- Roles
- Product Taxonomy
  - Sector
  - Industry
  - Company
  - Security

Example: Specific Web Services Properties Ontology Concepts

Stock Market Ontology (Alonso, 2005):

- Stock
- StockMarket
- BuySellOrder
- BestBuySellOrder
- ConditionedBuySellOrder
- LastPrice
- Session
- Index
- Volume
- IndexSession
- StockWeight
- Depositary

Figure 5. Web Services

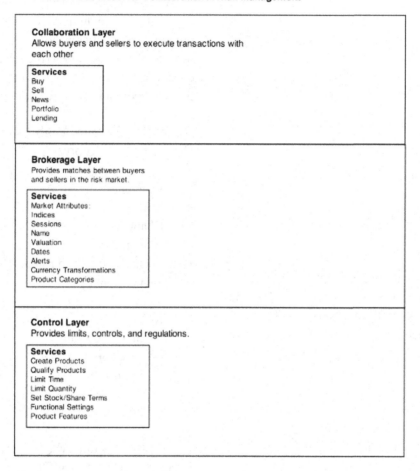

Web Services Model for Collaboration in Risk Management

Collaboration Layer
Allows buyers and sellers to execute transactions with each other

Services
Buy
Sell
News
Portfolio
Lending

Brokerage Layer
Provides matches between buyers and sellers in the risk market.

Services
Market Attributes:
Indices
Sessions
Name
Valuation
Dates
Alerts
Currency Transformations
Product Categories

Control Layer
Provides limits, controls, and regulations.

Services
Create Products
Qualify Products
Limit Time
Limit Quantity
Set Stock/Share Terms
Functional Settings
Product Features

- Broker
- Portfolio
- PriceInPeriod

Interactive Information design to Facilitate Risk Management

This system will support key tools in the knowledge management aspect of collaborative risk management. Several needs involving collaboration and risk management can be identified, along with requirements for interaction design and information design.

Discussion

Discussion of emerging or ambiguous forces can be brought to consensus via discussion, a form of 'collaborative persuasion'. Social networking schemes such as those used in online communities MySpace and Facebook have proven effective in encouraging participation. Collaboration can help to resolve disputes and highlight key issues (Figure 6).

Picturing can be enhanced via collaborative mapping used to connect the dots of the above discussion (Figure 7). Many pieces of information are available, but find no outlet, or are not

Figure 6. Discussion filtered by post with status symbols

Post	Name	Date	Symbol
Regarding the discrepency in the valuation.	Jrogers	10/10/08	▾
Regarding the discrepency in the valuation.	Jrogers	10/10/08	▾
Regarding the discrepency in the valuation.	Rsmith	10/10/08	▾
Regarding the discrepency in the valuation.	Jrogers	10/10/08	Ø
Regarding the discrepency in the valuation.	Janton	10/10/08	Ø

shared among individuals. It can be difficult for knowledge workers to *see the relationships* between different pieces of information. From a user interface issue, mapping schemes have been shown to be productive in helping users see relationships between known and lesser-known pieces of information.

A taxonomy can display the relationships between the above discussions and sectors, industries, companies, and products. It can also be used to enhance search.

Trust

A key issue in collaboration involves the role of individual trust. This is true due to privacy, time, and value/expertise considerations. Trust is important because users want to make sure their time and reputation are well considered before they take the time and effort to share, presumably in the expectation of getting something of value

in return. It has been shown that participation increases functionality as well; i.e. social computing environments fare better when a predefined need is addressed, as opposed to the approach "if we build it, they will come" (Nolan, 2008).

For example, projects such as A Small World, a social networking site for only the most elite world citizens, including former heads of state, have as one of their key challenges the development of trusted network models, and of complex permissions schemes to important documents.

Trusted networks can be used as information filters that provide context. XHTML Friends Network (XFN) is a microformat that can show human relationships in links, and has been used to enable social search. Filtering large amounts of information is key in providing context in risk environments (Figure 8).

Fluidity can be increased via a more efficient, unified system than the one currently in place, including a peer-to-peer e-Marketplace. A Web

Figure 7. Picturing: A map of terms associated with a query

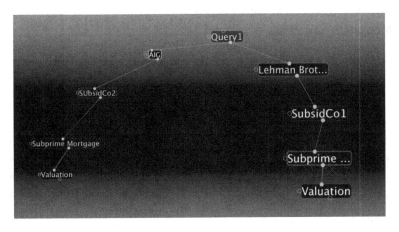

Figure 8. Filter Widget in which a user clicks on groups or users to narrow information display

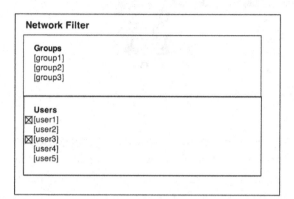

Services model can make it possible for collaborators to trade amongst themselves, rather than go through intermediaries, each of which may have redundant, unique, or incompatible systems (Chen, 2006).

Example: Finance

Finance has always been a collaborative effort because assumptions of value are based on collaborative input into financial systems. As financial markets become more complex and interdependent, collaboration becomes more important. A trading system using Web Services can be set up to facilitate transactions. While certain sectors can immediately benefit from this scheme, such as hedge funds and energy traders, it potentially has broader applicability.

In our example, risk is assumed in the form of a time bound stock purchase contract or other control. Stocks are bought and sold as currently except it is easier for organizations to trade risk amongst themselves rather than through brokers. Groups can create stock indices, which are sold as financial products. In this more fluid environment, investors already committed to risk can improve the liquidity of capital.

Where risk is a collaborative effort, it would be less likely that a situation like the recent finan-cial crisis would have transpired. Because there are fewer brokerage layers, and clearer roles, the transparency of transactions would increase. Organizations trading with peers have better market knowledge because they know the sellers, which automatically reduces risk.

If AIG and Lehman Brothers had been exchanging mortgage-backed securities risk with others in a collaborative environment, the market would likely have been more transparent and more accurately valued. Increased transparency would also make it easier to apply market controls.

The information architecture of the simplest possible user experience example is shown in Figure 9, which illustrates a means in which known 'red flags' regarding the discrepancies in financial product valuations might clearly be brought to attention:

While it has often been reported that many knew, or should have known, about these risks, there has been little discussion of **how** this information would have been represented. An integrated collaborative system can help address these 'gray areas', which frequently exist in risk environments. **Note:** the implication here for compliance may be the reason this type of system is ultimately never adopted. The current system's opaque paper trail may be seen as less risky to organizations from a legal standpoint because it makes it difficult to make the case that collaboratively-available risk information is generally known.

FUTURE DIRECTIONS

Any new approach to complex industries is associated with challenges. Several are anticipated in this case:

(1.) **Fraud.** There is always the risk of gaming the system. The most obvious problem occurred with Enron, which did not own any assets but profited from the trades, and counted potential future earnings as present earnings.

Figure 9. User interface for interactive information design for risk information

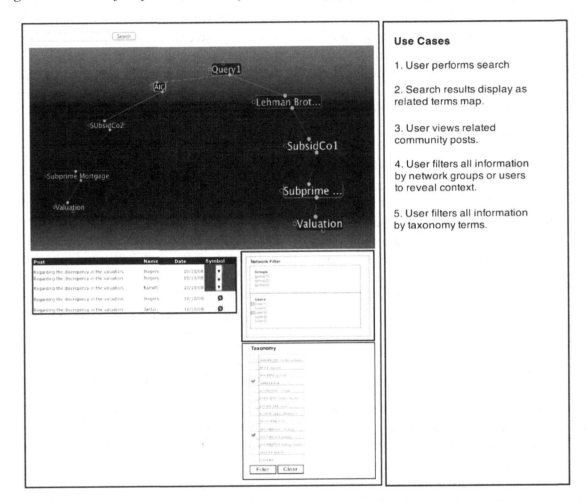

However, in that case Enron was the owner and operator of the trading platform, which was mixed up with sundry endeavors. This highlights the importance of the separation of roles among the three layers of collaboration described here.

(2.) **Business modeling.** Collaborating in this mode will have to be modeled so that the dynamics of buying, selling, and trading are better understood. In particular, the role of legislation, the politics of standards and compliance agreements, and the economic viability of these transactions for all parties will have to be worked through.

For example, many credit derivatives were put together via proprietary information and analytics obtained from Bloomberg Terminals. Mr. Bloomberg, a former Wall Street executive, and now mayor of New York City, has his former Deputy Mayor as head of Bloomberg LP. Although these parties are above reproach, one can see the daunting task in attempting to change regulations and information economics when there are various perspectives involved. One could make the case for having a cabinet-level Information Resources Management post at the White House for a person who would take an information science-based approach to these types of issues (Rummler, 2007). In fact, it is shocking that there is no such person who can bridge the gaps between policy, regulation, and technology.

Most parties would agree, however, that as a general rule, conventions not based on objective best practices (such as lack of transparency, pseudo-monopolies of information, etc.) should be candidates for consideration in any information system redesign.

(3.) **Technical.** The practical issues involved in building new risk systems are considerable but should be weighed against the current and future costs associated with maintaining numerous duplicate and incompatible systems. In addition, growth in this industry would help the economy by both creating jobs and fixing some of the original risk-based problems.

CONCLUSION

Collaboration has the potential to improve risk management. It is important to have the right business environment. A collaborative environment based on Web Services and Ontologies can foster productive risk exchange, reduce risk, and enhance risk knowledge management.

This environment would incentivise collaboration by making companies responsible for managing risk by trading it with peers. It improves transparency around complex, dependent risk products through role clarification and a less redundant data model. An ontology makes it easier for critical information to be recognized and shared. For example, the relationships between products in a huge mix of subsidiaries would be clearer for complex companies like AIG.

In the future, collaboration may be used to readily create indices or other products that can be sold directly to peers, or be a factor used to calculate the future value of a risk product. In the distant future one might imagine a system in which positive and negative risks are treated

even more programmatically. Actuarial science and market risk control mechanisms currently in place to adhere insurance, credit, and financial markets perform much the same function, albeit in an uncoordinated, risky, and inefficient fashion, with many complex workarounds. If a collaborative approach to risk environments were adopted it would be a new approach to the economy.

REFERENCES

Aklouf, Y. (2005, July). *Design of a web service platform for B2B products exchange based on PLIB ontology, RosettaNet PIPs and ebXML Registry.* Presented at Proceedings of the International Conference on Product Lifecycle Management: Emerging solutions and challenges for Global Networked Enterprise, Lyon, France.

Alonso, S.L. (2005, October). *WP10: Case study eBanking D 10.7 Financial Ontology.* Document presented for Project DIP, Galway, Ireland.

Androutsellis-Theotokis, S. (2004, December). Performing Peer-to-Peer E-Business Transactions: A Requirements Analysis and Preliminary Design Proposal. In *Proceedings of the IADIS eCommerce 2004 conference.* Lisbon, Portugal: IADIS Press.

Arpinar, B. I. Ontology-Driven Web Services Composition Platform. *Proceedings of the IEEE International Conference on E-Commerce Technology* (pp. 146-152). Athens, GA: University of Georgia.

Barrett, M. I. (1999). Challenges of EDI adoption for electronic trading in the London Insurance Market. *European Journal of Information Systems, 8,* 1–15. doi:10.1057/palgrave.ejis.3000313

Boff, E., et al. (2007). A collaborative Bayesian net editor to medical learning environments. In *Proceedings of the 25th IASTED International Multi-Conference: artificial intelligence and applications* (pp. 208-213). Insbruck, Austria: IASTAD.

Chen, I. Y. L., & Yang, S. J. H. (2006). Peer-to-Peer Knowledge Sharing in Collaboration Supported Virtual Learning Communities. In *Proceedings of the Sixth IEEE International Conference on Advanced Learning Technologies* (pp. 807-809). Washington, DC: IEEE Computer Society.

Davis, B. (2008, August 26). Shaky Economy Challenges Ambitious Obama Agenda. *The Wall Street Journal Eastern Edition*, A1-A18.

Desmond, B. (2006). Claims processing using Service Oriented Architecture and Web-services based technologies. *Risk & Insurance Online*, December 1, 2006. Retrieved November 22, 2008, from: http://www.riskandinsurance.com/issue.jsp?issueId=13604945&currentFlag=0

Dogac, A. (2006, February). *Untangle the Web: Communicating Through the Web Services Using Semantics.* Paper presented at HIMSS 2006, San Diego, CA.

Dogac, A. (2008, October). *A Brief Introduction to the Semantic Representations of the UN/CEFACT CCTS-based Electronic Business Document Artifacts.* Paper presented at OASIS Semantic Support for Electronic Business Document Interoperability (SET) TC, Teleconference, Billerica, MA.

Dogac, A. (2008, October). *Conformance and Interoperability Testing of NHIS, Turkey: Test-BATN Framework and NHIS Test Scenarios.* Paper presented at 9th International HL7 Interoperability Conference 2008 - IHIC 2008, Crete, Greece.

Giudici, P., Figini, S. (2008, May). *Knowledge management for effective risk governance.* Presentation given at Executive Workshop: Turning data into risk knowledge, London, England.

Noolan, T. (2008). The Role of Individual Trust in e-Collaboration. In N. Kock, (Ed.) *Encyclopedia of E-Collaboration* (pp. 534-539). Hershey, PA: Information Science Reference.

Oster, C., & Brown, K. (2002, January 23). AIG: A complex industry, a very complex company. *The Wall Street Journal Western Edition*, (p. C16).

Pathak, J. (2004). *Peer-to-Peer Semantic Web Services: A Symbiotic*

Relationship for Knowledge Sharing. Term Project Work for Theory of Distributed Algorithms, Iowa State University, Ames, IA.

Rodriguez-Martinez, M. (2004). *Smart Mirrors: Peer-to-Peer Web Services for Publishing Electronic Documents.* Presented at International Workshop on Research Issues on Data Engineering: Web Services for E-Commerce and E-Government Applications (RIDE'04), Boston, MA.

Rummler, S. (2007, March). *After EIA: Post-Methodology IA.* Poster presentation at the Information Architecture Summit sponsored by the American Society for Information Science and Technology, Las Vegas, NV.

Sa, E., Teixeira, J., & Fernandes, C. (2007). Towards a Collaborative Learning Flow Pattern using Educational Games in Learning Activities. In G. Richards (Ed.), *Proceedings of World Conference on E-Learning in Corporate, Government, Healthcare, and Higher Education 2007* (pp. 6483-6488). Chesapeake, VA: AACE.

Switzer, J. (2008). Ecollaboration Using Group Decision Support in Virtual Meetings. In N. Kock (Ed.), *Encyclopedia of E-Collaboration* (pp. 204-209). Hershey, PA: Idea Group Inc.

van Grinsven, J. H. M., Janssen, M., et al. (2008). Collaboration Methods and Tools for Operational Risk Management. In N. Kock, (Ed.) *Encyclopedia of E-Collaboration, Information Science Reference* (pp. 68-72). Hershey, PA: Information Science Reference.

Wistow, G. (1990). *Collaboration under financial constraint.* Aldershot, UK: Avebury.

Ziekow, H. (2007). In-Network Event Processing in a Peer to Peer Broker Network for the Internet of Things. In *On the Move to Meaningful Internet Systems 2007: OTM 2007 Workshops,* (pp. 970-979). Berlin / Heidelberg: Springer.

ADDITIONAL READINGS

Balka, E., & Bjorn, P. (2008). Steps toward a typology for health informatics. In *CSCW '08: Proceedings of the ACM 2008 conference on Computer supported cooperative work* (pp. 515-524). New York: ACM.

Bjerkestrand, A.A. & Zeid, Amir L. (2007). Fifth international workshop on SOA & web services best practices. In *Companion to the 22nd ACM SIGPLAN conference on Object-oriented programming systems and applications companion* (pp. 746 –746). New York: ACM.

Moriyama, M. (2004). Innovation, management & strategy. In *ACM International Conference Proceeding Series: Vol. 60. Proceedings of the 6th international conference on Electronic commerce* (pp. 213-218). New York: ACM.

Pautasso, C., & Zimmermann, O. (2008). Restful web services vs. "big"' web services: making the right architectural decision. In *WWW '08: Proceedings of the 17th international conference on World Wide Web* (pp. 805-814). New York: ACM.

Sell, D., da Silva, D. C., et al. (2008). SBI: a semantic framework to support business intelligence. In *Proceedings of the first international workshop on Ontology-supported business intelligence* (Article 11). New York: ACM.

Section 4
Selected Readings

Chapter 15
Collaborative Design:
An SSM–Enabled Organizational Learning Approach

Anita Mirijamdotter
Växjö University, Sweden

Mary M. Somerville
University of Colorado, Denver, USA

ABSTRACT

Within the context of a three year applied research project conducted from 2003-2006 in a North American university library, staff were encouraged to reconsider organizational assumptions and design processes. The project involved an organizational leader and an external consultant who introduced and collaboratively applied Soft Systems Methodology (SSM) practice. Project results suggest the efficacy of using 'soft' systems thinking to guide interaction (re)design of technology-enabled environments, systems, and tools. In addition, participants attained insights into their new roles and responsibilities within a dynamically changing higher education environment. Project participants also applied SSM to redesign 'in house' information systems. The process of employing systems thinking practices to activate and advance organizational (re)learning, and initiating and elaborating user-centered interaction (re) design practices, culminated in a collaborative design (co-design) approach that readied participants for nimble responsiveness to continuous changes in the dynamic external environment.

INTRODUCTION

Amidst rapid technological change, aggravating financial uncertainty, and escalating community expectations, librarians at California Polytechnic State University in San Luis Obispo (Cal Poly, USA) recognized that nimble organizational responsiveness required reinventing library processes, procedures, and services. They understood that this would require changing how they think and what they think about, as they readied themselves for new roles in the academic enterprise.

Concurrently, librarians in this comprehensive polytechnic teaching university observed a consistent pattern of declining gate counts and diminishing transactions, despite student enrollment increases. These data suggested that even the traditional "library as place" role was eroding at this institution, which offers a wide range of bachelor's and master's degree programs. Librarians were not alone in recognizing that the library was increasingly marginalized on campus: when campus administrators announced permanent budget cuts, the library's share was consistently greater than other academic support units.

So when a new group leader was hired in September 2003, public services librarians agreed to examine the underlying assumptions that historically guided organizational decision making. Systems thinking was used to reconsider the academic library's purpose(s), including project participants' roles and relationships, within the context of the university mission. This exploration also benefited from learning-centered consultation with user communities, which served to refine the alignment between organizational intentions, actions, and outcomes.

Within the systems thinking community, 'soft' systems thinking is widely recognized for its contributions to organizational learning through revisiting workplace assumptions (e.g., Ackoff, 1998; 1999; Ackoff *et al.*, 2006; Checkland, 1981; 2000; Flood & Jackson, 1991; Flood & Romm, 1996; Jackson, 2000; 2003; Midgley, 2000; Checkland & Winter, 2006). For this project, Soft Systems Methodology (SSM) was selected because of its proven usefulness in building larger frames of reference (Checkland, 1981; 2000; Checkland & Holwell, 1998a; Checkland & Poulter, 2006; Checkland & Scholes, 1990; Checkland & Winter, 2006), which librarians recognized as necessary to bridge boundaries within the library and across the campus.

During a three year project conducted between 2003 and 2006, nineteen university librarians and thirteen support staff were led by the group leader (Somerville) through an organizational learning initiative facilitated by an external trainer and project evaluator (Mirijamdotter), who introduced both Soft Systems Methodology and also Scandinavian 'participatory design' (Bansler, 1989; Bratteteig, 2004; Iivari & Lyytinen, 1998; Jansson, 2007; Langefors, 1995; Löwgren & Stolterman, 1998; 2004). Library leaders asked the external trainer and evaluator to deliver systems thinking workshops and conduct regular outcomes evaluations over the course of the project. Mirijamdotter was selected because her participatory design and user involvement orientation were compatible with the strong collective bargaining (labor union) orientation of the library workplace.

In this instance, Somerville and Mirijamdotter aimed to depart from typical SSM interventions in which a consultant enters the workplace for the life of the project and then, upon her departure, SSM usage ceases. Therefore, in addition to advancing SSM-guided projects, the leader and the consultant articulated a transferable leadership model for readying a workplace environment for rethinking, repurposing, and relearning. Thus, the purpose of this paper is to offer an account of using soft systems ideas to generate user-centric collaborative design ideas. The paper also illustrates the benefits of reflective practice focused on organizational learning. Finally, the efficacy of this interaction approach—which transformed organizational outcomes—inspired creation of a transferable leadership model.

In the following section, we introduce the underlying assumptions of our participatory action research approach followed by the guiding SSM framework. Next, we present student-generated studies that provided initial 'finding out' data and dialogue-based modeling practice, using Rich Pictures to represent various perspectives. Results fortified library staff resolve to engage in the change initiative, fueling their continuation of this user-generated approach, as illustrated by the example of a content architecture design project. Over the life of the three year initiative, these SSM-enabled projects served to produce organization wide re-design of work roles and tasks, including considerably extended interactions based on participants' perceptions of enlarged boundaries of concern and influence. To conclude the paper, we present and discuss a process model for organizational leadership, which surfaced during the project, that aims to use systems thinking to advance workplace learning.

PARTICIPATORY ACTION RESEARCH

In the Cal Poly project, systems thinking benefited from a participatory action research orientation (Agryris & Schön, 1991; Ghaye, 2007; Heron & Reason, 2001; Jacobs, 2006; Jansson, 2007). "Action research aims to contribute both to the practical concerns of people in an immediate problematic situation and to the goals of social science by joint collaboration within a mutually acceptable ethical framework" (Rapoport, 1970, 499). In other words, action research aims to solve a practical problem and at the same time increase scientific knowledge. The usefulness of combining systems thinking and action research has been well elaborated by leading systems thinkers (e.g., Checkland, 1985; Flood, 1998; Midgley, 2000; Stowell & West, 1994; Wilson, 2001).

In action research, the researcher's role is to create organizational change while simultaneously studying the process (Baskerville & Wood-Harper, 1998; Champion & Stowell, 2003; Checkland & Holwell, 1998b; Dick, 2004). Hence, the action researcher becomes part of the study and interprets the inter-subjective meaning of the observations. Although there is significant variety among action research approaches, they have in common a cyclic process where, following Susman and Evered (1978), the 'systemic' research cycle consists of situation diagnosis, action planning, and action

taking (intervening), followed by evaluating and reflecting - i.e., learning.

Participatory action research is a form of action research that involves practitioners as both subjects and co-researchers (Agryris & Schön, 1991). This is in contrast to other types of applied research where the researcher is seen as the expert (Whyte, *et al.*, 1991). In contrast, participatory action research aims to construct an environment where participants freely exchange information and make informed choices, thereby promoting commitment to the investigation results (Agryris & Schön, 1991). Through co-constructing, testing and improving theories about particular interpretations and experiences, people learn by interacting with each other that they can better control their social world (Elden & Levin, 1991). Thus, following Checkland and Holwell's (1998b) illustration of an action research situation, the ideas inherent in participatory action research, in which research subjects act as both practitioners and researchers, are inherent in the framework of ideas that guides this intervention. In a complementary fashion, the underlying philosophy of SSM, which is both interpretivistic and constructivistic, reinforces the notion that people who want to improve a situation perceived as problematic can make improvements, or changes, through learning their way. In this journey of discovery, SSM-enabled systems thinking guided the dialogue-based (Banathy & Jenlick, 2005) appreciative inquiry (Checkland & Casar, 1986; Vickers, 1983a; 1983b) which furthers organizational learning.

In this case, to encourage the university library's assumption of a new role as a dynamic center of instruction, exploration and learning, we introduced the participants to systems thinking tools which activated and challenged their prior understandings. The iterative learning cycle characteristic of Soft Systems Methodology (SSM), including Rich Picture modeling (Checkland, 1979; 1981; Lewis, 1992), aided librarians to, for example, (re)design web based pages, portals, and personas. In a complementary fashion, additional

SSM tools, particularly the Processes for Organizational Meanings (POM) model (Checkland & Holwell, 1993; 1998a; Rose, 2002), were used by the external consultant and organizational leader for direction setting and project planning (Mirijamdotter & Somerville, 2005 - i.e., used on a meta-level to plan or design, carry out, evaluate and reflect. In combination, as the following sections illustrate, these process tools supported participatory, collaborative systems thinking activities focused on advancing emergent insights from user-generated research projects. This resultant organizing model for encouraging interaction and transformation is presented as Figure 5.

RESEARCH PROJECT FRAMEWORK

Soft Systems Methodology (SSM), the main research framework around which we organize our change process, was development for management and information systems development by Dr. Peter Checkland and his associates at the University of Lancaster in the United Kingdom. Typically, SSM is facilitated by an external consultant who departs at the conclusion of the design activities. In this case, participants aimed to embed systems thinking processes into ongoing workplace practices. Therefore, in addition to advancing systems design projects, the external consultant and organizational leader also evolved an SSM-inspired leadership model (Figure 5) which guided the process and enabled continuation of systems thinking.

The SSM systems thinking approach is commonly described as comprising an iterative four-stage process—finding out, modeling, comparison, and taking action. See Figure 1.

Project participants were prepared to implement these iterative SSM processes through training by the external consultant supplemented by coaching from the organizational leader. However, they did not utilize the traditional sequence of SSM modeling techniques since learning the rules would have diverted attention from inquiring into the content of the situation. Therefore, Rich Pictures were used to visualize different

Figure 1. Soft systems methodology basic process (after Checkland, 2000)

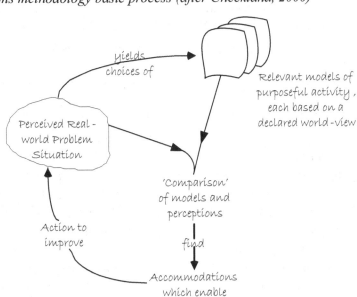

perspectives, or 'world-views', on user experiences and library services, for the purpose of initiating reflective dialogue aimed at comparing perceptions and mental models for subsequent action taking.

Over time and with experience, participants increased their working knowledge of Soft Systems Methodology ideas and participatory action research. Workplace learning was advanced through SSM training complemented by both formal and informal socialization activities. For instance, the organizational leader integrated systems thinking concepts into internal e-newsletters and other organizational communications. She also used face-to-face information sharing opportunities to summarize group successes in confronting long standing assumptions and moving beyond insular behaviors. These accomplishments were also noted in annual performance appraisals, which constitute an important part of the organization's 'reward structure'—i.e., rankings convert to salary increases. In addition, the leader cultivated dialogue-based social relationships among participants and with users to ensure satisfying inter-subjective 'meaning making' experiences. In a variety of ways, then, participants gained SSM conversance adequate to produce shared practices, vocabulary, competencies, and memories. This led them to question existing ways of seeing and doing things and to "open up novel and elegant proposals for ... advancing thinking and taking action" (Jackson, 2003, 208).

INITIAL 'FINDING OUT'

In January 2004, following an introduction to SSM 'thinking terminology', the process of 'finding out' about library users' needs and preferences commenced in advance of participants' introduction to SSM tools. The initial activity required librarians' consideration of research data generated from open-ended phenomenographic interviews with nineteen representative polytechnic students. The

aim of the interviews was to learn about undergraduate college students' conceptions of both information and also information usage.

Phenomenographic studies explore differing ways in which people experience, perceive, apprehend, understand, and conceptualize various phenomena in and aspects of the world. Since Bruce (1997a) introduced it into educational research in Australia, Lupton (2004) and Edwards (2006) in Australia and Limberg (1999) in Sweden have used the methodology to investigate students' conceptions of information literacy, information searching, and research processes.

With supervision from Somerville, graduate student Maybee modified Bruce's research questions to explore the differing ways that students experience, perceive, apprehend, understand, and conceptualize information. He asked subjects: "How do you use information to complete class assignments?" "How do you use information outside of your coursework?" "Tell a story of a time when you used information well." "Describe your view of someone who used information well." "Describe your experience using information." Recorded interview data was transcribed in preparation for interpretative analysis which focused on aggregated data—i.e., individual interview transcripts were analyzed as a whole. Categories were assigned to describe students' varying ways of experiencing the phenomenon of information usage and its advancement (Maybee, 2006).

As librarians reflected and created meanings based on Maybee's research findings, they recognized the importance of considering undergraduates' perceptions in designing information services and systems. They also recognized that "to adequately address the needs of student learners, a user-centered approach must be adopted that reflects the complexities inherent in the current information environment" (Maybee, 2006, 79). In addition, they were convinced that learning is about changes in conceptions, that learning always has a content as well as a process, that learning is about relations with the learner and the subject matter, and that improving learning depends on understanding students' perspective (Bruce, 1997a). These compelling insights fueled participants' subsequent exploration of user-centric design methods. And it moved them, over the course of the project, to reject the traditional 'library centric' information gatekeeper role in favor of assuming 'user centered' responsibilities as designers of knowledge enabling systems and services. During the life of the three year project, aspects were reported in conference proceedings and journal articles (Mirijamdotter & Somerville, 2004; Somerville, Huston, & Mirijamdotter, 2005; Somerville & Mirijamdotter, 2005; Mirijamdotter & Somerville, 2005; Somerville, Schader, & Huston, 2005; Somerville, Mirijamdotter, & Collins, 2006; Somerville & Brar, 2006; Somerville & Brar, 2007; Somerville & Brar, 2008).

SSM RICH PICTURES

Maybee's phenomenographic research results revealed three primary ways in which undergraduate students conceptualize information and its usage. His depictions of student conceptions introduced librarians to the function of a model as "an analytical tool to help precipitate a debate about the 'whats and hows' of a situation" (West & Stowell, 2000, 295). These new understandings whetted librarians' appetites to know more. So, in a series of workshops, the external consultant introduced them to SSM philosophy and tools, including the Rich Picture modeling technique. A Rich Picture is defined as "the expression of a problem situation ... often by examining elements of *structure*, elements of *process*, and the situation *climate*" (Checkland, 1981, 317). In relation to the SSM basic process, Figure 1, Rich Pictures are traditionally used to express the perceived real world situation. Here we used Rich Pictures as a modeling tool where each picture aimed at capturing the perspective of main actors involved in the situation. These pictures were then contrasted and compared with the real world situation rather than further exploring their content through SSM modeling techniques.

Librarians first practiced Rich Picture technique on themselves—i.e., they depicted the 'real-world problem situation' of their personal practices of information search and retrieval. Although the workshop participants worked in three groups, the drawings were all quite alike and reflected the 'ideal' information literacy model adopted by the professional association of North American academic librarians (ACRL, 2000). In subsequent discussion, however, the librarians 'admitted' that they had not depicted what they actually did. Rather, they presented an ideal model of information search and retrieval which placed the library at the center of the process.

In modeling how their professional association felt people ought to search for information, rather than how they actually conducted research, participants presented 'what it should look like' from their viewpoint. Surfacing this 'should' assumption served to create some additional 'healthy doubt' about the adequacy of the library's current approach to enabling students' information finding and using—since it failed to consider students' viewpoints and behaviors. Subsequently, candid dialogue—within a 'safe' reflective workplace environment—served to move participants from mimicking professional assumptions to sharing authentic perceptions. Building on this, the external consultant then asked participants to construct Rich Pictures based on the phenomenographic study results. As an example, see Figure 2.

Rich Picture results acknowledge the considerable information proficiencies that freshmen students possess when they enter college. The main information sources were categorized as Google, peers, and television. Upon entry to the university, however, students must acquire an expanded set of capabilities—including conversance with peer reviewed scholarship.

In the weeks following creation of the Rich Pictures, librarians considered how best to

Figure 2. Rich picture of student processes

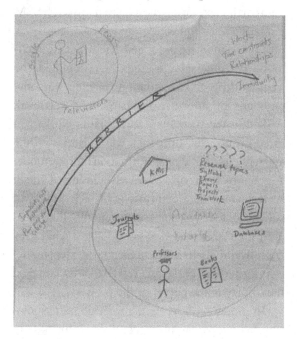

transition students from 'where they were' to 'where they needed to be' upon graduation. Their growing appreciation for students' rich interactions with (nonacademic) information sources prompted librarians to build—in a constructivist fashion—upon students' prior learning. This required identifying the ways in which students use information within different disciplines and at different stages—from first to final year of study. Known as 'relational information literacy', this approach recommends that domain knowledge advance concurrently with information proficiencies (Bruce, 1997b). Finally, given students' usage of the Internet, librarians recognized that they needed to enhance librarian and library web presence. Hence, in this instance, the Rich Picture technique was used to illustrate student perspectives on information search and retrieval and on library services, and the action outcome of the subsequent debate was to continue to explore student behavior with the purpose of finding ways to better serve their needs.

In building upon baseline phenomenographic findings, librarians decided to adopt a radically different approach as they continued their finding out process. They asked computer science professors teaching Human-Computer Interaction (HCI) courses to invite their students to assume responsibilities for problem definition, methodological implementation, and data analysis. This proved to be a fortuitous decision: from 2004 to 2006, reliance on student-framed, student-conducted, and student-reported research results produced rich evidence about different types of students, their information use at various stages—and why this is so, and their learning style and delivery media preferences.

USER-CENTERED PROJECTS

Enabled by SSM thinking tools, librarians worked with students over a three year period to (re)design several digital initiatives, including an academic research guide, a digital research portal, and a website persona prototype. In keeping with their commitment to learn from students about students, librarians relinquished control of the research process: students were supervised by their professors as they generated problem definitions, chose research methodologies, conducted data analysis, and reported research results.

Students' initial research explored: "What do Cal Poly students know about library resources? What do they want to know? And how do they want to learn it?" Students employed a variety of quantitative and qualitative methods to obtain a rich profile of student behaviors. For instance, they conducted interviews, administered paper and pencil surveys, facilitated focus groups, and implemented usability tests. Results revealed that seventy-two percent of student respondents used the Internet for research while only four percent reported using the library. Given the Net Generation's Web usage patterns, student researchers advised librarians to improve their digital discovery tools. They urged librarians to discontinue their 'library centric' (structure of bibliography) assumptions and adopt a more 'student centric' design perspective. In return, students offered to explore form and content issues in support of librarians' new roles as content providers for Web-based learning environments. Hence, in this phase of the project, student generated data and interaction led to an intention to improve the web site design to better support students' information search and retrieval preferences and needs.

In continuing exploration of student research habits, research skills, and learning styles, two new lines of inquiry evolved—effects of learning styles and implications of class level (years toward graduation). In response, student researchers decided to use preliminary findings to create a two-dimensional (2-D) model for content architecture. The emphasis on learning styles emerged out of the recognition that the Web honors multiple forms of intelligence—e.g., abstract, textual, visual, musical, social, and kinesthetic. Therefore, digital technologies offer opportunities for higher educators to construct tools, systems, and

environments that enable individuals to experience information in preferred learning modes. "The Web affords the match we need between a medium and how a particular person learns" (Brown, 2002). In addition, student researchers reasoned that students early in their college career needed to receive foundational information for required liberal arts and general studies coursework. Then, beginning in the third year of a four year undergraduate degree program (when most students declare their academic degree/major), students needed discipline-specific resources and research navigation assistance appropriate to the knowledge building traditions of the academic field. See Table 1.

The design concept acknowledged the 'dimensionality' of the target audience, including academic level considerations and other user attributes which produce different needs at various stages in students' careers. Students also recommended that viewing experiences accommodate learning style differences. The study and design work are reported in more detail in Rogers *et al.* (2005) and Somerville *et al.* (2007).

Table 1. 2-D content architecture model excerpt (adapted from Somerville et al., 2007)

	Lower Years (first two of four year program)	Intermediate Year (third)	Advanced Year (fourth)
Visual and Kinesthetic	More research content breadth but less depth and basic research strategies needed, paired with visual and kinesthetic presentation elements – e.g., use graphics and demonstrations and replace textual information with visual representations (graphs or diagrams)	Discipline-based coursework and higher order thinking experiences require more in depth information resources and research strategies, with continued application of visual and kinesthetic design elements	More depth topical content, presented within disciplinary framework, to enable more ambitious research purposes, with consistent application of visual and kinesthetic design elements
Auditory and Read/Write	More research content breadth but less depth and basic research strategies needed, paired with audio and read-write presentation elements – e.g., re-organize diagram or graph content into statements and offer both textual narrative and audio recordings, such as podcasts	Discipline-based coursework and higher order thinking experiences require more in depth information resources and research strategies, with continued application of audio and read-write elements	More depth topical content, presented within disciplinary framework, to enable more ambitious research purposes, with consistent application of audio and read-write elements

Data collection and interpretation required frequent face-to-face communication between university librarians and student researchers throughout iterative design processes. This ongoing dialogue served to advance mutual 'sense making' during decision making and 'action taking' designed to improve user experiences. During these discussions, librarians obtained valuable 'voiced' insights into user constituency perspectives which corroborated the wisdom of applying relational information literacy tenets to advance both domain mastery and information proficiencies. Continuing relationships with supervising faculty also ensured opportunities to study different aspects of particularly perplexing problems in subsequent academic quarters.

To sum up, this user-centric project resulted from participatory and collaborative systems thinking activities. It demonstrates that the evolving SSM-enabled collaborative design (co-design) approach reflects both a philosophy and a process in which the needs, wants and limitations of end users play a central role at each stage of the design process (Somerville & Brar, 2008). While quantitative methods are sometimes included in these approaches, a key feature of all these design methodologies is the integral and extensive use of qualitative data collection and analysis methodologies, including dialogue-based appreciative inquiry. Finally, interaction and collaboration produce the shared vision, mutual empathy, and committed focus to sustain continuous dialogue-based relationships with system beneficiaries and other campus stakeholders (Somerville & Nino, 2007). The action orientation further encourages quick prototype problem solutions as well as library service improvements and other organizational changes. As evidence of its transferability, co-design now informs creation of virtual and physical 'learning commons' at a university library in California's Silicon Valley (Somerville & Collins, 2008).

ORGANIZATIONAL SYSTEM RE-DESIGN

The leader and the consultant next decided to expand participation and include library support staff. These paraprofessional staff carry out day-to-day operational tasks, which free librarians for more high level, subject specific responsibilities. Having observed from afar the benefits of a user-centered design approach, staff were eager to rethink 'in house' information systems. Encouraged by the results of the student generated projects reported in previous sections, they began the 'finding out' phase by establishing and analyzing a transaction log at the reference desk. Preliminary findings were then extended through examination of assignments provided by librarians, who acquired the documents from faculty in advance of delivering information competence instruction sessions. Results informed the design of an information capture and exchange system to support problem solving at the reference desk (Somerville & Vazquez, 2004), for which staff had assumed responsibility as one result of an SSM-guided organizational redesign (Somerville, Huston, *et al.*, 2005). Over time, through application of the iterative SSM process of finding out, modeling, comparison, and taking action, library support staff experienced empowerment and efficacy, anchored in common understandings and interactive relationships, as reflected in Figure 3.

This figure illustrates library support staff members' conceptions of the interaction between themselves, now termed 'information and instructional service support staff', and university librarians, termed 'information specialists'. The interaction is formalized in a proposed Research and Information Service and Education (RISE) workplace learning system. The change in terminology is significant—as it replaces the traditional word 'reference desk' which connotes esoteric scholarly consultation on bibliographic references at a single physical service point within

Figure 3. Interactive processes of the research and information service and education (RISE) system

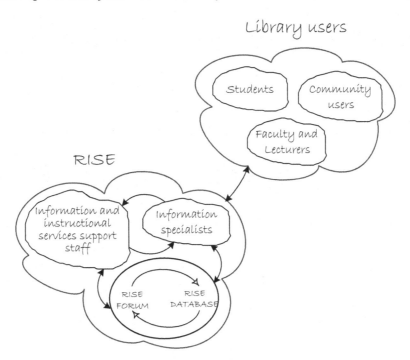

the library, isolated from the learning activities of the academic community. The technology-enabled component of the holistic RISE system is also significant, as it reflects both the need for a domain knowledge database (course assignments) as well as continuous information exchange (RISE forum). The knowledge base continues to grow as information specialists acquire, annotate, and contribute the documents that enable information and instructional service support staff to apply 'solutions and strategies' at the newly constituted 'research help desk'—a term recommended by students. Intentional virtual and face-to-face exchanges fuel continuous workforce learning.

Finally, the two-way communication between librarians and support staff is expressed through ongoing education, informally occurring throughout the workplace and formally provided in weekly training and education sessions which anticipate students' assignment-based needs. This outward looking, technology-enabled decision-support

system presents a sharp contrast to traditional professional assumptions whereby questioners were expected to come to librarians 'sitting at the reference desk'. Instead, information specialists now move beyond library walls to forge relationships that influence faculty members' assignments and thereby enrich student learning experiences. In addition to coaching the library staff members who assist students in completion of their assignments, information specialists also design and deliver disciplinary web pages complemented by digital learning objects that introduce essential information resources and search strategies. Now they also offer virtual research 'live chat' services that provide personalized 24/7 online advisement to students, any time, any place. In these various ways, librarians have fulfilled their shared aspiration to increase the library's web presence. Their co-design activities with students gave them the necessary expertise and confidence. In addition, through SSM practice, librarians have forged

Figure 4. Perception of interactive processes

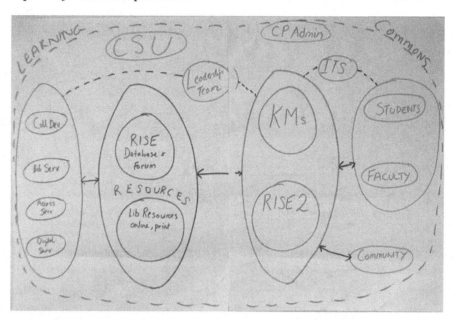

satisfying relationships with library staff, whose work has also been transformed in the process.

ORGANIZATIONAL LEARNING ASSESSMENT

In an evaluation session held at the end of this three year action research study, the external consultant invited all library participants to apply 'soft' systems principles and practices to depict their enlarged workplace context. Their conceptions were captured in visual SSM-like drawings which provided a common reference for renegotiating increasingly more complex and better contextualized organizational effectiveness, as well as larger boundaries of influence and concern. Illustrative of the renderings, the Rich Picture in Figure 4 presents an enterprise level model of university interactions—including consideration of what parts and relations to include—e.g., hierarchical levels, main processes, primary beneficiaries, relevant perspectives, and leading questions.

The figure illustrates the workplace learning enabled by SSM rethinking activities. For instance, the librarians refer to themselves as Knowledge Managers (KMs). They reside in the same circle as RISE 2, an enlarged group of information and instructional services support staff whose transformation processes were reported in the earlier section. To the right, the importance of relationships with students and faculty are recognized. Another circle indicates the need to also serve the community. The drawing on the left indicates recognition that both these groups, librarians/knowledge managers and research information and instructional services/support staff, interact with (increasingly digital) information resources which, the left most drawing illustrates, are acquired and organized by collection development and bibliographic services staff and made accessible by information technology specialists. Finally, at the top of the figure, the relationships with university administrators, campus information technologists, and library leaders are acknowledged, as is the California State University (CSU) system in which Cal

Poly serves as one of twenty three campuses. This high level 'system' is termed 'Learning Commons' - a phrase which refers to a physical, technological, social, and intellectual place (or space) for collaborative learning (Somerville & Harlan, 2008; Somerville & Collins, 2008). In the view of project participants, the Cal Poly library environment had become a learning commons over the course of the project.

Before this project began, workplace participants had never collectively reflected on their roles in a holistic context. As Figure 4 demonstrates, one of the most profound outcomes of this three year rethinking project is clarification of workplace participants' relationships to internal and external stakeholders. These insights emerge quite naturally, as one of the defining characteristics of SSM practice is intentionally entertaining multiple perspectives. Furthermore, by its very nature, Soft Systems Methodology creates a relational context that encourages individuals' recognition of the aspects of their workplace expertise which, when shared, advances collective knowledge creation and integration (Checkland, 2000), even as it extends boundaries of influence and concern.

Organizational learning is also revealed through comparison of the Rich Pictures generated by project participants. These images demonstrate the maturation indicators that, early on, librarians agreed were significant to student learning. They were therefore able, at project's end, to appreciate their own learning in these terms: learning is about change in conceptions, learning always has a content as well as a process, learning is embodied in the relationship between the learner and the subject matter, and advancement of learning depends on the readiness to change perspectives.

LIBRARY ORGANIZATION LEADERSHIP

The transformation of the workplace environment was orchestrated by the organizational leader. She served as creator of the contexts for the conversation-based relational information experiences that fueled collaborations with campus partners—i.e., co-design activities. In doing so with coaching from the external consultant, she advanced SSM's learning orientation to enable librarians and staff to become both reflective (re)learners and also responsive action-takers (Somerville, Huston, *et al.*, 2005; Somerville, Schader, *et al.*, 2005). Organizational purposes were revisited, constituency relationships were reinvented, and workplace roles were re-imagined within the context of a 'big picture' appreciation for the larger academic enterprise. Through this organizational discovery process, librarians and staff developed a shared vision for a repurposed organization. They came to appreciate and embrace new applications for their expertise within the larger context of the university's core knowledge creation and dissemination mission.

In recognition of the considerable organizational benefits achieved through embedding SSM in the workplace culture, the leader and consultant anticipate that leaders in other libraries and information organizations will choose to involve external SSM consultants in context specific projects. Therefore, they developed an activity model to enable organizational leaders to embed SSM philosophy and practices within the workplace and thereby facilitate recoverability according to principles suggested by Checkland and Holwell (1998b). The model in Figure 5 is based on the experience and learning which we now recognize accrued during the three year project. In short, it illustrates the aspects we found necessary for enabling staff engagement in participatory and collaborative re-designing processes. This model evolved over the life of the project; a first version to guide the intervention was developed and reported in Mirijamdotter and Somerville (2004). Subsequently, facets of the multi-dimensional approach represented in this model have been reported in conference papers and journal articles (Somerville & Mirjamdotter, 2005; Somerville *et*

Figure 5. Process model for library organization leadership

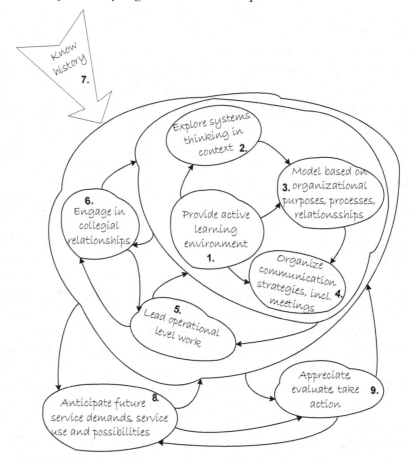

al., 2006; Davis & Somerville, 2006; Somerville & Howard, 2008). By providing this model, which complements the case description, the aim is to further establish the authenticity of the inquiry process (Champion & Stowell, 2003).

The model, Figure 5, illustrates the responsibilities of the organizational leader who chooses to enable, employ, and operationally implement systems thinking practices and processes. It represents layers of activities that interact with each other. At the very center of the figure, activity 1 represents the activities that are involved in providing an active learning environment. Its placement at the very heart of the model conveys the belief that a contemporary organization should be designed so as to be able rapidly to learn from

and adapt to its own successes and failures, and those of relevant others. It should also be capable of adapting to internal and external changes that affect its performance, and of anticipating such changes and taking appropriate action before these changes occur. This requires, among other things, that the organization be susceptible to continual redesign by its internal and external stakeholders (Ackoff *et al.*, 2006). Therefore, the organizational leader should create the conditions for employees to easily access and exchange information in terms that extend their interpretive and appreciative capabilities. Accomplishing this requires understanding "the process through which an organization (re)constructs knowledge"

(Huysman & de Wit, 2003, 29)—i.e., organizational learning.

The figure recognizes that active learning environments allow practice in systems thinking, activity 2. The leader advances systems thinking within the organizational context to further the understanding of its parts and their interrelations. Linked to systems thinking and also team success is a shared vision (Senge, 1990). Activity 3 represents modeling the organizational mission within the wider system. This visualization is to be co-developed and further evolved through conversations among staff. The final activity on this level, activity 4, illustrates that physical and virtual meetings are vital for facilitating active and dynamical engagement in information exchange as depicted in the interactions of SSM. To create adequate infrastructure, SSM is utilized to both define the purpose of the organization and also design the intentional learning environment, including its processes, in which organizational purposes are reconsidered (Checkland & Winter, 2006).

For the sake of model completeness, activity 5 recognizes the importance of leading operational level work. Its counterpart, activity 6, refers to engagement in internal and external relationship building. Historical context, activity 7, represents understanding how and why the present situation has come into being. This perspective offers relational context for envisioning the future, activity 8, including anticipated services and systems.

Finally, processes and outcomes need to be appreciated in the light of organizational purpose and vision, activity 9. In the Cal Poly example, the leader focused on systems thinking, problem solving, team building, and information sharing. Evaluation involved assessing how well these factors were represented in the active learning environment and how well the activities supported the development and sustainability of learning. SSM-guided systems thinking, in this instance, served both as the process tool for inquiry learning, i.e., "SSMp" and, ultimately, organizational

transformation based on "SSMc" (Checkland & Winter, 2006, 1435).

REFLECTIONS AND CONCLUSION

This action research project involved an organizational leader coached by an external SSM consultant. Nineteen library professionals and thirteen library staff were trained to use Soft Systems Methodology (SSM) philosophy, methodology, and tools during a three-year participatory action research project. As described in the preceding sections, library employees used systems thinking to invent workplace purposes, processes, and practices 'with and for' an ever expanding set of organizational beneficiaries. In so doing, they experienced the social nature of learning—i.e., that "all learning derives from experience, own and others" (Ackoff, 1998, 35) and that learning is about change of conceptions.

From the earliest finding out activities, employees found that cherished assumptions were challenged by user-generated research results which urged them to assume new roles and responsibilities. Systems thinking tools prompted their recognition that the organization's role had shifted from archiving print collections for potential usage to ensuring information access and enabling information usage for knowledge creation. When employees acquired new knowledge, skills, and abilities through co-design with faculty and students, they extended their boundaries of concern and influence to participate more fully in the teaching and learning activities of the university. As Midgley (2000) explains it, systems thinking philosophy highlights the bounded nature of all understandings and refocuses attention on comprehensiveness as an ideal.

In addition, because authority for problem identification was delegated to student beneficiaries and supervising professors, the content of the problematical situation (SSMc) as well as the intellectual process of the intervention itself (SSMp) enabled students to experience extra-ordinary inclusion—i.e., they directed the 'way finding' to agreed upon actions perceived as improvements in the situation. While this collaborative design (co-design) approach certainly informed library participants' systems thinking—"seeing the world in a holistic way" (Mingers, 2007, 84), the classic Analysis One (finding out about the problem) roles of client, problem solver, and problem owner (as described in lay terms by Checkland & Winter, 2006) were transformed. This proved convenient, however, in realizing the ultimate aim of the action research project—to apply systems approaches to information systems (Stowell, 2007) in terms that enhance and extend (over temporal time) action research outcomes, especially the culminating fifth phase of learning (Susman & Evered, 1978).

The quintessential elements of systems thinking—processes, purposes, relationships, and emergent properties—comprised the 'learning tool kit', corroborating Jackson's observation that "perhaps the main strength of systems ideas ... is the guidance they offer to practitioners" (2000, 423). In this case, SSM provided an excellent basis for real world problem identification, exploration, implementation, and evaluation. Relatedly, appreciation for multiple perspectives served to considerably extend organizational boundaries. Consequently, expanded boundaries of design processes were used to incorporate user 'needs finding' results into system interfaces, research portals, and library websites. These choices affirmed that "no matter what the previous history, every influence and concern produced new conversations and collaborations. As a result, interaction system can be altered and reinvented" (Norum, 2001, 325)—i.e., "if organizations are constructed, they can be reconstructed." (Norum, 2001, 324) Growing conversance with a variety of user-centered (re)design strategies also enabled librarians to fulfill their expanded responsibilities as collaborative architects of digital information and knowledge enabling spaces. They learned to

approach their new responsibilities with confidence, grounded in collaborative SSM-enabled evidence-based practices for decision making and action taking.

Of perhaps greatest significance, at the conclusion of this three year action research project, SSM-enabled systems thinking guided day-to-day workplace decision making. Project participants shared a common language and tools for discussing and analyzing complexities and interdependencies, using the thinking framework of finding out, modeling, comparing, and taking action. Furthermore, they were able to adapt these precepts to further co-design relationships through initiating dialogue, creating meaning, forming intentions, and taking action. Organizational learning advanced naturally through new 'habits of mind'—i.e., evaluating meaningful data, comparing and contrasting multiple interpretations, and infusing reflective insights and unsolved curiosities into perpetual discovery. By reflecting on the learning process and its crucial elements, such as methods and tools employed to engage participants, and also evaluating anticipated outcomes of the participatory action research approach, the authors follow recommendations advanced by Champion and Stowell (2003) for making evident the authenticity and credibility of the inquiry process. Doing so facilitates recoverability for participants and interested others, with the aim of enabling more organizational learning grounded in Soft Systems Methodology.

In summation, this paper gives an account of using soft systems ideas in a participatory and collaborative organizational design project in which inexperienced participants employed SSM tools to interpret what they found meaningful and useful in coming to a new understanding of organizational purpose. The paper delineates a process which combines the SSM elements of interaction and transformation into a transferable leadership model for guiding organizational re-design of work roles and tasks, including interactions based on perceptions of extended boundaries. Its expression is conveyed through description of user-centric and user-led (re)design of the organizational website, which benefited from user-generated research results.

Overall, participants learned from this project that it is rewarding for change initiatives to use systems thinking processes in organizational settings when the tools are adapted to the needs and preferences of the participants. Additionally, results suggest that leadership responsibilities include collaborative design of a learning environment which is rich in interactions and conversations and that, concurrently, advance information sharing and exchange relationships which purposefully extend collective interpretive and appreciative qualities and capabilities.

REFERENCES

Ackoff, R. L. (1999). *Re-creating the corporation: A design of organizations for the 21st century.* New York: Oxford University Press

Ackoff, R., Magidson, J., & Addison, H. J. (2006). *Idealized design: Creating an organization's future.* Philadelphia, Pennsylvania: Wharton School Publishing.

Argyris, C., & Schön, D. (1991). Participatory action research and action science compared: A Commentary. In W. F. Whyte (Ed.), *Participatory action research*, pp. 85-96. Newbury Park, CA: Sage Publications.

Association of College and Research Libraries (ACRL). (2000). *Information literacy competency standards for higher education*, Chicago, Illinois: American Library Association. Retrieved from http://www.ala.org/ala/acrl/acrlstandards/standards.pdf

Banathy, B. H., & Jenlink, P. M., (Eds.) (2005), *Dialogue as a means of collective communication.* New York City, New York: Kluwer Academic/Plenum Publishers.

Baskerville, R. L., & Wood-Harper, A. T. (1998). Diversity in information systems action research methods. *European Journal of Information Systems, 7,* 90-107.

Bansler, J. (1989). Systems development research in Scandinavia: Three theoretical schools. *Scandinavian Journal of Information Systems, 1,* 3-20.

Bratteteig, T. (2004). *Making change. Dealing with relations between design and use.* Doctoral Dissertation, No 332, Department of Informatics, University of Oslo, Oslo, Norway.

Brown, J. S. (2002), "Growing up digital - How the Web changes work, education, and the ways people learn", *Journal of the United States Distance Learning Association,* 16(2). Retrieved from http://www.usdla.org/html/journal/FEB02_Issue/article01.html

Bruce, C. (1997a). *The seven faces of information literacy.* Blackwood, South Australia: Auslib Press.

Bruce, C. (1997b) The relational approach: A new model for information literacy. *The New Review of Information and Library Research, 3,* 3—22.

Champion, D., & Stowell, F. A. (2003). Validating action research field studies: PEARL, *Systemic Practice and Action Research,* 16(1), 21-36.

Checkland, P. B. (1979). Techniques in 'soft' systems practice part 1: Systems diagrams - some tentative guidelines. *Journal of Applied Systems Analysis, 6,* 33-40.

Checkland, P. B. (1981). *Systems thinking, systems practice.* Chichester: John Wiley & Sons.

Checkland, P. B. (1985). From optimizing to learning: A development of systems thinking for the 1990s. *Journal of the Operational Research Society, 36*(9), 757-767.

Checkland, P. B. (2000). Soft systems methodology: A thirty year retrospective. *Systems Research and Behavioral Science, 17*(S1), 11-58.

Checkland, P. B., & Casar, A. (1986). Vickers' concept of an appreciative system: A systemic account. *Journal of Applied Systems Analysis, 13*, 3-17.

Checkland, P. B., & Holwell, S. (1993). Information management and organizational processes: An approach through soft systems methodology. *Journal of Information Systems, 3*, 3-16.

Checkland, P. B., & Holwell, S. (1998a). *Information, systems and information systems - Making sense of the field.* Chichester, England: John Wiley & Sons.

Checkland, P. B., & Holwell, S. (1998b). Action research: Its nature and validity. *Systemic Practice and Action Research, 11*(1), 9-21.

Checkland, P. B., & Poulter, J. (2006). *Learning for action. A short definitive account of soft systems methodology and its use for practitioners, teachers and students.* Chichester, England: John Wiley & Sons.

Checkland, P.B., & Scholes, J. (1990). *Soft Systems Methodology in action.* Chichester, England: John Wiley & Sons.

Checkland, P. B., & Winter, M. (2006). Process and content: Two ways of using SSM. *Journal of Operational Research Society, 57*, 1435-1441.

Churchman, C. W. (1984). *The systems approach.* New York: Dell Publishing Co.

Davis, H. L., & Somerville, M. M. (2006). Learning our way to change: Improved institutional alignment. *New Library World, 107*(3/4), 127-140.

Dick, B. (2004). Action research literature. Themes and trends. *Action Research, 2*(4), 425-444.

Edwards, S. L. (2006) *Panning for gold: Information literacy and the Net Lenses Model.* Blackwood, Australia: Auslib Press.

Elden, M., & Levin, M. (1991). Cogenerative learning: Bringing participation into action research. In W. F. Whyte (Ed.), *Participatory action research.* Newbury Park, CA: Sage Publications.

Flood, R. L. (1998). Action research and the management and systems sciences. *Systemic Practice and Action Research, 11*(1), 79-101.

Flood, R. L., & Jackson, M. C. (Eds.) (1991). *Creative problem solving: Total systems intervention.* Chichester, England: John Wiley & Sons.

Flood, R. L., & Romm, N. R. A. (1996). *Diversity management: Triple loop learning.* Chichester: John Wiley & Sons.

Ghaye, T. (2007). *Building the reflective healthcare organisation.* Oxford, England: Blackwell.

Heron, J. & Reason, P. (2001) The practice of co-operative inquiry: research 'with' rather than 'on' people. In P. Reason, P. & H. Bradbury (Eds) *Handbook of Action Research: Participative Inquiry & Practice,* pp. 179-188. Newbury Park, CA: Sage Publications.

Huysman, M., & de Wit, D. (2003) A critical evaluation of knowledge management practices. In M. S. Ackerman, V. Pipek, and V. Wulf (Eds.) *Sharing knowledge: Beyond knowledge management,* (pp. 27-55). Cambridge, MA: The MIT Press.

Iivari, J., & Lyytinen, K. (1998). Research on information systems development in Scandinavia—Unity in plurality. *Scandinavian Journal of Information Systems, 10*, 135-186.

Jackson, M. C. (2000). *Systems approaches to management.* New York: Kluwer Academic/ Plenum Publishers.

Jackson, M. C. (2003). *Systems thinking: Creative holism for managers.* Chichester, England: John Wiley & Sons.

Jacobs, G. (2006). Imagining the flowers, but working the rich and heavy clay: Participation and empowerment in action research for health. *Educational Action Research,* 14(4), 569—581.

Jansson, M. (2007). *Participation, knowledges and experiences: Design of IT-Systems in e-home health care.* Doctoral Thesis, Department of Business Administration and Social Science, Luleå University of Technology, Luleå, Sweden.

Langefors, B. (1995). *Essays on infology.* Lund, Sweden: Studentlitteratur.

Lewis, P. J. (1992). Rich picture building in the Soft Systems Methodology. *European Journal of Information Systems, 1,* 351-360.

Limberg, L. (1999). Three conceptions of information seeking and use. In T.D. Wilson & D. K. Allen (Eds.), *Exploring the contexts of information behaviour. Proceedings of the Second International Conference on Research in Information Needs, Seeking, and Use in Different Contexts,* (pp. 116-135). London: Taylor Graham.

Löwgren, J., & Stolterman, E. (1998). *Design av Informationsteknik - materialet utan egenskaper.* Lund, Sweden: Studentlitteratur.

Löwgren, J., & Stolterman, E. (2004). *Thoughtful interaction design. A design perspective on information technology.* Cambridge, MA: MIT Press.

Lupton, M. (2004). *The learning connection. Information literacy and the student experience.* Blackwood, Australia: Auslib Press.

Maybee, C. (2006). Undergraduate perceptions of information use: The basis for creating user-centered student information literacy instruction. *Journal of Academic Librarianship,* 32(1), 79-85.

Midgley, G. (2000). *Systemic intervention: Philosophy, methodology, and practice.* New York: Kluwer Academic/Plenum Publishers.

Mingers, J. (2007). Pluralism, realism, and truth: The keys to knowledge in information systems research. *International Journal of Information Technologies and the Systems Approach,* 1(1), 79-90.

Mirijamdotter, A., & Somerville, M. M. (2004). Systems thinking in the workplace: Implications for organizational leadership. In *Proceedings of the 3rd International Conference on Systems Thinking and Management (ICSTM),* Philadelphia, PA.

Mirijamdotter, A., & Somerville, M. M. (2005). Dynamic action inquiry: A systems approach for knowledge based organizational learning. In *Proceedings of the 11th International Conference on Human-Computer Interaction (HCI'05).* Las Vegas, NV.

Norum, K. E. (2001). Appreciative design. *Systems Research and Behavioural Science, 18,* 323-333.

Rapoport, R. (1970). Three dilemmas of action research. *Human Relations, 23,* 499-513.

Rogers, E., Somerville, M. M., & Randles, A. (2005). A user-centered content architecture for an academic digital research portal. In P. Kommers & G. Richards (Eds.), *Proceedings of ED-MEDIA 2005—World Conference on Educational Multimedia, Hypermedia, & Telecommunications,* Montreal, Canada, (pp. 1172-1177). Chesapeake, VA: Association for the Advancement of Computing in Education.

Rose, J. (2002). Interaction, transformation and information systems development - an extended application of soft systems methodology. *Information Technology & People, 15*(3), 242-268.

Senge, P.M. (1990). *The Fifth Discipline. The Art & Practice of The Learning Organization.* New York: Dubbleday/Currency

Somerville, M. M., & Brar, N. (2006). Collaborative co-design: The Cal Poly digital teaching library user centric approach. In *Information Access for Global Access: Proceedings of the*

International Conference on Digital Libraries (ICDL 2006), (pp. 175-187). New Delhi, India.

Somerville, M. M., & Brar, N. (2007). *Toward co-creation of knowledge in the Interaction Age: An organisational case study.* (Eds.) H. K. Kaul and S. Kaul, *Papers of the Tenth National Convention on Knowledge, Library and Information Networking* (NACLIN 2007), (pp. 367-376). New Delhi, India: DELNET.

Somerville, M. M., & Brar, N. (2008). A user-centered and evidence-based approach for digital library projects. *The Electronic Library* (in press).

Somerville, M. M., & Collins, L. (2008). Collaborative design: A learner-centered library planning approach. *The Electronic Library* (in press).

Somerville, M. M., & Harlan, S. (2008). From information commons to learning commons and learning spaces: An evolutionary context. In B. Schader (ed.), *Learning Commons: Evolution and Collaborative Essentials*, (pp. 1-36). Oxford, England: Chandos Publishing.

Somerville, M. M., & Howard, Z. (2008). Systems thinking: An approach for advancing workplace information literacy. *Australian Library Journal.* (in press)

Somerville, M. M., Huston, M. E., & Mirijamdotter, A. (2005). Building on what we know: Staff development in the digital age. *The Electronic Library*, 23(4), 480-491.

Somerville, M. M., & Mirijamdotter, A. (2005). Working smarter: An applied model for 'better thinking' in dynamic information organizations. *Currents and Convergence - Navigating the Rivers of Change. Proceedings of the 12th National Conference of the Association of College and Research Libraries (ACRL)*, (pp. 103-111). Chicago: Association of College and Research Libraries.

Somerville, M. M., Mirijamdotter, A., & Collins, L. (2006). Systems thinking and information literacy: Elements of a knowledge enabling workplace environment. In *Proceedings of the 39th Annual Hawaii International Conference on Systems Sciences (HICSS-39)*. Los Alamitos, CA: IEEE Computer Society. Retrieved from http://csdl2.computer.org/comp/proceedings/hicss/2006/2507/07/250770150.pdf

Somerville, M. M., & Nino, M. (2007). Collaborative co-design: A user-centric approach for advancement of organizational learning, *Performance Measurement and Metrics: The International Journal for Library and Information Services*, 8(3), 180-188.

Somerville, M. M., Rogers, E., Mirijamdotter, A., & Partridge, H. (2007), Collaborative evidence-based information practice: The Cal Poly digital learning initiative. In E. Connor, (Ed.). *Case Studies in Evidence-Based Librarianship*, (pp. 141-161). Oxford, England: Chandos Publishing.

Somerville, M. M., Schader, B., & Huston, M. E. (2005). Rethinking what we do and how we do it: Systems thinking strategies for library leadership. *Australian Academic and Research Libraries*, 36(4), 214-227.

Somerville, M. M., & Vazquez, F. (2004). Constructivist workplace learning: An idealized design project. In P. A. Danaher, C. Macpherson, F. Nouwens, & D. Orr (Eds.), *Proceedings of the 3rd International Lifelong Learning Conference.* Yeppoon, Queensland, Australia, (pp. 300-305 plus errata page). Rockhampton, Australia: Central Queensland University.

Stowell, F. (2007). Do we mean information systems or systems of information? International *Journal of Information Technologies and the Systems Approach*, 1(1), 25-36.

Stowell, F., & West, D. (1994). *Client-led design: A systemic approach to information system definition.* Berkshire, England: McGraw-Hill.

Susman, G., & Evered, R. (1978). An assessment of the scientific merits of action research. *Administrative Science Quarterly, 23*(4), 582-603

Vickers, G. (1983a). *The art of judgment. A study of policy making.* London: Harper & Row Ltd.

Vickers, G. (1983b). *Human systems are different.* London: Harper & Row Ltd.

West, D., & Stowell, F. (2000). Models, diagrams, and their importance to information systems analysis and design. In D. Bustard, P. Kawalek, & M. Norris (eds.) *For business improvement*, (pp. 295-311). Norwood, MA: ARTECH House, Inc.

Whyte, W. F., Greenwood, D. J., & Lazes, P. (1991). Participatory action research through practice to science in social research. In W. F. Whyte (Ed.), *Participatory action research.* Newbury Park, CA: Sage Publications.

Wilson, B. (2001). Soft systems methodology: Conceptual model building and its contribution. Chichester, England: John Wiley & Sons.

This work was previously published in the International Journal of Information Technologies and Systems Approach, Vol. 2, Issue 1, edited by D. Paradice and M. Mora, pp. 48-69, copyright 2009 by IGI Publishing (an imprint of IGI Global).

Chapter 16
How do Collaborative Technologies Affect Innovation in SMEs?

Angel Luis Meroño-Cerdán
Universidad de Murcia, Spain

Pedro Soto-Acosta
Universidad de Murcia, Spain

Carolina López-Nicolás
Universidad de Murcia, Spain

ABSTRACT

This study seeks to assess the impact of collaborative technologies on innovation at the firm level. Collaborative technologies' influence on innovation is considered here as a multistage process that starts at adoption and extends to use. Thus, the effect of collaborative technologies on innovation is examined not only directly, the simple presence of collaborative technologies, but also based on actual collaborative technologies' use. Given the fact that firms can use this technology for different purposes, collaborative technologies' use is measured according to three orientations: e-information, e-communication, and e-workflow. To achieve these objectives, a research model is developed for assessing, on the one hand, the impact of the adoption and use of collaborative technologies on innovation and, on the other hand, the relationship between adoption and use of collaborative technologies. The research model is tested using a dataset of 310 Spanish SMEs.

INTRODUCTION

Emerging powerful Information Technologies (ITs), such as the Intranet, allow people to collaborate and share their complementary knowledge (Bhatt, Gupta, & Kitchens, 2005). These technologies are responsible for e-collaboration, which can be defined as the collaboration among individuals engaged in a common task using electronic technologies (Dasgupta, Granger, & McGarry, 2002). As an intranet evolves, it increases in sophistication and complexity and can be used for advanced applications such as collaborative design, concurrent engineering, and workflow support (Duane & Finnegan, 2003). Thus, intranets are diverse and can integrate different collaborative technologies (CTs).

CTs can be oriented to different, but compatible, uses. These are related to the offering of information online, communications and information exchange, and the automation of internal business processes. Hamel (2002) emphasizes the role of IT as an enabler of product and process innovation. Innovation process requires the support of CTs since they help in the efficient storage and retrieval of codified knowledge (Adamides & Karacapilidis, 2006), get different people together to innovate (Bafoutsou & Mentzas, 2002), enable the formation of virtual teams to execute the innovation process (Adamides & Karacapilidis, 2006; Kessler, 2003), and create an organizational climate favourable to product innovation. Thus, e-collaboration is expected to have a positive impact on firm innovation. The reverse direction of causality could exist as well, that is, causality may flow also from innovation to CTs' adoption. However, this article focuses on analyzing the impact of CTs on innovation.

Computer systems cannot improve organizational performance if they are not used (Davis, Bagozzi, & Warshaw, 1989). Recently, Devaraj and Kohli (2003) showed that actual use may be an important link to IT value. Thus, we need to view CTs' impact on innovation as a multistage process

that starts at adoption and extends to use. Since knowledge will not necessarily circulate freely firm-wide just because accurate IT to support such circulation is available (Brown & Duguid, 2000), actual CTs' utilization may be a critical phase. In an attempt to address this issue, this research examines the effect of CTs on innovation not only directly, the simple presence of CTs, but also based on actual CTs' use. In this regard, this study will explore the direct relationship between CTs' adoption and innovation, as well as the indirect relationship from CTs' adoption, through CTs' use, to innovation.

The article consists of six sections and is structured as follows. The next section offers a classification of CTs and a framework differentiating three CTs' uses. In the third section, the theoretical model is proposed and hypotheses are stated. Following that, the methodology used for sample selection and data collection is discussed. Then, data analysis and results are examined. Finally, the article ends with a discussion of research findings and concluding remarks.

LITERATURE REVIEW

Collaborative Technologies

CTs are applications where ITs are used to help people coordinate their work with others by sharing information or knowledge (Doll & Deng, 2001). They are critical in KM programs (Alavi & Leidner, 2001; Marwick, 2001; Skyrme, 1998). Different technologies are used in e-collaborations (Dasgupta et al., 2002). A review of the literature reveals several CTs' classifications. DeSanctis and Gallupe (1987) discuss a taxonomy based on group size (smaller, larger) and task type (planning, creativity, intellective, preference, cognitive, conflict, mixed motive). According to Pinsonneault and Kraemer (1990), there are two categories of group support systems: group decision support systems and group communication support systems. Ellis,

Gibbs, and Rein (1991) describe a taxonomy based on application-functionality and Coleman (1995) also provides twelve categories of CTs in the same domain. Mentzas (1993) classifies CTs' software based on four major criteria: coordination model characteristics, type of processing, decision support issues, and organizational environment.

This study focuses on a classification of CTs based on the work of Nunamaker, Briggs, Mittleman, Vogel, and Balthazard (1997), DeSanctis and Gallupe (1987) and Pinsonneault and Kraemer (1990). In this sense, Table 1 shows that CTs may be grouped into two types of systems: (1) electronic communication systems (ECS), whose purpose is to facilitate information exchange; and (2) teamwork systems (TS), where teamwork (processes and decision-making) is structured and done. ECS aim at enabling relationships among individuals or institutions, employees or customers, while TS' objective is to integrate information and predefined work processes, as is the case with workflow tools. According to the expected frequency of use, the present study considers four CTs (two for each category), namely, discussion forums, repositories, shared databases, and document management systems/workflows.

Discussion forums: Due to their simplicity, discussion forums have been one of the earliest technologies for collaborative knowledge creation and knowledge sharing (Wagner & Bolloju, 2005). The subject is set and the discussion is carried on, either with all participants online, or over time, where anyone can share his or her opinion at any time (Bafoutsou & Mentzas, 2002).

Repositories: Valuable knowledge can be collected and placed into repositories for use by others (Gunnlaugsdottir, 2003). Document repositories are a collection of relevant documents that list tacit and articulated knowledge from the experts about the project using textual, picture, and diagrammatic forms (Fernandes, Raja, & Austin, 2005).

Shared databases: They are databases whose data may be consulted and modified by different authorized users within a company or a team. Shared databases are necessary to reduce or prevent the repeated typing of data, but in addition they supplement the system with a wealth of update information, thus building the organizational memory (Gunnlaugsdottir, 2003).

Document management systems/workflows: Document management systems handle documents, storing them in a central server where users can access and work on them. Occasionally, there is a possibility for version control, search, electronic signing, and access control (Bafoutsou & Mentzas, 2002). Workflows may be defined as the automation of a business process, in whole or part, during which documents, information, or tasks are passed from one participant to another for action, according to a set of procedural rules (WFMC, 2004). Thus, regarding process automation, workflows seem to be more advanced than document management systems.

Table 1. Collaborative technologies classification

	Electronic communication systems (ECS)	Teamwork systems (TS)
Concept	They support the exchange of information, documents, and opinions.	Work is done through them.
Aim	Relationship	Integration
Tools	Email; Discussion forums; Repositories; Yellow pages (experts directories)	Workflows/ Document management systems; Project management; Shared databases; Group decision support systems

Collaborative Technologies' Use

Firms can use CTs for different purposes. Soto-Acosta and Meroño-Cerdan (2006) identified three Website orientations: e-information, e-communication, and e-transaction. Based on this classification, three CTs' use orientations have been identified: e-information, e-communication, and e-workflow.

E-information: CTs can be used as a corporate channel for information dissemination and data access across functional boundaries and organizational levels. As a result, CTs may reduce the cost and effort associated with corporate information searches. Thus, e-information is considered as the use of CTs to provide one-way company electronic information.

E-communication: CTs, besides allowing cost reduction in comparison to traditional communication tools, offer a unique and integrated opportunity for interacting with several business agents (both internal and external to the organization). In this way, these technologies facilitate the exchange of information, collaboration, and the possibility of establishing close relationships based on trust and mutual commitment. Thus, e-communication is considered as the use of CTs for two-way information exchange.

E-workflow: In the new economy, work has shifted from the creation of tangible goods to the flow of information through the value chain (Basu & Kumar, 2002). The establishment and development of workflow processes has played a fundamental role in this transition. CTs provide great opportunity for automation of processes and workgroup. Thus, e-workflow is considered as the use of CTs for the establishment of predefined electronic processes through CTs.

MODEL

As mentioned in the introduction, the present study focuses on analyzing the impact of CTs on firm innovation. This effect is evaluated directly from the simple presence of IT, but also according to CTs' actual use. In addition, the relationship between adoption and use of CTs is examined in order to specify the indirect relationship of CTs' adoption and innovation through CTs' use.

Collaborative Technologies' Adoption and Innovation

Innovation can be defined as the search for, the discovery, and the development of new technologies, new products and/or services, new processes, and new organizational structures (Carneiro, 2000). It is the implementation of new ideas generated within the organization (Borghini, 2005;

Figure 1. Research model

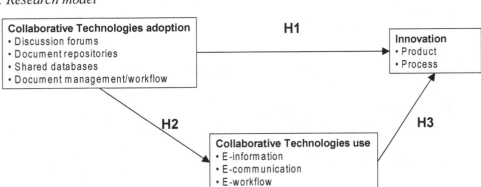

Gurteen, 1998). IT is considered a key facilitator of innovation. Many researchers are focused on analysis of how the Web will change innovation within and between companies (Sawhney & Prandelli, 2000). CTs are Web-based tools that allow information and knowledge exchange (electronic communication systems), as well as work execution by integrating information, documents, and employees (teamwork systems). Thus, intranets and other CTs can be used to distribute and share individual experience and innovation throughout the organization (Bhatt et al., 2005) and offer the chance of applying knowledge for the creation of new products. Also, users and partners from remote places may need to participate in the innovation process. This further emphasizes the instrumental role of IT as enabler for the formation of virtual teams to execute the innovation process (Adamides & Karacapilidis, 2006; Kessler, 2003). In summary, the benefits from Web collaboration, which include efficient information and knowledge sharing as well as working with no distance limitations, are expected to be positively related to the introduction of process and product innovations. Thus, the following hypothesis is proposed:

Hypothesis 1: *CTs' adoption is positively related to innovation:*

H_{1a}: *The adoption of discussion forums is positively related to innovation;*

H_{1b}: *The adoption of repositories is positively related to innovation;*

H_{1c}: *The adoption of shared databases is positively related to innovation; and*

H_{1d}: *The adoption of document management systems is positively related to innovation.*

Collaborative Technologies' Adoption and Collaborative Technologies' Use

Distinct CTs are expected to be more suitable for different purposes. However, all those technologies provide information that can be accessed by employees. Discussion forums, although intended to be convenient for e-communication (Hayes & Walsham, 2001; Rubenstein-Montano, Liebowitz, Buchwalter, McCaw, Newman, Rebeck, & The Knowledge Management Methodology Team, 2001), can be also used as an information tool, since online forums afford a larger and more diverse set of information resources, and also offer an enhanced opportunity for information exchange and communication (DeSanctis, Fayard, Roach, & Jiang, 2003; Walsham, 2001). Repositories store documents (Kwan & Balasubramanian, 2003) and information (Ackerman, 1998), facilitating access to stored knowledge from experts (Fernandes et al., 2005). In the case of CTs labelled as TS, both shared databases and document management systems/workflows are expected to support information and workflow roles. Shared databases include any data and information stored in the business, and make it available to third parties so that they can make decisions and process their transactions (Shah & Murtaza, 2005). Workflow technologies are natural repositories for organizational memory (Zhao, Kumar, & Stohr, 2000) and allow the inspection of information about the current status of the process of innovation (Chung, Cheung, Stader, Jarvis, Moore, & Macintosh, 2003), as well as the automation of processes and transactions. Thus, the following hypothesis is formulated:

Hypothesis 2: *Distinct CTs are expected to be associated to different uses:*

H_{2a}: *ECS are positively associated with e-information and e-communication uses; and*

H$_{2b}$: *TS are positively associated with e-information and e-workflow uses.*

Collaborative Technologies' Use and Innovation

The presence of ITs does not guarantee any effect on performance if they are not used (Davis et al., 1989; Forgionee & Kohli, 1996). Since knowledge will not necessarily circulate freely firm-wide just because accurate information technology to support such circulation is available (Brown & Duguid, 2000), actual CTs' utilization may be a critical phase. Thus, this research considers CTs' impact on innovation as a multistage process that starts at adoption and extends to use. That is, this study, besides testing the direct relationship between CTs' presence and innovation, also examines the influence of actual CTs' use on innovation. Actual CTs' use is expected to have a positive impact on innovation. CTs' use is measured according to three orientations: e-information, e-communication, and e-workflow.

Hypothesis 3: *There is a positive relationship between CTs' use and innovation:*

H$_{3a}$: *There is a positive relationship between e-information and innovation;*

H$_{3b}$: *There is a positive relationship between e-communication and innovation; and*

H$_{3c}$: *There is a positive relationship between e-workflow and innovation.*

METHODOLOGY

The organizations selected for this study are SMEs (small- and medium-sized enterprises) from Spain. SMEs were considered because of their importance for economic growth, employment, and wealth creation in economies both large and small. Currently, SMEs represent around 99% of the total number of firms in Spain (INE, 2005). SMEs are characterized by having fewer financial, technological, and personnel resources than their higher-level counterparts (large firms). Nonetheless, to ensure a minimum firm complexity in which CTs may be relevant, only firms with at least 10 employees were used.

Sample and Data Collection

The target population consisted of SMEs from the Region of Murcia (Spain), with at least 10 employees. Three hundred and ten valid responses were obtained from different industries. The study assumed an error of 5.4% for p=q=50 and a confidence level of 95.5%. A structured questionnaire consisting of close-ended questions was developed. Face-to-face surveys with the key informant person in each company were conducted in May, 2005. The studied companies are mainly SMEs, and most of the interviewees were CEOs. Table 2 shows the characteristics of the sample.

Measures of Variables

This section describes the variables used for measuring the presence of CTs, CTs' use, and innovation. The formulation and criteria for answering the questionnaire is defined in the Appendix.

Collaborative technologies: Using a dichotomous scale, CEOs assessed the presence of four tools in their firms: discussion forums, shared databases, repositories, and document management systems/workflows.

Collaborative technologies' use: One item (five-point Likert-type scale) was used for measuring each collaborative technology use. Firms were requested to value their CTs' degree of use in order to inform their employees (e-information), to debate or receive employees' suggestions (e-communication), and to support the automation of internal business processes (e-workflow).

Table 2. Sample characteristics (N = 310)

Business Industry	%	#	Respondent title	%	#
Textile	12.6	39	Managing director, CEO	58.4	181
Food and Agriculture	40.0	124	Human resources manager	8.7	27
ICTs	1.6	5	Business operations manager	5.2	16
Services to businesses	15.2	47	Administration/Finance manager	23.5	73
Retail	17.7	55	Others	4.2	13
Others	12.9	40			
Number of employees	%	#			
10-49	71.3	221			
50-249	24.5	76			
More than 249	4.2	13			

Table 3. Presence of collaborative technologies

Collaborative technology	Total % (n=310)	At least one CT% (n=115)
Discussion forums	9.4%	25.2%
Repositories	21.9%	59.1%
Shared databases	34.2%	92.2%
Document management systems/ Workflows	21.3%	57.4%

Innovation: Two items based on Choi and Lee's (2003) research were developed, distinguishing the firm's situation re new products and new processes with respect to the industry average. That distinction is based on previous literature, such as Damanpour and Gopalakrishnan (2001) who found differences in companies when adopting product versus process innovations.

ANALYSES AND RESULTS

With regard to CTs, 37.1% out of all analyzed firms (310) had at least one type of CT within their intranet. Table 3 shows detailed results. Shared databases were the most frequently-found technology, with 34.2% of the total number of firms containing it. This technology was also found in almost all

firms that had at least one type of CT (92.2%). The second and third technologies in importance were document repositories and document management systems/workflows, respectively. Less than 10% of all analyzed companies presented discussion forums, while 25.2% of firms containing at least one CT had them. Descriptive statistics and bivariate correlation coefficients are presented in Table 4. Although significant correlations among many of the variables were found, to test casual relationships, regression analysis was used.

Collaborative Technologies' Adoption and Innovation

Analysed firms claimed to innovate slightly above the industry average. Also, the degree of product innovation and process innovation were very simi-

Table 4. Descriptive statistics and bivariate correlation coefficients

Variables	Mean	S.D.	Correlation							
			1	2	3	4	5	6	7	8
1. Discussion forums	0.09	0.29	1							
2. Shared databases	0.34	0.47	0.39***	1						
3. Document repositories	0.22	0.41	0.44***	0.65***	1					
4. Document management systems/Workflows	0.21	0.41	0.42***	0.63***	0.69***	1				
5. E-information	2.96	1.57	0.30***	0.18*	0.26**	0.34***	1			
6. E-communication	2.47	1.41	0.36***	0.13	0.18*	0.23**	0.79***	1		
7. E-workflow	4.07	1.14	0.04	0.37***	0.15	0.19*	0.13	0.04	1	
8. Product innovation	3.24	1.01	0.05	0.14**	0.13**	0.13**	0.24**	0.15	0.08	1
9. Process innovation	3.34	0.98	0.04	0.16***	0.13**	0.16***	0.28***	0.19*	0.05	0.68***

$p<0.1*$; $p<0.05**$; $p<0.01***$

Table 5. Collaborative technologies adoption and innovation

	All variables		Stepwise method	
Independent variables	**New products**	**New processes**	**New products**	**New processes**
Discussion forums	-0.028	-0.049		
Repositories	0.048	-0.002		
Shared databases	0.076	0.099	0.139**	
Document management systems/ Workflows	0.068	0.128		0.169***
F	1.933*	2.768**	6.091**	9.025***
R²	0.012	0.022	0.016	0.025

$p<0.1*$; $p<0.05**$; $p<0.01***$

lar, with 3.2 and 3.3, respectively. As presented in Table 4, all CTs, except for the discussion forums, had significant correlations with both types of innovation. Regression results (see Table 5) showed that, although statistically significant coefficients were not found for any CT, CTs' adoption was associated with innovation. When doing the analysis by the stepwise procedure, it was found that shared databases were positively associated with product innovation (supporting H1c) and document management systems/workflows were positively related to process innovation (supporting H1d). Thus, H1 is partially supported; only TS (shared databases and document management

systems/workflows) were found to be associated with innovation.

Collaborative Technologies' Adoption and Collaborative Technologies' Use

As shown in Table 6, the most predominant collaborative technology used was e-workflow (mean= 4.21), while the least was e-communication (mean= 2.54). Only a few companies allow electronic employee participation through suggestions or debates. Regression results reveal different CTs were associated to different CTs' uses,

Table 6. Collaborative technologies adoption and use

Independent variables	Collaborative technologies use (dependent variables)		
	E-information	E-communication	E-workflow
	(Mean=3.06)	(Mean=2.54)	(Mean=4.21)
Discussion forums	0.215**	0.323***	-0.078
Repositories	0.061	0.013	0.017
Shared databases	0.069	0.049	0.348***
Document management systems/Workflows	0.233*	0.120	0.112
F	4.481***	3.866	3.857
R2	0.137	0.115	0.115

p<0.1*; p<0.05**; p<0.01***

Table 7. Collaborative technologies use and innovation

Independent variables	New products	New processes
E-information	0.331*	0.374**
E-communication	-0.090	-0.112
E-workflow	0.100	0.073
F	2.575*	2.877**
R²	0.091	0.101

p<0.1*; p<0.05**; p<0.01***

thus, supporting Hypothesis 2. More specifically, discussion forums and document management systems/workflows were positively associated with e-information, while discussion forums were positively related to e-communication, and shared databases were positively related to e-workflow. This confirms that ECS are more e-information- and e-communication-oriented, as posited in Hypothesis 2a, particularly when considering discussion forums, whereas TS are used for e-information, in the case of document management systems/workflows, and for e-workflow when considering shared databases, as posited in Hypothesis 2b.

Collaborative Technologies' Use and Innovation

The relationship between actual CTs' use and organizational innovation was tested through regression analysis. As shown in Table 7, CTs' e-information use was statistically significant with a positive impact on innovation (support for Hypothesis 3a was provided). The only differences between product and process innovation were that e-information had a greater positive impact on product innovation and, while the influence on product innovation was statistically significant at 5% level, for process innovation it was significant at 10% level. These results indicate that companies which use CTs as informative mediums achieve higher innovation levels. Conversely, e-communication and e-workflow coefficients were not found to be statistically significant (Hypotheses 3b and 3c were rejected). Through this analysis, support for Hypothesis Hypothesis 3a was provided, whereas support for Hypotheses Hypothesis 3b and Hypothesis 3c was not found.

DISCUSSION AND CONCLUSION

The present research examines the impact of CTs on innovation. This effect is evaluated directly from the mere presence of those technologies, but also indirectly through CTs' use. Given the fact that firms can use this technology for different purposes, CTs' use is measured according to three orientations: e-information, e-communication, and e-workflow. In this regard, this research tests three relationships: CTs' adoption and CTs' use, the influence of CTs' adoption on innovation, and the effect of CTs' use on innovation.

The results indicate that CTs are not widespread among SMEs, since only 37.1% out of all analyzed firms (310) had at least one type of CT within their intranet. The most frequently-found CT was shared databases. Specifically, 34.2% of the sample had shared databases. Also, this technology was found in almost all firms that have at least one type of CT (92.2%). These results confirm previous research studies. For instance, Bafoutsou and Mentzas (2002) found that shared databases are clearly the most common and needed collaboration tools for sharing information. Recently, Meroño-Cerdan (2005) also found that shared databases were the most-adopted CT at the firm level. On the contrary, results showed discussion forums were the least-presented CT. Although discussion forums have been one of the earliest technologies for collaborative knowledge creation and knowledge sharing (Wagner & Bolloju, 2005), firms seem to relegate this technology to an anecdotal use.

The empirical results demonstrate that CTs classified as Teamwork Systems (TS), shared databases and document management systems/workflow, are directly related to process and product innovation, respectively, since work is done through them. On the contrary, Electronic Communication Systems (ECS), discussion forums and repositories, characterized by supporting individual and group work, are not associated with innovation. Thus, apparently, ECS' adoption per se has no effect on innovation.

The results showed, as hypothesized, that distinct CTs are associated with different CTs' uses. Specifically, it was found that ECS are more e-information- and e-communication-oriented (particularly when considering forums), whereas TS are used for e-information (document management/workflow) and e-workflow (shared databases). The lack of relationship between document management/workflow and e-workflow leads us to believe that this technology has been considered, mainly, as a document management system, which does not necessarily include the automation of internal processes.

With regard to the contribution of CTs' use to innovation, only e-information has a significant impact on innovation. Initially, it might be logical to think of a possible influence from e-communication as well. As this is not the case, it could be interpreted that participation and discussion processes, fundamental to innovation, are done outside the intranet. A possible explanation of this can be found in the characteristics of the firms analyzed (SMEs).

In sum, results show that TS are the only CTs that directly influence innovation. The adoption of these technologies involves changing organizational practices, since work is done through them. Research findings also suggest that indirect effects on innovation exist through the influence of e-information. Considering that e-information is significantly influenced by discussion forums and document management systems/workflows, here it is possible to make several recommendations. Document management systems/workflows are found to be the CT that most contributes to innovation. The adoption of this technology influences process innovation, but also influences product innovation when used with an informative orientation (e-information). The case of discussion forums is particularly interesting. It is the least-presented CT and, as an ECS which supports work realization, the simple presence of this technology does not guarantee effects on innovation. However, when they are employed with an informative orientation, influences on innovation are found. Therefore, this study demonstrates that, when considering TS, CTs have a direct influence on innovation. Also, a mediating effect of e-information exists between document management systems/ workflow and process innovation, although this effect is not stronger than the direct effect. Thus, the presence of that technology is important, and, in addition, process innovation is improved when related to e-information. Finally, it is worthy of note that the size of analyzed firms may influence CTs' use. The use of CTs as informative mediums (e-information) in SMEs is possible and was found to contribute to innovation. However, the limited size of firms may imply that collaboration and debate among employees is done outside the intranet. This argument could explain why significant influences on innovation were not found from e-communication.

While this study presents some interesting findings, it has some obvious limitations which can be addressed in future research. First, the sample was obtained from the Region of Murcia (Spain). In this sense, findings may be extrapolated to other Spanish areas and other countries, since economic and technological development in Murcia and Spain is similar to other OECD Member countries. However, in future research, a sampling frame that combines firms from different countries could be used in order to provide a more international perspective on the subject. Second, the sample consisted of SMEs and, according to Spanish Statistics National Institute, large companies are more used to implementing Intranets (INE, 2006). This segment merits a special analysis. Third, the key informant method was used for data collection. This method, while having its advantages, also suffers from the limitation that the data reflects the opinions of one person (not necessarily the user). Future studies could consider research designs that allow data collection from multiple respondents within an

organization. Fourth, the variables used for measuring innovation may be too general. However, basing on literature, they reflect the two main outcomes of innovating efforts: new products and new processes. Finally, it could be interesting to complete this research about the influence of CTs on innovation by studying the relationship between innovation and CTs' adoption, that is, analyzing to what extent innovative firms adopt more CTs.

REFERENCES

Ackerman, M. (1998). Augmenting organizational memory: A field study of answer garden. *ACM Transactions on Information Systems, 16*(3), 203–224.

Adamides, E. D., & Karacapilidis, N. (2006). Information technology support for the knowledge and social processes of innovation management. *Technovation, 26*, 50-59.

Alavi, M., & Leidner, D. (2001). Knowledge management and knowledge management systems: Conceptual foundations and research issues. *MIS Quarterly, 23*(1), 107-125.

Bafoutsou, G., & Mentzas, G. (2002). Review and functional classification of collaborative systems. *International Journal of Information Management, 22*(4), 281-305.

Basu, A., & Kumar, A. (2002). Research commentary: Workflow management issues in e-business. *Information Systems Research, 13*(1), 1-14.

Bhatt, G. D., Gupta, J. N. D., & Kitchens, F. (2005). An exploratory study of groupware use in the knowledge management process. *Journal of Enterprise Information Management, 8*(1), 28-46.

Borghini, S. (2005). Organizational creativity: Breaking equilibrium and order to innovate. *Journal of Knowledge Management, 9*(4), 19-33.

Brown, J. S., & Duguid, P. (2000). Balancing act: How to capture knowledge without killing it. *Harvard Business Review, 78*(3), 73-80.

Carneiro, A. (2000). How does knowledge management influence innovation and competitiveness? *Journal of Knowledge Management, 4*(2), 87-98.

Carvalho, R., & Ferreira, M. (2001). Using information technology to support knowledge conversion processes. *Information Research, 7*(1). Retrieved from http://InformationR.net/ir/7-1/paper118.html

Choi, B., & Lee, H. (2003). An empirical investigation of KM styles and their effect on corporate performance. *Information & Management, 40*(5), 403-417.

Chung, P., Cheung, L., Stader, J., Jarvis, P., Moore, J., & Macintosh, A. (2003). Knowledge-based process management—An approach to handling adaptive workflow. *Knowledge-Based Systems, 16*(2), 149–160.

Coleman, D. (1995). *Groupware: Technology and applications.* Englewood Cliffs, NJ: Prentice Hall.

Damanpour, F., & Gopalakrishnan, S. (2001). The dynamics of the adoption of product and process innovations in organizations. *Journal of Management Studies, 38*(1), 45-65.

Dasgupta, S., Granger, M., & McGarry, N. (2002). User acceptance of e-collaboration technology: An extension of the technology acceptance model. *Group Decision and Negotiation, 11*(2), 87-100.

Davis, F. D., Bagozzi, R. P., & Warshaw, P. R. (1989). User acceptance of computer technology: A comparison of two theoretical models. *Management Science, 35*(8), 982-1003.

DeSanctis, G., Fayard, A. L., Roach, M., & Jiang, L. (2003). Learning in online forums. *European Management Journal, 21*(5), 565–577.

DeSanctis, G., & Gallupe, R. B. (1987). A foundation for the study of group decision support system. *Management Science, 33*(5), 589-609.

Devaraj, S., & Kohli, R. (2003). Performance impacts of information technology: Is actual usage the missing link? *Management Science, 49*(3), 273-289.

Doll, W. J., & Deng, X. (2001). The collaborative use of information technology: End-user participation and systems success. *Information Resources Management Journal, 14*(2), 6-16.

Duane, A., & Finnegan, P. (2003). Managing empowerment and control in an intranet environment. *Information Systems Journal, 13*(2), 133-158.

Ellis, L., Gibbs, S. J., & Rein, G. L. (1991). Groupware: Some issues and experiences. *Communications of the ACM, 34*(1), 38-58.

Fernandes, K., Raja, V., & Austin, S. (2005). Portals as a knowledge repository and transfer tool—VIZCon case study. *Technovation, 25*(11), 1281–1289.

Forgionne, G., & Kohli, R. (1996). HMSS: A management support system for concurrent hospital decision-making. *Decision Support Systems, 16*(3), 209-229.

Gunnlaugsdottir, J. (2003). Seek and you will find, share and you will benefit: Organising knowledge using groupware systems. *International Journal of Information Management, 23*(5), 363-380.

Gurteen, D. (1998). Knowledge, creativity, and innovation. *Journal of Knowledge Management, 12*(1), 5-13.

Hamel, G. (2002). *Leading the revolution.* New York: Plume.

Hayes, N., & Walsham, G. (2001). Participation in groupware-mediated communities of practice: A socio-political analysis of knowledge working. *Information and Organization, 11*(4), 263-288.

INE (2005). Estructura y demografía empresarial. *Directorio Central de Empresas* (DIRCE). Retrieved April, 2006, from www.ine.es/inebase

Kessler, E. H. (2003). Leveraging e-R&D processes: A knowledge-based view. *Technovation, 23*, 905-915.

Marwick, A. (2001). Knowledge management technology. *IBM Systems Journal, 40*(4), 814-830.

Mentzas, G. (1993). Coordination of joint tasks in organizational processes. *Journal of Information Technology, 8*, 139-150.

Meroño-Cerdan, A. (2005). Uso de tecnologías de grupo en pymes e influencia sobre el desempeño. *4th International Conference of the Iberoamerican Academy of Management, Lisbon, December.*

Nunamaker, J., Briggs, R., Mittleman, D., Vogel, D., & Balthazard, P. (1997). Lessons from a dozen years of group support systems research: A discussion of lab and field findings. *Journal of Management Information Systems, 13*(3), 63-207.

Pinsonneault, A., & Kraemer, K. L. (1990). The effects of electronic meetings on group processes and outcomes: An assessment of the empirical research. *European Journal of Operations Research, 46*(2), 143-161.

Rubenstein-Montano, B., Liebowitz, J., Buchwalter, J., McCaw, D., Newman, B., Rebeck, K., & The Knowledge Management Methodology Team (2001). A system thinking framework for knowledge management. *Decision Support Systems, 31*(1), 5-16.

Sawhney, M., & Prandelli, E. (2000). Communities of creation: Managing distributed innovation in turbulent markets. *California Management Review, 42*(4), 24-54.

Shah, J., & Murtaza, M. (2005). Effective customer relationship management through Web services. *The Journal of Computer Information Systems, 46*(1), 98-109.

Soto-Acosta, P., & Meroño-Cerdan, A. (2006). An analysis and comparison of Web development between local governments and SMEs in Spain. *International Journal of Electronic Business, 4*(2), 191-203.

Skyrme, D. (1998). Knowledge management solutions - The IT contribution. Retrieved May, 2006, from http://www.skyrme.com/pubs/acm0398.doc

Wagner, C., & Bolloju, N. (2005). Supporting knowledge management in organizations with conversational technologies: Discussion forums, Weblogs, and wikis. *Journal of Database Management, 16*(2), 1-8.

Walsham, G. (2001). Knowledge management: The benefits and limitations of computer systems. *European Management Journal, 19*(6), 599–608.

WFMC (2004). *Workflow Management Coalition.* Retrieved from http://wfmc.org

Zhao, J. L., Kumar, A., & Stohr, E. A. (2000). Workflow-centric information distribution through e-mail. *Journal of Management Information Systems, 17*(3), 45–72.

APPENDIX. MEASURES

Indicators	Description
<u>CTs Adoption</u>	
Discussion forums	Does your company have discussion forums within the Intranet? (Y/N)
Shared databases	Does your company have shared databases within the Intranet? (Y/N)
Repositories	Does your company have document repositories within the Intranet? (Y/N)
Document management systems/ Workflows	Does your company have document management systems/workflows within the Intranet? (Y/N)
<u>CTs use</u>	
E-information	Use of CTs within the Intranet to inform employees (1-5)
E-communication	Use of CTs within the Intranet to receive/debate suggestions from employees (1-5)
E-workflow	Use of CTs within the Intranet to support internal processes automation (1-5)
Product innovation	The number of new or improved products and/or services, launched by your company, is greater than the sector's average (1-5).
Process innovation	The number of new or improved internal processes is greater than the sector's average (1-5).

Note. Y/N, dummy variable; 1-5, five-point Likert-type scale

This work was previously published in the International Journal of e-Collaboration, Vol. 4, Issue 4, edited by N. Kock, pp. 33-50, copyright 2008 by IGI Publishing (an imprint of IGI Global).

Chapter 17
Enabling On-Line Deliberation and Collective Decision-Making through Large-Scale Argumentation:
A New Approach to the Design of an Internet-Based Mass Collaboration Platform

Luca Iandoli
University of Naples Federico II, Italy

Mark Klein
Massachusetts Institute of Technology, USA

Giuseppe Zollo
University of Naples Federico II, Italy

ABSTRACT

The successful emergence of on-line communities, such as open source software and Wikipedia, seems due to an effective combination of intelligent collective behavior and internet capabilities However, current internet technologies, such as forum, wikis and blogs appear to be less supportive for knowledge organization and consensus formation. In particular very few attempts have been done to support large, diverse, and geographically dispersed groups to systematically explore and come to decisions concerning complex and controversial systemic challenges. In order to overcome the limitations of current collaborative technologies, in this article, we present a new large-scale collaborative platform based on argumentation mapping. To date argumentation mapping has been effectively used for small-scale, co-located groups. The main research questions this work faces are: can argumentation scale? Will large-scale argumentation outperform current collaborative technologies in collective problem solving and deliberation? We present some preliminary results obtained from a first field test of an argumentation platform with a moderate-sized (few hundred) users community.

THE CHALLENGE: TOWARDS INTERNET-ENABLED COLLECTIVE INTELLIGENCE

The spectacular emergence of the Internet has enabled unprecedented opportunities for large scale interactions, via email, instant messaging, news groups, chat rooms, forums, blogs, wikis, podcasts, and the like. Using such technologies, it is now feasible to draw together knowledgeable and interested individuals and huge information sources on a scale that was impossible a few short years ago. We believe that it is possible to harness these new potentialities to enable "collective intelligence", i.e. the synergistic and cumulative channeling of the vast human and technical resources now available over the internet (Klein, Cioffi and Malone, 2007) – to address what we call "systemic" problems, i.e. highly complex and widely impactful problems such as climate change, where the nature of the solution depends on the problem setting and the level of analysis (Rosenhead and Mingers, 2001). Reframing the issue in computational terms, we can say that such problems have a very large, unexplored and partially unknown solution space. Through the contributions of large numbers (up to many thousands) of knowledgeable users, a virtual community can enable unprecedented breadth of exploration of the solution space and, if adequately motivated and supported, convergence on high-quality and widely-supported solutions through collective deliberation.

The successful emergence of on-line peer production communities, e.g. for Linux and Wikipedia, seems due to an effective combination of intelligent collective behavior and Internet capabilities (Surowiecki, 2004). In a nutshell, openness, large scale, self-organization and the support offered by adequate, low-cost technologies have allowed large groups of users to achieve outstanding results in knowledge creation, sharing and accumulation, to the point that such virtual communities have become a source of inspiration for both organizational scholars and companies (Gloor, 2006; Raymond, 2001; Tapscott and Williams, 2006; von Hippel, 2001; von Krogh and von Hippel, 2006).

However, current technologies, such as forums, wikis and blogs, while enabling effective information sharing and accumulation, appear to be less supportive of knowledge organization, use and consensus formation. In particular, little progress has been made to date in providing virtual communities with suitable tools and mechanisms for collective decision-making around complex and controversial problems.

In this article we argue that a new kind of web-mediated platform is needed in order to overcome the limitations of current technologies in this regard and to properly exploit the potential of collective intelligence on the Internet. We present the design for such a platform, which we call the Deliberatorium, which applies a knowledge organization and visualization approach based on argument mapping to help large, diverse, and geographically-dispersed groups systematically explore, evaluate, and come to decisions concerning systemic challenges. We will argue that the argumentation approach, by providing a logical rather than a time-based debate representation, and by encouraging evidence-based reasoning and critical thinking, should significantly reduce the prevalence of some critical pitfalls (such as low signal to noise ratios, digression, hidden assumptions, low information disclosure, and so on) often faced by traditional technologies such as forum and wikis, and avoid many of the pitfalls that lead to deliberation failures in small scale groups as well.

The article is structured as follows. In the next section we outline the factors that have a major influence on group deliberation failures and discuss the limits faced by current technologies from the perspective of supporting collective deliberation around complex systemic problems. In the second part of the article we outline the design of a large-scale deliberation platform that we believe can transcend these limitations. In the third part we report some preliminary results obtained from a first field test of the Deliberatorium with a community of more than 200 users.

In the conclusions we introduce and discuss several research hypotheses we intend to test for in next experiments about how on-line large scale argumentation may improve collective deliberation compared to other technologies, like wikies and forums.

SUPPORTING ON-LINE DELIBERATION: PROS AND CONS OF CURRENT INTERNET TECHNOLOGIES

In the design of a platform for large-scale collective deliberation, it is critical to design effective countermeasures to limit the risk of group deliberation failures. In his book Infotopia, Sunstein (2006) outlines several causes that can induce deliberating groups to fail in making accurate, truthful and reliable decisions as well as some conditions under which group deliberation can work. He points out that deliberating groups typically suffer from three major problems:

- they do not elicit all the relevant information that their members have because of social pressure (low *information disclosure*);
- they are subject to cascade effects: sequential information propagation in the group may produce errors amplification and premature convergence (contributions that happen to have been made early in the group deliberation process can have a disproportionate impact on the final outcome, eclipsing more accurate or useful contributions that came later in the process);
- they show a tendency toward group polarization: often deliberating groups may assume a position on an issue which is even more extreme than the average opinion, in

particular when they are very homogeneous and when the issue is related to values and social identity.

The following conditions, in contrast, seem to help deliberating groups outperform even their best members:

- people believe that the issue has a correct, demonstrable solution (e.g. for so-called "eureka problems", i.e. where a self-evident superior solution exists)
- the correct solution enjoys a certain degree of support by the group members before deliberation starts (in the extreme case, at least one of the group members knows the right solution and is able to *persuade* the other members).

The deliberation failure causes outlined above have been detected in experiments in which groups were required to deliberate about an issue and reach a collective decision. It is important to remark that this huge literature, developed mostly in the '80s and '90s, is largely concerned with small scale, closed, physically co-located groups of individuals involved in direct interaction in typical social situations, such as political and management committees, juries, assemblies, focus groups, meetings, etc.

While there are reasons to believe that the above problems could also appear in groups collaborating through the Internet, to our knowledge no systematic evidence is available to assess the extent to which those effects can be found in large-scale on-line deliberation communities. However, some evidence exists for on-line prediction markets. Participants to a prediction market bet on the supposed best candidate and receive a money prize if their bet is correct, or lose their money in the opposite case. Prediction markets have proven to be a reliable approach for harnessing collective intelligence for such uses as predicting the winners of political elections (University of IOWA prediction market) or forecasting the success of new products (Google), but they cannot be used to deliberate collectively about complex problems for which no obvious limited set of solutions can be pre-defined.

The reason for the good performance of prediction markets lies first in the simplicity of the problems they can deal with (there is a known and limited set of possible alternatives), and, second, on the presence of market incentives that motivate individuals to search for more information and prefer rational choices. The more informed the decision makers, the higher the probability that their majority guess is correct, by virtue of the well-known Condorcet's Jury theorem. This appears to represent a major difference with other on-line collaborative communities, like Wikipedia or the open-source movement, in which many different kind of both extrinsic (e.g. being paid) and intrinsic incentives (reputation, reciprocity, entertainment, voluntary contributions, etc.) are at work (Shah, 2006).

Following de Moor and Aakhus (2006), Klein, Cioffi and Malone (2007) classify on-line deliberation support technologies into three groups: sharing, funneling, and issue networking technologies.

By far the most commonly used technologies, including wikis, blogs, and discussion forums, are what we can call *sharing* tools (Jøsang, Ismail and Boyd, 2007). While such tools have been remarkably successful at enabling a global explosion of idea and knowledge sharing, they face serious shortcomings. One is the signal-to-noise ratio. The content captured by such tools, especially forums, is notorious for often being unsystematic, repetitive, and of highly variable quality. Sharing systems do not inherently encourage or enforce any standard concerning what constitutes valid argumentation, so postings are often bias- rather than evidence- or logic-based. A second issue involves the weakness of sharing-type systems when applied to controversial topics with many diverging perspectives, often leading to such

phenomena as forum "flame wars" and wiki "edit wars". Sharing tools are thus ill-suited to identifying a group's consensus on a given issue.

Funneling technologies, which include group decision support systems, prediction markets, and e-voting, have proven effective at aggregating individual opinions to determine the most widely/strongly held view, but provide little or no support for identifying what the alternatives selected among should be, or what their pros and cons are.

Issue networking tools (also known as argumentation or rationale capture technologies, Kirshner, Buckingham Shum and Carr, 2005) fill this gap by helping groups define networks of *issues* (questions to be answered), *options* (alternative answers for a question), and *arguments* (statements that support or detract from some other statement, see Figure 1). Such tools help make deliberations, even complex ones, more systematic and complete. The central role of argument entities encourages careful critical thinking, by implicitly requiring that users express the evidence and logic in favor of the options they prefer. The results are captured in a compact form that makes it easy to understand what has been discussed to date and, if desired, add to it without needless duplication, enabling increased synergy across group members as well as cumulativeness across time.

Current issue networking systems do face some important shortcomings, however. A central problem is ensuring that people enter their thinking as well-formed argument structures – a time and skill-intensive activity - when the benefits thereof often accrue mainly to *other* people at some time in the future. Most issue networking systems have addressed this challenge by being applied in physically co-located meetings where a single facilitator captures the free-form deliberations of the team members in the form of an commonly-viewable argument map. Issue networking systems have also been used, to a lesser extent, to enable non-facilitated deliberations, over the Internet, with physically distributed

Figure 1. An example of argument map

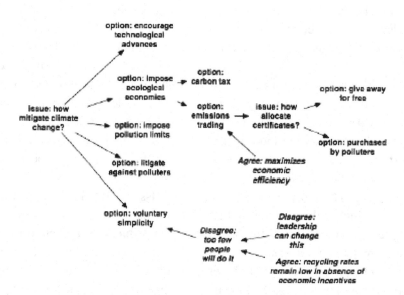

participants (Buckingham Shum, 2006; Verheij, 2003). With only one exception that we know of[1], however, the scale of use has been small, with on the order of 10 participants or so working together on any given task, far less than what is implied by the vision of large-scale collective intelligence introduced in this article.

Since the set up and large scale testing of a collaborative deliberation platform requires considerable effort and higher costs than a traditional experiment with a small group, the risk of ex-post deliberation failure should be reduced by suitable pre-emptive countermeasures. In the next section we present an approach to the design of an on-line argumentation collaborative platform and propose several implementation solutions aimed at ensuring effective deliberation. The proposed approach is centered around argumentation: we claim that an argument-based format for knowledge representation and a deliberation process developing through a debate characterized by a dynamic exchange of arguments can improve deliberation performances compared to those obtained by small, physically co-located groups and enhance deliberation performance in the

solution of complex problems compared to other more traditional internet collaborative technologies such as forums, wikis and blogs.

THE DESIGN OF A LARGE SCALE ARGUMENTATION COMMUNITY

The Proposed Framework

One possible way to cope with the complexity arising in large scale on-line deliberation is to move from the issue of designing a platform to the more general problem of organizational design. In other words, we need to figure out how the virtual community will (and should) work. We can model the virtual community as a kind of organization characterized by (Figure 2):

- a mission to realize
- one or more goals coherent with the mission
- a large group of participants offering portions of their time and attention to the achievement of the goal through information search,

Figure 2. Components for the design of an on line virtual community

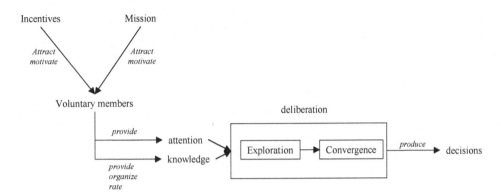

knowledge sharing and creation, consensus achievement acting under suitable incentives

• a set of processes through which members explore the solution space and converge to a decision

• rules governing the access to the community and proper interaction roles charged with certain responsibilities.

There are many differences between an on-line virtual community and a traditional organization. First, in the virtual community interaction happens mainly or solely through the internet medium; second, individual contribution is mainly voluntary and limited to three forms: knowledge provision, knowledge rating, and knowledge organization (e.g. classification). Third, a virtual community is a self-organized system in which top-down management and centralization are present to only a very limited extent and to which people join on a voluntary basis, propose and share ideas, form spontaneous teams and proceed to achieve goals pursuing recognition from the outside world (Gloor, 2007). In order for this kind of organizations to work properly, three major governance problems have to be dealt with:

• *participation goverance* involves attracting, retaining, and motivating a critical mass of users with the right skills

• *attention governance* involves mediating how that community explores the design and decision space when at work

• *community governance* involves the definition of the organizational structure and processes in terms of hierarchy, rules and incentives

In the following we address these three problems in the context of designing an argument based platform.

The On-Line Argumentation Process

The platform is aimed at supporting an on-line collective argumentative debate: ideas submitted by users are supported and attacked by arguments through a dynamic debate whose aim is to uncover chains of pros and cons behind each ideas. Knowledge is structured and organized through argument mapping and visualization (Figure 3).

Ideas and arguments are rated by users through voting. It is important to distinguish between the voting process and the way scores are expressed, computed and aggregated. The idea is to have three types of scores: argument scores (where

Figure 3. An example of an on-line argument maps

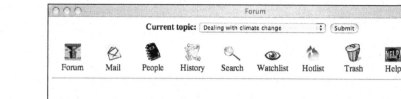

users vote how well grounded and convincing an argument is), idea scores (where users rate how promising and high-impact an idea is), and author scores (where users vote for the reputation of an author).

Voting can take place either in a "direct democracy" scenario, i.e. where all users are allowed to participate in the deliberation process without intermediation/delegation, or through proxy democracy. A pure direct democracy approach has several shortcomings: first, not all people who express their preferences will be adequately knowledgeable about the specific topic; second, a high number of participants could post too many arguments and ideas of poor quality, producing a fragmented, low quality debate. A proxy democracy solution with some degree of moderation has, indeed, proved successful in some large-scale implementations (see the Slashdot.org meta-moderators system described in Jøsang et al., 2007 or the proxy-voting in smartocracy.org).

In both cases it will be important to ensure the presence of a positive feedback between author reputation, idea and argument quality. For instance, suppose one voter likes the idea "support the implementation of a hydrogen economy" so that s/he wants to vote for it to increase the idea score. A possible option is to have a rigid scoring method ensuring that if the idea is not adequately supported by good arguments this and other votes should not affect significantly the idea score. Alternatively, a softer rule could be for the system to simply make it clear, through analysis tools, when people have voted for ideas that don't have strong logical support: this will hopefully encourage them to look at the argument structure, but without imposing a kind of automatic censoring process that many users may rebel against. Whichever the way, voters and authors will look at the available arguments. The following cases are possible:

1. voters can endorse the existing arguments to support the idea;
2. authors can propose new supporting arguments;
3. voters can read the attacking arguments and get convinced that the Hydrogen economy is not such a good idea, so they can change their mind and reconsider their support for the idea.

Argument Representation

There is a huge body of research about argument analysis and structure with implications for mapping and representation. We can classify this research into two major branches:

- *philosophical inquiries* (e.g. the New Rhetoric of Perelman, the Informal Logic of Toulmin, Habermas' Theory of Communicative Action);
- *artificial intelligence and computer science*, starting from the early efforts of the so called Yale School (Galambos, Abelson and Black, 1986; Schank, 1986) on case based reasoning to more recent works on argumentative agents and the use of arguments in hypertext, knowledge management and the semantic web (see the recent special issue on Argumentation published by the journal Artificial Intelligence in 2007).

The applications related to the first area are mainly in the field of education and legal argumentation, while the second stream has elicited a remarkable degree of attention in different areas of artificial intelligence. In the last decade, considerable effort has been invested by several researchers in the attempt to find a synthesis of these two schools of thought, and to consider several internet related emerging phenomena as field of application. We can call this attempt a socio-technical perspective on argumentation (Carter, 2000; Chesnevar et al., 2006; de Moor

and Aakhus, 2006; Kirschner et al. 2003; Mancini and Buckingham Shum, 2006; Rawhan, Zablith and Reed, 2007). The majority of works in this area shares a focus on the use of internet related technologies to implement argumentation frameworks and environments aimed at improving the quality of collective debates and decisions and, more generally, knowledge representation, sharing and transfer. The idea is to exploit the intrinsic structure of argumentation:

- to represent knowledge in a compact and structured way compared to traditional textual representation (knowledge summarization),
- to retrieve knowledge and connections among pieces of information (creating knowledge networks),
- to foster debate through argumentative dialogues on the net between users in which ongoing "mass conversations" made by arguments, endorsements and attacks should favor the emergence of more plausible, convincing and shared conclusions about a given topic (convergence) by allowing at the same time a certain amount of conflict.

Several attempts have been made to propose suitable argument representations to achieve these aims. We can classify these attempts using a continuum defined by the degree of formalization, and by the standardization of the proposed argument format. For instance, Rahwan et al. (2007) propose a highly structured formalization called the Argument Interchange Format (AIF), based on a RDF Schema Semantic Web-based ontology language. Such formats have the advantage of being understood by the machines that are supposed to process such information, such as argumentative agents, but are hard for humans to use. In cases where human involvement is high, we need to look for less-formal argument representations that let people easily perform typical argumentative routines and tasks (posting, editing, elaborating, reading, attacking, etc.).

Our proposal in this context involves integrating three approaches: the IBIS approach (Issue based information system, Conklin, 2006), the Toulmin argument analysis structure (1959) and the concept of argument schemes proposed by Walton (1989, 2006). The proposed representation aims to be very close to what people usually mean by argumentation, keeping formalization at a minimum without losing the structuring power of arguments.

The IBIS approach represents arguments using three basic elements: Questions, which pose a problem or issue, Ideas, which offer possible solutions or explanations, and pro/con Arguments, which support or reject an idea or other argument. In the IBIS framework arguments develop as trees (as in Figure 3). Several software tools for argument mapping have been developed, but their application has largely been limited to small scale, physically co-located groups, usually requiring the presence of a facilitator.

According to Toulmin (1959), Toulmin, Rieke & Janik (1979) an argument is a sequence of interconnected affirmations (claims) that establish the content and the strength of the position of the orator (Hitchcock and Verheij, 2005). As a consequence, argumentative speech can be broken down into a series of claims. Claims can be classified into the following categories, with respect to the functions that they have in the speech:

- the key *claim*, or conclusion of an argumentation;
- the *grounds*, such as the facts, common sense, and opinions of influential people offered to support a key claim;
- *warrants*, meaning the rules that demonstrate how the grounds support the claims;
- *qualifiers*, which are expressions or terms that limit the validity of the claims, such as "usually", "rarely", "according to what we know", etc.

Following Toumin's framework we can define an argument as an inference mechanism (warrant) capable of transferring the degree of truth of a set of premises (grounds) to a conclusion.

Walton (2006) classifies arguments in three categories: deductive, inductive, plausible: *Deductive* arguments (modus ponens, modus tollens, syllogism) are such that if the premises are true, the conclusion must be true (e.g. Portland is in Maine, Maine is in the US, then Portland must be in the US). *Inductive* arguments are such that if the premises are true, the conclusion is probably true (Most American cats are domestic, Bill is an American cat, Bill is (with high probability) a domestic cat). *Plausible* arguments are such that if the premises are true then a weight of plausibility is shifted to the conclusion. Plausible arguments are used when not all needed information is available (or is made explicit): "To say that a statement is plausible we mean that it seems to be true based on the data known and observed so far in a kind of situation we are familiar with" (Walton, 2006: 83).

Plausible arguments can be classified into "schemes". Schemes represent stereotypical, commonly-used ways of drawing inferences (Rahwan et al., 2007) that can be considered acceptable in absence of complete information. Structures and taxonomies of schemes have been proposed by many theorists, such as Perelman and Olbrechts-Tyteca (1969). Walton's exposition is very appealing since his classification is drawn from the everyday use of arguments. A second desirable characteristic of Walton's schemes is that they are each assigned a set of critical questions enabling contenders to identify the weaknesses of an argument and potentially attack it (see some examples in table 1). Compared with deductive and inductive arguments we can say that the critical questions can be viewed as "premises that need to be verified", as they are usually implicit or taken for granted in everyday reasoning.

Walton's scheme theory could be used by readers to recognize and classify arguments pro-

Table 1. Examples of argument schemes (our adaptation from Walton, 2006)

Argument scheme	Argument Structure	Critical questions
Expert opinion	**Ground**: E is an expert in the domain A is in **Warrant**: trust what expert says	How credible is E (reliable, free of conflict of interests, authoritative, etc.)? Is E an expert in the field A is in? Is E's assertion based on evidence?
Popular opinion	**G**: A is generally accepted as true **W**: Believe what is generally accepted as true	What evidence (e.g. polls) supports that A is generally accepted? Even if A is generally accepted, there are any reason for doubting it is true?
Analogy	**G**: Case C1 is similar to case C2, A is true in C1 **W**: repeat things that have proven to work well in the past	Are there differences between C1 and C2? Was A correct (true) in C1? Is there any other case C3 similar to C1 in which A was not correct/true?
Causal (contains as variant the argument form consequences and the slippery slope argument)	**G:** there is a positive correlation between A and B **W**: find out causal relationships between things happening together	Is the correlation supported by credible evidence? Is the correlations due to coincidence? Could there be some factor C causing both A and B? Are there any other consequences to A that should be taken in the account? What evidence support that given A, B will really occur? What factors can prevent the causal chain to happen and how much are they probable? What is the weakest link of this chain? How much is the probability that the chain will actually start?

posed by users and check if critical questions are adequately answered, and to help authors to check if their arguments are defendable with respect to the critical questions and, if not, to revise.

By merging the IBIS, Toulmin and Walton approaches we represent arguments through argument nets. We define and argument net as a directed graph made up of nodes (claims) and arcs (relationship between claims). A claim can be the premise or conclusion of an argument and can be considered to be true to a *certain degree* (e.g. based on the level of consensus assigned to it by an audience). An arc links two claims, specifically a premise to a conclusion. It transfers the degree of truth of the premise to the conclusion. Arcs have a semantics related to the specific argument scheme through which they transfer the truth from the premise to the conclusion (e.g. a "causal" semantic according to which a premise

A causes a conclusion B, as in "wet weather will make you sick").

The arc semantics, assigned by users, describes the way the conclusion is "inferred" from the premise. Even if argumentative reasoning is not logical reasoning, one can assume the two are similar in that they aim to convince viewers about the truth of a proposition, by "proving" it on the basis of given premises. An example of argument net is shown in figure 4.

The proposed representation is aimed at helping people distinguish between the input (*grounds*) *of* an argument (i.e. facts, evidence, shared opinions, values, etc.) and the reasoning scheme through which an acceptable conclusion is obtained from the available inputs. This critical distinction is made for two reasons: i) to encourage evidence-based reasoning; and ii) to induce users to consider the validity of an argument by

Figure 4. A proposal for the representation of argument nets

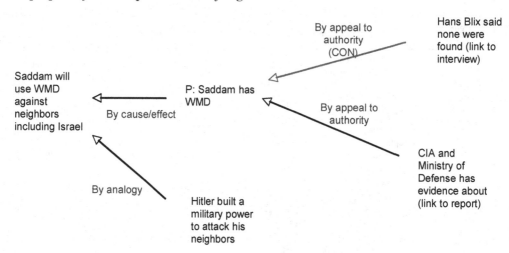

assessing the credibility of both the grounds *and* the reasoning scheme. In other words, an argument's pitfalls can be found in the supporting evidence, or in the scheme, or in both.

THE EMPIRICAL TEST OF THE PLATFORM: PRELIMINARY RESULTS

Software Implementation Overview

The Deliberatorium is a Common Lisp application developed on top of cl-http, an open source web server developed at MIT (http:/www.cl-http. org:8001/). It provides a simple and consistent web-based user interface that allows users to navigate and edit the argument map as well as communicate with each other. The system's capabilities is made accessible via a set of tool icons arrayed across the toolbar at the top of the page (figure 5).

The tools include:

• the argument map: this allows users to browse and edit the argument map. The argument map, as much as possible, attempts to provide "social translucence" (Erikson et al., 2002), allowing members of the user community get a sense of what other community members are doing, thereby fostering emergent self-organization. This is achieved by providing visual cues concerning which branches of the argument map are most active, which posts are the most highly-rated, and so on. The system preserves the edit history for all articles in the argument map, which allows one to quickly "roll back" an article to a previous version if desired.

• search, bookmarks and history: these allow users to find the posts that have given keywords or edit histories, were bookmarked for future reference, or were looked at recently by that user

• people and home: every user has a customizable home page which lists which articles and comments they have contributed. These allow users to to develop, if they wish, an on-line presence, facilitating reputation-building, networking, and community-building. The people tool provides links to the home pages for all the users registered for the current topic.

Figure 5. A snapshot of the Collaboratorium user interface.

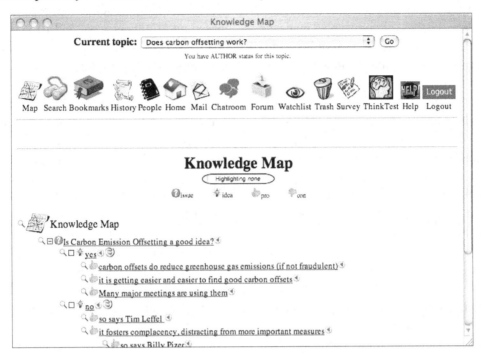

- mail, chatroom and forum: these tools allow users to communicate 1-to-1 (mail), in a public synchronous context (chatroom), or via a public asynchronous threaded discussion (forum).

- watchlist: this allows users to specify which articles or comments they are interested in, so they can be automatically notified (by email) when any changes are made thereto. When coupled with easy rollbacks, this helps make the knowledge-base "self-healing": if an article is compromised in some way, this can be detected and repaired rapidly.

- survey and thinktest: these allow users to provide feedback on the system (survey) as well as take an analytic reasoning test derived from the widely-used Graduate Management Admissions Test (GMAT). The latter allows us to better understand individual differences in successful use of the argument map, as well as assess whether argument map use improves critical reasoning skills.

- the help tool: this tool provides a set of textual user guidelines (describing how to participate in an argument-mapping community) as well as help videos (describing how to use the user interface, including all the tools listed here).

See Klein (2007) for a more detailed discussion of the design of the Deliberatorium.

The Set Up of the Experiment

A first test of the deliberatorium was performed in December of 2007 at the University of Naples Federico II (Italy) with a community of 220 graduate students, which was asked to deliberate on the topic "the future of biofuels". The students were all part of a same class from a graduate program in Industrial Engineering, age 23-25, 55% male. Students selected from that class helped to coordinate and manage the experiment, and were required as a result to deal with social pressures from their fellow students and with the fact that most students inevitably felt the experiment was a course task for which they will be evaluated by their professor. All these circumstances made the context different from a fully open online community and represent a significant limitation of this study. On the other hand, going large scale in these early steps within an uncontrolled experimental setting might not have attracted a critical mass of users and would have prevented us from having a direct contact with them, which has proven to be very useful for debugging, improving and upgrading the software from users' feedback.

The test developed in four phases, starting from early November 2007:

1. Phase 1: preparatory work
2. Phase 2: a three weeks period, in which students were requested to populate the deliberatorium with contents
3. Phase 3: one week for consolidating the knowledge map produced by the community
4. Phase 4: data analysis

In the preparatory phase, the students had four 2 hours seminars from external experts about:

1. collective intelligence and its current internet applications
2. argumentation, with focus on the IBIS approach
3. major issues in energy governance with a country focus on Italy and UE policies
4. an instructional demo of the deliberatorium beta version

The students were also given a few reading materials: two newspaper and magazine articles about the topic and the IBIS manual available at http://touchstone.com/wp/IBIS.html (Conklin, 2003).

We decided to keep at a minimum both the knowledge of the topic and of the platform the students were required to have before starting the experiment since two main objectives of the

experiment were to evaluate i) how easy it is for new users to approach a collaborative platform based on argumentation, and ii) how much the platform helps users improve their knowledge and understanding of the topic.

As a discussion topic we chose "the future of biofuels". The criteria we used to select the topic were: 1) it had to be a relevant topic in the current debate about a systemic complex challenge, like for instance how to reduce global warming; 2) it had to be focused enough to help students not get lost into a too wide a debate, considering they had limited time, attention and expertise; 3) it had to be controversial and multifaceted so that the community could explore possible different solutions and perspectives.

Instead of giving students an empty argument map, we set up two framing, first level questions and options: 1) what percentage of transportation energy needs in Italy will come from biofuel consumption twenty years from now? (options: limited (less than 20%), moderate (between 20 and 30%), substantial (more than 30%)); 2) how can Italy get the biofuels it needs? (no options). The first was a kind of prediction market question while the second was an open design question. We did not prevent users from adding further first level questions.

Before starting phase 2 we prepared two tests to be given to the students before and after the experiment. The first test was aimed at evaluating their knowledge of the topic, and the second was a critical thinking test. Our aim was to see if and to which extent the deliberatorium helps the students improve their knowledge of the topic and their critical thinking skills.

Designing the Argumentation Community: Roles, Rules & Incentives

In the design of the deliberatorium virtual community we adopted the framework described in figure 2. In particular, in the deliberatorium case there are three roles: moderators, authors and readers/voters. Moderators are charged with the usual tasks of filtering out noise and rejecting off-topic posts. They, in addition, were charged with ensuring that the argument map was well-structured, i.e. that all posts were properly divided into individual and non-redundant issues, ideas, and arguments, and were located in the relevant branch of the argument map. This involved classifying and sometimes editing posts, offering suggestions to authors, aggregating similar arguments, and occasionally re-organizing the overall argument map so that related topics are grouped into the same branch. A team of 4 student moderators was selected and trained in argument mapping before the test. One of the authors also joined the moderators team.

The on-line argumentation process developed as follows:

1. Authors posted and edited questions, ideas, and pro/con arguments and produced an argument map similar to that in figure 3. While questions and ideas could be posted only as single short sentences, arguments were posted using an on-line form that helped them structure their post in argument form (conclusion, argument scheme and critical questions, argument content, possibility to attach links, references and documents); the form was designed because otherwise people tended to bundle a mishmash of issues ideas and arguments within individual issues and ideas;

2. All users (including moderators, authors and readers) rated arguments and ideas and could send comments to authors through threaded discussion forums associated, like wiki talk pages, with each post. Rating was anonymous;

3. Posts were initially given a status of "pending", and could only be certified by moderators. Until a post was certified, it could not be rated and nobody, except its author, could link any other posts to it. We also explained

that only certified posts will appear in the final, publicly available, version of the argument map. Moderators also left comments, edited, moved, trashed and classified posts. Usually moderators would leave a comment to explain changes. Authors would receive an alert email when their post was modified or trashed (but the trash was never emptied).

In the experiment we established a single authorship rule: nobody, except moderators, was allowed to edit a post authored by someone else.

Several countermeasures and incentives were set up to limit the negative effects due to limited scale and presence of social and informational pressure usually absent or limited in Internet communities. In particular, we used several extrinsic incentives such as minor awards and five scholarships for the best participants thanks to the support of the Naples City Science Museum with the aim of improving post quality. To limit the negative influence of social pressure on the rating process, a kind of prediction market incentive for voters was set up according to which votes would have been converted at the end of the experiments into awards financed by the sponsor organization in the following way: at the end of phase 2, a team of independent external experts would have identified and ranked the best posts. Then voters would have been assigned a score based on how closely their votes correlated with the expert ratings. The voters with the highest correlation score would have been selected and awarded with educational gadgets.

Preliminary Results

Since phase 2 terminated at the end of December 2007, at the time of writing this article, the data analysis had just begun. We are currently collecting and analyzing three types of data:

1. statistics about tool usage and information accumulation (number of ideas, number of arguments, total volume of inputs, etc.),

2. effects on users in terms of users satisfaction as well as impact on topic knowledge and critical thinking skills,
3. quantity and quality of contents.

Consequently we can report only some preliminary results. Nevertheless the experiment was very useful for observing the behavior of users in the field and for improving the software based on users feedback. These changes will help to plan and design future experiments.

Among the more relevant modifications to the software there were: the introduction of a chat room for users, changes to the argument map visualization to facilitate content searching and display, introduction of a search functions whose algorithm helped to find "similar" posts (and thus help avoid redundant posts as well as assure new posts are properly located), the ability to upload files, and the addition of new features for moderators such as a merge tool to aggregate overlapping posts and a queue tool to show the queue of uncertified posts.

We observed a very high level of user participation as we achieved thousands of posts in just a few days (Figure 6).

Remarkably, the deliberatorium was active almost 24 hours per day, except for a hiatus between roughly 3 and 6 am. About 180 out of 220 users

Figure 6. Number & kinds of posts after two weeks

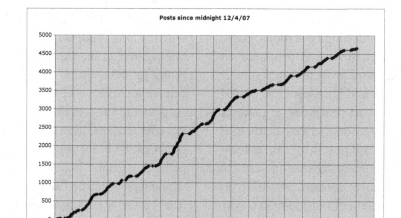

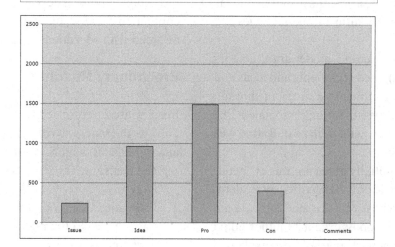

participated with at least a few postings. In two weeks they posted nearly 3000 issues ideas and arguments (of which roughly 1900 were eventually certified) in addition to over 2000 comments (table 2). They were, however, relatively few ratings, notwithstanding the presence of extrinsic incentives: each post received an average of only 2.2 ratings.

The intensity of participation was very heterogeneous among users, as shown in Figure 7. This distribution of posts per users shows a thick middle of users and it vaguely recalls the power law distribution that has instead been found to be typical of many on-line communities (Madey et al., 2002; Healy and Schussman, 2003).

The breadth of coverage, as well as the efficiency of the platform in terms of knowledge accumulation, was quite good: a non-expert community of students was able to create a remarkably comprehensive map of the current debate on biofuels in just a couple of weeks, exploring topics ranging from technological issues to environmental, economic and socio-political impacts of the widespread diffusion of biofuels. Moreover, the proportion of out-of-topic posts was negligible – about 0.1%. The dominant argument scheme was "by authority", followed by analogy, deductive, and inductive schemes (table 3). It also appears that users were generally not able to associate the

Table 2. Number and kind of posts

Type of Post	Number of Posts	Number of Certified Posts	% (certified)
Issue	242	89	5%
Idea	962	452	24%
Pro	1488	1045	55%
Con	402	325	17%
Comments	2009	n/a	n/a
Grand total	5003	1911	100%

Figure 7. Distribution of number of posts per user

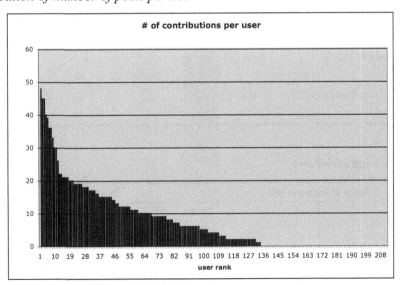

251

right scheme to their arguments, which increased the moderators' workload.

Though students participation may have been influenced by their perception that the experiment was a course task for which they could be evaluated by their professor, their informal face-to-face and on-line comments, posted on the deliberatorium as well as on a threaded discussion forum run independently by a students association web site, showed that they found the experiment interesting and appreciated the innovative characteristics of the deliberatorium.

As expected, at the beginning of the experiment most users really did not grasp the IBIS logic. Rather, many users adopted a kind of forum frame in which they tended to publish posts as news articles (e.g. "France creates incentives for biofuel") rather than as IBIS entities. Common mistakes were: difficulties in distinguishing between ideas and arguments, the tendency to put multiple arguments into a single argument post, linking arguments to a logically irrelevant location in the

argument map, questions and ideas proliferating without any associated pro/con arguments, and difficulties in selecting the right kind of scheme for arguments. After a while we observed an improvement in the use of the platform, as users developed confidence, profited from moderator feedback, and learned to use the tool.

The level of direct debate was moderate. Users did attach many arguments to each other's posts (72% of all certified posts were arguments, and 70% of these arguments were attached to posts authored by someone else) but the great majority of all arguments (again, 70%) were pros rather than cons. The depth of the argument trees was relatively small (table 4).

Most arguments (85%) were attached directly to ideas, with the remainder attached to other arguments. This relative dearth of debate may have been an outcome of the student's reluctance to criticize the contributions of their peers, and thus may be an artifact of the co-located nature of the user population. Other possible explanations

Table 3. Most popular argument schemes

Scheme Type	# times used
APPEAL TO AUTHORITY	760
ANALOGY	280
DEDUCTIVE ARGUMENT	204
BY INDUCTION	171
FROM CONSEQUENCES	102
CAUSAL	61
APPEAL TO POPULAR OPINION	49
AD HOMINEM	35

Table 4. Depth of the argument tree

Depth of argument tree	% of all arguments
1	85%
2	12%
3	2%
4	1%

include: i) inertia deriving from the predominant use of forums and wikis, ii) the short time window compared to the learning curve of users with the new tools, iii) the lack of specific expertise and motivation of the students on the topic leading to fast content saturation and inability to explore in-depth specific subtopics; iv) the use of individual awards and prizes together with the single autorship rules may have fostered competition over collaboration; this aspect could explain a certain level of redundancy in contents, emphasis on authoring rather than on debating to maximize individual exposure, fear of being involved into sub-discussions potential characterized by high-conflicting evolution.

Other important lessons were learned concerning the moderators and, more generally, community governance. Moderators played a crucial role: in an important sense they led the community. They supported users with comments and suggestions and, by ensuring a logically-organized argument map, helped users rapidly locate the contexts where their piece of knowledge can best be linked. For these reasons it is crucial to have enough moderators working to ensure fast certification and timely reorganization of the argument map. With the existing data we can roughly estimate the requisite number of moderators per users. A cadre of from 2 to 5 moderators (the number varied from day to day according to their other commitments during the course of the experiment) was able to more or less keep up with 180 active authors, but only by dint of an unsustainably heavy investment of their time. We estimate that a more realistic time commitment would require that between 5 and 10% of the active users be moderators.

CONCLUSION

Limitations of this Study

In this article we have presented a new mass collaboration platform we call the deliberatorium.

The aim of the deliberatorium is to support large, geographically dispersed communities of users in collective deliberation about complex and controversial issues. The key difference between the deliberatorium and other large-scale collaboration tools like forums, blogs, chat rooms, and wikis is that it supports a logic- rather than time-based knowledge organization structure, based on argument maps. In this article we have argued that this structure makes the deliberatorium a superior tool for supporting large-scale collective deliberation. We have also reported some preliminary results of a first field experiment with a community of about 220 users. To our knowledge the deliberatorium represents the first argumentation platform to be applied successfully at this scale. The experiment permitted us to build what is to our knowledge one of the largest argument maps ever built, on a complex topic, over the course of two weeks, starting with novice users.

Many more lessons almost certainly remain to be gleaned from the test dataset. The deliberatorium software recorded essentially every user interaction with the knowledge base, including every view or modification or rating of any post, so we have a complete time-stamped record of the evolution of the argument map and what the users did while creating it, a database of over 110,000 distinct events. The results of a thorough analysis of this data will be presented in future publications.

The field evaluation was limited in several important ways. One major limitation was the disproportionate use of extrinsic incentives (awards for best participants). It is highly probable that this, in combination with the single author rule, fostered competition over collaboration among users, leading them to focus on authoring rather than on reading, rating and improving what others have authored. This probably encouraged needless redundancy, low information disclosure, produced a relatively moderate level of debate, and did not fully exploit the power of the community to improve the quality of the posts. One of the major changes we will introduce in the next evaluation, therefore, is to enact an open authorship rule, such as that used in Wikipedia, and to rely mostly on intrinsic incentives (like voluntarism and reputation).

Another open issue is the rating procedure. The rating procedure can play a critical role in promoting high-quality contributions and convergence in collective deliberation. In the experiment presented in this article the rating tool was extremely simple: users votes expressed how much a user liked a post through a five point scale ranging from 1 (poor) to excellent (5). Further research developments will concern the design of a more articulated rating procedure aimed at evaluating ideas and argument quality, author reputation, and the community consensus.

The experiment involved a relatively small number of users, by Internet standards, and the way students approached the experiment was distorted, no doubt, by the fact that they were co-located peers. Social pressure, for instance, may have had a role in limiting the number of cons compared to pro's and reduce the number of poor rating, coupled with the students' low expertise in the topic. The experiment also ran, perforce, over a limited time window. Further evaluations will aim to remove these artificial constraints by assessing the platform with much larger, and truly open, more intrinsically motivated user communities. Increased scale will probably require qualitative changes in design choices and user incentives. Among the most critical improvements we underline: designing mechanisms and rules able to generate a self-organized hierarchy of user roles (readers, authors, and moderators), improving the design of the platform in terms of browsing, Information visualization & retrieval, providing on-line support to users (such as on line help and training tools), and building tools to increase moderators productivity. We are currently identifying other possible contexts for assessing and applying the deliberatorium, ranging from problem solving within companies and profes-

sional communities of practice, to learning and education with communities of young students.

Research Implications and Next Steps

The experiment presented in this article was the very first test of the Deliberatorium. The main aim of the test was to observe users' first hand reactions to large scale, internet-based argument debate to improve the design of the platform for the next experiments in which our aim will be to compare the deliberatorium performances with other current sharing tools based on different technologies. A first attempt has been done in a second test scheduled in the late Spring of 2008 with a group of 300 students at the University of Zurich. The aim of this test was to compare the new release of the deliberatorium with more traditional technologies, in particular with forums and wikis, given the same structure of solely intrinsic incentives. For this purpose, we created three groups of users debating on a same topic but using, respectively, the deliberatorium, a forum and a wiki. The analysis of the data of this test was still in progress during the writing and reviewing of this article and results will be the object of a future publication.

Starting from the empirical results and lessons-learned obtained in the Naples test, in this section we present several research hypotheses for the next test, clustered into three groups: *effects on users skills and participation*, *effects on quality and quantity of knowledge contents*, and *effects on group deliberation*.

Effects on Users Skills and Participation

H1: *A large-scale collaborative argumentation platform improves users' critical thinking skills compared to forum and wikis.*

While in forum and wikis people express themselves freely, the deliberatorium requires that users post their contributions through a specific argumentative format. By its very nature, argumentation should encourage critical thinking and evidence-based reasoning through the use of claims, rebuttals, pros and cons, explicit opinions, facts and figures. We expect that after the learning process needed to become confident with the IBIS logic and intense use of the platform, users will improve their critical thinking skills. In order to test this hypothesis users can be given, before and after the experiment, a critical thinking test aimed at measuring if critical thinking skills have improved. A possibility is to use existing standard critical thinking tests, like those employed for graduate program admission or recruitment purposes, consisting of a set of multiple-choice questions that evaluate if users are able to recognize valid arguments and reasoning fallacies and produce correct deductions.

H2: *The deliberatorium supports users in gaining and developing greater knowledge of the discussion topic compared to forum and wikis.*

On-line argumentation should foster debate through internet-enabled "mass conversations" made up of arguments, endorsements and attacks, and should favor the emergence of the most plausible, convincing and widely-shared conclusions about a given topic. To correctly post their contribution, users are required to understand the structure of the discussion with the help of the argument map and other knowledge visualization facilities, to read other users' contributions which are properly located in the current debate, look for additional information to improve, attack or endorse existing arguments and ideas, and/or create new ones. Even for passive users, the mere browsing of a well organized argument map should help them to develop at least a basic, but critical, understanding of the main issues related to the topic. In order to test this hypothesis we will develop, with the help of experts of the field, a structured multiple-choice test to evaluate topical

knowledge before and after the experiment.

H3: *The level of participation of users decreases compared to forums and wikis due to the difficulties of using argumentation rules to post their contributions.*

Previous studies with the IBIS logic show that people encounter difficulties in using the argumentation format, especially if they lack previous experience and specific skills (Conklin, 2003). At the small scale this problem is solved by human facilitators who are charged with the task of identifying arguments in the discussion and "coding" them into an argument map. On the other hand, forums and wikis pose no constraints to the way people wish to express their ideas. Consequently, we expect that, on average, less experienced and occasional users may be discouraged from participating. User participation can be measured by several quantitative indicators such as number of log-ins, number and kind of posts, number of post revisions, number of feedback comments given to other users, etc.

Quality and Quantity of Knowledge Contents

H4: *The quality of the contents posted by users of the deliberatorium will be higher than in forums and wikis*

While on one hand the argumentation formalism can represent an obstacle to participation, on the other hand committed users together with a handful of moderators endowed with above-average argument mapping skills should increase the quality and organization of the contents. Content quality and proper knowledge organization would, in turn, increase the pay-off for new users in terms of the knowledge they gain from using the system, so, in the long term, the level of participation could recover. Measuring contribution quality is definitely critical. Content quality indicators can be *intrinsic* or *extrinsic*. Intrinsic indicators can be related to redundancy, signal-to-noise ratio, presence of fallacious arguments, and coherence (Lih, 2004; Storrer, 2002; Stvilia et al., 2005). Extrinsic indicators can be defined in terms of users satisfaction or judgments by panels of topic experts through ad hoc surveys.

H5: *The deliberatorium will underperform forums and wikis in the sheer volume of information*

H6: *The deliberatorium will outperform forums and wikis in the volume of non-redundant information, in the breadth of problem space exploration, and will limit off-topic posts and digression*

When assessing the quantity of posted information, one should consider several variables: the sheer volume of posted information, the volume of non-redundant information, the extent to which users are able to explore the problem space, and the level of digression in the discussion. The rationale for H5 is that posting in forum and wikis is definitely simpler, so in the short term a larger amount of contributions can be expected. In the longer term, as the discussion develops more in depth and become more specialized, common users may find it increasingly difficult to contribute with novel information.

The rationale for H6 is the following. First, in an argument map multiple posting should be considerably limited by the fact that a post about a specific issue will be just published once and possibly improved by successive revisions. Second, the IBIS logic should encourage users to explore the problem space both vertically (in terms of variety) and horizontally (in terms of depth of discussion about a given issue or idea), since it is probable that arguments and ideas can generate new issues as long as the discussion develops in depth. Third, since the argument map will provide a more rational organization of contents and more focus, it will be easier to identify and marginalize digressions from the main discussion. We expect

that the IBIS logic should increase diversity and/ or depth because people will find it much easier to know whether or not an idea or argument has been proposed yet, or not. Instead, if there is a huge corpus of text, like in more traditional text-based media, people may simply assume that their point has already been made, because it is too time-consuming for them to check.

Effects on Group Deliberation

H7: *Compared to wikis and forums the deliberatorium is expected to produce less polarization, more information disclosure and less error propagation*

We expect that the deliberatorium will contribute to improve collective deliberation by reducing the negative effects of social and informational pressures that are typical of small scale, co-located group decision-making. Large scale on-line communities have a set of desirable characteristics from this perspective:

1. **impersonality:** anonymity or the fact that members do not know each other can ensure some protection from social pressure and higher decisional independence of participants;

2. **asynchronicity:** people can enter the debate when they want and are not forced to provide an answer immediately as in face-to-face situations. Users may have, as a result, more time for information search, reflection, and exploration;

3. **greater information access:** the internet is a formidable low-cost tool for access to a large body of information and evidence that can then immediately being referenced in the deliberatorium discussion

4. **greater diversity & turnover:** large scale communities have a higher chance to attract diverse, independent and heterogeneous perspectives, thus preserving diversity; on-line

large groups are not closed but characterized by variable degrees of participation and high rate of participants turnover; one further advantage of turnover is that it helps keep the discussion vital and less likely to get locked into a rut, e.g. someone new may come a login that opens up a new line of inquiry.

5. **parallelism:** with large-scale social software, people can make contributions in parallel, so there is little opportunity for a single individual or ideology to dominate the debate, unlike contexts with serial, limited bandwidth, interactions, like forums.

To our knowledge, however, there is no empirical evidence to prove that large scale, internet mediated interaction and greater information availability will lower social pressure and improve collective deliberation. On the contrary, some kinds of on-line communities and platforms (e.g. blogs) appear to suffer from polarization, and others (such as wikipedia and forums) often flounder with controversial issues (Sunstein, 2006). We expect that on-line, large-scale argumentation can at least partly avoid these shortcomings: i) by inducing critical thinking and evidence-based reasoning; ii) by encouraging users to look for additional information to support their claims and become more informed about a topic as well as aware of possible different and even contrasting perspectives, iii) by contributing to greater information disclosure since, in order to be convincing, an argument has to be supported by convincing explicit premises; iv) by improving the quality of arguments, since the weaker, more fallacious schemes will be uncovered and easily defeated by a large audience. Finally, critical evaluation of alternative/conflicting solutions should help the community be less inclined to balkanization. In a logically-organized argument map, contrasting perspectives may better coexist that in other collaborative tools like wikies and forums, in which the presence of conflict usually brings about editorial wars. In an argument map, moreover, a

given issue and its adversary claim can be closely co-located and are much more difficult to overlook than in traditional blogs and wikis which typically are focused, by self-selection, on just a subset of the possible perspectives.

ACKNOWLEDGMENT

The authors wish to gratefully acknowledge the Naples City Science Museum (Città della Scienza) sponsorship for the test implementation and the support in the dissemination of the first research results. The authors also wish to thank Livio Ferraro, Fabiana Ippolito, Samantha Lamberti and Vincenzo Leone for their valuable help as community moderators and research assistantship during the field test.

REFERENCES

Buckingham Shum, S. 2006. Hypermedia Support for Argumentation-Based Rationale: 15 Years on from gIBIS and QOC. In A. Dutoit (ed.). *Rationale Management in Software Engineering*, 111-132. Berlin: Springer-Verlag.

Carter, L.M. 2000. *Arguments in Hypertext: a Rhetorical approach.* Proceedings of the Hypertext 2000 Conference, San Antonio (TX), 85-91.

Chesnevar, C., McGinnis, J., Modgil, S., Rahwan, I., Reed, C., Simari, G., South, M., Vreeswijk, G., Willmott, S. 2006. Towards an argument interchange format. *The knowledge Engineering Review*, 21(4), 293-316.

Conklin, J. 2003. *The IBIS Manual: A Short Course in IBIS Methodology*, http://cognexus.org/id26.htm#the_ibis_manual.

Conklin, J. 2006. *Dialogue Mapping: Building Shared Understanding of Wicked Problems.* Chichester (UK): Wiley.

de Moor, A, Aakhus, M. 2006. Argumentation support from technologies to tools. *Communication of the ACM*, 49(3): 93-98.

Erickson, T., Halverson C., Kellogg, W.A., Laff, M. and T. Wolf 2002. *Social Translucence: Designing Social Infrastructures that Make Collective Activity Visible.* Communications of the ACM, 45(4): 40-44.

Galambos, J.A., Abelson, R.P., Black, J.B. (eds.) 1986. *Knowledge Structures*, Hillsdale (NJ): Lawrence Earlbaum Associates.

Gloor, P. 2006. *Swarm Creativity - Competitive advantage through collaborative networks.* New York: Oxford University Press.

Gloor, P. 2007. Coolfarming, http://scripts.mit.edu/~pgloor/coolfarming/index.php?title=Main_Page.

Healy, K. and A. Schussman 2003. *The Ecology of Open-Source Software Development.* Working paper, http://kb.cospa-project.org/retrieve/3150/healyschussman.pdf

Hitchcock, D., Verheij B. 2005. The Toulmin model today: Introduction to special issue of Argumentation on contemporary work using Stephen Edelston Toulmin's layout of arguments. *Argumentation*, 19(3): 255-258.

Jøsang, A., Ismail, R. and C. Boyd 2007. A survey of trusts and reputation systems for online service provision. *Decision Support Systems*, 43: 618-644.

Kirschner, P.A, Buckingham Shum, S.J. and C.S. Carr (eds.) 2003. *Visualizing Arguentation.* Spinger Verlag.

Klein, M. (2007). *The MIT Deliberatorium: Enabling Effective Large-Scale Deliberation for Complex Problems.* MIT Sloan School of Management, Research Paper 4679-08. http://ssrn.com/abstract=1085295

Klein, M., Cioffi, M. and T. Malone 2007. *Achieving Collective Intelligence via Large Scale On-line Argumentation.* Working paper, MIT Center for Collective Intelligence, Cambridge (MA).

Lih, A. 2004. *Wikipedia as Participatory Journalism: Reliable Sources? Metrics for evaluating collaborative media as a news resource.* 5th International Symposium on Online Journalism (April 16-17, 2004), University of Texas at Austin.

Mancini, C., Buckingham Shum, S. 2006. Modelling Discourse in Contested Domains: a Semiotic and Cognitive Framework. *Int. J. of Human Computer Studies* (in press).

Madey, G., V. Freeh, and R. Tynan 2002. *The open source software development phenomenon: An analysis based on social network theory.* Americas Conference on Information Systems (AMCIS-2002).

Perelman, C., Olbrecths-Tyteca, L. 1969. *The New Rhetoric: A Treatise on Argumentation.* Notre Dame (IN): University of Notre Dame Press.

Rahwan, I., Zablith, F. and C. Reed (2007). Laying the foundations for a World Wide Argument Web. *Artificial Intelligence* (in press).

Raymond, E.S. 2001. *The cathedral and the bazaar.* Sebastopol (CA): O'Reilly.

Rosenhead, J., Mingers, J. 2001. *Rational analysis for a problematic world revisited: Problem structuring method for uncertainty and conflict.* Chichester (UK): John Wiley & Son.

Shah, S.K 2006. Motivation, governance and the viability of hybrid forms in open source development. *Management Science*, 52(7): 1000 -1014.

Schank, R.C. 1986. *Explanation Patterns: Understanding Mechanically and Creatively.* Hillsdale (NJ): Lawrence Erlbaum.

Storrer, A. 2002. Coherence in text and hypertext. *Document Design*, 3: 156 - 168.

Stvilia, B., Twidale, M. B., Smith, L. C., Gasser, L. 2005. *Assessing information quality of a community-based encyclopedia.* In Proc. ICIQ, 442-454.

Sunstein, C.R. 2006. *Infotopia.* New York: Oxford University Press

Surowiecki, J. 2004. *The Wisdom of the Crowds.* New York: Doubleday.

Tapscott, D., Williams, A.D. 2006. *Wikinomics.* New York: Penguin Book.

Toulmin, S. 1959. *The Uses of Arguments.* Cambridge (MA): Cambridge University Press.

Toulmin, S., Rieke, R. and Janik, A. 1979. *An Introduction to Reasoning.* New York: Macmillan.

Verheij, B. 2003. Dialectical Argumentation with Argumentation Schemes: An Approach to Legal Logic. *Artificial Intelligence and Law,* 11(2): 167-195.

von Hippel, E. 2001. Open Source Shows the Way: Innovation by and for Users – No Manufacturer Required! *Sloan Management Review,* Summer.

Von Krogh, G., von Hippel, E. 2006. The Promise of Research on Open Source Software. *Management Science,* 52(7): 975-983.

Walton, D.N. 1989. *Informal Logic – A handbook of critical argumentation,* Cambridge (MA): Cambridge University Press.

Walton, D.N. (2006). *Fundamentals of Critical Argumentation - Critical Reasoning and Argumentation.* Cambridge (MA): Cambridge University Press.

ENDNOTE

[1] This exception (the Open Meeting Project's mediation of the 1994 National Policy Review (Hurwitz 1996)) was effectively a comment collection system rather than a deliberation system, since the participants were predominantly engaged in offering reactions to a large set of pre-existing policy documents, rather than interacting with each other to create new policy options.

This work was previously published in the International Journal of Decision Support System Technology, Vol. 1, Issue 1, edited by G. Forgionne, pp. 69-92, copyright 2009 by IGI Publishing (an imprint of IGI Global).

Chapter 18
Gender and Diversity in Collaborative Virtual Teams

Anna Michailidou
University of Macedonia, Greece

Anastasios Economides
University of Macedonia, Greece

ABSTRACT

Computer supported collaborative learning environments (CSCLEs) is one of the innovative technologies that support online education. Successful design and implementation of such environments demand thorough analysis of many parameters. This chapter studies the impact of diversity in learner-learner interactions in collaborative virtual teams through a social and cultural perspective. Social differences include gender, race, class, or age. Cultural differences refer to matters like how an individual's cognition, values, beliefs, and study behaviors are influenced by culture. Instructors must take into consideration the factors that influence individuals' diversity, and invent new ways to implement successful collaboration. This is crucial, especially regarding teams scattered on different countries or even continents. Social and cultural differences influence an individual's performance in a learning environment. Such differences must be adequately studied by both the educational organization and the instructors in such a way that the learning procedure will become a positive experience for all the members involved.

INTRODUCTION

It is beyond any doubt that adequate education is one of the key factors for successful embedment of the synchronous man to a world that becomes increasingly digitalized. The increased use of information and communication technologies (ICTs) generated a major modification in both the pedagogical and educational methodologies (Andrews & Schwarz, 2002). This refers to the teacher-learner relationship and embraces matters like personalized learning, collaboration, interaction, and evaluation.

The approach of participative learning offers the possibility of developing novel learning environments that support collaboration, rapid interaction and feedback, real time communication, information seeking, and problem solving. The learner has the opportunity to construct knowledge through a process of discussion and interaction with both other learners and teachers (Michailidou & Economides, 2003).

Diversity in computer supported collaborative learning environments (CSCLEs) is a complex concept. It is one thing to create diversity by recruiting learners—of different nationality, cultural background, race, gender, sexual orientation, religion, discipline, and another thing to develop a supportive educational environment in which individuals of diverse backgrounds can perform at their highest levels and contribute fully to the learning procedure (Chen, Czerwinski, & Macredie, 2000). Even more challenging is the task of fully integrating the varied knowledge experiences, perspectives, and values that learners of diverse backgrounds bring into the educational environment.

This chapter begins with a discussion concerning the issue of collaboration in virtual teams. Afterwards, diversity in collaborative virtual teams is being studied, along with its impact in learner-learner interactions. Some suggestions to the instructors for facilitating effective learning in a collaborative computer-supported environment are also included. Finally, the conclusions are presented along with future trends.

COLLABORATION IN VIRTUAL TEAMS

A virtual team is a group of people who work interdependently across space, time, cultures, and organizational boundaries on temporary, nonoccurring projects with a shared purpose, while using technology (Lipnack & Stamps, 2000). Virtual teams are utilized in multiple settings, including education (teams formed among students of distance learning classes), professional development, as well as corporate and community organizations.

The use of virtual teams is growing in popularity, especially in work-related and educational organizations. There are many advantages for using virtual teams in an educational setting. These include the creation of learning communities and the opportunity to work collaboratively to generate new knowledge. Working in virtual teams presents unexplored opportunities for peer interaction as teams create new knowledge to resolve the problem assigned. Additionally, it asserts that the best conditions for intellectual accomplishment are environments that are motivated by discovery, the reciprocal feedback between mutually-respected individuals, and the free exchange of ideas. Conclusively, virtual teams have become a vehicle for distance education, through which group work is accomplished in demanding learning environments (Anderson & Garrison, 1998).

The current chapter analyzes the gender and diversity impact in collaborative computer-mediated environments formed basically for educational purposes. Therefore, if the instructors study the diversity issue in a potential learning virtual team, then some solutions might occur, concerning the embodiment of diversity parameters and their impact in the success factors of a collaborative task.

Diversity intensively influences the performance of a virtual team in an educational setting. Many significant factors constitute diversity like those related to differences in social and cultural characteristics, gender, ethics, knowledge, educational experiences, and future expectations. For most virtual teams to be effective, some degree of diversity is both desirable and necessary. If all the team members have the same perspectives, histories, work experience, and academic training, then, theoretically, the creativity and problem solving potential of the team is limited. When facilitated properly, a team will be more effective than a single person will. For example, virtual teams that develop new ideas and problem solving are often composed deliberately of people of various ages, interests, religious backgrounds, or academic disciplines. Therefore, diversity on learning virtual teams has been shown to be positively associated with performance if process challenges are addressed (Chen et al., 2000; Paulus, Legett, Dzindolet, Coskun, & Putman, 2002).

Although diversity is connected to positive outcomes, it also has been linked to negative ones, like difficulties in managing cooperation. While a diverse team can generate a wider array of ideas, solutions, and perspectives, it may also require special management to both release and harness that diverse energy. The collection of differences in a diverse virtual team may bring more conflict within the team if these differences are not managed with insight to the idiosyncrasies of the team membership.

Gender is among the characteristics associated with diversity and is known to influence team behaviours (Barrett & Lally, 1999). Many surveys were designed to explore whether men and women feel differently about being part of a learning team. More specifically, some questions arose: Are there differences in the degree to which men and women are satisfied with team performance? Are there differences between what men and women see as the primary difficulties faced by a team? And if gender differences exist, how do they influence team performance? The assessment of gender and diversity influence in learner-learner interactions in a CSCLE is a crucial issue concerning the determination of the educational value of such an environment (Gunn & McSporran, 2003). In order for educators to balance the benefits of diversity with its possible costs, they must be aware of the factors that constitute diversity and their influence on team performance.

THE IMPACT OF GENDER AND DIVERSITY IN LEARNER-LEARNER INTERACTIONS

In the current section, the discussion focuses on the social and cultural differences of individuals that shape diversity in a collaborative virtual team.

Social Differences

Social differences focus on race, gender, class, age, or sexual orientation. The individual's identity in these social categories is derived both from the knowledge of what it is like to be part of a particular group (e.g., women) and from the way others view the value of being a member of that group (Abnett, Stanton, Neale, & O'Malley, 2001).

Gender-based differences in performance and communication style in computer supported learning environments were deemed as an important element for research (Blum, 1999; Gunn & McSporran, 2003; McLean & Morrison, 2000).

Fewer girls and women study or have jobs in engineering or computer science; in schools and homes, boys often dominate computer use, while females are typically less confident about using technology and have less experience with it (Blum, 1999; Brosnan & Davison, 1994; Ford & Miller, 1996; Hatton, 1995). There have been identified common differences in the behavior of male and female students in technology-based instructions. These differences include self-reported levels of confidence in ability to work successfully with technology, and patterns of interaction. It was found that women talked less, contributed less frequently, did not receive positive feedback to their contributions, and did not appeal to the same sources of support (Ausburn, 2004; Barrett & Lally, 1999).

Similarly, Gunn and McSporran's (2003) study found gender differences in motivation, confidence level, flexibility, and access. Men stated that they were very confident and enjoyed using the online materials, whereas women stated they were apprehensive about using the materials and about their overall ability for the technical aspects of the course. In addition, women reported that they had more problems with access, such as having to share the computer with other family members or friends. Richardson and Turner (2000) also stated that females responded significantly more negatively toward CSCLEs than males. This outcome may arise from the fact that female students are not as computer-literate as male students, and therefore less confident. Another explanation may be that some elements of working in such an environment may not be compatible with the needs of female students.

There are also several research studies that found gender differences in the learning outcomes. Studies of gender-related patterns in epistemological knowledge demonstrated that female students tend to view learning from a connected and relational path, rather than an individualistic perspective (Baxter-Magolda, 1992). It was also found that females performed better than males in mixed-gender online courses, and generally, female groups demonstrate a more positive attitude towards teamwork and collaboration tasks, as compared to males (McSporran & Young, 2001; Young, Dewstow, & McSporran, 1999). However, these studies show mixed results. Some found that women are more successful in Web-based learning, while others found that men performed as well too (McSporran & Young, 2001; Mehlenbacher, Miller, Covington, & Larsen, 2000). This is partly due to culture's role as a moderating factor affecting gender differences (Mortenson, 2002). In individualistic cultures, people tend to be opinion-oriented and straight-forward, whereas in collectivistic cultures, task dominates over personal relationships (Chang & Lim, 2002). Countries such as Canada and USA are typically associated with individualistic cultures, while most Asian countries, such as Singapore and Taiwan, are inclined towards collectivism (Hofstede, 1991). Mortenson (2002) found that the typical gendered behavior was only supported in Euro-American

subjects. Males were as likely as females in using supportive modes of communication in Asian subjects. In addition, Watkins, Adair, Akande, Cheng, Fleming, Gerong, Ismail, McInerney, Lefner, Mpofu, Regmi, Singh-Sengupta, Watson, Wondimu, and Yu (1998) discovered that the gender stereotypes, with females valuing social relationships more, apply only to individualistic western countries.

The existing literature concerning gender differences in a computer conferencing environment has evidently addressed variations in terms of communication styles and participation rates between males and females (McLean & Morrison, 2000). Females tend to display a more socio-emotional behavior, nonaggressive strategies, and a stronger compliance concerning others' differentiations. In contrast, males are typically associated with aggressive and active strategies. Generally, they support their opinion in a stronger manner and express independence (Ausburn, 2004; Barrett & Lally, 1999). Furthermore, research suggests that women are more comfortable than men with team-based evaluations and rewards. This may be partly due to findings by gender theorists that men's relationships tend to be defined by role and status, while women tend to value relationships based on communication and understanding (Bostock & Lizhi, 2005; Gunn & McSporran, 2003; Herring, 2000).

Analysis of written dialogue in computer mediated communication systems reveals gender variations in message style. In particular, females tend to be more punctual and use frequently apologies, questions, personal orientation, and support. Males' language includes strong assertions, self-promotion, challenges, and sarcasm (Herring, 2000). Bostock and Lizhi, (2005) studied the gender differentiations that occurred in student asynchronous online discussions. The research findings indicated that female groups had significantly more messages per student than male groups. Mixed groups were more variable than single-gender groups, while the messages contributed by males in mixed groups were especially changeable. More females were less confident of using computer applications and less positive regarding new technology challenges. They also demonstrated higher average final report marks, although they had expressed fears about finding the course difficult.

Clearly, gender is one of the many factors associated with team performance and cohesion in CSCLEs. Concerning the role of the instructor in managing gender differences in virtual teams with the purpose of promoting collaboration and influencing learner-learner interactions, the following list is presented (Barrett & Lally, 1999; Johnson & Aragon, 2003; Knight, Pearce, Smith, Olian, Sims, Smith, & Flood, 1999; Potter & Bathazard, 2002):

- Gender differences and needs may be addressed by tailoring distance programs or by creating peer groups with similar learning backgrounds and interests. The instructor would organize discussions about gender similarities and differences.
- Strategies for promoting inclusion regarding gender issues suggest equally profiling men and women in curriculum illustration in both traditional and nontraditional roles. Care should be taken to be sensitive to diversity in sexual orientation. The instructor would create mixed teams and ask them to play a game or to develop a project.
- An instructor should keep in mind that male participants will tend to be most comfortable when team's objectives are clarified to the greatest possible extent, and the individual roles of team members are defined. Whilst female participants appear to be most comfortable when communication and other group maintenance activities are clearly valued, along with task activities.
- Instructors might choose to discuss common gender differences with their team members to raise awareness and understanding. For

this purpose, they can use teambuilding exercises with discussions of differences in personality types, levels of participation, technology issues, and so on.

Ethnic-racial, economic-class differences and barriers occur in most learning groups, since it is common for individuals initiated from different races or social classes to participate in the same computer-mediated learning environment. Wegerif (1998) showed, through a study of a multicultural computer-mediated course, that social factors, like ethnicity, have an impact upon the learning procedure. In particular, he stated that when ethnicity differentiations corresponding to language or race differences are not taken under account, lead to decreased participation rates, and willingness in collaboration. Similar studies had also been conducted by other researchers (Kember, 2000; Kennedy, 2002; Vogel, Lou, van Eekhout, van Genuchten, Verveen, & Adams, 2000). In cases where the learning environment allows racist hints concerning racial or economic-class backgrounds, individuals hurt demonstrate negativism, unwillingness in participation, and abstention to any collaborative task. As a result, the team coherence is damaged, and the whole learning procedure fails.

One of the key issues facing all educational environments, both traditional and computer mediated (and indeed lifelong learning), is how to create tolerance for minorities in an environment characterized by diversity (Obidah, 2000; Volet, 1999). Intolerance is conceptualized basically as a matter of attitudes, and is said to be constituted by prejudice.

The instructor should confront ethnic or racial differences within the members of a virtual team by using information summarized below (Chow, Shields, & Wu, 1999; Chen et al., 2000; Bonner, Marbley, & Agnello, 2004):

- The context supporting the courses in such an environment should be adequate and neutral in terms of ideas and learning outcomes. This develops a sense of equal confrontation among the participants, resulting in an increase of involvement in the learning procedure, and in satisfactory collaboration terms.

- If racism is an issue in a learning environment, then participants must become acquainted with other cultures and find the courage to challenge stereotypes and appreciate others. The instructor would:
  ° Enable learners to share personal photos (e.g., family, friends, and place of origin), videos, ethnic-traditional music, tourist information about their countries, and so on.
  ° Provide information about learners' ethnicities and races.
  ° Organize discussions about learners' ethnic-racial similarities and differences.
  ° Create a common basis of views accepted by all.
  ° Unify and integrate opposing views and ideas.

- Illustrations in distance learning delivery can include culturally appropriate personal names and culturally accepted phrases. This illustration embraces the students' background and serves as an engaging point to keep their interest.

- Matters that relate to prejudice and attitudes must be confronted through teaching about "other cultures." That requires a dismantling of institutionalized practices of racism—whether in employment or education or in social welfare. It also entails a direct confrontation with racist ideologies—for example, in curricula. The instructor would:
  ° Find common ground among conflicting opinions (e.g., two learners from different nations describe a battle between their nations from a single compromised point of view).

° Create mixed teams and ask them to complete a project.
° Ask learners to collaboratively develop concept maps on controversial issues.

Concerning economic class differences, an instructor would (Howard & Levine, 2004; Paulsen & St. John, 2002; Walpole, 2004):

- Enable the participation of the lowest economic class learners by either encouraging scholarships or tailoring the required economic resources of a project to these learners.
- Provide the appropriate background information to students lacking it, due to their economic situation.
- Create mixed teams and ask them to complete a project.
- Encourage learners to share their living experiences.
- Foster mutual understanding and respect.

Age differences and barriers correspond mainly to different life experience, educational background, professional status, and maturity (Gaskell, 2000). Age should be taken under consideration in group formation, especially when it influences team effectiveness due to differences that might occur in prior educational background and technology adequacy. For example, it is evident that all participants should be familiarized with technology demands and frustrations, especially in a virtual learning environment.

Turner (2000) conducted a research with the purpose of investigating individual difference factors with respect to computer use generally, as a means of informing e-learning instructional design. The learning team included 170 undergraduate students (103 Chinese and 67 UK) who completed tasks, and also a questionnaire on their knowledge of the Internet and how effectively they used it. The results indicated a difference in the affective and cognitive components of attitudes between different age groups, such that the younger age group (17-19 years) reported more positive attitudes than the older age group (21-32 years). It is possible that this may relate to differences in education and exposure to the Internet.

In some cases (Chioncel, Van Der Veen, Nildemeersch, & Jarvis, 2003; Mehrotra, 2003), both younger and older learners with the same educational background reported that participating in an age-diverse group was a positive experience. Older learners felt that the younger group respected their opinions, and the age mix in the virtual classroom finally provides a multitude of ideas. Instructors noted that older learners fear failure, more than younger learners (Chioncel et al., 2003). There has also been expressed the opinion that older learners have difficulty with multitasking, and as a result, require more understanding from other learners regarding their capabilities. Furthermore, older adult learners are less confident in using information and communication technologies and need more time to remember the necessary information for understanding the material. Consequently, if they feel confident and relaxed, being a part of the educational environment, they will learn more.

Older adult learners most commonly have their own views and opinions on certain subjects, and therefore, they will challenge teachers on the information that they give. The teacher has to invent ways in order to get older adults to challenge their ways of thinking and open their minds to new ways of perceiving knowledge (Mehrotra, 2003). Older adults also have a lot of maturity regarding their studies and will give help and advice to younger students. They have better attendance, are more mannerly, and in most cases are more grateful for the opportunity to learn.

The instructor would confront age differences within the members of a virtual team by using information summarized below (Liang & McQueen, 1999; Merriam & Simpson, 2000):

- Age differences and barriers may be addressed by tailoring distance programs or by creating peer groups with similar learning backgrounds and interest.
- Delivery systems for different age groups relate most prominently to the amount of—and degree of—interactivity. Therefore, instructors must facilitate interactivity procedures between the participants of different age groups, introducing both synchronous (e.g., chat) and asynchronous (e.g. e-mail) ways of communication.
- Instructors must also analyze all the evidence concerning the individual characteristics of any participant related to age, like prior educational background, professional skills, and expectations, and suggest realistic solutions that confront any potential learning issue on an equal basis for each and every learner. In order for this to happen, instructors should receive feedback information (with interviews, interactive exercises, etc.) throughout the learning procedure.
- Since older adult learners are more sensitive to failure, they need more individual or one-to-one attention.

The above discussion concerning the social differences among learners in a CSCL educational environment is being summarized in Table 1. The first column contains the Differential Factor corresponding to Social Differences and the second column the Behavioral Attitude affecting Learner- Learner Interactions that might occur in a CSCLE.

CULTURAL DIFFERENCES

Cultural differences focus on how individuals' values, beliefs, norms, communication styles, and study behaviours are influenced by the culture in which they grew up or live. Cultural differences may help the instructors to understand

Table 1. Social differences and behavioral attitude affecting learner-learner interactions

Social Differences		Behavioral Attitude affecting Learner-Learner Interactions
Differential Factor		
Gender Differences	**Females**	• They display more socio-emotional behavior, non-aggressive strategies and a stronger compliance concerning others' differentiations. • They usually perform better than males in mixed-gender online courses. • They demonstrate a more positive attitude towards teamwork and collaboration tasks. • In dialogues, they tend to be more punctual and use frequently apologies, questions, personal orientation and support. • Analysis of written dialogue in computer mediated communication systems revealed that female groups write more massages per student than male groups. • They have lower confidence with IT applications.
	Males	• They are associated with aggressive and active strategies. • In dialogues, they use language with strong assertions, self-promotion, challenges and sarcasm. • According to some studies males were as likely as females in using supportive modes of communication in collectivistic countries. • They are more confident about using technology.
Ethnic-Racial, Economic-Class Discrimination	**Present**	• Individuals are being hurt and demonstrate negativism, unwillingness in participation and abstention to any collaborative task. • The team coherence is damaged and the whole learning procedure fails.
	Not present	• There is a sense of equal confrontation among the participants resulting in an increase of involvement in the learning procedure and in satisfactory collaboration terms. • The learners become acquainted with other cultures and find the courage to challenge stereotypes and appreciate others. • The learners form a harmonious, democratic educational environment that supports cultural pluralism.
Age Differences (when prior educational background and technology adequacy are not at the same level among individuals)	**Taken under consideration**	• Team members will correspond better in learning tasks. • Team members may feel more comfortable with each other.
	Not taken under consideration	• Team coherence will be jeopardized. • Many difficulties will occur concerning the achievement of a learning task.
Age Differences (when prior educational background and technology adequacy are at the same level among individuals)		• Both younger and older learners with the same educational background, find that participating in an age diverse group is a positive experience. • Older learners fear failure, more than younger learners. • Older learners are less confident in using information and communication technologies. • It is common for older learners to challenge teachers on the information that they give. • Older learners and in particular adults have a lot of maturity regarding their studies.

how students can best adapt to new educational environments (Hughes, Wickersham, Ryan-Jones, & Smith, 2002). Cultural differences are harder to "see," but may be much more important causes of misunderstanding among learners participating in multicultural educational organizations. Taking under consideration relevant cultural differences and preconceptions is a crucial step into creating effective international learning teams (Myers & Tan, 2002).

Hofstede (1991) defined a cultural model in which cultures vary along five dimensions: Power distance, collectivism/ individualism, femininity/masculinity, uncertainty avoidance, and long term/ short term orientation. Taken together, these dimensions provide a means of characterizing and comparing different cultures, as well as providing a meaning for the use or nonuse of computer-mediated software. For example, cultures reflecting more "collectivist" tendencies, such as Chinese and those in the Middle East may actually use collaborative software more effectively than individualistic cultures like those of the U.S. or Australia (Chung & Adams, 1997).

Cultures can be learned and reflect the patterns of thinking, feeling, and acting (Harris, 1987). The underlying theme is that culture is an abstraction from concrete behaviour, but not behaviour itself. Culture is transmitted mainly by symbols, constituting distinctive achievement of human groups, including the embodiments in artifacts (Chow et al., 1999). It is in this sense that culture characterizes the whole way of life of a group. It is a pattern of traditions that can be transmitted over time and space. Three qualities underlie its centrality: it is learned, much of it exists at a non- or unconscious level, and it helps structure thought perception and identity (Mayers & Tan, 2002).

Cultural sensitivity must be included in the initial design stages of a collaborative virtual learning environment (Rovai, 2002). A level of cultural sensitivity could be incorporated into the design of the system, such that users' individual identities can be expressed, while simultaneously supporting community development. For example, cultural sensitivity is paramount in designing interaction systems (Mudur, 2001; Raybourn, 2001). In answer to this call, data collected from ethnography, questionnaires, and persona development provide the basis for designing cultural and organizational cues into the community-based system, in order to engender identification among the members of the community of practice.

Lessons learned both from face-to-face and computer-mediated communication tell us that the quality of successful collaborations depends largely on sharing cultural information like this concerning the values, beliefs, and norms of individuals. That minimizes uncertainty in interpersonal relationships and enhances interaction and collaboration among the participants (Chow et al., 1999). In much the same way, collaborating organizations, individuals, or communities of practice share cultural information to reduce uncertainty and strengthen notions of common ground (Wenger, 1998). Cultural information often shared across and within members of organizations includes values, goals, and histories that are shared, negotiated, and cocreated by the members. The future success of collaborative work in community-based virtual environments requires not only understanding the sociocultural dynamics that manifest in online communication and communities of practice, but also considering how the design of these environments can support intercultural communication with cultural of organizational contextual cues (Leevers, 2001).

A significant factor relative to the development of a collaborative community is the mutual engagement of participants. Mutual engagement refers to participants' cocreation and negotiation of actions or meanings, and relates to communication styles that each participant has developed. Consequently, mutual engagement is facilitated by communication, whether occurring in the face-to-face context, or virtually (Fai Wong & Trinidad, 2004). Observations of heterogeneous groups, whose members are of different (national) cultural backgrounds, revealed a wider variety of skills, information and experiences that could potentially improve the quality of collaborative learning (Rich, 1997). An improvement such as this could be obtained in a CSCLE, since the number of concurrent conversations that a medium can support, along with the reprocessing of messages during communication, can help learners of different cultures to gain a more accurate understanding of each other, thus improving performance (Yu, 2001). Additionally, it has been demonstrated that designing subtle cultural and contextual cues into a text-based collaborative virtual environment such as a multi-user dimension, object-oriented (MOO) is an effective way to encourage collaboration and awareness of intercultural communication, including the negotiation of power and exploration of identity (Raybourn, 2001). This aspect is particularly important for non-native speakers. Nevertheless, a direct consequence of cultural diversity is communication distortion, because basic modes of communication differ among people from different cultural backgrounds (Easley, Devaraj, & Crant, 2003).

Learners have different strategies, approaches, and capabilities for learning that are a function of prior experience and heredity. Individuals are born with and develop their own capabilities and talents. In addition, through learning and social acculturation, they have acquired their own preferences for how they like to learn, and the pace at which they learn (Ford, 2000).

Therefore, a learner's study behavior, especially when he is a part of a heterogeneous group, becomes more positive in the case of his participation in the cultural cocreation process. The cultural cocreation process includes the formation of a "new culture," which arises from the interactions in the educational setting between all the participating cultures. In effect, together, users co-create a "new culture" that is neither one nor the other, but a combination of the two, or three, and so on (Lim & Zhong, 2005). The successful

future design of intelligent community-based systems requires considering how the design of these environments support intercultural communication and a greater awareness of cultural orientations in both the organizational and educational context.

Several studies indicate that individual success or failure on a learning task depends upon the level to which learners are able to cross a threshold from feeling like an outsider to feeling like an insider (Muirhead, 2000; Wegerif, 1998). In collaborative learning, students learn by recognizing flawed reasoning of others during a discussion. Prior studies have highlighted the importance of the discussion session in collaborative learning activities (Lave & Wenger, 1991). However, text-based computer mediated communication facilitates important features with respect to communication that are radically different from the face-to-face setting (Dennis & Valacich, 1999). The parallelism afforded by collaborative learning systems is expected to help learners of different cultures to gain a more accurate understanding of each other, thus improving performance. This aspect is particularly salient for nonnative speakers, since the spoken language disappears altogether after the utterance (Herring, 1999).

Conclusively, a significant factor that increases the feeling of alienation between the participants in a learning procedure is the different native **language**. This means that there must be defined a common communication language for the course, something that corresponds to a different level of adequate language knowledge for the participants. Although this may always be a problem, it is possible that with a sufficiently strong sense of community, learners with less experience on the language being used would be able to overcome their fears (Myers & Tan, 2002).

Table 2 summarizes some of the outcomes corresponding to cultural differences and their impact on learner-learner interactions. The first column contains the Differential Factor related to Cultural Differences, and the second column,

Table 2. Cultural differences and their impact on learner-learner interactions

Cultural Differences			Impact on Learner-Learner Interactions
Values, beliefs, norms (when shared among the participants)			• Minimize uncertainty in interpersonal relationships. • Enhance collaboration tasks. • Better implementation of interaction techniques and feedback among the participants in a virtual learning environment.
Communication styles	**When they are developed in a way that enhance communication among the participants.**		• Support information sharing. • Support real time spontaneous communication. • Enhance mutual engagement between the participants (mutual engagement refers to participants' co-creation and negotiation of actions or meanings). • Heterogeneous groups, whose members are of different (national) cultural backgrounds, reveal a wider variety of skills, information and experiences that could potentially improve the quality of collaborative learning. • Multiple concurrent conversations that a medium can support are expected to help learners of different cultures to gain a more accurate understanding of each other, thus improving performance.
	When they are not taken under consideration.		• Communication distortion may appear because basic modes of communication differ among people from different cultural backgrounds.
Study behaviors (when taken under consideration)			• A learner's study behavior especially when he/she is a part of a heterogeneous group becomes more positive in the case of his/hers participation in the cultural co-creation process. • The cultural co-creation process includes the formation of a 'new culture' which arises from the interactions in the educational setting between all the participating cultures. This new culture is accepted by all members and helps in the development of any study behavior that affects positively the learning procedure.
Language			• Different level of adequate language knowledge for the participants results to limited participation. • With a sufficiently strong sense of community, learners with less experience on the language being used would be able to overcome their fears.

the Impact on Learner- Learner Interactions that might occur in a CSCLE.

From the above discussion, it has become clear that cultural diversity plays an important role in implementing successful collaboration in virtual environments. Therefore, the instructor could follow some of the recommendations listed below:

- The instructor needs to foster critical engagement, to help people to connect with, and own, those aspects which accord with their sense of themselves, and of what is good and right. At the same time, it is to reject certain things, to encourage the desire and ability to change values, behaviors, ideas that are unjust or that inhibit well being (Swigger, Alpaslan, Brazile, & Monticino, 2004).

- Many people do not explicitly share information about their cultural background or educational organization for a variety of reasons, including diverse orientations toward privacy and public versus private information (Raybourn, 2001). Therefore, the instructor must invent ways to motivate users to identify more strongly with their community of practice, and take the first steps towards opening a chat with others whom they may share common interests with, but do not know well enough to feel comfortable communicating with in a virtual environment. In order for this to happen:

  ○ The instructor could organize a discussion forum supporting themes of common interest among the participants.

  ○ A set of educational tasks (e.g., exercises) given by the instructor would motivate the participants to increase e-mail or chat communication. This would reduce nervousness among the participants, and encourage them to support and share their own cultural background.

- Most users who inhabit virtual worlds like to leave their mark on the shared space, whether it is through building artifacts (objects) or becoming influential members of the community (Selim, 2003). Allowing each person to contribute to development or design of the space creates more community, which could help individuals to surpass cultural differences that hinder collaboration, like language barriers. A graffiti board, or bulletin board, arouses curiosity and participation among the community by arousing interest among teammates—whether it is curiosity about other members of the community, or the shared space itself. The instructor could participate in creating more motivating environments by designing for user fun, curiosity, and fantasy exploration.

- Both designers and instructors could consider giving the right to participating members to express themselves anonymously in a virtual setting—for example, only for a few sessions at the beginning of a learning procedure. Certain anonymity can create more equitable communication (especially for newcomers) reducing the appearance of hierarchy and power in a collaborative environment, and fostering more peer-based communication events (Volet, 1999). A virtual tour of the learning space, and perhaps a FAQ on the formal and informal cultural norms, will help a participant to feel more like part of the team, and thus identify more strongly with the community. A team gallery of interests might be an informal mechanism for obtaining meta-level information on the team culture and individual identities.

- Avatar movement may be based on common cultural attributes, or common social interests, in addition to movement throughout the space based on keywords and common work products. Educational agents could connect users of common social and cultural interests, and provide reasons for the movement in the space. Cultural information about the team (hobbies, families, etc.) may be made available in the learning space via interactive objects (Myers & Tan, 2002). The instructor should encourage learners to interact in real time where there are mutual concerns or interests, and evaluate certain cultural characteristics, incorporating them into an adaptive community-based virtual environment in order to offer enhanced support for intercultural communication among remote learners.

- Different national cultures emphasize distinct values and are associated with diverse languages. It is apparent that the presence of different languages, and the inability to speak and comprehend these different languages, creates barriers to efficient knowledge sharing throughout the organization. In the case of multinational learning groups, a lot of knowledge might be lost in translation, or due to the inability to articulate the knowledge in the project's working language (Myers & Tan 2002). A good way to diminish the negative consequences of language barriers is to emphasize active listening skills, patience, and understanding. Despite language differences, it is important to enable all members an equal opportunity to be heard. The difficulty of studying and communicating in a second language exacerbates the problem of equal participation, especially in the case of a CSCLE. Until students have built up sufficient fluency in the lower-level language skills (Raybourn, Kings, & Davies, 2003) to be able to express their understanding in their own words in the language of instruction, they may find it difficult to display their newly acquired knowledge. Therefore, the instructor must encourage learners with less language experience, and help them to overcome their difficulties in expressing their opinion, and actively participate in the learning procedure.

- Learners have different strategies, approaches, and capabilities for learning that are a function of prior experience and heredity. Individuals are born with and develop their own capabilities and talents (Ford, 2000). Instructors need to help students examine their learning preferences and expand or modify them, if necessary. They also need to attend to learner perceptions, as long as

these differences are adapted to by varying instructional methods and materials.

CONCLUSION AND FUTURE RESEARCH

As several studies have observed (Adler, 1997; Watson, Kumar, & Michaelsen, 1993), diversity within teams is a reality for educators and organizations. It is also an important social value for synchronous society. For these reasons, it is important that research clearly and accurately elucidate the true impact of diversity in learning-teams. This requires moving beyond studies of simple demographic effects and broad generalizations about the effects of diversity on teams, to understanding how these differences arise and are experienced in specific contexts. Only then, both learners and instructors will be able to manage differences effectively and understand in detail how diversity really affects individuals in different types of educational organizations.

In the current chapter, diversity issues that arise from both social and cultural differences are analyzed. Social differences focus mainly on race, gender, class and age. While cultural differences focus on how individuals' cognition, values, beliefs, communication styles, and study behaviors are influenced by their culture. The impact of these factors on the learner-learner interactions are being summarized in Tables 1-2.

Online learning and virtual learning environments demand that the role of the instructor will be the one of the facilitator in the learning process, rather than that a of knowledge dispenser. Conclusively, in order for the instructor to attain successful collaboration, diversity and all its factors that affect learners' interactions must be adequately analyzed and studied. A number of constructive suggestions to be used by the instructor in both the design and the implementation of learning activities are presented in the bulleted paragraphs throughout the "The Impact of Gender and Diversity in Learner-Learner Interactions" section.

A teaching and learning environment located within a technological context can be used to support instructor-learner and learner-learner communication, and to aid collaborative learning across different cultures. An individual's learning process, combined with synchronous or even asynchronous interactivity with other learners, can be enhanced with the proliferation of communication technologies. Such technologies can strengthen and increase additional communication cues during group activities (Aviv, 2000). Due to their unique features, CSCLEs provide strong support for the collaborative learning process. They help in teaming up groups of people who are unable to meet face-to-face and facilitate group interactions.

By using CSCLEs, learners from an individualistic cultural context might emphasize more on group achievement or relationship than before, and learners from a collectivistic context might become more independent and insistent on their own opinion during the reasoning process. Future research should work toward greater understanding of this aspect. In addition, problems of cross-cultural learning might be due to differences in language, cultural values, and the types of learning strategies preferred.

Recent technological developments have opened new perspectives for the cooperation between human learners, virtual humans, and anthropomorphic robots, especially in an augmented virtual reality environment. This kind of learning environments can be defined as Digi-Mech learning environments (DMLE) (La Russa & Faggiano, 2004; Nijholt, 2005). The richness and variety of users' possible interactions in such environments go far beyond the simple sensorial use of the virtual realities. The existing research, literature, experiences, practices and academic know-how support that DMLEs have extensive educative and cognitive potentials, especially in distant education context, and need further

explorations. In addition, the associated social awareness mechanisms and diversity factors need to be explored further, including the issue of how robots and virtual humans perceive and interpret the social situations in the community they are a part of.

REFERENCES

Abnett, C., Stanton, D., Neale, H., & O'Malley. (2001, March 22-24). The effect of multiple input devices on collaboration and gender issues. In *Proceedings of European Perspectives on Computer-Supported Collaborative Learning (EuroCSCL) 2001*, Maastricht, The Netherlands (pp. 29-36).

Adler, N. J. (1997). *International dimensions of organizational behavior.* Cincinnati, OH: South-Western College Publishing.

Anderson, T. D., & Garrison, D. R. (1998). Learning in a networked world: New roles and responsibilities. In C. C. Gibson (Ed.), *Distance learners in higher education* (pp. 97-112). Madison, WI: Atwood.

Andrews, T., & Schwarz, G. (2002). Preparing students for the virtual organization: An evaluation of learning with virtual learning technologies. *Educational Technology & Society, 5*(3).

Ausburn, L. (2004). Gender and learning strategy differences in non-traditional adult students' design preferences in hybrid distance courses. *The Journal of Interactive Online Learning, 3*(2), 1-17.

Aviv, R. (2000). Educational performance of ALN via content analysis. *Journal of Asynchronous Learning Networks, 4*(2).

Barrett, E., & Lally, V. (1999). Gender differences in an online learning environment. *Journal of Computer Assisted Learning, 15*, 48-60.

Baxter-Magolda, M. B. (1992). *Knowing and reasoning in college: Gender-related patterns in student's intellectual development.* San Francisco: Jossey-Bass Publishers.

Blum, K. D. (1999). Gender differences in asynchronous learning in higher education: Learning styles, participation barriers and communication patterns. *Journal of Asynchronous Learning Networks, 3*(1), 46-66.

Bonner, F., Marbley, A., & Agnello, M. F. (2004). The diverse learner in the college classroom. *E-Journal of Teaching and Learning in Diverse Settings, 1*(2), 246-255.

Bostock, S. J., & Lizhi, W. (2005). Gender in student online discussions. *Innovations in Education and Teaching International, 42*(1), 73-85.

Brosnan, M. J., & Davison, M. J. (1994, February). Computerphobia: Is it a particularly female phenomenon? *The Psychologist,* pp. 74-78.

Chang, T., & Lim, J. (2002). Cross-cultural communication and social presence in asynchronous learning processes. *e-Service Journal, 1*(3).

Chen, C., Czerwinski, M., & Macredie, R. (2000). Individual differences in virtual environments. Introduction and overview. *Journal of the American Society for Information Science, 51*(6), 499-507.

Chioncel, N. E., Van Der Veen, R. G. W., Nildemeersch, P., & Jarvis, P. (2003). The validity and reliability of focus groups as a research method in adult education. *International Journal of Lifelong Education, 22*(5), 495-517.

Chow, W. C., Shields, M. D., & Wu, A. (1999). The importance of national culture in the design of and preference for management controls for multi-national operations. *Accounting Organizations and Society, 24,* 441-461.

Chung, K., & Adams, C. (1997). A study on the characteristics of group decision-making behaviour: Cultural difference perspective of Korea vs.

US. *Journal of Global Information Management, 5*(3), 18-29.

Dennis, A. R., & Valacich, J. S. (1999). Rethinking media richness: Towards a theory of media synchronicity. In *Proceedings of the 32nd Hawaii International Conference on System Sciences,* Hawaii.

Easley, R. F., Devaraj, S., & Crant, J. M. (2003). Collaborative technology use to teamwork performance: An empirical analysis. *Journal of Information Systems, 19*(4), 247-268.

Fai Wong, L., & Trinidad, S. G. (2004). Using Web-based distance learning to reduce cultural distance. *The Journal of Interactive Online Learning, 3*(1).

Ford, N. (2000). Cognitive styles and virtual environments. *Journal of American Society for Information Science, 51*(6), 543-557

Ford, N., & Miller, D. (1996). Gender differences in Internet perceptions and use. In *Proceedings of the Elvira Conference* (pp.87-100). London: ASLIB. Retrieved November 9, 2007, from http://www.shef.ac.uk/~is/home_old/gender.htm

Gaskell, T. (2000). The process of empirical research: A learning experience? *Research in Post-Compulsory Education, 5*(3), 349-360.

Gunn, C., & McSporran, M. (2003). Dominant or different? Gender issues in computer supported learning. *Journal of Asynchronous Learning Networks, 7*(1), 14-30.

Harris, M. (1987). *Cultural anthropology* (2nd ed.). Harper and Ross.

Hatton, D. (1995, November 18-21). Women and the "L": A study of the relationship between communication apprehension, gender and bulletin boards. In *Proceedings of the 81st Annual Meeting of the Speech Communication Association,* San Antonio, TX.

Herring, S. C. (1999). Interactional coherence in CMC. In *Proceedings of the* 32nd *Hawaii International Conference on System Sciences (HICSS).*

Herring, S. C. (2000). Gender differences in CMC: Findings and implications. *The CPSR Newsletter, 18*(1). Retrieved November 9, 2007, from http://www.cpsr.org/publications/newsletters/issues/2000/Winter2000/herring.htm

Hofstede, G. (1991). *Cultures and organizations: Software of the mind.* McGraw-Hill.

Howard A., & Levine, A. (2004). Where are the poor students? A conversation about social class and college attendance. *About Campus, 9*(4), 1924.

Hughes, S. C., Wickersham, L., Ryan-Jones, D. L., & Smith, A. (2002). Overcoming social and psychological barriers to effective on-line collaboration. *Educational Technology & Society, 5*(1).

Johnson, S. D., & Aragon, S. A. (2003). An instructional strategy framework for online learning environments. In S. A. Aragon (Ed.), *Facilitating learning in online environments, new directions for adult and continuing education* (pp. 10, 31-44). San Francisco: Jossey-Bass.

Kember, D. (2000). Misconceptions about the learning approaches, motivation and study practices of Asian students. *Higher Education, 40,* 99-121.

Kennedy, P. (2002). Learning cultures and learning styles: Myth-understandings about adult (Hong Kong) Chinese learners. *International Journal of Lifelong Education, 21*(5), 430-445.

Knight, D., Pearce, C. L., Smith, K. G., Olian, J. D., Sims, H. P., Smith, K. A., & Flood, P. (1999). Top management team diversity, group process, and strategic consensus. *Strategic Management Journal, 20,* 445-465.

La Russa, G., & Faggiano, E. (2004). Robo-eLC: Enhancing learning hypermedia with robotics. In *Proceedings of ICALT, Joensuu, Finland* (pp. 465-469).

Lave, J., & Wenger, E. (1991). *Situated learning: Legitimate peripheral participation.* Cambridge, UK: Cambridge University.

Leevers, D. (2001). Collaboration and shared virtual environments—from metaphor to reality. In R. Earnshaw, R. Guedj, A. van Dam, & J. Vince (Eds.), *Frontiers of human-centered computing, online communities and virtual environments* (pp. 278–298). Springer.

Liang, A., & McQueen, R. J. (1999). Computer assisted adult interactive learning in a multi-cultural environment. *Adult Learning, 11*(1), 26-29.

Lim, J., & Zhong, Y. (2005). Cultural diversity, leadership, group size and collaborative learning systems: An experimental study. In *Proceedings of the 38th Hawaii International Conference on System Sciences.*

Lipnack, J., & Stamps, J. (2000). *Virtual teams people working across boundaries with technology* (2nd ed.). New York: John Wiley & Sons.

Mayers, M., & Tan, F. (2002). Beyond models of national culture in information systems research. *Journal of Global Information Management, 10*(1), 24-32.

McLean, S., & Morrison, D. (2000). Sociodemographic characteristic of learners and participation in computer conferencing. *Journal of Distance Education, 15*(2).

McSporran, M., & Young, S. (2001). Does gender matter in online learning? *Association for Learning Technology Journal (Alt-J), 9*(2), 3-15.

Mehlenbacher, B., Miller, C. R., Covington, D., & Larsen, J. S. (2000). Active and interactive learning online: A comparison of Web-based and conventional writing classes. *IEEE Transactions on Professional Communication, 43*(2), 166-184.

Mehrotra, C. M. (2003). In defense of educational programs for older adults. *Educational Gerontology, 29,* 645-655.

Merriam S. B., & Simpson, E. L. (2000). *A guide to research for educators and trainers of adults* (2nd ed.). Krieger Publishing Company.

Michailidou, A., & Economides, A. (2003). El-earn: Towards a collaborative educational virtual environment. *Journal of Information Technology Education, 2,* 131-152.

Mortenson, S. T. (2002). Sex, communication and cultural values: Individualism-collectivism as a mediator of sex differences in communication in two cultures. *Communication Reports, 15*(1).

Mudur, S. (2001). On the need for cultural representation in interactive systems. In R. Earnshaw, R. Guedj, A. van Dam, & J. Vince (Eds.), *Frontiers of human-centered computing, online communities and virtual environments* (pp. 299-310). Springer.

Muirhead, B. (2000). Enhancing social interaction in computer-mediated distance education. *Educational Technology & Society, 3*(4), 4-11.

Myers, M., & Tan, F. (2002). Beyond models of national culture in information systems research. *Journal of Global Information Management, 10*(1), 24-32.

Nijholt, A. (2005). Human and virtual agents interacting in the virtuality continuum. In *Proceedings of ACTAS II: IX Symposio Internacional de Comunicacion Social, Centro de Linguistica Aplicade, Santiago de Cuba* (pp. 551-558).

Obidah, J. (2000). Mediating boundaries of race, class and professorial authority as a critical multiculturalist. *Teachers College Record, 102,* 1035-1061.

Paulsen, M., & St. John, E. P. (2002). Social class and college costs: Examining between college choice and persistence. *The Journal of Higher Education, 73*(2), 189-236.

Paulus, P. B., Legett, K., Dzindolet, M. T., Coskun, H., & Putman, V. L. (2002). Social and cognitive influences in group brainstorming: Prediction of production gains and losses. In W. Stroebe & M. Hewstone (Eds.), *European review of social psychology* (pp. 299-325). London: Wiley.

Potter, R. E., & Bathazard, P. A. (2002). Understanding human interactions and performance in the virtual team. *Journal of Information Technology Theory and Application (JITTA), 4*(1), 1-23.

Raybourn, E. M. (2001). Designing an emergent culture of negotiation in collaborative virtual communities: The DomeCityMOO simulation. In E. Churchill, D. Snowden, & A. Munro (Eds.), *Collaborative virtual environments* (pp. 247-264). Springer.

Raybourn, E. M., Kings, N. J., & Davies, J. (2003). Adding cultural signposts in adaptive community-based environments [Special issue on intelligent community-based systems]. *Interacting With Computers: The Interdisciplinary Journal of Human-Computer Interaction, 15*(1), 91-107. Elsevier Science Ireland Ltd.

Rich, M. (1997). A learning community on the Internet: An exercise with masters students. In *Proceedings of Americas Conference on Information Systems,* Indianapolis.

Richardson, J. A., & Turner, A. (2000). A large-scale "local" evaluation of students' learning experiences using virtual learning environments. *Educational Technology & Society, 3*(4).

Rovai, A. A. P. (2002). A preliminary look at the structural differences of higher education classroom communities in traditional and ALN courses. *Journal of Asynchronous Learning Networks, 6*(1), 41-56.

Selim, H. M. (2003). An empirical investigation of student acceptance of course Websites. *Computers & Education, 40,* 343-360.

Swigger, K., Alpaslan, F., Brazile, R., & Monticino, M. (2004). Effects of culture on computer-supported international collaborations. *International Journal of Human-Computer Studies, 60,* 365-380.

Turner, Y. (2000). When an unstoppable force meets an immovable object: Chinese students in the UK university system. In *Proceedings of the 5th International Conference on Learning Styles* (pp. 353-384).

Vogel, D. R., Lou, D., van Eekhout, M., van Genuchten, M., Verveen, S., & Adams, T. (2000). Distributed experiential learning: The Hong Kong-Netherlands project. In *Proceedings of the 33rd Annual Hawaii International Conference on System Sciences* (pp. 1-9).

Volet, S. (1999). Learning across cultures: Appropriateness of knowledge transfer. *International Journal of Educational Research, 31,* 625-643.

Walpole, M. (2004). Socioeconomic status and college: How SES affects outcomes. *The Review of Higher Education, 27*(1), 4573.

Watkins, D. A., Adair, J., Akande, A., Cheng, C., Fleming, J., Gerong, A., et al. (1998). Cultural dimensions, gender and the nature of self-concept: A fourteen-country study. *International Journal of Psychology, 33*(1).

Watson, W. E., Kumar, K., & Michaelsen, L. K. (1993). Cultural diversity's impact on interaction process and performance: Comparing homogeneous and diverse task groups. *Academy of Management Journal, 36*(3), 590-602.

Wegerif, R. (1998). The social dimension of asynchronous learning networks. *Journal of Asynchronous Learning Networks, 2*(1), 34-49.

Wenger, E. (1998). *Communities of practice: Learning, meaning, and identity.* Cambridge University Press.

Young, S., Dewstow, R., & McSporran, M. (1999, July). Who wants to learn online? What types of students benefit from the new learning environment? In *Proceedings of the NACCQ.*

Yu, F. (2001). Competition within computer-assisted cooperative learning environments: Cognitive, affective, and social outcomes. *Journal of Educational Computing Research, 24*(2), 99-117.

This work was previously published in Computer-Supported Collaborative Learning: Best Practices and Principles for Instructors, edited by K. Orvis and A. Lassiter, pp. 199-224, copyright 2008 by Information Science Publishing (an imprint of IGI Global).

Compilation of References

109th Congress. (2005). *The National Innovation Act of 2005.*

Abnett, C., Stanton, D., Neale, H., & O'Malley. (2001, March 22-24). The effect of multiple input devices on collaboration and gender issues. In *Proceedings of European Perspectives on Computer-Supported Collaborative Learning (EuroCSCL) 2001,* Maastricht, The Netherlands (pp. 29-36).

Ackerman, M. (1998). Augmenting organizational memory: A field study of answer garden. *ACM Transactions on Information Systems, 16*(3), 203–224.

Ackoff, R. L. (1978). *The Art of Problem Solving:* New York: John Wiley & Sons.

Ackoff, R. L. (1999). *Re-creating the corporation: A design of organizations for the 21st century.* New York: Oxford University Press

Ackoff, R., Magidson, J., & Addison, H. J. (2006). *Idealized design: Creating an organization's future.* Philadelphia, Pennsylvania: Wharton School Publishing.

Adamides, E. D., & Karacapilidis, N. (2006). Information technology support for the knowledge and social processes of innovation management. *Technovation, 26,* 50-59.

Adler, N. J. (1997). *International dimensions of organizational behavior.* Cincinnati, OH: South-Western College Publishing.

Aklouf, Y. (2005, July). *Design of a web service platform for B2B products exchange based on PLIB ontology, RosettaNet PIPs and ebXML Registry.* Presented at

Proceedings of the International Conference on Product Lifecycle Management: Emerging solutions and challenges for Global Networked Enterprise, Lyon, France.

Alavi, M., & Leidner, D. E. (2001). Review: Knowledge management and knowledge management systems: Conceptual foundations and research issues. *MIS Quarterly, 25*(1), 107–136. doi:10.2307/3250961

Alexander, C. (1964). *Notes on the Synthesis of Form* (7th Ed.). Cambridge, MA: Harvard University Press.

Alexander, C. (1979). *The timeless way of building.* New York: Oxford University Press.

Alexander, C., Ishikawa, S., Silverstein, M., Jacobson, M., Fiksdahl-King, I., & Angel, S. (1977). *A pattern language.* New York: Oxford University Press.

Alexander, C., Silverstein, M., Angel, S., Ishikawa, S., & Abrams, D. (1980). *The Oregon Experiment.* New York: Oxford University Press.

Alonso, S.L. (2005, October). *WP10: Case study eBanking D 10.7 Financial Ontology.* Document presented for Project DIP, Galway, Ireland.

Ambrozek, J., & Cothrel, J. (2004). Online communities in business: Past progress, future directions. In *Proceedings of the 7th International Conference on Virtual Communities.* The Hague, Netherlands.

Anderson, A., McEwan, R., & Carletta, J. (2007). Virtual team meetings: An analysis of communication and context. *Computers in Human Behavior, 23,* 2558–2580. doi:10.1016/j.chb.2007.01.001

Anderson, P. (2007). *What is web 2.0? ideas, technolo-*

gies and implications for education,' JISC Technology & Standards Watch. Retrieved, July 19, 2008, from http://www.jisc.ac.uk/media/documents/techwatch/tsw0701b.pdf

Anderson, T. D., & Garrison, D. R. (1998). Learning in a networked world: New roles and responsibilities. In C. C. Gibson (Ed.), *Distance learners in higher education* (pp. 97-112). Madison, WI: Atwood.

Anderson, T., Howe, C., Soden, R., Halliday, J., & Low, J. (2001). Peer interaction and the learning of critical thinking skills in further education students . *Instructional Science, 29*, 1–32. doi:10.1023/A:1026471702353

Andrews, T., & Schwarz, G. (2002). Preparing students for the virtual organization: An evaluation of learning with virtual learning technologies. *Educational Technology & Society, 5*(3).

Androutsellis-Theotokis, S. (2004, December). Performing Peer-to-Peer E-Business Transactions: A Requirements Analysis and Preliminary Design Proposal. In *Proceedings of the IADIS eCommerce 2004 conference.* Lisbon, Portugal: IADIS Press.

Antoniou, G., & van Harmelen, F. (2004). *A Semantic Web Primer.* Cambridge, MA: The MIT Press.

Argamon, S., Koppel, M., Fine, J., & Shimoni, A. R. (2003). Gender, Genre, and Writing Style in Formal Written Texts. *Text, 23*(3). doi:10.1515/text.2003.014

Argyris, C., & Schön, D. (1991). Participatory action research and action science compared: A Commentary. In W. F. Whyte (Ed.), *Participatory action research*, pp. 85-96. Newbury Park, CA: Sage Publications.

Arpinar, B. I. Ontology-Driven Web Services Composition Platform. *Proceedings of the IEEE International Conference on E-Commerce Technology* (pp. 146-152). Athens, GA: University of Georgia.

Association of College and Research Libraries (ACRL). (2000). *Information literacy competency standards for higher education*, Chicago, Illinois: American Library Association. Retrieved from http://www.ala.org/ala/acrl/acrlstandards/standards.pdf

Ausburn, L. (2004). Gender and learning strategy differences in non-traditional adult students' design preferences in hybrid distance courses. *The Journal of Interactive Online Learning, 3*(2), 1-17.

Aviv, R. (2000). Educational performance of ALN via content analysis. *Journal of Asynchronous Learning Networks, 4*(2).

Babco, E. (2004). *Skills for the Innovation Economy: What the 21st Century Workforce Needs and How to Provide It.* Washington, DC: Commission on Professionals in Science and Technology.

Backstrom, L., Cynthia, D., & Kleinberg, J. (2007). Wherefore art thou R3579X? Anonymized social networks, hidden patterns, and structural steganography. *Proceedings of the WWW 2007 conference*, May 8-12, 2007, Alberta, Canada.

Bafoutsou, G., & Mentzas, G. (2002). Review and functional classification of collaborative systems. *International Journal of Information Management, 22*(4), 281-305.

Bai, B., Ng, K. B., Sun, Y., Kantor, P., & Strzalkowski, T. (2004). The institutional dimension of document quality judgments. *In the Proceedings of the 2004 Annual Meeting of American Society for Information Science and Technology.*

Bailey, A., Tell, L., & Walker, H. (2007). Librarian to Librarian Networking Summit: Collaboratively providing professional development for school media personnel. *Southeastern Librarian, 55*(1), 3–13.

Balka, E., & Bjorn, P. (2008). Steps toward a typology for health informatics. In *CSCW '08: Proceedings of the ACM 2008 conference on Computer supported cooperative work* (pp. 515-524). New York: ACM.

Banathy, B. H., & Jenlink, P. M., (Eds.) (2005), *Dialogue as a means of collective communication.* New York City, New York: Kluwer Academic/Plenum Publishers.

Bansler, J. (1989). Systems development research in Scandinavia: Three theoretical schools. *Scandinavian Journal of Information Systems, 1*, 3-20.

Barnes, S. B. (2006). A privacy paradox: Social networking in the United States. *First Monday, 1*(9). Retrieved July 19, 2008, from http://firstmonday.org/issues/issue11_9/barnes/index.html

Barouni-Ebrahimi, M., & Ghorbani, A. A. (2008). An interactive search assistant architecture based on intrinsic query stream characteristics. *Computational Intelligence, 24*(2), 158–190. doi:10.1111/j.1467-8640.2008.00326.x

Barrett, E., & Lally, V. (1999). Gender differences in an online learning environment. *Journal of Computer Assisted Learning, 15*, 48-60.

Barrett, M. I. (1999). Challenges of EDI adoption for electronic trading in the London Insurance Market. *European Journal of Information Systems, 8*, 1–15. doi:10.1057/palgrave.ejis.3000313

Barry, C. L. (1994). User-defined relevance criteria: An exploratory study. *Journal of the American Society for Information Science American Society for Information Science, 45*(3), 149–159. doi:10.1002/(SICI)1097-4571(199404)45:3<149::AID-ASI5>3.0.CO;2-J

Baskerville, R. L., & Wood-Harper, A. T. (1998). Diversity in information systems action research methods. *European Journal of Information Systems, 7*, 90-107.

Basu, A., & Kumar, A. (2002). Research commentary: Workflow management issues in e-business. *Information Systems Research, 13*(1), 1-14.

Baxter-Magolda, M. B. (1992). *Knowing and reasoning in college: Gender-related patterns in student's intellectual development.* San Francisco: Jossey-Bass Publishers.

Becker, H. S., Geer, B., & Hughes, E. C. (1968). *Making the grade: the academic side of college life.* New York: Wiley

Bennett, R. (2000). Om'nium [vds]: Presenting an On-Line Future for Tertiary [Design] Education. *Outline 9,* (winter 9), 17-24.

Bennett, R., Chan, L. K., & Polaine, A. (2004). *The Future Has Already Happened: Dispelling some myths of online education.* Proceedings of the Australian Council of University Art and Design Schools Annual Conference 2004, Canberra, Australia. Retrieved from http://www.acuads.com.au/conf2004/conf2004.htm.

Benson, C., Adam, E., Nickell, S., & Robertson, C. Z. (2002). *GNOME Human Interface Guidelines 1.0.* Retrieved July 2, 2007 from http://developer.gnome.org/projects/gup/hig/1.0.

Bentley, F., Metcalf, C., & Harboe, G. (2006). Personal vs. commercial content: The similarities between consumer use of photos and music. *Proceedings of the SIGCHI conference on Human Factors in computing systems,* April 22-27, 2006, Montréal, Québec, Canada

Berners-Lee, T. (1998). *Semantic Web Roadmap,* January 14, 2004. Retrieved from http://www.w3.org/DesignIssues/Semantic.html

Berners-Lee, T., Fensel, D., Hendler, J. A., Lieberman, H., & Wahlster, W. (2005). *Spinning the Semantic Web: Bringing the World Wide Web to Its Full Potential.* Cambridge, MA: The MIT Press.

Bhatt, G. D., Gupta, J. N. D., & Kitchens, F. (2005). An exploratory study of groupware use in the knowledge management process. *Journal of Enterprise Information Management, 8*(1), 28-46.

Biggerstaff, T., & Richter, C. (1987). Reusability Framework, Assessment, and Directions. *IEEE Software, 4*(2): 41–49. doi:10.1109/MS.1987.230095

Bikson, T. K., & Eveland, J. D. (1996). Groupware implementation: reinvention in the sociotechnical frame. In *CSCW '96: Proceedings of the 1996 ACM conference on Computer supported cooperative work* (pp. 428-437). New York: ACM Press.

Bjerkestrand, A.A. & Zeid, Amir L. (2007). Fifth international workshop on SOA & web services best practices. In *Companion to the 22nd ACM SIGPLAN conference on Object-oriented programming systems and applications companion* (pp. 746 –746). New York: ACM.

Black, A. (2005). The use of asynchronous discussion: Creating a text of talk. *Contemporary Issues in Technology & Teacher Education, 5*(1), 5–24.

Blake, P. (2006). Using a wiki for information services:

Principles and practicalities. In *Proceedings of New Librarians Symposium*. Sydney: Australian Library and Information Association.

Blum, K. D. (1999). Gender differences in asynchronous learning in higher education: Learning styles, participation barriers and communication patterns. *Journal of Asynchronous Learning Networks, 3*(1), 46-66.

Boff, E., et al. (2007). A collaborative Bayesian net editor to medical learning environments. In *Proceedings of the 25th IASTED International Multi-Conference: artificial intelligence and applications* (pp. 208-213). Insbruck, Austria: IASTAD.

Bonner, F., Marbley, A., & Agnello, M. F. (2004). The diverse learner in the college classroom. *E-Journal of Teaching and Learning in Diverse Settings, 1*(2), 246-255.

Borges, J., & Levene, M. (1999). Data mining of user navigation patterns. In *Revised Papers from the International Workshop on Web Usage Analysis and User Profiling*, (pp. 92-111). Berlin: Springer.

Borghini, S. (2005). Organizational creativity: Breaking equilibrium and order to innovate. *Journal of Knowledge Management, 9*(4), 19-33.

Bostock, S. J., & Lizhi, W. (2005). Gender in student online discussions. *Innovations in Education and Teaching International, 42*(1), 73-85.

Boud, D. (2000). Sustainable Assessment: Rethinking assessment for the learning society. *Studies in Continuing Education, 22*(2), 151–167. doi:10.1080/713695728

Box, G. E. P., & Draper, N. R. (1987). *Empirical Model-Building and Response Surfaces*. Hoboken, NJ: Wiley.

Boyd, D. (2004). Friendster and publicly articulated social networking. *CHI 2004,* April 24-29, 2004, Vienna, Austria.

Boyd, D. (2007). Social network sites: public, private or what? *Knowledge Tree*, 13, Retrieved Dec 12, 2007, from http://kt.flexibelearning.net.au/tkt2007/?page_id=28

Boyd, D., & Ellison, N. B. (2007). Social networking sites: Definition, history and scholarship. *Journal of Computer Mediated Communication, 13*(1), 11. Retrieved Dec 12, 2007, from http://jcmc.indiana.edu/vol13/issue1/boyd.ellison.html

Boyd, D., & Heer, J. (2006). Profiles as conversation: Networked identity performance on friendster. *Proceedings of the Hawaii International Conference on System Sciences (HICSS-39)*, January 4-7, Persistent Conversation Track, Kauai, Hawaii.

Bratteteig, T. (2004). *Making change. Dealing with relations between design and use.* Doctoral Dissertation, No 332, Department of Informatics, University of Oslo, Oslo, Norway.

Briggs, R. O. (2006). *The Value Frequency Model: Towards a Theoretical Understanding of Organizational Change.* Paper presented at the International Conference on Group Decision and Negotiation, Karlsruhe, Germany.

Briggs, R. O., de Vreede, G. J., & Nunamaker, J. F. Jr. (2003). Collaboration Engineering with ThinkLets to Pursue Sustained Success with Group Support Systems. *Journal of Management Information Systems, 19*(4), 31–63.

Briggs, R. O., de Vreede, G. J., Nunamaker, J. F., Jr., & David, T. H. (2001). *ThinkLets: Achieving Predictable, Repeatable Patterns of Group Interaction with Group Support Systems.* Paper presented at the Hawaii International Conference on System Sciences, Waikoloa, HI.

Briggs, R. O., Kolfschoten, G. L., de Vreede, G. J., & Dean, D. L. (2006). *Defining Key Concepts for Collaboration Engineering.* Paper presented at the Americas Conference on Information Systems, Acapulco, Mexico.

Brosnan, M. J., & Davison, M. J. (1994, February). Computerphobia: Is it a particularly female phenomenon? *The Psychologist*, pp. 74-78.

Brown, J. S. (2002), "Growing up digital - How the Web changes work, education, and the ways people learn", *Journal of the United States Distance Learning Association*, 16(2). Retrieved from http://www.usdla.org/html/journal/FEB02_Issue/article01.html

Brown, J. S., & Duguid, P. (2000). Balancing act: How to capture knowledge without killing it. *Harvard Business Review, 78*(3), 73-80.

Bruce, C. (1997). *The seven faces of information literacy.* Blackwood, South Australia: Auslib Press.

Bruce, C. (1997) The relational approach: A new model for information literacy. *The New Review of Information and Library Research, 3,* 3—22.

Bruce, H. W. (1994). A cognitive view of the situational dynamism of user-centered relevance estimation. *Journal of the American Society for Information Science American Society for Information Science, 45*(3), 142–148. doi:10.1002/(SICI)1097-4571(199404)45:3<142::AID-ASI4>3.0.CO;2-6

Brugali, D., & Sycara, K. (2000). Frameworks and pattern languages: an intriguing relationship. *ACM Computing Surveys, 32*(1es), 2. doi:10.1145/351936.351938

Buckingham Shum, S. 2006. Hypermedia Support for Argumentation-Based Rationale: 15 Years on from gIBIS and QOC. In A. Dutoit (ed.). *Rationale Management in Software Engineering,* 111-132. Berlin: Springer-Verlag.

Budinsky, F.J., Finnie, M.A., Vlissides, J.M., & Yu, P.S. (1996). Automatic Code Generation from Design Patterns. *Object technology, 35*(2), 151-172.

Burnett, G., & Buerkle, H. (2004). Information exchange in virtual communities: A comparative study. *Journal of Computer-Mediated Communication, 9*(2).

Butler, K. (1996). Usability engineering. *Interaction, 3*(1), 58–75. doi:10.1145/223500.223513

Byrne, M. D., Wood, S. D., Foley, J. D., Kieras, D. E., & Sukaviriya, P. N. (1994). Automating interface evaluation. *CHI '94: Proceedings of the SIGCHI conference on Human factors in computing systems,* (New York,pp. 232–237 NY, USA)., New York: ACM, pp. 232–237.

Carneiro, A. (2000). How does knowledge management influence innovation and competitiveness? *Journal of Knowledge Management, 4*(2), 87-98.

Carter, L.M. (2000). *Arguments in Hypertext: a Rhetorical approach.* Proceedings of the Hypertext 2000 Conference, San Antonio (TX), 85-91.

Carvalho, R., & Ferreira, M. (2001). Using information technology to support knowledge conversion processes. *Information Research, 7*(1). Retrieved from http://InformationR.net/ir/7-1/paper118.html

Castano, S., de Antonellis, V., & Melchiori, M. (1999). A methodology and tool environment for process analysis and reengineering. *Data & Knowledge Engineering, 31*(3), 253–278. doi:10.1016/S0169-023X(99)00028-2

Castells, M. (2000). *The Rise of the Network Society: The Information Age: Economy, Society and Culture Vol 1 (The Information Age).* London: Blackwell Publishers.

Caverlee, J., Liu, L., & Webb, S. (2008). Towards robust trust establishment in web-based social networks with social trust. [Beijing, China.]. *WWW, 2008*(April).

Cayzer, S. (2004). Semantic blogging and decentralized knowledge management. *Communications of the ACM, 47*(12), 47–52. doi:10.1145/1035134.1035164

Çetin, G., Verzulli, D., & Frings, S. (2007). An Analysis of Involvement of HCI Experts in Distributed Software Development: Practical Issues. *Online Communities and Social Comput., HCII 2007,* (LNCS 4564, pp. 32–40). Springer-Verlag Berlin: Springer-Verlag. Heidelberg

Chabert, A., Grossman, E., Jackson, L., Pietrovicz, S., & Seguin, C. (1998). Java Object-Sharing in Habanero. *Communications of the ACM, 41*(6), 69–76. doi:10.1145/276609.276622

Champion, D., & Stowell, F. A. (2003). Validating action research field studies: PEARL, *Systemic Practice and Action Research,* 16(1), 21-36.

Chang, T., & Lim, J. (2002). Cross-cultural communication and social presence in asynchronous learning processes. *e-Service Journal, 1*(3).

Chapman, C., & Lahav, M. (2008). International ethnographic observation of social networking sites. *Proceedings of the CHI 2008 conference on Human Factors in Computing Systems,* April 5-10, 2008, Florence, Italy.

Charman, S. (2006). An adoption strategy for social software in the enterprise. *Corante*. Retrieved May 13, 2008, from http://strange.corante.com/archives/2006/03/05/an_adoption_strategy_for_social_ software_in_enterprise.php

Chaski, C. (2001). Empirical evaluations of language-based Author identification techniques. *Forensic Linguistics . The International Journal of Speech Language and the Law, 8*(1).

Chatraborty, M., & Victor, S. (2004). Do's and don't's of simultaneous instruction to on-campus and distance students via video conferencing. *Journal of Library Administration, 41*(1/2), 97–112.

Chau, T., & Maurer, F. (2005). A case study of wiki-based experience repository at a medium-sized software company. In *Proceedings of the 3rd International Conference on Knowledge Capture* (pp 185-186), Banff, Alberta, Canada.

Chauvel, D., & Despres, C. (2002). A review of survey research in knowledge management: 1997-2001. *Journal of Knowledge Management, 6*(3), 207–223. doi:10.1108/13673270210434322

Checkland, P. B. (1979). Techniques in 'soft' systems practice part 1: Systems diagrams - some tentative guidelines. *Journal of Applied Systems Analysis, 6*, 33-40.

Checkland, P. B. (1981). *Systems thinking, systems practice*. Chichester: John Wiley & Sons.

Checkland, P. B. (1985). From optimizing to learning: A development of systems thinking for the 1990s. *Journal of the Operational Research Society, 36*(9), 757-767.

Checkland, P. B. (2000). Soft systems methodology: A thirty year retrospective. *Systems Research and Behavioral Science, 17*(S1), 11-58.

Checkland, P. B., & Casar, A. (1986). Vickers' concept of an appreciative system: A systemic account. *Journal of Applied Systems Analysis, 13*, 3-17.

Checkland, P. B., & Holwell, S. (1993). Information management and organizational processes: An approach through soft systems methodology. *Journal of Information Systems, 3*, 3-16.

Checkland, P. B., & Holwell, S. (1998). *Information, systems and information systems - Making sense of the field*. Chichester, England: John Wiley & Sons.

Checkland, P. B., & Holwell, S. (1998). Action research: Its nature and validity. *Systemic Practice and Action Research, 11*(1), 9-21.

Checkland, P. B., & Poulter, J. (2006). *Learning for action. A short definitive account of soft systems methodology and its use for practitioners, teachers and students*. Chichester, England: John Wiley & Sons.

Checkland, P. B., & Winter, M. (2006). Process and content: Two ways of using SSM. *Journal of Operational Research Society, 57*, 1435-1441.

Checkland, P.B., & Scholes, J. (1990). *Soft Systems Methodology in action*. Chichester, England: John Wiley & Sons.

Chen, C., Czerwinski, M., & Macredie, R. (2000). Individual differences in virtual environments. Introduction and overview. *Journal of the American Society for Information Science, 51*(6), 499-507.

Chen, I. Y. L., & Yang, S. J. H. (2006). Peer-to-Peer Knowledge Sharing in Collaboration Supported Virtual Learning Communities. In *Proceedings of the Sixth IEEE International Conference on Advanced Learning Technologies* (pp. 807-809). Washington, DC: IEEE Computer Society.

Chesnevar, C., McGinnis, J., Modgil, S., Rahwan, I., Reed, C., Simari, G., South, M., Vreeswijk, G., Willmott, S. 2006. Towards an argument interchange format. *The knowledge Engineering Review, 21*(4), 293-316.

Chin, J. P., Diehl, V. A., & Norman, K. L. (1988). Development of an instrument measuring user satisfaction of the human-computer interface. *Proceedings of CHI Conference on Human Factors in Computing Systems* (pp. 213-218). New York: ACM, 213-218.

Chioncel, N. E., Van Der Veen, R. G. W., Nildemeersch, P., & Jarvis, P. (2003). The validity and reliability of focus groups as a research method in adult education. *Interna-*

tional Journal of Lifelong Education, 22(5), 495-517.

Choi, B., & Lee, H. (2003). An empirical investigation of KM styles and their effect on corporate performance. *Information & Management, 40*(5), 403-417.

Chow, W. C., Shields, M. D., & Wu, A. (1999). The importance of national culture in the design of and preference for management controls for multi-national operations. *Accounting Organizations and Society, 24,* 441-461.

Chung, K., & Adams, C. (1997). A study on the characteristics of group decision-making behaviour: Cultural difference perspective of Korea vs. US. *Journal of Global Information Management, 5*(3), 18-29.

Chung, P., Cheung, L., Stader, J., Jarvis, P., Moore, J., & Macintosh, A. (2003). Knowledge-based process management—An approach to handling adaptive workflow. *Knowledge-Based Systems, 16*(2), 149–160.

Churchman, C. W. (1984). *The systems approach.* New York: Dell Publishing Co.

Clagg, M. (2002). Why beginning teachers stay in the profession: Views in a Kansas school district, (Doctoral dissertation, Wichita State University, 2002). *Dissertation Abstracts International, 63*(4), 1197.

Coates, T. (2006). *Greater than the sum of its parts.* Paper presented at the Future of Web Apps, San Francisco.

Coleman, D. (1995). *Groupware: Technology and applications.* Englewood Cliffs, NJ: Prentice Hall.

Collins, A., Brown, J. S., & Newman, S. E. (1987, January). *Cognitive apprenticeship: Teaching the craft of reading, writing and mathematics* (Technical Report No. 403). BBN Laboratories, Cambridge, MA & Centre for the Study of Reading, University of Illinois.

Conklin, J. (1987). Hypertext: An Introduction and Survey. *IEEE Computer, 20*(9), 17–41.

Conklin, J. (2003). *The IBIS Manual: A Short Course in IBIS Methodology,* http://cognexus.org/id26.htm#the_ibis_manual.

Conklin, J. (2006). *Dialogue Mapping: Building Shared Understanding of Wicked Problems.* Chichester (UK):

Wiley.

Conway, M. E. (1968). How do committees invent? *Datamation, 14*(4), 28–31.

Coplien, J. O., & Harrison, N. B. (2004). *Organizational Patterns of Agile Software Development.* Upper Saddle River, NJ: Prentice Hall.

CosmoCode. (2008). *WikiMatrix: Compare them all.* Retrieved May 10, 2008, from http://www.wikimatrix.org

Couger, J. D. (1995). *Creative Problem Solving and Opportunity Finding.* Danvers, MA: Boyd and Fraser.

Council on Competitiveness. (2005). *National Innovation Initiative (NII) Final Report - Innovate America: Thriving in a World of Challenge and Change.*

Cox, M. (2008). Faculty learning communities: Recommendations for initiating and implementing an FLC at your campus. *Faculty Learning Communities.* Miami, OH: Miami University. http://www.units.muohio.edu/flc/recommendations.php

Cress, U., & Kimmerle, J. (2008). A systemic and cognitive view on collaborative knowledge building with wiki. In *Computer-Supported Collaborative Learning (3),* (pp. 105-122). Berlin: Springer.

Cunningham, J. (1998, Feb). *The workplace: A learning environment.* Paper delivered at the First Annual Conference of the Australian Vocational Education and Training Research Association, Sydney.

Cutter, C. A. (1875). *Rules for a printed dictionary catalogue.* Washington, DC: Government Printing Office.

CXO CIO Media Custom Solutions Group. (2007, February 13). *Collaborative Efforts: Survey Reveals Clear Business Acceleration Using On-demand Collaboration Technology.*

Daggett, W. R. (2005, June). *Preparing Students for Their Future.* Presented at June 2005 Model Schools Conference

Dall'Alba, G., & Sandberg, J. (2006). Unveiling professional development: A critical review of stage models.

Review of Educational Research, 76(3), 383–412. doi:10.3102/00346543076003383

Damanpour, F., & Gopalakrishnan, S. (2001). The dynamics of the adoption of product and process innovations in organizations. *Journal of Management Studies, 38*(1), 45-65.

Dasgupta, S., Granger, M., & McGarry, N. (2002). User acceptance of e-collaboration technology: An extension of the technology acceptance model. *Group Decision and Negotiation, 11*(2), 87-100.

Davenport, T. H., & Prusak, L. (2000). *Working Knowledge*, (2nd Ed.). Boston: Harvard Business School Press.

Davis, A. M. (1990). *Software Requirements: Analysis and Specification.* New York: Prentice-Hall.

Davis, B. (2008, August 26). Shaky Economy Challenges Ambitious Obama Agenda. *The Wall Street Journal Eastern Edition*, A1-A18.

Davis, F. D., Bagozzi, R. P., & Warshaw, P. R. (1989). User acceptance of computer technology: A comparison of two theoretical models. *Management Science, 35*(8), 982-1003.

Davis, H. L., & Somerville, M. M. (2006). Learning our way to change: Improved institutional alignment. *New Library World*, 107(3/4), 127-140.

de Moor, A, Aakhus, M. 2006. Argumentation support from technologies to tools. *Communication of the ACM*, 49(3): 93-98.

De Vel, O., & Nesbitt, S. (1997). A Collaborative Filtering Agent System for Dynamic Virtual Communities on the Web. *Working notes of Learning from Text and the Web, Conference on Automated Learning and Discovery CONALD-98,* Carnegie Mellon University, Pittsburgh, 1998.

de Vreede, G. J., & Briggs, R. O. (2001). *ThinkLets: Five Examples Of Creating Patterns Of Group Interaction.* Paper presented at the International Conference on Group Decision and Negotiation, La Rochelle, France.

de Vreede, G. J., & Briggs, R. O. (2005). *Collaboration Engineering: Designing Repeatable Processes for High-Value Collaborative Tasks.* Paper presented at the Hawaii International Conference on System Science, Los Alamitos.

de Vreede, G. J., Briggs, R. O., & Kolfschoten, G. L. (2006). ThinkLets: A Pattern Language for Facilitated and Practitioner-Guided Collaboration Processes. *International Journal of Computer Applications in Technology, 25*(2/3), 140–154. doi:10.1504/IJCAT.2006.009064

de Vries, S., & Kommers, P. (2004). Online knowledge communities: Future trends and research issues. *International Journal of Web Based Communities, 1*(1), 115–123.

DeGraff, J., et al. (2002). *Creativity at Work.* New York: Wiley & Sons.

Del Galdo, E. M., Williges, R. C., Williges, B. H., & Wixon, D. R. (1987). A critical incident evaluation tool for software documentation. In L. S. Mark, J. S. Warm, & R. L. Huston (Eds.), *Ergonomics and Human Factors*, (pp. 253-258). New York: Springer-Verlag, 253-258

DeMarco, T., & Lister, T. (1999). *Peopleware: Productive Projects and Teams.* New York: Dorset House.

Deming, W. E. (2000). *Out of the Crisis: For Industry, Government, Education.* Cambridge, MA: MIT Press.

Dennis, A. R., & Valacich, J. S. (1999). Rethinking media richness: Towards a theory of media synchronicity. In *Proceedings of the 32nd Hawaii International Conference on System Sciences*, Hawaii.

DeSanctis, G., & Gallupe, R. B. (1987). A foundation for the study of group decision support system. *Management Science, 33*(5), 589-609.

DeSanctis, G., Fayard, A. L., Roach, M., & Jiang, L. (2003). Learning in online forums. *European Management Journal, 21*(5), 565–577.

Desilets, A., Paquet, S., & Vinson, N. G. (2005). Are wiki usable? *WikiSym 2005 – Conference Proceedings of the 2005 International Symposium on Wikis*, (pp 3-15).

Desmond, B. (2006). Claims processing using Service Oriented Architecture and Web-services based technologies. *Risk & Insurance Online*, December 1, 2006. Retrieved November 22, 2008, from: http://www.riskandinsurance.com/issue.jsp?issueId=13604945&currentFlag=0

Devaraj, S., & Kohli, R. (2003). Performance impacts of information technology: Is actual usage the missing link? *Management Science, 49*(3), 273-289.

Diani, M. (2000). Social movement networks: Virtual and real. *Information Communication and Society, 3*(3), 386–401. doi:10.1080/13691180051033333

Dick, B. (2004). Action research literature. Themes and trends. *Action Research, 2*(4), 425-444.

DiMicco, J., & Millen, D. (2007). Identity management: multiple presentations of self in facebook. *Group '07, Conference on Supporting Group Work*, November 4-7, 2007, Sannibel Island, Florida, USA.

Dogac, A. (2006, February). *Untangle the Web: Communicating Through the Web Services Using Semantics.* Paper presented at HIMSS 2006, San Diego, CA.

Dogac, A. (2008, October). *A Brief Introduction to the Semantic Representations of the UN/CEFACT CCTS-based Electronic Business Document Artifacts.* Paper presented at OASIS Semantic Support for Electronic Business Document Interoperability (SET) TC, Teleconference, Billerica, MA.

Dogac, A. (2008, October). *Conformance and Interoperability Testing of NHIS, Turkey: TestBATN Framework and NHIS Test Scenarios.* Paper presented at 9th International HL7 Interoperability Conference 2008 - IHIC 2008, Crete, Greece.

Doll, W. J., & Deng, X. (2001). The collaborative use of information technology: End-user participation and systems success. *Information Resources Management Journal, 14*(2), 6-16.

Donath, J. (1998). Identity and deception in the virtual community. In P. Kollock, & M. Smith (Eds.), *Communities in cyberspace* (29-59). London: Routledge.

Donath, J., & Boyd, D. (2004). Public displays of connection. *BT Technology Journal, 22*(4), 71–81. doi:10.1023/B:BTTJ.0000047585.06264.cc

Drucker, P. F., Garvin, D., Leonard, D., Straus, S., & Brown, J. S. (1998) *Harvard Business Review on Knowledge Management.* 6th ed. Boston, MA: Harvard Business School Press.

Duane, A., & Finnegan, P. (2003). Managing empowerment and control in an intranet environment. *Information Systems Journal, 13*(2), 133-158.

Duarte, D. L., et al. (2006). *Mastering Virtual Teams.* New York: Wiley & Sons.

Duarte, D., & Snyder, N. (2000). *Mastering Virtual Teams: Strategies, Tools, and Techniques that Succeed,* (2nd Ed.). Hoboken, NJ: Jossey-Bass.

Duyne, D. K. V., Landay, J., & Hong, J. I. (2002). *The Design of Sites: Patterns, Principles, and Processes for Crafting a Customer-Centered Web Experience.* Reading MA: Addison-Wesley.

Easley, R. F., Devaraj, S., & Crant, J. M. (2003). Collaborative technology use to teamwork performance: An empirical analysis. *Journal of Information Systems, 19*(4), 247-268.

Ebersbach, A., Glaser, M., & Heigl, R. (2005). *Wiki: Web Collaboration.* Berlin, Germany: Springer.

Ebersbach, A., Glaser, M., Heigl, R., & Warta, A. (2008). *Wiki Web Collaboration, 2 Ed.* Berlin: Springer-Verlag.

Economist Intelligence Unit (2007). Enterprise Knowledge Workers: Understanding Risks and Opportunities.

Edwards, S. L. (2006) *Panning for gold: Information literacy and the Net Lenses Model.* Blackwood, Australia: Auslib Press.

Egan, J. P. (1975). *Signal detection theory and ROC analysis.* New York: Academic Press.

Elden, M., & Levin, M. (1991). Cogenerative learning: Bringing participation into action research. In W. F.

Whyte (Ed.), *Participatory action research*. Newbury Park, CA: Sage Publications.

Ellis, C. A., Gibbs, S. J., & Rein, G. L. (1991). Groupware some issues and experiences. *Communications of the ACM, 34*(1), 39–58. doi:10.1145/99977.99987

Ellis, L., Gibbs, S. J., & Rein, G. L. (1991). Groupware: Some issues and experiences. *Communications of the ACM, 34*(1), 38-58.

Elovici, Y., & Kantor, P. B. (2003). Using the Information Structure Model to Compare Profile-Based Information Filtering Systems. *Information Retrieval, 6*(1), 75–97. doi:10.1023/A:1022952531694

Eppler, M. J., & Wittig, D. (2000). Conceptualizing information quality: A review of information quality frameworks from the last ten years. In B. D. Klein, D. F. Rossin, (Ed.), *Proceedings of the 2000 conference on information quality*, (pp. 83-96). Cambridge, MA: Massachusetts Institute of Technology.

Erickson, T. (2000). Lingua Francas for design: sacred places and pattern languages. In *Proceedings of the conference on Designing interactive systems* (pp. 357-368). New York: ACM Press.

Erickson, T., Halverson C., Kellogg, W.A., Laff, M. and T. Wolf (2002). *Social Translucence: Designing Social Infrastructures that Make Collective Activity Visible.* Communications of the ACM, 45(4): 40-44.

Ericsson, A., & Simon, H. (1984). *Protocol analysis: verbal reports as data.* Boston: The MIT Press.

Ertl, B., Fischer, F., & Mandl, H. (2006). Conceptual and socio-cognitive support for collaborative learning in video conferencing environments. *Computers & Education, 47*, 298–315. doi:10.1016/j.compedu.2004.11.001

Fai Wong, L., & Trinidad, S. G. (2004). Using Web-based distance learning to reduce cultural distance. *The Journal of Interactive Online Learning, 3*(1).

Falchikov, N., & Goldfinch, J. (2000). Student Peer Assessment in Higher Education: A Meta-Analysis Comparing Peer and Teacher Marks. *Review of Educational Research, 70*(3), 287–322.

Fayad, M. E., & Schmidt, D. C. (1997). Object-oriented Application Frameworks. *Communications of the ACM, 40*(10), 32–38. doi:10.1145/262793.262798

Fellbaum, C. (Ed.). (1998). *WordNet: An Electronic Lexical Database.* Cambridge, MA: The MIT Press.

Fenstermacher, K. D. (2005). Revealed processes in knowledge management. In *Professional Knowledge Management: Third Biennial Conference.* Berlin, Germany: Springer.

Fernandes, K., Raja, V., & Austin, S. (2005). Portals as a knowledge repository and transfer tool—VIZCon case study. *Technovation, 25*(11), 1281–1289.

Fichter, D. (2006). Using wikis to support online collaboration in libraries. *Information Outlook, 10*(1), 30–31.

Figallo, C., & Rhine, N. (2002) *Building the Knowledge Management Network: Best Practices, Tools, and Techniques for Putting Conversation to Work.* Hoboken, NJ: Wiley.

Fitzgerald, R. (2007). Wikis as an exemplary model of open source learning. In *Handbook of Research in Open Source Software*, (pp. 681-689), Hershey, PA: IGI Global.

Flood, R. L. (1998). Action research and the management and systems sciences. *Systemic Practice and Action Research, 11*(1), 79-101.

Flood, R. L., & Jackson, M. C. (Eds.) (1991). *Creative problem solving: Total systems intervention.* Chichester, England: John Wiley & Sons.

Flood, R. L., & Romm, N. R. A. (1996). *Diversity management: Triple loop learning.* Chichester: John Wiley & Sons.

Ford, N. (2000). Cognitive styles and virtual environments. *Journal of American Society for Information Science, 51*(6), 543-557

Ford, N., & Miller, D. (1996). Gender differences in Internet perceptions and use. In *Proceedings of the Elvira Conference* (pp.87-100). London: ASLIB. Retrieved November 9, 2007, from http://www.shef.ac.uk/~is/

home_old/gender.htm

Forgionne, G., & Kohli, R. (1996). HMSS: A management support system for concurrent hospital decision-making. *Decision Support Systems, 16*(3), 209-229.

Fradkin, D., & Kantor, P. B. (2004). A Design Space Approach to Analysis of Information Retrieval Adaptive Filtering Systems. *The 13th ACM Conference on Information and Knowledge Management* (CIKM). November 2004.

Fradkin, D., & Kantor, P. B. (2005). Methods for Learning Classifier Combinations: No Clear Winner. *Proceedings of ACM Symposium on Applied Computing 2005, Information Access and Retrieval Track.*

Franco, J. F., Sandra Regina da Cruz, S. R., & de Deus Lopes, R. (2006). *Computer Graphics, Interactive Technologies and Collaborative Learning Synergy Supporting Individuals' Skills Development.* Paper presented at ACM SIGRAPH2006, Boston, MA.

Frappaolo, C. (2006). *Knowledge Management,* (2nd Ed.). Mankato, MN: Capstone Press.

Friedland, L. A. (1996). Electronic democracy and the new citizenship. *Media Culture & Society, 18*, 185–212. doi:10.1177/016344396018002002

Froehlich, D., Kuchinsky, A., Pering, C., Don, A., & Ariss, S. (2002). Requirements for photoware. *Proceedings from the Conference on Computer Supported Cooperative Work: CSCW 2002.* New Orleans, LA.

Froomkin, A. (1995). Anonymity and its enmities. *Journal of Online Law, 4.* Retrieved Dec 12, 2007 from http://www.wm.edu/law/publications/jol/95_96/froomkin.html

Frost, & Sullivan. (2007). *Meetings around the World: The Impact of Collaboration on Business Performance.*

Fuchs-Kittowski, F., & Köhler, A. (2005). Wiki communities in the context of work processes. In *Proceedings of the 2005 International Symposium on Wikis, San Diego, CA* (pp 33-39). New York, NY: ACM Press.

Fung, Y. (2004). Collaborative online learning: interaction patterns and limiting factors. *Open Learning, 19*(2),

135–149. doi:10.1080/0268051042000224743

Galambos, J.A., Abelson, R.P., Black, J.B. (eds.) 1986. *Knowledge Structures*, Hillsdale (NJ): Lawrence Earlbaum Associates.

Gamma, E., Helm, R., Johnson, R., & Vlissides, J. (1995). *Design Patterns: Elements of Reusable Object-Oriented Software.* Reading, MA: Addison-Wesley.

Gamma, E., Helm, R., Johnson, R., & Vlissides, J. (1995). *Elements of Reusable Object-Oriented Software.* Reading, MA: Addison-Wesley Publishing Company.

Garshol, L. (2002). *Topic maps, RDF, DAML, OIL.* Retrieved March 14, 2007, from http://www.ontopia.net/topicmaps/materials/tmrdfoildaml.html

Gaskell, T. (2000). The process of empirical research: A learning experience? *Research in Post-Compulsory Education, 5*(3), 349-360.

Gauntlett, D., & Hill, A. (1999). *TV Living: TV, Culture and Everyday Life.* London: Routledge.

Geyer, W., Dugan, C., DiMicco, J., Millen., D., et al. (2008). Use and reuse of shared Lists as a social Content Type. *Proceedings of the CHI 2008, conference on Human Factors in Computing Systems,* April 5-10, 2008, Florence, Italy.

Ghaye, T. (2007). *Building the reflective healthcare organisation.* Oxford, England: Blackwell.

Ghosh, R. A. (2005). Cooking-pot markets and balanced value flows. In *CODE: Collaborative Ownership and the Digital Economy,* (pp. 153-168). Cambridge, MA: The MIT Press.

Ghosh, R. A. (Ed.). (2005). *CODE: Collaborative Ownership and the Digital Economy.* Cambridge, MA: MIT Press.

Gibbs, G., & Simpson, C. (2004). Does your assessment support your students learning? *Learning and Teaching in Higher Education, 1*(1), 3–31.

Gibbs, G., & Simpson, C. (2004-05). Conditions under which Assessment Supports Students' Learning. *Learning and Teaching in Higher Education, 1*, 1–29.

Gibs, J., Fields, N., Liang, P., & Plipre, A. (2005). SNIF: Social networking in Fur. *Proceedings of the CHI 2005 conference on Human Factors in Computing Systems*, April 2-7, 2005, Portland, Oregon, USA.

Gibson, R. (2007). Who's really in your top 8: Networking security in the age of social networking. *Proceedings of the SIGUCCS' 07, conference on user services*, October 7-10, 2007, Orlando, FL.

Gibson, W. (1984). *Neuromancer*. New York: Ace Books.

Giddens, A. (1990). *The Consequences of modernity*. Stanford, CA: Stanford University Press.

Gillingson, S., & O'Leary, D. (2006). *Working progress: how to reconnect young people and organisations.* London: Demos.

Giudici, P., Figini, S. (2008, May). *Knowledge management for effective risk governance.* Presentation given at Executive Workshop: Turning data into risk knowledge, London, England.

Glogowski, J., & Steiner, S. (2008). The life of a wiki: How Georgia State University Library's wiki enhances content currency and employee collaboration. *Internet Reference Services Quarterly*, *13*(1). doi:10.1300/J136v13n01_05

Gloor, P. 2006. *Swarm Creativity - Competitive advantage through collaborative networks.* New York: Oxford University Press.

Gloor, P. (2007). *Coolfarming*. http://scripts.mit.edu/~pgloor/coolfarming/index.php?title=Main_Page.

Göktürk, M., & Çetin, G. (2007). Out of Box Experience Issues of Free and Open Source Software. *HCI International Proceedings*, (Volume 1), (LNCS_4550). ISBN: 978-3-540-73104-7

Golbeck, J., & Wasser, M. (2007). Social browsing: Integrating social networks and web browsing. *Proceedings from CHI 2007, conference on Human Factors in Computing Systems*, April 28 – May 34, San Jose, CA.

Golbeck, J., Hendler, J., & Parsia, B. (2003). Trust networks on the semantic web. *Proceedings from Agents 2003, conference on cooperative information agents*, August 27-29, Helsinki, Finland.

Gonzolez-Reinhart, J. (2005). *Wiki and the wiki way: Beyond a knowledge management system.* C. T. Bauer College of Business, University of Houston. Retrieved May 10, 2008 from http://www.uhisrc.com/FTB/Wiki/wiki_way_brief[1]-Jennifer%2005.pdf

Goussevskaia, O. Kuhn. M., & Wattenhofer, R. (2007). Layers and hierarchies in real virtual networks. In *proceedings of IEEE/WIC/ACM International Conference on Web Intelligence* (pp 89-94). IEEE Computer Society: Washington, DC.

Granollers, T., Lorès, J., & Perdrix, F. 2002. Usability Engineering Process Model. – Integration with Software Engineering. *Proceedings of HCI International 2003*. Crete, Greece.

Grant, L. (2006). Using Wikis in Schools: A Case Study. *Futurelab-Innovation in Education*, Retrieved August 23, 2008, from http://www.futurelab.org.uk/resources/documents/discussion_papers/Wikis_in_Schools.pdf

Green, H., & Hannon, C. (2007). *Their Space: Education for a Digital Generation.* London: Demos.

Green, M., & Cifuentes, L. (2008). An exploration of online environments supporting follow-up to face-to-face professional development. *Journal of Technology and Teacher Education*, *16*(3), 283–306.

Greenberg, S., & Roseman, M. (2003). Using a Room Metaphor to Ease Transitions in Groupware. In M. Ackermann, V. Pipek & V. Wulf (Eds.), *Sharing Expertise: Beyond Knowledge Management* (pp. 203-256). Cambridge, MA: MIT Press.

Gross, R., & Acquisti, A. (2005). Information revelation and privacy in online social networks. *Workshop on Privacy in the Electronic Society* (WPES). Retrieved from Dec 4, 2007 from http://privacy.cs.cmu.edu/dataprivacy/projects/facebook/facebook1.html

Grover, V., & Kettinger, W. J. (1995). *Business Process Change; Reengineering Concepts, Methods and Tech-*

nologies. Hershey, PA: Idea Group Publishing.

Grudin, J. (2006). Enterprise knowledge management and emerging technologies. In *Proceedings of the 39th Annual Hawaii International Conference on System Sciences,* (track 3, p 57a). University of Hawaii at Manoa.

Guha, S., Kettinger, W. J., & Teng, T. C. (1993). Business Process Reengineering: Building a Comprehensive Methodology. *Information Systems Management, 10*(3), 13–22. doi:10.1080/10580539308906939

Gunn, C., & McSporran, M. (2003). Dominant or different? Gender issues in computer supported learning. *Journal of Asynchronous Learning Networks, 7*(1), 14-30.

Gunnlaugsdottir, J. (2003). Seek and you will find, share and you will benefit: Organising knowledge using groupware systems. *International Journal of Information Management, 23*(5), 363-380.

Gurteen, D. (1998). Knowledge, creativity, and innovation. *Journal of Knowledge Management, 12*(1), 5-13.

Haake, A., Lukosch, S., & Schümmer, T. (2005). Wiki-Templates: Adding Structure Support to Wikis On Demand. In *WikiSym 2005 - Conference Proceedings of the 2005 International Symposium on Wikis* (pp. 41-51). New York: ACM Press.

Haake, J. M., Haake, A., Schümmer, T., Bourimi, M., & Landgraf, B. (2004). End-User Controlled Group Formation and Access Rights Management in a Shared Workspace System. In *CSCW '04: Proceedings of the 2004 ACM conference on Computer supported cooperative work* (pp. 554-563). New York: ACM Press.

Haake, J. M., Schümmer, T., Haake, A., Bourimi, M., & Landgraf, B. (2004). Supporting flexible collaborative distance learning in the CURE platform. In *Proceedings of the Hawaii International Conference On System Sciences (HICSS-37).* New York: IEEE Press.

Hakiel, S. (1997). Delivering ease of use. *Computing & Control Engineering Journal,* April 1997.

Hamel, G. (2002). *Leading the revolution.* New York: Plume.

Hamel, G., et al. (2007). *The Future of Management.* Cambridge, MA: Harvard Business School Press.

Hann, I. H., Roberts, J. A., Slaughter, S. A., & Fielding, R. (2002) Why do developers contribute to open source projects? First evidence of economic incentives. In *Proceedings of the 2nd Workshop on Open Source Software Engineering, The 24th International Conference on Software Engineering, Orlando, FL.* New York, NY: ACM Press.

Hansen, M. T., Nohria, N., & Tierney, T. (1999). What's your strategy for managing knowledge? *Harvard Business Review, 77*(2), 106–116.

Harris, M. (1987). *Cultural anthropology* (2nd ed.). Harper and Ross.

Hatton, D. (1995, November 18-21). Women and the "L": A study of the relationship between communication apprehension, gender and bulletin boards. In *Proceedings of the 81st Annual Meeting of the Speech Communication Association,* San Antonio, TX.

Hayes, C. (2006). *Position Paper: Collaboration Challenges in Distributed Engineering Design Projects.* University of Minnesota.

Hayes, N., & Walsham, G. (2001). Participation in groupware-mediated communities of practice: A socio-political analysis of knowledge working. *Information and Organization, 11*(4), 263-288.

Haythornthwaite, C., Kazmer, M. M., Robins, J., & Shoemaker, S. (2000). Community Development Among Distance Learners: Temporal and Technological Dimensions. *Journal of Computer-Mediated Communication, 6*(1).

Head, G. (2003). Effective collaboration: deep collaboration as an essential element of the learning process. *Journal of Educational Enquiry, 4*(2), 47–62.

Healy, K. and A. Schussman 2003. *The Ecology of Open-Source Software Development.* Working paper, http://kb.cospa-project.org/retrieve/3150/healyschussman.pdf

Helfert, M. (2001). Managing and Measuring Data

Quality in Data Warehousing. *Proceedings of the World Multiconference on Systemics, Cybernetics and Informatics*, (pp. 55-65).

Henri, F. (1991). Computer Conferencing and Content Analysis. In A.R. Kaye (Ed.) *Collaborative Learning Through Computer Conferencing. The Najaden Papers.* Berlin: Springer Verlag.

Hepp, M., Siorpaes, K., & Bachlechner, D. (2007). Harvesting wiki consensus: Using Wikipedia entries as vocabulary for knowledge management. *IEEE Internet Computing, 11*(5), 54–65. doi:10.1109/MIC.2007.110

Heron, J. & Reason, P. (2001) The practice of co-operative inquiry: research 'with' rather than 'on' people. In P. Reason, P. & H. Bradbury (Eds) *Handbook of Action Research: Participative Inquiry & Practice*, pp. 179-188. Newbury Park, CA: Sage Publications.

Herring, S. C. (1999). Interactional coherence in CMC. In *Proceedings of the 32nd Hawaii International Conference on System Sciences (HICSS)*.

Herring, S. C. (2000). Gender differences in CMC: Findings and implications. *The CPSR Newsletter, 18*(1). Retrieved November 9, 2007, from http://www.cpsr.org/publications/newsletters/issues/2000/Winter2000/herring.htm

Higgs-Horwell, M., & Schwelik, J. (2007). I got by with a little help from my friends. *Library Media Connection* (Nov./Dec.), 36-38.

Hillside. (2008). *hillside pattern languages.* Unpublished manuscript.

Hillside. (2008). Wiki for pattern sharing. Retrieved August 26, 2008, from http://hillside.net/Wiki/

Hitchcock, D., Verheij B. (2005). The Toulmin model today: Introduction to special issue of Argumentation on contemporary work using Stephen Edelston Toulmin's layout of arguments. *Argumentation*, 19(3): 255-258.

Hof, R. D. (2004). Something wiki this way comes. *Business Week*, (June): 7.

Hofstede, G. (1991). *Cultures and organizations: Software of the mind.* McGraw-Hill.

Holden, J. (2007). *Logging On: Culture, Participation and the Web.* London: Demos.

Holm, J. (2001). *Real World Applications of Topic Maps.* Paper presented at the XML 2001, Florida, USA.

Holmes, D. (1985). The Analysis of Literary Style – A Review. *Journal of the Royal Statistical Society. Series A (General), 148*(4), 328–341. doi:10.2307/2981893

Holsapple, C. W., & Joshi, K. D. (2000). An investigation of factors that influence the management of knowledge in organizations. *The Journal of Strategic Information Systems, 9*(2-3), 235–261. doi:10.1016/S0963-8687(00)00046-9

Horrocks, I., Parsia, B., Patel-Schneider, P., & Hendler, J. (2005). Semantic Web Architecture: Stack or Two Towers? In F. Fages & S. Soliman (Eds.), *Principles and Practice of Semantic Web Reasoning* (pp. 37-41). Dagstuhl Castle, Germany: Springer.

Horst, S. A., & Miller, D. (2006). *The Cell Phone: An Anthropology of Communication.* Oxform, UK: Berg.

Hough, A. (2007, November 23). Fraud warning for users of social networking sites. *Reuters.* Retrieved Dec 4, 2007, from http:today.reuters.co.uk/misc/

Howard A., & Levine, A. (2004). Where are the poor students? A conversation about social class and college attendance. *About Campus, 9*(4), 1924.

Huberty, C. J. (1994). *Applied Discriminant Analysis.* Hoboken, NJ: Wiley-Interscience.

Hughes, S. C., Wickersham, L., Ryan-Jones, D. L., & Smith, A. (2002). Overcoming social and psychological barriers to effective on-line collaboration. *Educational Technology & Society, 5*(1).

Hult, A. (2005). *Examination över nätet - en studie av 10 nätuniversitetskurser.* Umea, Sweden: UCER/ Umea Centre for Evaluation Research.

Hult, A. (2007). *Examinationen är kursen - En analys av examination i kurser över nätet.* Swedish Agency for Networks and cooperation in Higher Education.

Huysman, M., & de Wit, D. (2003) A critical evaluation of knowledge management practices. In M. S. Ackerman, V. Pipek, and V. Wulf (Eds.) *Sharing knowledge: Beyond knowledge management*, (pp. 27-55). Cambridge, MA: The MIT Press.

IBM & Cisco (2007). *Enhancing the Way People Work Through Unified Communication*, [White paper].

IEEE Std 1348. (1995). IEEE Recommended Practice for the Adoption of Computer-Aided Software Engineering (CASE) Tools.

Iivari, J., & Lyytinen, K. (1998). Research on information systems development in Scandinavia—Unity in plurality. *Scandinavian Journal of Information Systems*, 10, 135-186.

INE (2005). Estructura y demografía empresarial. *Directorio Central de Empresas* (DIRCE). Retrieved April, 2006, from www.ine.es/inebase

International Technology Education Association. (2000/2002). *Standards for technological literacy: Content for the study of technology*. Reston, VA: Author.

Jackson, M. C. (2000). *Systems approaches to management*. New York: Kluwer Academic/ Plenum Publishers.

Jackson, M. C. (2003). *Systems thinking: Creative holism for managers*. Chichester, England: John Wiley & Sons.

Jacobs, G. (2006). Imagining the flowers, but working the rich and heavy clay: Participation and empowerment in action research for health. *Educational Action Research*, 14(4), 569—581.

James Rhem & Associates, LLC., (1996-2003). *Active Learning: Creating Excitement in the Classroom, The National Teaching & Learning Forum*. Retrieved August 11, 2008, from http://www.ntlf.com/html/lib/bib/91-9dig.htm

Jansson, M. (2007). *Participation, knowledges and experiences: Design of IT-Systems in e-home health care*. Doctoral Thesis, Department of Business Administration and Social Science, Luleå University of Technology, Luleå, Sweden.

Jensen, C., & Scacchi, W. (2007). Role migration and advancement processes in OSSD projects: A comparative case study. In *Proceedings of the 29th International Conference on Software Engineering*, (pp 364-374). Washington, DC: IEEE Computer Society.

John, M. (2008). Mind the Gap-Open Source is a Player. *Futurelab-Innovation in Education*. Retrieved August 23, 2008, from http://www.futurelab.org.uk/resources/publications_reports_articles/web_articles/Web_Article1065

Johnson, B. (2007, Aug 13). Facebook's Code Leak Raises Fears of Fraud. *Guardian Unlimited*. Retrieved April 12, 2007, from http://www.guardian.co.uk/technology/2007/aug/13/internet

Johnson, R. E. (1997). Frameworks = (Components + Patterns). *Communications of the ACM*, 40(10), 39–42. doi:10.1145/262793.262799

Johnson, S. (2001). *Emergence: the connected lives of ants, brains, cities, and software*. London: Scribner.

Johnson, S. D., & Aragon, S. A. (2003). An instructional strategy framework for online learning environments. In S. A. Aragon (Ed.), *Facilitating learning in online environments, new directions for adult and continuing education* (pp. 10, 31-44). San Francisco: Jossey-Bass.

Joinson, A. (2008). 'Looking at,' 'looking up' or 'keeping up with people?' motives and uses of facebook. *Proceedings from CHI 2008, conference on human factors in computing systems*, April 5-10, Florence, Italy.

Jordan, T. (1999). *Cyberpower: the culture and politics of cyberspace and the internet*. London: Routledge.

Jøsang, A., Ismail, R. and C. Boyd 2007. A survey of trusts and reputation systems for online service provision. *Decision Support Systems*, 43: 618-644.

Kantor, P. B. (1989). Scholars Cross Reference System. In *Annual Research Report of OCLC*, OCLC, Dublin, OH (pp. 26-27).

Kantor, P. B. (1993). The Adaptive Library Network

Interface: A Historical Overview and Interim Report. *Library Hi Tech, 11*, 81–92. doi:10.1108/eb047897

Kantor, P. B. Melamed, B., Boros, E., & Menkov, V. (1999). The Information Quest: A Dynamic Model of User's Information Needs. In L. Woods, (Ed.) *Proceedings of the 62nd Annual Meeting of the American Society for Information Science,* (pp. 536-545).

Kantor, P. B., Boros, E., Melamed, B., Meñkov, V., & Shapira, B. (2000). ANTWORLD: Capturing Human Intelligence in the Net. *Communications of the ACM, 43*(8), 112–115. doi:10.1145/345124.345162

Karamuftuoglu, M. (1998). Collaborative information retrieval: Toward a social informatics view of IR interaction. *Journal of the American Society for Information Science and Technology, 49*(12), 1070–1080. doi:10.1002/(SICI)1097-4571(1998)49:12<1070::AID-ASI3>3.0.CO;2-S

Kember, D. (2000). Misconceptions about the learning approaches, motivation and study practices of Asian students. *Higher Education, 40*, 99-121.

Kendall, L. (2002). *Hanging out in the virtual pub: identity, masculinities, and relationships online.* Berkeley, CA: University of California Press.

Kennedy, P. (2002). Learning cultures and learning styles: Myth-understandings about adult (Hong Kong) Chinese learners. *International Journal of Lifelong Education, 21*(5), 430-445.

Kessler, E. H. (2003). Leveraging e-R&D processes: A knowledge-based view. *Technovation, 23*, 905-915.

Khazanchi, D., & Zigurs, I. (2007). *An Assessment Framework for Discovering and Using Patterns in Virtual Project Management.* Paper presented at the Hawaii International Conference on System Science, Waikoloa, HI.

King, W. R., Marks, P. V. Jr, & McCoy, S. (2002). The most important issues in knowledge management. *Communications of the ACM, 45*(9), 93–97. doi:10.1145/567498.567505

Kirschner, P.A, Buckingham Shum, S.J. and C.S. Carr (eds.) 2003. *Visualizing Arguentation.* Spinger Verlag.

Kjeldskov, J., & Stage, J. (2004). New Techniques for Usability Evaluation of Mobile Systems. *International Journal of Human-Computer Studies, 60*(5-6): 599–620. doi:10.1016/j.ijhcs.2003.11.001

Klecka, W. R. (1980) *Discriminant analysis.* Sage University Paper series on quantitative applications in the social sciences, series no. 07-019. Thousand Oaks, CA: Sage.

Klein, M. (2007). *The MIT Deliberatorium: Enabling Effective Large-Scale Deliberation for Complex Problems.* MIT Sloan School of Management, Research Paper 4679-08. http://ssrn.com/abstract=1085295

Klein, M., Cioffi, M. and T. Malone (2007). *Achieving Collective Intelligence via Large Scale On-line Argumentation.* Working paper, MIT Center for Collective Intelligence, Cambridge (MA).

Kleinberg, J. (2006). Distributed social systems. *Proceedings from PODC'06, conference on principles of distributed computing,* July 22-26, Denver, CO.

km Sciences, Inc. (2006). *Knowledge and Collaboration for Project Managers.* Retrieved August 1, 2008 from http://whitepapers.itbusinessnet.com/whitepaper812/

Knight, D., Pearce, C. L., Smith, K. G., Olian, J. D., Sims, H. P., Smith, K. A., & Flood, P. (1999). Top management team diversity, group process, and strategic consensus. *Strategic Management Journal, 20*, 445-465.

Koenig, M. (2001). User education for KM: The problem we won't recognize. *KM World*, December.

Koh, J., Kim, Y.-G., Butler, B., & Bock, G.-W. (2007). Encouraging participation in virtual communities. *Communications of the ACM, 50*(2), 68–73. doi:10.1145/1216016.1216023

Kohavi, R., & Provost, F. (1998). Special issue on Applications of Machine Learning and the Knowledge Discovery Process. *Machine Learning, 30*(2-3).

Kohl, D. F. (2008). From the editor: Sacajawea, wikis and trusted guides. *Journal of Academic Librarian-*

ship, 34(5), 387-388.

Kolfschoten, G. L., & de Vreede, G. J. (2007). *The Collaboration Engineering Approach for Designing Collaboration Processes.* Paper presented at the CRIWG Conference, Bariloche, Argentina.

Kolfschoten, G. L., & Rouwette, E. (2006). *Choice Criteria for Facilitaition Techniques.* Paper presented at the First HICSS Symposium on Case and Field Studies of Collaboration, Kauai, HI.

Kolfschoten, G. L., & Rouwette, E. (2006). *Choice Criteria for Facilitation Techniques: A Preliminary Classification.* Paper presented at the International Conference on Group Decision and Negotiation, Karlsruhe, Germany.

Kolfschoten, G. L., & Santanen, E. L. (2007). *Reconceptualizing Generate ThinkLets: the Role of the Modifier.* Paper presented at the Hawaii International Conference on System Science, Waikoloa, HI.

Kolfschoten, G. L., & van der Hulst, S. (2006). *Collaboration Process Design Transition to Practitioners: Requirements from a Cognitive Load Perspective.* Paper presented at the International Conference on Group Decision and Negotiation, Karlsruhe, Germany.

Kolfschoten, G. L., & van Houten, S. P. A. (2007). *Predictable Patterns in Group Settings through the use of Rule Based Facilitation Interventions.* Paper presented at the International Conference on Group Decision and Negotiation conference, Mt. Tremblant, Canada.

Kolfschoten, G. L., & Veen, W. (2005). *Tool Support for GSS Session Design.* Paper presented at the Hawaii International Conference on System Sciences, Waikoloa, HI.

Kolfschoten, G. L., Appelman, J. H., Briggs, R. O., & de Vreede, G. J. (2004). *Recurring Patterns of Facilitation Interventions in GSS Sessions.* Paper presented at the Hawaii International Conference on System Sciences, Waikoloa, HI.

Kolfschoten, G. L., Briggs, R. O., Appelman, J. H., & de Vreede, G. J. (2004). *ThinkLets as Building Blocks for Collaboration Processes: A Further Conceptualization.*

Paper presented at the CRIWG conference, San Carlos, Costa Rica.

Kolfschoten, G. L., Briggs, R. O., de Vreede, G. J., Jacobs, P. H. M., & Appelman, J. H. (2006). Conceptual Foundation of the ThinkLet Concept for Collaboration Engineering. *International Journal of Human Computer Science, 64*(7), 611–621. doi:10.1016/j.ijhcs.2006.02.002

Kolfschoten, G. L., de Vreede, G. J., Briggs, R. O., & Sol, H. G. (2007). *Collaboration Engineerability.* Paper presented at the Group Decision and Negotiation conference, Mt Tremblant, Canada.

Kolfschoten, G. L., de Vreede, G. J., Chakrapani, A., & Koneri, P. (2006). *A Design Approach for Collaboration Engineering.* Paper presented at the First HICSS Symposium on Case and Field Studies of Collaboration, Kauai, HI.

Kolfschoten, G. L., den Hengst, M., & de Vreede, G. J. (2007). Issues in the Design of Facilitated Collaboration Processes. *Group Decision and Negotiation, 16*(4), 347–361. doi:10.1007/s10726-006-9054-6

Kolfschoten, G. L., Kosterbok, J., & Hoekstra, A. (2008). *A Transferable ThinkLet based Process Design for Integrity Risk Assessment in Government Organizations.* Paper presented at the International Conference on Group Decision and Negotiation, Coimbra, Portugal.

Kollock, P. (1999). The production of trust in online markets. *Advances in Group Processes, 16*(1), 99–123.

Korfiatis, N., & Naeve, A. (2005). Evaluating wiki contributions using social networks: A case study on Wikipedia. In *Proceedings of the First Online Conference on Metadata and Semantics Research.* Association for Information Systems.

KPMG Consulting (2000). *Knowledge Management Research Report.* London: KPMG Consulting.

Kushner, H., & Pacut, A. (1982). A Simulation Study of Decentralized Detection Problem. *IEEE Trans. On Automatic Control, 27*(5), 1116–1119. doi:10.1109/TAC.1982.1103071

Kussmaul, C., & Jack, R. (2009) Wikis for knowledge

management: Business cases, best practices, promises, & pitfalls. *Web 2.0: The Business Model*, Lytras, M. D., Damiani, E. and Ordóñez de Pablos, P., editors. Berlin: Springer.

La Russa, G., & Faggiano, E. (2004). Robo-eLC: Enhancing learning hypermedia with robotics. In *Proceedings of ICALT, Joensuu, Finland* (pp. 465-469).

Lampe, C., Ellison, N., & Steinfield, C. A. (2006). Face(book) in the crowd: Social searching vs. social browsing. *Proceedings of the CSCW '06, Conference on Computer Supported Cooperative Work*, November 4-8, Banff, Alberta, Canada.

Lange, P. (2007). Publicly private and privately public: Social networking on youtube. *Journal of Computer-Mediated Communication, 13*(1), 18. Retrieved December 4, 2007, from http://jcmc.indianna.edu/vol113/issue1/lange/html

Langefors, B. (1995). *Essays on infology.* Lund, Sweden: Studentlitteratur.

Lave, J., & Wenger, E. (1991). *Situated learning: Legitimate peripheral participation.* Cambridge, UK: Cambridge University.

Leadbeater, C. (2008). *We-think: The Power of Mass Creativity.* London: Profile Books Ltd.

Leadbeater, C., & Miller, P. (2004). *The pro-am revolution: how enthusiasts are changing our society and economy.* London: Demos.

Lee, E. Y. C., Chan, C. K. K., & Van Aalst, J. (2006). Students assessing their own collaborative knowledge building. *International Journal of Computer-Supported Collaborative Learning, 1*, 57–58. doi:10.1007/s11412-006-6844-4

Leevers, D. (2001). Collaboration and shared virtual environments—from metaphor to reality. In R. Earnshaw, R. Guedj, A. van Dam, & J. Vince (Eds.), *Frontiers of human-centered computing, online communities and virtual environments* (pp. 278–298). Springer.

Lenhart, A., Madden, M., & Hitlin, P. (2005). *Teens and Technology: Youth are leading the transition to a fully wired and mobile nation.* Washington, DC: Pew Internet & American Life.

Lerner, J., & Tirole, J. (2002). Some Simple Economics of Open Source. *The Journal of Industrial Economics, 46*(2), 125–156.

Leuf, B., & Cunningham, W. (2001). *The Wiki Way: Quick Collaboration on the Web.* Boston: Addison-Wesley Professional.

Lewis, P. J. (1992). Rich picture building in the Soft Systems Methodology. *European Journal of Information Systems, 1*, 351-360.

Liang, A., & McQueen, R. J. (1999). Computer assisted adult interactive learning in a multi-cultural environment. *Adult Learning, 11*(1), 26-29.

Lih, A. (2004). *Wikipedia as Participatory Journalism: Reliable Sources? Metrics for evaluating collaborative media as a news resource.* 5th International Symposium on Online Journalism (April 16-17, 2004), University of Texas at Austin.

Lim, J., & Zhong, Y. (2005). Cultural diversity, leadership, group size and collaborative learning systems: An experimental study. In *Proceedings of the 38th Hawaii International Conference on System Sciences.*

Limberg, L. (1999). Three conceptions of information seeking and use. In T.D. Wilson & D. K. Allen (Eds.), *Exploring the contexts of information behaviour. Proceedings of the Second International Conference on Research in Information Needs, Seeking, and Use in Different Contexts,* (pp. 116-135). London: Taylor Graham.

Lin, S. C., Chen, Y. C., & Yu, C. Y. (2006). Application of wiki collaboration system for value adding and knowledge aggregation in a digital archive project. *Journal of Educational Media and Library Science, 43*, 285–307.

LinkedIn Answers (n.d.). Retrieved from http://www.linkedin.com

Lipnack, J., & Stamps, J. (2000). *Virtual teams people working across boundaries with technology* (2nd ed.). New York: John Wiley & Sons.

Logan, D., et al. (2008). *Tribal Leadership*. New York: Collins.

Louridas, P. (2006). Using wikis in software development. *IEEE Software, 23*(2), 88–91. doi:10.1109/MS.2006.62

Loveland, T., & Harrison, H. L. (2006). Video Production: A New Technological Curricula.Preview. *Technology Teacher, 66*(3), 7–13.

Löwgren, J., & Stolterman, E. (1998). *Design av Informationsteknik - materialet utan egenskaper*. Lund, Sweden: Studentlitteratur.

Löwgren, J., & Stolterman, E. (2004). *Thoughtful interaction design. A design perspective on information technology*. Cambridge, MA: MIT Press.

Lueg, C. (2003). Knowledge sharing in online communities and its relevance to knowledge management in the e-business era. *International Journal of Electronic Business, 1*(2), 140–151. doi:10.1504/IJEB.2003.002170

Lukosch, S. (2003). *Transparent and Flexible Data Sharing for Synchronous Groupware*. Köln, Germany: JOSEF EUL VERLAG GmbH Lohmar.

Lukosch, S. (2007). Facilitating shared knowledge construction in collaborative learning. *Informatica, Special Issue on 'e-Society', 31*(2), 167-174.

Lukosch, S. (2008). Seamless Transition between Connected and Disconnected Collaborative Interaction. *Journal of Universal Computer Science, 14*(1), 59–87.

Lukosch, S., & Bourimi, M. (2008). Towards an Enhanced Adaptability and Usability of Web-based Collaborative Systems. *International Journal of Cooperative Information Systems, Special Issue on 'Groupware: Implementation, Design, and Use'*.

Lukosch, S., & Leisen, A. (2008). Dealing with Conflicting Modifications in a Wiki. In *WEBIST 2008 - Proceedings of the 4th International Conference on Web Information Systems and Technologies* (Vol. 2, pp. 5-15). Madeira, Portugal: INSTICC - Institute for Systems and Technologies of Information, Control, and Communication, Universidade da Madeira.

Lukosch, S., & Schümmer, T. (2006). Groupware Development Support with Technology Patterns. *International Journal of Human Computer Systems, 64*(7), 599–610. doi:10.1016/j.ijhcs.2006.02.006

Lukosch, S., & Schümmer, T. (2006). Groupware Development Support with Technology Patterns. *International Journal of Human Computer Studies, Special Issue on 'Theoretical and Empirical Advances in Groupware Research', 64*(7), 599-610.

Lukosch, S., & Schümmer, T. (2006). Making exam preparation an enjoyable experience. *International Journal of Interactive Technology and Smart Education, Special Issue on 'Computer Game-based Learning', 3*(4), 259-274.

Lupton, M. (2004). *The learning connection. Information literacy and the student experience*. Blackwood, Australia: Auslib Press.

Lynch, M. (2002). *The online educator*. London: Routledge.

MacCormack, A., Forbath, T., Brooks, P., & Kalaher, P. (2007). *Innovation through Global Collaboration: A New Source of Competitive Advantage*. Cambridge, MA: Harvard Business School. Retrieved August 1, 2008 from http://hbswk.hbs.edu/item/5760.html

Macdonald, J. (2002). Exploiting Online Interactivity to Enhance Assignment Development and Feedback in Distance Education, Open Learning. *The Journal of Open and Distance Learning, 16*(2), 179–189.

MacInnes, I., & Hu, L. (2005). Business models for online communities: The case of the virtual worlds industry in China. In *Proceedings of the Proceedings of the 38th Annual Hawaii International Conference on System Sciences*, (track 7, volume 07). University of Hawaii at Manoa.

MacMillan, P. (2001). *The Performance Factor*. Nashville, TN: Broadman & Holman Publishers.

Macpherson, K. (1999). The Development of Critical Thinking Skills in Undergraduate Supervisory Management Units: efficacy of student peer assessment.

Assessment & Evaluation in Higher Education, 24(3), 273–284. doi:10.1080/0260293990240302

Mader, S. (2008) *Wikipatterns: A practical guide to improving productivity and collaboration in your organization.* Hoboken, NJ: Wiley.

Madey, G., V. Freeh, and R. Tynan 2002. *The open source software development phenomenon: An analysis based on social network theory.* Americas Conference on Information Systems (AMCIS-2002).

Majchrzak, A., Wagner, C., & Yates, D. (2006). Corporate wiki users: Results of a survey. In *Proceedings of the 2006 International Symposium on Wikis*, (pp 99-104), Odense, Denmark: ACM Press.

Mancini, C., Buckingham Shum, S. 2006. Modelling Discourse in Contested Domains: a Semiotic and Cognitive Framework. *Int. J. of Human Computer Studies* (in press).

Mannan, M., & Oorschot, P. (2008). Privacy-enhanced sharing of personal content on the web. *WWW '08,* April 21-25, 2008, Beijing, China.

Manns, M. L., & Rising, L. (2005). *Fearless Change: Patterns for Introducing New Ideas.* Reading, MA: Addison-Wesley.

Marca, D. A., & McGowan, C. L. (1987). *SADT: Structured Analysis and Design Technique.* New York: McGraw Hill, Inc.

Marwick, A. (2001). Knowledge management technology. *IBM Systems Journal, 40*(4), 814-830.

Mason, D., & Pauleen, D. J. (2003). Perceptions of knowledge management: A qualitative analysis. *Journal of Knowledge Management, 7*(4), 38–48. doi:10.1108/13673270310492930

Maxwell, J. C. (2003). *Relationships 101: what every leader needs to know.*

Maybee, C. (2006). Undergraduate perceptions of information use: The basis for creating user-centered student information literacy instruction. *Journal of Academic Librarianship, 32*(1), 79-85.

Mayer, R. (1990). *IDEF0 Functional Modeling.* College Station, TX: Knowledge Based Systems, Inc.

Mayers, M., & Tan, F. (2002). Beyond models of national culture in information systems research. *Journal of Global Information Management, 10*(1), 24-32.

McDonough, W., & Braungart, M. (2002). *Cradle to Cradle: Remaking the Way We Make Things.* New York: North Point Press.

McLean, S., & Morrison, D. (2000). Sociodemographic characteristic of learners and participation in computer conferencing. *Journal of Distance Education, 15*(2).

McMillan, S. J., & Morrison, M. (2006). Coming of age with the internet: A qualitative exploration of how the internet has become an integral part of young people's lives. *New Media & Society, 8*(1), 73–95. doi:10.1177/1461444806059871

McSporran, M., & Young, S. (2001). Does gender matter in online learning? *Association for Learning Technology Journal (Alt-J), 9*(2), 3-15.

Mehlenbacher, B., Miller, C. R., Covington, D., & Larsen, J. S. (2000). Active and interactive learning online: A comparison of Web-based and conventional writing classes. *IEEE Transactions on Professional Communication, 43*(2), 166-184.

Mehlman, B. P. (2003). *ICT Literacy: Preparing the Digital Generation for the Age of Innovation.* Retrieved August 11, 2008, from http://www.technology.gov/Speeches/p_BPM_030124-DigGen.htm

Mehrotra, C. M. (2003). In defense of educational programs for older adults. *Educational Gerontology, 29,* 645-655.

Menard, S. (1995) *Applied logistic regression analysis.* Sage University Paper series on quantitative applications in the social sciences, series no. 07-106. Thousand Oaks, CA: Sage.

Mentzas, G. (1993). Coordination of joint tasks in organizational processes. *Journal of Information Technology, 8,* 139-150.

Meroño-Cerdan, A. (2005). Uso de tecnologías de grupo en pymes e influencia sobre el desempeño. *4th International Conference of the Iberoamerican Academy of Management, Lisbon, December.*

Merriam S. B., & Simpson, E. L. (2000). *A guide to research for educators and trainers of adults* (2nd ed.). Krieger Publishing Company.

Michailidou, A., & Economides, A. (2003). Elearn: Towards a collaborative educational virtual environment. *Journal of Information Technology Education, 2,* 131-152.

Micheletti, G., Manenti, P., & Eibisch, J. (2007). *A Construction Industry Brief. Benefiting the Bottom Line: Collaboration and Collaborative Technologies.* IDC Executive Brief, IDC EMEA. Retrieved August 1, 2008 from http://www.idc.com

Microsoft & Verizon (2006). *Meetings Around the World: The Impact of Collaboration on Business Performance,* [White paper].

Midgley, G. (2000). *Systemic intervention: Philosophy, methodology, and practice.* New York: Kluwer Academic/Plenum Publishers.

Mika, P. (2004). Social networks and the semantic web. *Proceedings of the IEEE/WIC/ACM International Conference on Web Intelligence,* 20-24 September, Beijing, China.

Miller, C. M. L., & Parlett, M. (1974). *Up to the mark: a study of the examination game.* London: SRHE.

Miller, D., & Slater, D. (2000). *Internet: An Ethnographic Approach.* London: Berg.

Mingers, J. (2007). Pluralism, realism, and truth: The keys to knowledge in information systems research. *International Journal of Information Technologies and the Systems Approach,* 1(1), 79-90.

Miniwatts Marketing Group. (2008). *World Internet Users and Population Stats.* Retrieved August 1, 2008, from http://www.internetworldstats.com/stats.htm

Mirijamdotter, A., & Somerville, M. M. (2004). Systems thinking in the workplace: Implications for organizational leadership. In *Proceedings of the 3rd International Conference on Systems Thinking and Management (ICSTM),* Philadelphia, PA.

Mirijamdotter, A., & Somerville, M. M. (2005). Dynamic action inquiry: A systems approach for knowledge based organizational learning. In *Proceedings of the 11th International Conference on Human-Computer Interaction (HCI'05).* Las Vegas, NV.

Mislove, A., Marcon, M., & Gummadi, K. (2007). Measurement and analysis of online social networks. *Internet Measurement Conference '07,* October 24-26, San Diego, CA.

Mitroff, I. I., Betz, F., Pondly, L. R., & Sagasty, F. (1974). On Managing Science In The Systems Age: Two Schemas For The Study Of Science As A Whole Systems Phenomenon. *TIMS Interfaces, 4*(3), 46–58. doi:10.1287/inte.4.3.46

Montgomery, E. (2007). Facebook: Fraudsters' Paradise? *Money.UK.MSN.com,* November 20, 2007. Retrieved December 4, from http://money.uk.msn.com/banking/id-fraud/article.aspx?cp-documentid=5481130

Moore, T. D., & Serva, M. A. (2007). Understanding member motivation for contributin to different types of virtual communities: A proposed framework. In *Proceedings of the 2007 ACM SIGMIS Computer Personnel Research Conference: The Global Information Technology Workforce, SIGMIS-CPR 2007,* (pp. 153-157).

Mori, J., Sugiyama, T., & Matsuo, Y. (2007). Real-world oriented information sharing using social Networks. *Proceedings from SIGGROUP '07 conference on supporting group work,* Sannibel Island, FL.

Moriyama, M. (2004). Innovation, management & strategy. In *ACM International Conference Proceeding Series: Vol. 60. Proceedings of the 6th international conference on Electronic commerce* (pp. 213-218). New York: ACM.

Mortenson, S. T. (2002). Sex, communication and cultural values: Individualism-collectivism as a mediator of sex differences in communication in two cultures.

Communication Reports, 15(1).

Mudur, S. (2001). On the need for cultural representation in interactive systems. In R. Earnshaw, R. Guedj, A. van Dam, & J. Vince (Eds.), *Frontiers of human-centered computing, online communities and virtual environments* (pp. 299-310). Springer.

Muirhead, B. (2000). Enhancing social interaction in computer-mediated distance education. *Educational Technology & Society, 3*(4), 4-11.

Myers, B. A., & Rosson, M. B. (1992). Survey on user interface programming. In *Proceedings of CHI'92, Monterey, CA* (pp. 195-202). New York: ACM, pp. 195-202.

Myers, M., & Tan, F. (2002). Beyond models of national culture in information systems research. *Journal of Global Information Management, 10*(1), 24-32.

Nardi, B. A. (2005). Beyond bandwidth: Dimensions of connection in interpersonal communication. *Computer Supported Cooperative Work, 14*, 91–130. doi:10.1007/s10606-004-8127-9

National Academy of Sciences. (1997). *Preparing for the 21st Century: The Education Imperative.*

Naumann, F. (2002). *Quality-driven Query Answering for Integrated Information Systems.* Berlin: Springer-Verlag. Retrieved on November 9, 2002 from http://link.springer.de/link/service/series/0558/tocs/t2261.htm

Newman, R. (2006). Cybercrime, identity theft and fraud: practicing safe internet – Nework security threats and vulnerabilities. *InfoSecCD Conference '06*, September 22-23, 2006, Kennesaw, GA.

Ng, K. B., Kantor, P., Strzalkowski, T., Wacholder, N., Tang, R., & Bai, B. (2006). Automated Judgment of Document Qualities. [JASIS]. *Journal of the American Society for Information Science and Technology, 57*(9), 1155–1164. doi:10.1002/asi.20393

Ng, K. B., Kantor, P., Tang, R., Rittman, R., Small, S., Song, P., et al. (2003). Identification of effective predictive variables for document qualities. In R. J. Todd (Ed.) *Proceedings of 2003 Annual Meeting of American Society*

for Information Science and Technology (pp. 221-229.) Medford, NJ: Information Today, Inc.

Nichols, D. M., & Twidale, M. B. (2003). The usability of open source software. *First Monday 8*(1). Retrieved September 15, 2005 from: http://firstmonday.org/issues/issue81/nichols/, 15 September 2005)

Nichols, D. M., Thomson, A., Kirsten, T., & Yeates, S. (2001). Usability and open-source software development. In Elizabeth E. Kemp, Chris Phillips, Kinshuk, and & John J. Haynes, (Editors), *Symposium on Computer Human Interaction*, Palmerston North, New Zealand, (pp. 49–54). New York: ACM SIGCHI NZ.

Niegemann, H. M., & Domagk, S. (2005). *ELEN Project Evaluation Report.* Retrieved from http://www2tisip.no/E-LEN

Nielsen, J. (1990). Big playbacks from discount usability. *IEEE Software, 3*, 107–108.

Nielsen, J. (2006). Participation inequality: Lurkers vs. contributors in internet communities. *Jakob Nielsen's Alertbox.* Retrieved May 2008 from http://www.useit.com/alertbox/participation_inequality.html.

Nielsen, J., & Molich, R. (1990). Heuristic Evaluation of User Interfaces. *Proceedings of CHI Conference on Human Factors in Computing Systems,* (pp. 249-256). New York: ACM, 249-256.

Nijholt, A. (2005). Human and virtual agents interacting in the virtuality continuum. In *Proceedings of ACTAS II: IX Symposio Internacional de Comunicacion Social, Centro de Linguistica Aplicade, Santiago de Cuba* (pp. 551-558).

Noll, J. (2008). Open Source Development, Communities and Quality. In Barbara Russo, Ernesto E. Damiani, Scott S. Hissam, Björn B. Lundell, Giancarlo G. Succi (Eds.), *IFIP International Federation for Information Processing,* (Volume 275, pp. 69–79). Boston: Springer.

Nonaka, I. (1991). The knowledge-creating company. *Harvard Business Review, 69*(6), 96–104.

Nonaka, I., & Takeuchi, H. (1995) *The Knowledge-Creating Company: How Japanese Companies Cre-*

ate the Dynamics of Innovation. Oxford, UK: Oxford University Press.

Noolan, T. (2008). The Role of Individual Trust in e-Collaboration. In N. Kock, (Ed.) *Encyclopedia of E-Collaboration* (pp. 534-539). Hershey, PA: Information Science Reference.

Norum, K. E. (2001). Appreciative design. *Systems Research and Behavioural Science, 18*, 323-333.

Nunamaker, J., Briggs, R., Mittleman, D., Vogel, D., & Balthazard, P. (1997). Lessons from a dozen years of group support systems research: A discussion of lab and field findings. *Journal of Management Information Systems, 13*(3), 63-207.

O'Conner, M., & Herlocker, J. (1999). Clustering Items for Collaborative Filtering. In *Proceedings of the ACM SIGIR Workshop on Recommender Systems.*

O'Dell, C., & Grayson, C. J. (1998) *If Only We Knew What We Know: The Transfer of Internal Knowledge and Best Practice* (1st Ed). New York: Free Press.

O'Donovan, B., Price, M., & Rust, C. (2004). Know what I mean? Enhancing student understanding of assessment standards and criteria. *Teaching in Higher Education, 9*(3), 325–335. doi:10.1080/1356251042000216642

O'Mahony, S., & Ferraro, F. (2007). The emergence of governance in an open source community. *Academy of Management Journal, 50*(5), 1079–1106.

O'Neill, P., & Sohal, A. S. (1999). Business Process Reengineering, A Review of Recent Literature. *Technovation, 19*(9), 571–581. doi:10.1016/S0166-4972(99)00059-0

O'Reilly, T. (2005). *What Is Web 2.0: Design Patterns and Business Models for the Next Generation of Software.* Retrieved October 8, 2007, from http://www.oreillynet.com/pub/a/oreilly/tim/news/2005/09/30/what-is-web-20.html

Oberg, D. (1995). *Sustaining the vision: A selection of conference papers.* 24th International Association of School Librarianship Conference July 1995, (pp. 17-25). Worcester, UK: Worcester College of Higher Education.

Obidah, J. (2000). Mediating boundaries of race, class and professorial authority as a critical multiculturalist. *Teachers College Record, 102*, 1035-1061.

Oehlman, P., & Moore, R. (2007). Getting them to pay attention. *CSLA Journal, 31*(1), 11–13.

Olson, D. R. (1994), *The world on paper.* Cambridge, UK: Cambridge University press.

Ong, W. J. (1982) *Orality and literacy: The Technologizing of the Word.* New York: Methuen.

Orsmond, P., Merry, S., & Reiling, K. (1996). The importance of marking criteria in peer assessment. *Assessment & Evaluation in Higher Education, 21*(3), 239–249. doi:10.1080/0260293960210304

Orsmond, P., Merry, S., & Reiling, K. (1997). A study in self-assessment; tutor and students' perceptions of performance criteria. *Assessment & Evaluation in Higher Education, 22*(4), 357–369. doi:10.1080/0260293970220401

Oster, C., & Brown, K. (2002, January 23). AIG: A complex industry, a very complex company. *The Wall Street Journal Western Edition*, (p. C16).

Owens, T., & Kelley, R. (2006). The Next Job Boom: The 10 fastest-growing jobs. *Business 2.0 Magazine.* Retrieved August 22, 2008 from http://money.cnn.com/2006/05/02/technology/business2_nextjobboom_hotjobs/index.htm

Palloff, R. M., & Pratt, K. (1999). *Building Learning Communities in Cyberspace - Effective Strategies for the Online Classroom.* San Francisco: Jossey Bass Wiley.

Partnership for 21st Century Skills (2004). *Framework for 21st Century Learning.* Retrieved August 11, 2008 from http://www.21stcenturyskills.org/

Patel-Schneider, P. F. (2005). A Revised Architecture for Semantic Web Reasoning. In F. Fages & S. Soliman (Eds.), *Principles and Practice of Semantic Web Reasoning* (pp. 32-36). Dagstuhl Castle, Germany: Springer.

Pathak, J. (2004). *Peer-to-Peer Semantic Web Services: A Symbiotic*

Patrick, C. (1937). Creative Thought in Artists. *The*

Journal of Psychology, 4.

Patterson, J. F., Day, M., & Kucan, J. (1996). Notification Servers for Synchronous Groupware. In *Proceedings of the ACM 1996 Conference on Computer Supported Cooperative Work* (pp. 122-129), Boston.

Paulk, M. C., Weber, C. V., Curtis, B., & Chrissis, M. B. (1995). *The Capability Maturity Model: Guidelines for Improving the Software Process*. New York: Addison-Wesley.

Paulsen, M., & St. John, E. P. (2002). Social class and college costs: Examining between college choice and persistence. *The Journal of Higher Education, 73*(2), 189-236.

Paulus, P. B., Legett, K., Dzindolet, M. T., Coskun, H., & Putman, V. L. (2002). Social and cognitive influences in group brainstorming: Prediction of production gains and losses. In W. Stroebe & M. Hewstone (Eds.), *European review of social psychology* (pp. 299-325). London: Wiley.

Pausch, R. (1995). A Brief Architectural Overview of Alice, a Rapid Prototyping System for Virtual Reality. *IEEE Computer Graphics and Applications*. Retrieved August 11, 2008, from http://www.cs.cmu.edu/~stage3/publications/95/journals/IEEEcomputer/CGandA/paper.html

Pautasso, C., & Zimmermann, O. (2008). Restful web services vs. "big"' web services: making the right architectural decision. In *WWW '08: Proceedings of the 17th international conference on World Wide Web* (pp. 805-814). New York: ACM.

Pemberton, L., & Griffiths, R. (2003). Usability evaluation techniques for interactive television. *Proc. HCI International*.

Pennock, D., Horvitz, E., Lawrence, S. C., & Giles, L. (2000). Collaborative Filtering by Personality Diagnosis: A Hybrid Memory- and Model-Based Approach. *Proceedings of the 16th Conference on Uncertainty in Artificial Intelligence*, UAI 2000.

Pepper, S. (2002). *The TAO of Topic Maps*. Retrieved January 12, 2006, from http://www.ontopia.net/topic-maps/materials/tao.html

Pepper, S. (2002). *Ten Theses on Topic Maps and RDF*. Retrieved March 23, 2007, from http://www.ontopia.net/topicmaps/materials/rdf.html

Pepper, S., & Schwab, S. (2003). *Curing the Web's Identity Crisis*. Retrieved November 23, 2004, from http://www.ontopia.net/topicmaps/materials/identitycrisis.html#Pepper2003

Perelman, C., Olbrecths-Tyteca, L. (1969). *The New Rhetoric: A Treatise on Argumentation*. Notre Dame (IN): University of Notre Dame Press.

Perkowitz, M., & Etzioni, O. (2000). Towards adaptive web sites: Conceptual framework and case study. *Artificial Intelligence, 118*(1-2), 245–275. doi:10.1016/S0004-3702(99)00098-3

Pfister, H.-R., Schuckmann, C., Beck-Wilson, J., & Wessner, M. (1998). The Metaphor of Virtual Rooms in the Cooperative Learning Environment CLear. In N. Streitz, S. Konomi & H. Burkhardt (Eds.), *Cooperative Buildings - Integrating Information, Organization and Architecture. Proceedings of CoBuild'98* (pp. 107-113). Heidelberg, Germany: Springer.

Pinsonneault, A., & Caya, O. (2005). Virtual teams: What we know, what we don't know. *International Journal of e-Collaboration, 1*(3), 1–16.

Pinsonneault, A., & Kraemer, K. L. (1990). The effects of electronic meetings on group processes and outcomes: An assessment of the empirical research. *European Journal of Operations Research, 46*(2), 143-161.

Population Reference Bureau. (2002). *The Changing Age Structure of U.S. Teachers*. Retrieved on August 15, 2008 from http://www.prb.org/Articles/2002/TheChangingAgeStructureofUSTeachers.aspx

Potter, R. E., & Bathazard, P. A. (2002). Understanding human interactions and performance in the virtual team. *Journal of Information Technology Theory and Application (JITTA), 4*(1), 1-23.

Powell, A., Piccoli, G., & Ives, B. (2004). Virtual

teams: A review of current literature and directions for future research. *ACM SIGMIS Database*, *35*(1), 6–36. doi:10.1145/968464.968467

Preece, J. (2000). *Online Communities*. Chichester, UK: John Wiley & Sons, Inc.

Preibusch, S., Hoser, B., Gurses, S., & Berebdt, B. (2007, June). Ubiquitous social networks – opportunities and challenges for Privacy-aware user modelling. *Proceedings of the Data Modelling Workshop*, Corfu, Greece. Retrieved December 4, 2007, from http://vasarely.wiwi. hu-berlin.de/DM.UM07/Proceedings/05-Preibusch.pdf

Prensky, M. (2001). *Digital Game-Based Learning*. New York: McGraw-Hill Education.

Prensky, M. (2001). Do They Really Think Differently? *Horizon*, *9*(6).

Prensky, M. (2001). Digital Natives, Digital Immigrants. *Horizon*, *9*(5).

Prensky, M. (2008). *Programming: The New Literacy*. Retrieved August 13, 2008, from Edutopia website: http:// www.edutopia.org/programming

Priedhorsky, R., Chen, J., Lam, S. K., Panciera, K., Terveen, L., & Riedl, J. (2007). Creating, destroying, and restoring value in Wikipedia. In *Proceedings of the 2007 International ACM Conference on Supporting Group Work* (GROUP 2007), Sanibel Island, FL.

Prins, F. J., Sluijsmans, D., Kirschner, P. A., & Strijbos, J.-W. (2005). Formative peer assessment in a CSCL environment: a case study. *Assessment & Evaluation in Higher Education*, *30*(4), 417–444. doi:10.1080/02602930500099219

Rahwan, I., Zablith, F. and C. Reed (2007). Laying the foundations for a World Wide Argument Web. *Artificial Intelligence* (in press).

Raman, M., Ryan, T., & Olfman, L. (2005). Designing knowledge management systems for teaching and learning with wiki technology. *Journal of Information Systems Education*, *16*(3), 311–320.

Randerson, J. (2007). Social network sites do not deepen friendships. *The Guardian*, September 10. Retrieved December 4, 2007, from http://guardian.co.uk/science/2007/ sep/10/socialnetwork/print

Rapoport, R. (1970). Three dilemmas of action research. *Human Relations*, *23*, 499-513.

Raybourn, E. M. (2001). Designing an emergent culture of negotiation in collaborative virtual communities: The DomeCityMOO simulation. In E. Churchill, D. Snowden, & A. Munro (Eds.), *Collaborative virtual environments* (pp. 247-264). Springer.

Raybourn, E. M., Kings, N. J., & Davies, J. (2003). Adding cultural signposts in adaptive community-based environments [Special issue on intelligent community-based systems]. *Interacting With Computers: The Interdisciplinary Journal of Human-Computer Interaction*, *15*(1), 91-107. Elsevier Science Ireland Ltd.

Raymond, E. (1999). *The revenge of the hackers*. In M. Stone, S. Ockman, and & C. DiBona (Editors), *Open Sources: Voices from the Open Source Revolution* (pp. 207-219). Sebastopol, Calif.: O'Reilly & Associates.

Raymond, E.S. 2001. *The cathedral and the bazaar*. Sebastopol (CA): O'Reilly.

Relationship for Knowledge Sharing. Term Project Work for Theory of Distributed Algorithms, Iowa State University, Ames, IA.

Rheingold, H. (2000). *The virtual community*. Cambridge, MA: MIT Press.

Rheingold, H. (2003). *Smart Mobs: The Next Social Revolution*. New York: Perseus Books, U.S.

Rich, M. (1997). A learning community on the Internet: An exercise with masters students. In *Proceedings of Americas Conference on Information Systems*, Indianapolis.

Richardson, J. A., & Turner, A. (2000). A large-scale "local" evaluation of students' learning experiences using virtual learning environments. *Educational Technology & Society*, *3*(4).

Rising, L. (2001). *Design Patterns in Communication*

Software. Cambridge, UK: Cambridge University Press.

Riskin, S. (2005). The Chicago Ninety. *School Library Journal, 51*(11), 50–51.

Rittman, R., Wacholder, N., Kantor, P., Ng, K. B., Strzalkowski, T., & Sun, Y. (2004). Adjectives as indicators of subjectivity in documents. *Proceedings of the 67th Annual Meeting of the American Society for Information Science and Technology*, (pp. 349-359).

Rodriguez-Martinez, M. (2004). *Smart Mirrors: Peer-to-Peer Web Services for Publishing Electronic Documents*. Presented at International Workshop on Research Issues on Data Engineering: Web Services for E-Commerce and E-Government Applications (RIDE'04), Boston, MA.

Rogers, E., Somerville, M. M., & Randles, A. (2005). A user-centered content architecture for an academic digital research portal. In P. Kommers & G. Richards (Eds.), *Proceedings of ED-MEDIA 2005—World Conference on Educational Multimedia, Hypermedia, & Telecommunications*, Montreal, Canada, (pp. 1172-1177). Chesapeake, VA: Association for the Advancement of Computing in Education.

Rose, J. (2002). Interaction, transformation and information systems development - an extended application of soft systems methodology. *Information Technology & People, 15*(3), 242-268.

Roseman, M., & Greenberg, S. (1996). Building Real-Time Groupware with GroupKit, A Groupware Toolkit. *ACM Transactions on Computer-Human Interaction, 3*(1), 66–106. doi:10.1145/226159.226162

Rosen, C. (2007). Virtual friendship and the new narcissism. *New Atlantis (Washington, D.C.), 17*, 15–31.

Rosenhead, J., Mingers, J. 2001. *Rational analysis for a problematic world revisited: Problem structuring method for uncertainty and conflict*. Chichester (UK): John Wiley & Son.

Route 21 (2007). *21st Century Skills in West Virginia*. Retrieved August 12, 2008, from Welcome to Route 21: Retrieved August 11, 2008, from http://

www.21stcenturyskills.org/documents/p21_wv2008.pdf

Rovai, A. A. P. (2002). A preliminary look at the structural differences of higher education classroom communities in traditional and ALN courses. *Journal of Asynchronous Learning Networks, 6*(1), 41-56.

Rubenstein-Montano, B., Liebowitz, J., Buchwalter, J., McCaw, D., Newman, B., Rebeck, K., & The Knowledge Management Methodology Team (2001). A system thinking framework for knowledge management. *Decision Support Systems, 31*(1), 5-16.

Rudman, J. (1997). The state of authorship attribution studies: Some problems and solutions. *Computers and the Humanities, 31*(4), 351–365. doi:10.1023/A:1001018624850

Rummler, S. (2007, March). *After EIA: Post-Methodology IA*. Poster presentation at the Information Architecture Summit sponsored by the American Society for Information Science and Technology, Las Vegas, NV.

Sa, E., Teixeira, J., & Fernandes, C. (2007). Towards a Collaborative Learning Flow Pattern using Educational Games in Learning Activities. In G. Richards (Ed.), *Proceedings of World Conference on E-Learning in Corporate, Government, Healthcare, and Higher Education 2007* (pp. 6483-6488). Chesapeake, VA: AACE.

Sadler, R. D. (2005). Interpretations of criteria-based assessment and grading in higher education. *Assessment & Evaluation in Higher Education, 30*(2), 175–194. doi:10.1080/0260293042000264262

Sadler, R. D. (2008). Indeterminacy in the use of preset criteria for assessment and grading. *Assessment & Evaluation in Higher Education, iFirst Article*, April 2008, 1-20.

Sainsbury, E. J., & Walker, R. A. (2008). Assessment as a vehicle for learning: extending collaboration into testing. *Assessment & Evaluation in Higher Education, 33*(2), 103–117. doi:10.1080/02602930601127844

Sallnas, E. (2005). Effects of communication mode on social presence, virtual presence, and performance in collaborative virtual environments. *Presence, 14*(4),

434–449. doi:10.1162/105474605774785253

Salmon, G. K. (2000). *E-moderating the Key to Teaching & Learning Online*. London: RoutledgeFarmer.

Santanen, E. L., & de Vreede, G. J. (2004). *Creative Approaches to Measuring Creativity: Comparing the Effectiveness of Four Divergence ThinkLets*. Paper presented at the Hawaiian International Conference on System Sciences, Waikoloa, HI.

Saracevic, T. (1975). Relevance: A review of and a framework for the thinking on the notion in information science. *Journal of the American Society for Information Science American Society for Information Science, 26*(6), 321–343. doi:10.1002/asi.4630260604

Saracevic, T. (1996). Relevance reconsidered. Information science: Integration in perspectives. *Proceedings of the Second Conference on Conceptions of Library and Information Science*, Copenhagen, Denmark, (pp. 201-218).

Sawhney, M., & Prandelli, E. (2000). Communities of creation: Managing distributed innovation in turbulent markets. *California Management Review, 42*(4), 24-54.

Sawyer, K. (2007). *Group Genius: The Creative Power of Collaboration*. New York, NY: Perseus Books Group.

Scacchi, W. (2002). Understanding the Requirements for Developing Open Source Software Systems. *IEE Proceedings Software, 149*(1), pp. 24-39.

Schaffert, S. (2001). *RDF and RDF Schema: An Overview*. Retrieved October 3, 2006, from http://www.schaffert.eu/download/slides/rdf_overview.pdf

Schaffert, S. (2006). IkeWiki: A semantic wiki for collaborative knowledge management. *1st International Workshop on Semantic Technologies in Collaborative Applications (STIC'06)*, Manchester, UK.

Schank, R. C. (1986). *Explanation Patterns: Understanding Mechanically and Creatively*. Hillsdale (NJ): Lawrence Erlbaum.

Schiano, D., Nardi, B., Gumbrecht, M., & Swartz, L. (2004). Blogging by the rest of us. *Proceedings in CHI*

2004, Conference on Human Factors in Computing Systems, April 2004, Vienna, Austria.

Schuckmann, C., Kirchner, L., Schümmer, J., & Haake, J. M. (1996). Designing object-oriented synchronous groupware with COAST. In *Proceedings of the ACM 1996 Conference on Computer Supported Cooperative Work* (pp. 30-38), Boston.

Schümmer, T., & Lukosch, S. (2006). Structure-preserving transformations in pattern-driven groupware development. *International Journal of Computer Applications in Technology, Special Issue on 'Patterns for Collaborative Systems', 25*(2/3), 155-166.

Schümmer, T., & Lukosch, S. (2007). *Patterns for Computer-Mediated Interaction*. Chichester, UK: John Wiley & Sons, Inc.

Schümmer, T., Lukosch, S., & Haake, J. M. (2005). Teaching Distributed Software Development with the Project Method. In T. Koschmann, D. D. Suthers & T.-W. Chan (Eds.), *Computer Supported Collaborative Learning 2005: The Next 10 Years!* (pp. 577-586). Mahwah: Lawrence Erlbaum Associates.

Schümmer, T., Lukosch, S., & Slagter, R. (2006). Using Patterns to empower End-users - The Oregon Software Development Process for Groupware. *International Journal of Cooperative Information Systems, Special Issue on '11th International Workshop on Groupware (CRIWG'05)', 15*(2), 259-288.

Schwartz, J., Stagner, J., & Morrison, W. (2006). *Kid's Programming Language (KPL)*. Presented at ACM SIGRAPH2006, Boston, MA.

Schwarz, R. M. (1994). *The Skilled Facilitator*. San Francisco: Jossey-Bass Publishers.

Selim, H. M. (2003). An empirical investigation of student acceptance of course Websites. *Computers & Education, 40*, 343-360.

Sell, D., da Silva, D. C., et al. (2008). SBI: a semantic framework to support business intelligence. In *Proceedings of the first international workshop on Ontology-supported business intelligence* (Article 11). New York:

ACM.

Senge, P.M. (1990). *The Fifth Discipline. The Art & Practice of The Learning Organization*. New York: Dubbleday/Currency

Shah, J., & Murtaza, M. (2005). Effective customer relationship management through Web services. *The Journal of Computer Information Systems, 46*(1), 98-109.

Shah, S.K 2006. Motivation, governance and the viability of hybrid forms in open source development. *Management Science*, 52(7): 1000 -1014.

Sheffield, J. (2004). The Design of GSS-Enabled Interventions: A Habermasian Perspective. *Group Decision and Negotiation, 13*(5), 415–435. doi:10.1023/B:GRUP.0000045750.48336.f7

Shepherd, M. M., Briggs, R. O., Reinig, B. A., Yen, J., & Nunamaker, J. F. Jr. (1996). Social Comparison to Improve Electronic Brainstorming: Beyond Anonymity. *Journal of Management Information Systems, 12*(3), 155–170.

Sifry, D. (2007). *State of the Live Web*, April 2007. Retrieved November 3rd, 2007, from http://www.sifry.com/alerts/archives/000493.html

Simon, H. A. (1973). The Structure of Ill Structured Problems. *Artificial Intelligence, 4*(3-4), 181–201. doi:10.1016/0004-3702(73)90011-8

Siniscalco, M. T. (2002). *A Statistical Profile of the Teaching Profession*. International Labour Organization and United Nations Educational, Scientific and Cultural Organization.

Skyrme, D. (1998). Knowledge management solutions - The IT contribution. Retrieved May, 2006, from http://www.skyrme.com/pubs/acm0398.doc

Slater, D. (2002). Social relationships and identity on/off-line. In L. Lievrouw & S. Livingstone (Eds.), *Handbook of New Media: Social Shaping and Consequences of ICTs*. London: Sage.

Slevin, J. (2000). *The Internet and Society*. Cambridge, UK: Polity Press.

Small, S., et al. (2004). HITIQA: Towards Analytical Question Answering. In *the Proceedings of The 20th International Conference on Computational Linguistics (Coling 2004)*, Geneva, Switzerland, August 2004.

Smeaton, A. F., & Berrut, C. (1996). *Thresholding postings lists, query expansion by word-word distances and POS tagging of Spanish text*. Paper presented at the fourth text retrieval conferences, Gaithersburg, MD.

Smith, M., & Kollock, P. (Eds.). (1999). *Communities in cyberspace*. London: Routledge.

Smith, S., Engen, D., Mankoski, A., Frishberg, N., Pedersen, N., & Benson, C. (2001). GNOME Usability Study Report. *Sun GNOME Human Computer Interaction Laboratory*.

Smyth, B. (2004). Exploiting Query Repetition and Regularity in an Adaptive Community-Based Web Search Engine . *User Modeling and User-Adapted Interaction, 14*(5), 383–423. doi:10.1007/s11257-004-5270-4

Smyth, B., et al. (2003). I-SPY -- Anonymous, Community-Based Personalization by Collaborative Meta-Search. In *Proceedings of the 23rd SGAI International Conference on Innovative Techniques and Applications of Artificial Intelligence, 2003*.

Snee, R. D. (2004). Six-Sigma: the evolution of 100 years of business improvement methodology. *International Journal of Six Sigma and Competitive Advantage, 1*(1), 4–20. doi:10.1504/IJSSCA.2004.005274

Snowden, D. (2002). Complex acts of knowing: Paradox and descriptive self-awareness. *Journal of Knowledge Management, 6*(2), 100–111. doi:10.1108/13673270210424639

Snowden, D. (2006). Whence goeth KM? *Cognitive Edge*. Retrieved May 12, 2008, from http://www.cognitive-edge.com/2006/11/whence_goeth_km.php

Snyder, B. R. (1971). *The hidden curriculum*. New York: Knopf.

Sol, H. G. (1982). *Simulation in information systems development*. Groningen, the Netherlands: Rijksuniversiteit Groningen.

Somerville, M. M., & Brar, N. (2006). Collaborative co-design: The Cal Poly digital teaching library user centric approach. In *Information Access for Global Access: Proceedings of the International Conference on Digital Libraries (ICDL 2006)*, (pp. 175-187). New Delhi, India.

Somerville, M. M., & Brar, N. (2007). *Toward co-creation of knowledge in the Interaction Age: An organisational case study.* (Eds.) H. K. Kaul and S. Kaul, *Papers of the Tenth National Convention on Knowledge, Library and Information Networking* (NACLIN 2007), (pp. 367-376). New Delhi, India: DELNET.

Somerville, M. M., & Brar, N. (2008). A user-centered and evidence-based approach for digital library projects. *The Electronic Library* (in press).

Somerville, M. M., & Collins, L. (2008). Collaborative design: A learner-centered library planning approach. *The Electronic Library* (in press).

Somerville, M. M., & Harlan, S. (2008). From information commons to learning commons and learning spaces: An evolutionary context. In B. Schader (ed.), *Learning Commons: Evolution and Collaborative Essentials*, (pp. 1-36). Oxford, England: Chandos Publishing.

Somerville, M. M., & Howard, Z. (2008). Systems thinking: An approach for advancing workplace information literacy. *Australian Library Journal.* (in press)

Somerville, M. M., & Mirijamdotter, A. (2005). Working smarter: An applied model for 'better thinking' in dynamic information organizations. *Currents and Convergence - Navigating the Rivers of Change. Proceedings of the 12ᵗʰ National Conference of the Association of College and Research Libraries* (ACRL), (pp. 103-111). Chicago: Association of College and Research Libraries.

Somerville, M. M., & Nino, M. (2007). Collaborative co-design: A user-centric approach for advancement of organizational learning, *Performance Measurement and Metrics: The International Journal for Library and Information Services*, 8(3), 180-188.

Somerville, M. M., & Vazquez, F. (2004). Constructivist workplace learning: An idealized design project. In P. A.

Danaher, C. Macpherson, F. Nouwens, & D. Orr (Eds.), *Proceedings of the 3ʳᵈ International Lifelong Learning Conference.* Yeppoon, Queensland, Australia, (pp. 300-305 plus errata page). Rockhampton, Australia: Central Queensland University.

Somerville, M. M., Huston, M. E., & Mirijamdotter, A. (2005). Building on what we know: Staff development in the digital age. *The Electronic Library*, 23(4), 480-491.

Somerville, M. M., Mirijamdotter, A., & Collins, L. (2006). Systems thinking and information literacy: Elements of a knowledge enabling workplace environment. In *Proceedings of the 39ᵗʰ Annual Hawaii International Conference on Systems Sciences (HICSS-39).* Los Alamitos, CA: IEEE Computer Society. Retrieved from http://csdl2.computer.org/comp/proceedings/hicss/2006/2507/07/250770150.pdf

Somerville, M. M., Rogers, E., Mirijamdotter, A., & Partridge, H. (2007), Collaborative evidence-based information practice: The Cal Poly digital learning initiative. In E. Connor, (Ed.). *Case Studies in Evidence-Based Librarianship,* (pp. 141-161). Oxford, England: Chandos Publishing.

Somerville, M. M., Schader, B., & Huston, M. E. (2005). Rethinking what we do and how we do it: Systems thinking strategies for library leadership. *Australian Academic and Research Libraries*, 36(4), 214-227.

Soto-Acosta, P., & Meroño-Cerdan, A. (2006). An analysis and comparison of Web development between local governments and SMEs in Spain. *International Journal of Electronic Business,* 4(2), 191-203.

Stefani, L. (1998). Assessment in Partnership with Learners. *Assessment & Evaluation in Higher Education, 23*(4), 339–350. doi:10.1080/0260293980230402

Stefanone, M., Lackoff, D., & Rosen, D. (2008). We're all stars now: Reality television, web 2.0, and mediated identities. *HT'08*, June 19-21, Pittsburgh, PA.

Storrer, A. 2002. Coherence in text and hypertext. *Document Design*, 3: 156 - 168.

Stowell, F. (2007). Do we mean information systems

or systems of information? International *Journal of Information Technologies and the Systems Approach*, 1(1), 25-36.

Stowell, F., & West, D. (1994). *Client-led design: A systemic approach to information system definition.* Berkshire, England: McGraw-Hill.

Strater, K., & Richter, H. (2007). Examining Privacy and Disclosure in a Social Networking Community. *Symposium on Usable Privacy and Security* (SOUPS) 2007, July 18-20, 2007, Pittsburgh, PA.

Stvilia, B., Twidale, M. B., Smith, L. C., Gasser, L. 2005. *Assessing information quality of a community-based encyclopedia.* In Proc. ICIQ, 442-454.

Sun, Y. (2005). *An Investigation of Using Natural Language Features as Indicators for Automatic Document Classification on Non-Topical Properties —through Machine Learning Methods.* Unpublished doctoral dissertation, Rutgers University, New Brunswick, NJ.

Sundstrom, E., & Associates. (1998). *Supporting Work Team Effectiveness: Best Management Practices for Fostering High Performance.* Hoboken, NJ: Jossey-Bass.

Sunstein, C.R. 2006. *Infotopia.* New York: Oxford University Press

Surowiecki, J. 2004. *The Wisdom of the Crowds.* New York: Doubleday.

Susman, G., & Evered, R. (1978). An assessment of the scientific merits of action research. *Administrative Science Quarterly, 23*(4), 582-603

Swedish Agency for Networks and cooperation in Higher Education, homepage. The Swedish Higher Education act (n.d.). Retrieved January 7, 2009 from http://www.sweden.gov.se/sb/d/3288/a/19574

Swedish Higher Education Ordinance (n.d.). Retrieved January 7, 2009 from http://www.sweden.gov.se/sb/d/3288/a/19574

Swets, J. A. (1996). *Signal Detection Theory & ROC Analysis in Psychology & Diagnostics: Collected Papers.* Mahwah, NJ: Lawrence Erlbaum Associates, Inc.

Swigger, K., Alpaslan, F., Brazile, R., & Monticino, M. (2004). Effects of culture on computer-supported international collaborations. *International Journal of Human-Computer Studies, 60,* 365-380.

Swisher, K. (2004). 'Wiki' may alter how employees work together. *The Wall Street Journal,* July 29.

Switzer, J. (2008). Ecollaboration Using Group Decision Support in Virtual Meetings. In N. Kock (Ed.), *Encyclopedia of E-Collaboration* (pp. 204-209). Hershey, PA: Idea Group Inc.

Szomszor, M. (2008). Correlating user profiles from multiple folksonomies. *HT '08 Conference on Hypertext and Hypermedia,* June 19-21, 2008, Pittsburgh, PA.

Szulanski, G. (1994). *Intra-Firm Transfer of Best Practices Project.* Houston, TX: American Productivity and Quality Center.

Tang, R., Ng, K. B., Strzalkowski, T., & Kantor, P. (2003). Automatically predicting information quality. In D. Radev & S. Abney (Eds.), *Proceedings of Human Language Technology Conference of the North American Chapter of the Association for Computational Linguistics, Companion Volume* (pp. 97-99). East Stroudsburg, PA: Association for Computational Linguistics.

Tang, R., Ng, K.B., Strzalkowski, T., & Kantor, P. (2003) Automatically Predicting Information Quality. *HLT/NACCL'03.*

Tapscott, D., & Williams, A. (2006). *Wikinomics: How Mass Collaboration Changes Everything.* New York, NY: Portfolio Hardcover.

Task Force on the Future of American Innovation. (2005, February 16). *The Knowledge Economy: Is the United States Losing Its Competitive Edge?* Retrieved August 22, 2008 from www.futureofinnovation.org.

Taylor, C. (2007) Why commercial Wikis don't work. *CNN Money Business 2.0.* Retrieved May 12, 2008 from http://money.cnn.com/2007/02/21/magazines/business2/walledgardens.biz2/index.htm

Techquila. (2007). Retrieved from http://www.techquila.com/topicmaps.html

Texas Instruments (2003). *Engineering and Education Statistics: Fact Sheet*. Retrieved December 19, 2006 from http://www.ti.com/corp/docs/press/company/2003/c03033.shtml

The SIMILE Project Timeline Tool (n.d.). Retrieved from http://simile.mit.edu/timeline/

Tidwell, J. (2006). *Designing Interfaces*. Sebastopol, CA: O'Reilly.

Topping, K. (1998). Peer-assessment between students in colleges and universities. *Review of Educational Research*, (68): 249–276.

Torrance, H. (2007). Assessment as learning? How the use of explicit learning objectives, assessment criteria and feedback in post-secondary education and training can come to dominate learning. *Assessment in Education: Principles . Policy & Practice*, *14*(3), 281–294.

Toulmin, S. 1959. *The Uses of Arguments*. Cambridge (MA): Cambridge University Press.

Toulmin, S., Rieke, R. and Janik, A. 1979. *An Introduction to Reasoning*. New York: Macmillan.

Townes-Young, K., & Ewing, V. (2005). NASA live: Crating a clobal classroom. *T.H.E. Journal* (Nov.), 43-45.

Turner, Y. (2000). When an unstoppable force meets an immovable object: Chinese students in the UK university system. In *Proceedings of the 5ᵗʰ International Conference on Learning Styles* (pp. 353-384).

Tweedie, F., & Baayen, R. (1998). How variable may a constant be? Measure of lexical richness in perspective. *Computers and the Humanities*, *32*(5), 323–352. doi:10.1023/A:1001749303137

Ulicsak, M., Facer, K., & Sandford, R. (2007). Issues impacting games-based learning in formal secondary education. *International Journal on Advanced Technology for Learning (IJATL)*.

Usoro, A., Sharratt, M., Tsui, E., & Shekhar, S. (2007). Trust as an antecedent to knowledge sharing in virtual communities of practice. *Knowledge Management Research & Practice*, *5*, 199–212. doi:10.1057/palgrave.

kmrp.8500143

van der Aalst, W. M. P., ter Hofstede, A. H. M., & Kiepuszewski, B. (2003). Workflow Patterns. *Distributed and Parallel Databases*, *14*(1), 5–51. doi:10.1023/A:1022883727209

van Grinsven, J. H. M., Janssen, M., et al. (2008). Collaboration Methods and Tools for Operational Risk Management. In N. Kock, (Ed.) *Encyclopedia of E-Collaboration, Information Science Reference* (pp. 68-72). Hershey, PA: Information Science Reference.

Vanderbilt, T. (2008). *Traffic – Why we drive the way we do*. New York: Knopf.

Vassou, A. (2006). Social networking sites driving new wave of security. *Computeractive*, December 13, 2006. Retrieved Dec 4, 2007, from http://www.computeractive.co.uk/articles/print2170872

Verheij, B. (2003). Dialectical Argumentation with Argumentation Schemes: An Approach to Legal Logic. *Artificial Intelligence and Law*, 11(2): 167-195.

Vickers, G. (1983). *The art of judgment. A study of policy making*. London: Harper & Row Ltd.

Vickers, G. (1983). *Human systems are different*. London: Harper & Row Ltd.

Vickery, A., Brooks, H. M., Robinson, B., & Vickery, B. C. (1987). A Reference and Referral System Using Expert System Techniques. *The Journal of Documentation*, *43*, 1–23. doi:10.1108/eb026798

Viégas, F., Wattenberg, M., & Dave, K. (2004). Studying cooperation and conflict between authors with history flow visualizations. In *Proceedings of the SIGCHI Conference on Human Factors in Computing Systems*, (pp. 575-582). Vienna, Austria.

Viégas, F., Wattenberg, M., & McKeon, M. (2007). The hidden order of Wikipedia. In *Proceedings of the 12th International Conference on Human-Computer Interaction*, Beijing, P.R. China.

Vogel, D. R., Lou, D., van Eekhout, M., van Genuchten, M., Verveen, S., & Adams, T. (2000). Distributed experiential learning: The Hong Kong-Netherlands project. In *Proceedings of the 33rd Annual Hawaii International Conference on System Sciences* (pp. 1-9).

Volet, S. (1999). Learning across cultures: Appropriateness of knowledge transfer. *International Journal of Educational Research, 31*, 625-643.

Völter, M., Kircher, M., & Zdun, U. (2004). *Remoting Patterns - Foundations of Enterprise, Internet, and Realtime Distributed Object Middleware.* Chichester, UK: John Wiley & Sons, Inc.

Völter, M., Schmid, A., & Wolff, E. (2002). *Server Component Patterns: Component Infrastructures Illustrated with EJB.* Chichester, UK: John Wiley & Sons, Inc.

von Hippel, E. 2001. Open Source Shows the Way: Innovation by and for Users – No Manufacturer Required! *Sloan Management Review*, Summer.

von Krogh, G., Ichijo, K., & Nonaka, I. (2000). *Enabling Knowledge Creation: How to Unlock the Mystery of Tacit Knowledge and Release the Power of Innovation.* Oxford, UK: Oxford University Press.

Von Krogh, G., von Hippel, E. (2006). The Promise of Research on Open Source Software. *Management Science, 52*(7): 975-983.

Voorhees, E. M. (1994). *Query expansion using lexical-semantic relations.* Paper presented at the 17th ACM SIGIR conference on research and development in information retrieval.

Vygotskii, L. (1978). *Mind in Society: The Development of Higher Psychological Processes.* Cambridge, MA: Harvard University Press.

Wagner, C. (2004). Wiki: A technology for conversation knowledge management and group collaboration. *Communications of the Association for Information Systems, 13*, 265–289.

Wagner, C., & Bolloju, N. (2005). Supporting knowledge management in organizations with conversational technologies: Discussion forums, Weblogs, and wikis. *Journal of Database Management, 16*(2), 1-8.

Wagner, C., & Majchrzak, A. (2007). Enabling customer-centricity using wikis and the wiki way. *Journal of Management Information Systems, 23*, 17–43. doi:10.2753/MIS0742-1222230302

Wahren, H.-K. (2003). *Success Factor Innovation.* [trans. Erfolgsfaktor Innovation. Ideen systematisch generieren, bewerten und umsetzen]. Berlin: Springer.

Wallas, G. (1926). *The Art of Thought.* San Diego, CA: Harcourt Brace Jovanovich, Inc.

Walpole, M. (2004). Socioeconomic status and college: How SES affects outcomes. *The Review of Higher Education, 27*(1), 4573.

Walsham, G. (2001). Knowledge management: The benefits and limitations of computer systems. *European Management Journal, 19*(6), 599–608.

Walton, D.N. (2006). *Fundamentals of Critical Argumentation - Critical Reasoning and Argumentation.* Cambridge (MA): Cambridge University Press.

Walton, D.N. 1989. *Informal Logic – A handbook of critical argumentation,* Cambridge (MA): Cambridge University Press.

Wang, R. Y., & Strong, D. M. (1996). Beyond accuracy: What data quality means to data consumers. *Journal of Management Information Systems, 12*(4), 5–34.

Wasko, M. M., & Faraj, S. (2005). Why should I share? Examining knowledge contribution in networks of practice. *MIS Quarterly, 29*, 25–58.

Watkins, D. A., Adair, J., Akande, A., Cheng, C., Fleming, J., Gerong, A., et al. (1998). Cultural dimensions, gender and the nature of self-concept: A fourteen-country study. *International Journal of Psychology, 33*(1).

Watson, W. E., Kumar, K., & Michaelsen, L. K. (1993). Cultural diversity's impact on interaction process and performance: Comparing homogeneous and diverse task groups. *Academy of Management Journal, 36*(3), 590-602.

Wegerif, R. (1998). The social dimension of asynchronous learning networks. *Journal of Asynchronous Learning*

Networks, *2*(1), 34-49.

Weinberger, D. (2007). *Everything Is Miscellaneous: The Power of the New Digital Disorder*. New York: Times Books.

Weinfan, L., & Davis, P. (2004). *Challenges in virtual communication: Videoconferencing, audioconferencing, and computer-mediated communications*. Santa Monica, CA: RAND Corporation.

Weintraub, J., & Kumar, K. (Eds.). (1997). *Public and private in thought and practice*. Chicago: University of Chicago Press.

Wells, A. M., & Schorr, J. (2007). *Sales and Operations Planning: The Key to Continuous Demand Satisfaction. SAP Insight Business Process Innovations*. Retrieved August 1, 2008 from http://www.sap.com

Wendlandt, A. (2007). Web advertising to come under EU scrutiny. *Reuters*, November 23. Retrieved Dec 4, 2007, from http://www.reuters.com/articlePrint?articleI d=USL229260820071123

Wenger, E. (1998). *Communities of practice: Learning, meaning, and identity*. Cambridge University Press.

West, D., & Stowell, F. (2000). Models, diagrams, and their importance to information systems analysis and design. In D. Bustard, P. Kawalek, & M. Norris (eds.) *For business improvement*, (pp. 295-311). Norwood, MA: ARTECH House, Inc.

WFMC (2004). *Workflow Management Coalition*. Retrieved from http://wfmc.org

Wharton, C., Bradford, J., Jeffries, R., & Franzke, M. (1992). Applying Cognitive Walkthroughs to More Complex User Interfaces: Experiences, Issues, and Recommendations. *Proceedings of CHI Conference on Human Factors in Computing Systems*, (pp. 381-388). New York: ACM, 381-388.

White House Office of Communications. (2006). *The American Competitiveness Initiative: Encouraging Innovation*, April 18, 2006.

Whyte, W. F., Greenwood, D. J., & Lazes, P. (1991). Par-

ticipatory action research through practice to science in social research. In W. F. Whyte (Ed.), *Participatory action research*. Newbury Park, CA: Sage Publications.

WikiWikiWeb History. (2009). Cunningham & Cunningham, Inc. Retrieved from http://c2.com/cgi/wiki?WikiHistory

Wilson, B. (2001). Soft systems methodology: Conceptual model building and its contribution. Chichester, England: John Wiley & Sons.

Wistow, G. (1990). *Collaboration under financial constraint*. Aldershot, UK: Avebury.

Wong, K. Y., & Aspinwall, E. (2005). An empirical study of the important factors for knowledge-management adoption in the SME sector. *Journal of Knowledge Management*, *9*(3), 64–82. doi:10.1108/13673270510602773

Wurman, R. S. (1989). *Information Anxiety*. New York: Doubleday.

Wynn, E., & Katz, J. E. (1997). Hyperbole over cyberspace: Self-presentation and social boundaries in internet home pages and discourse. *The Information Society*, *13*(4), 297–327. doi:10.1080/019722497129043

Yahoo. (2008). *Design Pattern Library*. Retrieved from http://developer.yahoo.com/ypatterns/atoz.php

Yi, M. (2008). Information organization and retrieval using a topic maps-based ontology: Results of a task-based evaluation. *Journal of the American Society for Information Science and Technology*, *59*(12), 1898–1911. doi:10.1002/asi.20899

Yi, M. (2008). *Topic Maps-based Ontology and Semantic Web - Ontology-Driven Information Retrieval System*. Saarbrücken, Germany: VDM Verlag.

Young, S., Dewstow, R., & McSporran, M. (1999, July). Who wants to learn online? What types of students benefit from the new learning environment? In *Proceedings of the NACCQ*.

YouTube. (2006). *YouTube Fact Sheet*. Retrieved 8th October, 2006, from http://www.youtube.com/t/fact_sheet/

Yu, F. (2001). Competition within computer-assisted

cooperative learning environments: Cognitive, affective, and social outcomes. *Journal of Educational Computing Research, 24*(2), 99-117.

Zeng, M. L. (2005). Using software to teach thesaurus development and indexing in graduate programs of LIS and IAKM. *Bulletin of the American Society for Information Science and Technology*, (pp. 11-13).

Zhao, J. L., Kumar, A., & Stohr, E. A. (2000). Workflow-centric information distribution through e-mail. *Journal of Management Information Systems, 17*(3), 45–72.

Zhu, Z. (2004). Knowledge management: Towards a universal concept or cross-cultural contexts? *Knowledge Management Research & Practice, 2*(2), 67–79. doi:10.1057/palgrave.kmrp.8500032

Ziekow, H. (2007). In-Network Event Processing in a Peer to Peer Broker Network for the Internet of Things. In *On the Move to Meaningful Internet Systems 2007: OTM 2007 Workshops*, (pp. 970-979). Berlin / Heidelberg: Springer.

Zigurs, I., & Buckland, B. (1998). A Theory of Task/Technology Fit and Group Support Systems Effectiveness. *Management Information Systems Quarterly, 22*(3), 313–334. doi:10.2307/249668

About the Contributors

Scott Rummler (laserthread.com) holds a Master of Science in information and library science from Pratt Institute, a Master of Fine Art from Rochester Institute of Technology, a computer certificate in Internet technology from Baruch College, a Bachelor of Arts from the University of Rochester, and did an internship at Merrill Lynch. He is a business consultant and designer in New York City in the areas of information architecture and user experience design. His areas of focus include social networking/collaboration, business consulting for distressed industsy sectors, financial applications, metrics improvement for online publications, e-business for the insurance industry, and healthcare information management. He has worked for clients including Sapient, Razorfish, Hearst Digital, Schering-Plough, and Standard & Poor's. He has published articles in the areas of information architecture and library science.

Kwong Bor Ng (PhD) is an associate professor at the Graduate School of Library and Information Studies of Queens College, CUNY, where he teaches advanced level technologies courses like "Metadata and XML", "Database Construction" and "Web Programming". Besides teaching, Dr. Ng has also been working as a consultant for research projects, including projects sponsored by the National Science Foundation and DARPA (Defense Advanced Research Projects Agency). His research interests are in the technical and technological areas of knowledge representation and organization. Dr. Ng has published more than 20 academic papers in refereed journals. His book, Using XML, was published by Neal Schuman in 2007.

* * *

Rick Bennett, raised and educated in South London, England, Rick's undergraduate education specialised in sculpture. He spent eight years within the UK TV & film industry before moving to Australia in 1990. In 1991 he began working for the University of New South Wales and was later appointed Coordinator of the first year Bachelor of Design program. Through ongoing links and consulting roles with the international digital media industry he was appointed the first Creative Director of a newly formed commercial graphic design consultancy in 1999. He undertook this role for two years before returning to his research through The Omnium Project that he had founded in 1998. His Master of Higher Education investigated the current teaching practice and future possibilities of 'Design Studio' subjects. The Omnium Research Group was founded to progress this area and in 2003, Rick was appointed Head of COFA Online: a newly formed academic unit established to design, produce and facilitate a suite of online courses across a range of art and design disciplines. The international reputation of Omnium's research led to a three-year Australian Research Council (ARC) Discovery Grant. Rick and The Omnium Project have been honoured to received several national and international awards and accolades. He presents at numerous design and education conferences and publishes in journals and other publications worldwide.

Robert O. Briggs is Professor in the Management and Marketing department at the University of Nebraska at Omaha, where he is also the director of academic affairs for the Center for Collaboration Science. He researches the theoretical foundations of collaboration and learning, and applies his findings to the design and deployment of new collaboration technologies and concepts of operation. He has published more than 100 scholarly works on team productivity, technology-supported learning, creativity, satisfaction, and technology transition. He is co-founder of the Collaboration Engineering field and co-inventor of the thinkLets concept. He lectures worldwide on collaboration theory and practice, and on the philosophy of science. He earned his doctorate Management Information Systems at the University of Arizona in 1994.

Görkem Çetin is an open source evangelist, training manager and university instructor. His current doctorate studies in Gebze Institute of Technology focus on human computer interaction issues of open source software. Çetin has authored 5 books, written numerous articles for technical and sector magazines and spoken at various conferences. Working in TUBITAK/UEKAE, he acts as coordinator and co-coordinator of two EU FP6 projects, as well as Pardus Linux.

Marjorie Darrah has a BS, MS, and Ph.D. in Mathematics and a BA in Education with a 5-12 specialization in Mathematics. She is currently an Associate Professor of Mathematics at West Virginia University. In the past, Darrah was the Principal Investigator on three National Science Foundation education related projects totaling over two million dollars. She has also served as an external evaluator on a Department of Education grant and many state and local grant projects. Before coming to West Virginia University, she was a Principal Scientist and the Director of Computer Sciences at the West Virginia High Technology Consortium and before that an Associate Professor and the Chair of the Natural Sciences Department at Alderson Broaddus College, in Phillipi, West Virginia.

Angie Dowling, originally from Racine, Wisconsin, Dowling earned a BS in Life Sciences from the University of Wisconsin. She also attended West Virginia University where she earned a MA in Secondary Education. Dowling is presently completing her doctoral coursework in the Instructional Design and Technology EdD program at West Virginia University in Morgantown, WV. She currently is in her 14th year at Suncrest Middle School in Morgantown, WV. Dowling teaches 8th grade Science and is a contributing member of the school's Technology Team. She has collaborated in the writing of grants and has been awarded a $30,000.00 Tech Connect grant. Dowling has been a presenter at various state and national level educational conferences, including the West Virginia Science Teachers Association Conference, the West Virginia State Technology Conference and the National Educator's Computer Conference. In recent years, Dowling has become extensively involved in technology integration at the middle school level. She has taught Photoshop, HTML and VRML programming languages. She also is web master for one of the few middle schools in West Virginia that have a completely student-generated web site. In 2007, her 7th and 8th grade students constructed a scale model of Suncrest Middle School using entirely VRML programming language and it is now showcased on the school's web site. Dowling strongly believes that the integration of 21st Century and IT Skills is essential in preparing middle school students for the increasingly digital age.

Lesley Farmer coordinates the Librarianship program at California State University Long Beach. She earned her M.S. Library Science at the University of North Carolina Chapel Hill, and her Adult Education doctorate from Temple University. Dr. Farmer worked as a K-12 teacher-librarian, and as a public, special and academic librarian. She is IASL VP Association Relations, Special Library Association Education Division chair, and presents and writes frequently. Dr. Farmer's most recent book is *Teen Girls and Technology* (Teachers College Press, 2008). Her research includes information literacy, collaboration, library service equity, and educational technology.

Mehmet Gokturk has been working at Gebze Institute of Technology, Turkey since his graduation from the Computer Science Department of The Washington University with his doctoral study on Human Computer Interaction. His dissertation titled The Significance Of Selection Method In Computer Pointing Tasks, focused on the relationship between the selection methods and interaction device performance. Dr. Gokturk holds B.Sc. degree from Bogazici University Electrical and Electronics Engineering Department and M.Sc. degree from The George Washington University on Computer Graphics. Among his current research interests are human computer interaction, usability, interaction devices, universal access, attentive computing and software engineering. He has been involved in various projects funded by Department of Defense of Turkey, NASA JPL and Department of Education of United states. He currently is an Assistant Professor of Computer Engineering, head of Informatics Department and directs Human Computer Interaction Laboratory in Gebze Institute of Technology.

Jay Heuer provides executive leadership in the areas of Product Development and Technology Management. His specialty lies in digital convergence products (hardware & software), where he has a wealth of experience in the global team leadership for rapid prototyping, concept cars and market pilots. Currently, he serves as a consultant by helping his clients improve their strategic innovation capabilities. J. was globally responsible for the Software R&D for a Fortune 500 corporation and founded three software and consulting companies in his career. He has developed and worked with online collaboration system for almost 15 years. J. holds a PhD in Economics and an MBA in Production Management & IT from the University of Paderborn, Germany. He currently resides in Northern Germany.

Yasmin Ibrahim is a Senior Lecturer in the Division of Information and Media Studies at the University of Brighton where she lectures on globalisation and political communication. Her main research interests include the use of the Internet for empowerment and political communication in repressed polities and diasporic communities, global governance and the development of alternative media theories in non-Western contexts.

Gwendolyn L. Kolfschoten is an assistant Professor at Delft University of Technology in the Netherlands. She is an experienced facilitator of thinkLets-based Group Support Systems workshop having worked with numerous public and private organizations. Her research focuses on the quality of thinkLet-based collaboration process design for complex tasks. She developed the first example of Computer Supported Collaboration Engineering (CACE) technology – an integrated support suite to assist collaboration engineers in process design. She has organized successful minitracks and tutorials at HICSS for the past four years. Her research has been presented at HICSS, CRIWG, AMCIS, EE and GDN conferences and has been published in the *International Journal of Computer Application in Technology, International Journal of Human-Computer Studies, Journal of the AIS, and Group Decision and Negotiation.*

Clif Kussmaul is Associate Professor of Computer Science at Muhlenberg College and Chief Technology Officer for Elegance Technologies, Inc., which develops software products and provides software development services. His previous positions include Senior Member of Technical Staff with NeST Technologies, and Assistant Professor of CS at Moravian College. He has a PhD in Computer Science from the University of California, Davis, master's degrees in CS and Electro-acoustic Music from Dartmouth College, and bachelor's degrees in Engineering and Music from Swarthmore College. His professional interests and activities include software engineering, entrepreneurship, digital signal processing, cognitive neuroscience, and music.

Monica Liljeström is a junior lecturer at the Department of Education, Umeå University, Sweden. She has been an educator in online and distance courses for the past10 years and has a great interest in human interaction and learning trough ICT in both formal and informal contexts. At the moment she is participating in a peer assessment project aimed to explore if this can enhance collaboration and learning in online and distance education. She is also a PhD-student in pedagogy, and is at current working on her thesis about collaborative learning in online and distance education.

Stephan Lukosch is since 2008 an assistant professor at the Delft University of Technology. His current research interests include service-oriented infrastructures for collaborative systems, development processes for collaborative applications, design patterns for computer-mediated interaction, and tool and process support for collaborative storytelling. In 1998, he received a Diploma in Computer Science from the University of Dortmund. From 1998 to 2003, he was working as a researcher at the chair for Cooperative Systems at the FernUniversität in Hagen. In 2003, he received a Dr. rer. nat. in Computer Science with distinction from the FernUniversität in Hagen. From 2003 to 2008, he was working as assistant professor for the FernUniversität in Hagen. His articles appeared in various journals including Journal of Universal Computer Science, Informatica, International Journal of Cooperative Information Systems, International Journal of Human Computer Studies, and International Journal of Computer Applications in Technology.

In 1994, **Andy Polaine** co-founded the award-winning new-media collective Antirom in London and worked with clients such as the BBC, Levis Strauss and Co. and The Science Museum as well exhibiting several interactive installations and performances around the world. Andy was a producer at dotcom giant Razorfish in the UK before moving to Australia where he started the interactive department of visual effects company, Animal Logic. He was a Senior Lecturer in Interactive Media at the College of Fine Arts, The University of New South Wales, Sydney, and formerly the Head of the School of Media Arts. Now living in Germany, Andy has been a Guest Professor at the Bauhaus University and continues to work as a lecturer, interaction designer and writer. He is the founder and editor of The Designer's Review of Books. He has published over 160 articles and papers and regularly speaks at a range of international conferences and institutions.

Ying Sun received a B.S. in Information Science from the Peking University, Beijing, China, and a Ph.D. in Library and Information Science from Rutgers, the State University of New Jersey in 2005 for a dissertation on automatic assessment of document non-topical properties. She is a member of the Association for Computing Machinery (ACM) and the American Society of Information Science and Technologies (ASIST). Her research interests encompass topics in Information Retrieval, text mining, natural language processing and human computer interaction. An assistant Professor of Library and Information Department at University at Buffalo, Dr. Ying Sun is an educator and researcher. Her work has been published and presented. Before joining UB, she worked at RelevantNoise Inc. as a senior data mining engineer, where she leaded researches on automatic identification of Blog sentiment orientations.

Gert-Jan de Vreede is the Kayser Distinguished Professor at the Department of Information Systems & Quantitative Analysis, at University of Nebraska at Omaha where he is the director of the Center for Collaboration Science and affiliated with the Faculty of Technology, Policy and Management, at Delft University of Technology in the Netherlands where he received his PhD. His research focuses on the design of transferable practitioner-driven collaboration processes and the application, adoption, and diffusion of collaboration technology and facilitation in organizations. He is co-founder of the Collaboration Engineering field and co-inventor of the thinkLets concept. His articles have appeared in journals, including *Journal of Management Information Systems, Communications of the ACM, Small Group Research, DataBase, Group Decision and Negotiation, International Journal of e-Collaboration, Group Facilitation, Journal of Creativity and Innovation Management, Journal of Decision Systems, Simulation & Gaming, Simulation, Journal of the AIS* and *Journal of Simulation Practice and Theory.*

Moyongho "Lee" Yi is an Assistant Professor at the School of Library and Information Studies, Texas Woman's University, where he teaches Information Storage and Retrieval Systems and Web development for the Information Professions. Yi's research focuses on information organization and retrieval (implementation and evaluation of traditional and alternative information organization approaches such as index, thesaurus, taxonomy, semantic web, and ontology) to enhance information access. The goal is to evaluate and develop information systems that return "relevant resources," not merely "irrelevant/ lengthy hits" and to manage digitally stored information. Yi is also interested in information security to ensure integrity of digital resources.

Index

A

altruism 107
American Competitiveness Initiative (ACI)
68, 69
anthropomorphic robots 273
AntWorld 129, 130
asynchronous discussion 58, 65

B

balanced value flows 106, 112
bottom up 97, 106
business process change 4, 15
business process reengineering 4, 16, 17

C

CACE tool 1, 8, 9, 10, 11, 12, 13, 14
Capability Maturity Model 4, 17
certification model 176
closed model 42
cognitive apprenticeship 71, 75, 77
cognitive overload 116
collaboration engineering
1, 3, 4, 5, 6, 8, 14, 15, 16
collaboration process design
1, 3, 6, 8, 9, 12, 13
collaborative filtering 41
collaborative information retrieval 126
collaborative knowledge building
137, 139, 140, 141, 145, 146
collaborative learning 52, 74, 75
collaborative retrieval systems 126
collaborative risk management 194
collaborative search 126, 129, 134
collaborative virtual team xiii, 260, 261, 262

collaborative work practice 1, 2, 5, 6, 8, 9
community-based system 268
community-based virtual environment 271
community of practice (CoP) 71, 179, 180,
181, 182, 186, 187
computer aided process engineering (CAPE)
3, 7, 8, 14
computer aided software engineering (CASE)
3, 7, 16
computer enhanced learning 52
computer-literate 263
computer mediated communication (CMC)
83, 84, 268
computer-mediated course 264
computer-mediated environment 261, 264
computer-mediated interaction 19, 20, 21,
22, 23, 24, 25, 30, 32, 34, 35
computer-mediated software 268
computer supported collaborative learning environments (CSCLEs) xiii, 260, 261
content generation divide 155
course management system (CMS) 182
Creative Waves 39–51
cue-seekers 54
CURE 25, 26, 27, 28, 29, 30, 31, 32, 33,
34, 35, 36
cyberspace 83, 84, 87, 93, 94, 95
cyclic design approach 5

D

data consistency 21
data model 191, 193, 198
decision tree 143
deep collaboration 52, 56, 65, 189, 190

V

Value Frequency Model 2, 15
video conferencing 179, 180, 182, 183,
        184, 185, 186, 187, 188
virtual humans 273
virtuality 82, 83, 84
virtual learning environments (VLE) 268
virtual reality environment 273
virtual reality modeling language (VRML)
        74, 76, 77, 78
virtual teams 261

W

Web-based learning 263
Web ontology language (OWL) 118, 119
wiki 97, 98, 99, 100, 101, 102, 103, 104,
        105, 106, 108, 109, 110, 111, 112,
        113, 114, 115, 137, 138, 139, 140,
        141, 142, 143, 144, 145, 146, 147
Wikipedia 100, 101, 102, 103, 112, 113,
        115
WikiWikiWeb 137, 138, 147
workflow 160
workflow management 3, 4
worldstorming 49
WYSIWYG 104